The
Punter's
Friend

This book is dedicated to the memory of Maxie Read –
the best friend on a racecourse that ever was.

The
Punter's
Friend

A GUIDE TO RACING AND BETTING

Jack Waterman

Published in Great Britain in 2005 by
Virgin Books
Thames Wharf Studios
Rainville Road
London W6 9HA

First published in Great Britain in 1987 by
Queen Anne Press, a division of
Lennard Associates Limited

© Jack Waterman 1987, 1989, 1994, 1996, 1999, 2001, 2005

The right of Jack Waterman to be identified as the author of this
work has been asserted in accordance with the Copyright Designs
and Patents Act 1988

First paperback edition 1994
Second revised paperback edition 1996
Third revised paperback edition 1999
Fourth revised paperback edition 2001
Fifth revised paperback edition 2005

A CIP catalogue record for this book
is available from the British Library

ISBN 0 7535 1045 6

Editor: Chris Marshall

Printed and bound in Italy by
L.E.G.O. - S.p.a.

CONTENTS

INTRODUCTION

The English believe that racing is sinful ... Perhaps that is the secret of its appeal. I fail to see the sin myself, in watching a marvellous horse perform deeds of wonder. People also believe that gambling is sinful. It is not even enjoyable. It is winning that is enjoyable. Mostly, gambling is an exciting way of making yourself depressed.

I had already written this introduction when I read in *The Times* Simon Barnes's rave notice of *Dancing Brave*'s performance in the 1986 Prix de l'Arc de Triomphe. The words he wrote, quoted above, tie in with what I wish to make clear about *The Punter's Friend*. It is not a gospel for the gone gambler. There is quite enough evidence on the sad fact and incidence of compulsive gambling to dissuade anything that might be construed as encouragement in that direction. This book, therefore, nowhere suggests that there is a copperbottom, unsinkable method of finding winners all the time. Equally, those who consider they know everything about racing are excused all further reading beyond this point.

What I have attempted to do is largely for the benefit of those who would like to go racing, and have an occasional bet either on the racecourse or in the local betting shop, but are so put off by the mystique surrounding the whole business and its impenetrable terminology, that they find the effort is beyond them. At the same time, experienced racegoers may also find certain sections of interest and use. From them, however, a certain amount of indulgence is asked for, when what to their eyes appears self-evident is given a basic explanation. Chapter One, therefore is devoted at length in a 'Glossary' section, to de-mystifying the Turf as far as possible.

Above all, I have tried to suggest that horses should not be treated simply as names in a newspaper, or, worse, as a kind of homogeneous breed of racing Daleks, running their races like automata. A few examples will suffice to show that horses are as different in personality and characteristics as human beings, and this fairly naturally affects their racecourse performances: *St Paddy* was scared of birds and *Silver Buck* a bundle of nerves until solaced by a Trebor Mint; and *Mandarin* was always more amenable after a pint of Guinness. A horse called *Woodburn* was so spoilt and almost ruined when very young he use to take it out of other horses round him on the racecourse, to the extent of biting a bit of the rump of the horse in front (which did not have an effect *Woodburn* desired – it simply made the other horse go faster). *Hyperion* when at home on the gallops used to decide not to do any work and would stand stock still for as much as half an hour. When he was at stud he was fascinated by aeroplanes crossing the Newmarket sky. Another great horse, *Le Moss*, had to be fooled into working by Henry Cecil. Many horses like a travelling companion, and 'peerless' *Pretty Polly* was only one who had a pony to keep her company. Strangest of all, perhaps, that good old jumper *Pelican's Pay* had a telly installed in his box to keep him amused. And not all horses like to be retired from the racing scene: one of the greatest of Grand National winners, *Freebooter*, was put out in a paddock away from Robert Renton's Yorkshire stables where he used regularly to get out and swim a canal; back in the yard he just used to stand looking wistfully at the door of his old box.

Finally, my acknowledgements, first to Toby Roxburgh who originally approached me with the idea of doing the book for Queen Anne Press. Next, to some other old friends: George Ennor, formerly of *The Sporting Life*, later of the *Racing Post* who has been unstinting of time and encouragement, information and loan of material, and his daughter Charlotte who, with Theo Barr, gave great help with the statistical side; to Doug Newton, senior *Sporting Life* man on the racecourse, and to John Sharratt, senior race-reader for *Raceform* who both gave their time and knowledge generously. Richard Lancelyn Green very kindly loaned the 1879 copy of *The Times*, while Ian Clark of the *Manchester Evening News*, Jane McKerron, Tony Fairbairn, former Director of the Racing Information Bureau, and Geoffrey Webster of the Tote must be thanked for supplying invaluable material. Specimen pages from *Raceform*, *Chaseform*, the *Notebook* and *Private Handicap* are reproduced by kind permission of their publishers, Raceform Ltd, and the kind help of *Timeform* in reprinting material and giving permission for use is also gratefully acknowledged. In making clear one or two difficult settlements for the 'Compendium of Bets' section, I am indebted to Max Thomas bookmakers of Archway Road, London. Lastly, thanks must go to my wife, Penny, on whom the ideas were first tried, and who undertook the arduous task of helping to proof-read the race statistics in Chapter Eight.

Jack Waterman
June 1987

PREFACE TO THE PAPERBACK EDITION

Racing is a highly perishable subject to write about. No sooner is a book in the shops than events on and off the racecourse immediately begin to overtake what is in print; rising stars among horses, trainers, jockeys; new results of big races; changes in the endless politics of the Turf; all sorts of fresh developments and sometimes innovation. When the second printing of the hardback edition of *The Punter's Friend* came out in 1989, two years after the original, it contained two whole extra pages with details of various changes. Some of these, in turn, are now themselves out of date. With this new paperback edition, the opportunity has been taken to incorporate those changes which remain relevant as well as many others that have taken place in recent years. In addition, what one otherwise favourable reviewer called 'a few irritating errors' have been excised, as far as I could detect them; if any still endure, my apologies herewith. The book has also been partially restructured, while mainly historical references have been expanded and several extra important races included. In addition, a new chapter has been added dealing with the ever-expanding British interest in racing abroad. Also, since the first edition of this book, three outstanding anthologies of writing about the Turf, in all its aspects, have appeared. They are *The Faber Book of the Turf* edited by two peerless and knowledgeable men of racing, who have both since, sadly, died: John Hislop and David Swannell; *A Racing Companion* edited by Lord Oaksey and Bob Rodney (Lennard Books for W.H. Smith); and *Runners & Riders* edited by Sean Magee (Methuen). These are required (and immensely enjoyable and illuminating) reading as considerable back-up to what I have attempted to sketch in this book. From the last of the three volumes, I found that what my colleague, Alastair Down, vividly had to say in *The Sporting Life Weekender* on 21 February 1991 on the subject of horses chimed very much with my own views, as well as touching on the subject of old, retired campaigners for whom, as might be deduced from what I have written in later pages, I hold a great affection and respect. On a visit to Kingsclere in 1989, Ian Balding thoughtfully took me up to a paddock to see (and give a mint to) *Aldie, Mill Reef*'s grey travelling companion and relentlessly front-running winner of 20 races at 1 m 2 f on his own account. He was then almost white at 23 years, and the meeting gave me immense pleasure as well as a sense of being privileged and honoured as I had been when having an audience with *Red Rum* (also then 23 years young) in his box the previous year when there was likewise cause for shares in Polo Mints to take a dramatic upturn. Another trainer, the late Ryan Price, also faithfully looked after his pensioners, all of them old favourites of mine and retired heroes of the Cheltenham Gold Cup, Whitbread Gold Cup, Chester Cup, Cesarewitch (two of them), Schweppes Gold Trophy and Mackeson Gold Cup: *What a Myth, Major Rose, Persian Lancer, Le Vermontois* and *Charlie Worcester.* This is what Alastair Down wrote about a visit with Ryan Price to those pensioners (reprinted with permission): 'I recall racing up a rough old cart track in a large Merc at what seemed about 60 mph and getting out at the edge of an apparently empty field. But after an ear-splitting shout of "Come on you boys" the place suddenly came to life as the horses responded to that inimitable roar and ambled up over the skyline to greet him. He loved those horses and his obvious affection for them and gratitude for what they had done for him taught me an important lesson about racing and racing people. It is important because it helps draw a crucial line between those who love racing and those who love racehorses. To most trainers – and it is usually the best trainers – the horses are more important than the racing. But to many people involved with the Turf, the racing is more important than the horses.' To conclude, my thanks once again to some of my friends for the help they have generously given: George Ennor of the *Racing Post*, Geoffrey Hamlyn of Tattersalls' Committee, Dick Hinder, Racing Editor of *The Times*, Doug Newton of *The Sporting Life*, Geoffrey Webster of the Tote, and, not least, invaluable statistical aid as ever from Theo Barr.

Jack Waterman
October 1994

PREFACE TO THE 2001 PAPERBACK EDITION

Much was encompassed in the 1999 revision of this book, not least the demise of both *The Sporting Life* and *Ruff's Guide To The Turf*, a much-missed annual still, as well as the rapid rise of racing interests on the Internet. The present revision covers another two years of extensive changes including the ever-growing expansion of racing websites, far-reaching changes in racecourse betting rings and the abolition of betting tax and all that implies. My warmest thanks, once again, continue to go to friends for their generous help: Reg Griffin for *Timeform* details; Wally Pyrah and Ms N. Gordon for the Sporting Index entry; John Gallimore for the Weatherbys article; Sue Bainbridge of the Tote and, most particularly, George Ennor, for his many valuable amendments and additions. Also my wife, Penny, for unfailing encouragement and suggestions, plus much statistical research once more from Theo Barr.

Jack Waterman
June 2001

PREFACE TO THE 2004 PAPERBACK EDITION

The warmest of thanks go to George Ennor, once again, for his quite invaluable help and time spent in preparing this edition, particularly in the matter of race results.

Jack Waterman
November 2004

CHAPTER ONE

An Alphabet of Racing Terms

Acceptor *See ENTRIES.*

Added money *See PRIZE-MONEY.*

Age All horses share the same birthday irrespective of the exact date of their foaling. This is fixed to facilitate the framing of races according to age groups, and is 1 January each year in the Northern Hemisphere. (In the Southern Hemisphere 1 August is the equivalent birthday.) Until 1834, the fixed date was 1 May, in line with the end, more or less, of the foaling season. In that year the official date was shifted, for Newmarket horses, to the present one, which occurs before the foaling season has properly got under way. It was not until nearly a quarter of a century later that the rest of the country followed suit.

The majority of races on the Flat are for two-year-olds (2-y-o) only or three-year-olds (3-y-o) only, with a fair proportion also confined to three-year-olds and four-year-olds only, or three-year-olds and upwards. A horse of either sex, before its first birthday, is known as a foal; between that date and its next birthday, a yearling. (*See also COLT, FILLY, GELDING, MARE and WEIGHT FOR AGE.*)

Aged A term not as insulting as it might be when applied to human beings. Once past the age of six, all racehorses are officially 'aged'. Because of the use of this description in very early records, it is sometimes impossible to determine exactly how old a horse was when he or she won a particular contest. Today, however, exact ages are used for the purposes of records, whether or not the horse is officially 'aged'. Most horses have finished their careers on the Flat by the time they are rising five-year-olds, and often earlier in the case of winners of Classics and other important races, and in the case of fillies. Many horses go to stud; others continue racing over hurdles and fences. But a proportion of racehorses on the Flat continue long after becoming officially 'aged', and when the runners for a race are assessed, a horse should by no means be overlooked solely because it is (literally) long in the tooth (as well as having a full set of teeth).

The five oldest winners in Turf history were all 18 years of age. Three only were on the Flat, and all in the 18th and 19th centuries: *Revenge, Marksman* and, in Australia, *Jorrocks*. The other winners at the age of 18 were over the jumps: *Wild Aster* succeeded no fewer than three times in 1919, and that old favourite, *Sonny Somers*, trained by Fred Winter, won two chases within a fortnight in February 1980. Among those within a year of the record, *De Pluvinel* must be mentioned as one of the most remarkable horses ever to have taken part in the Royal Artillery Gold Cup. Between 1982 and 1990 he ran nine times in this historic Sandown race, winning three times, being second three times and never failing to complete. In 1989, when *De Pluvinel* was 16, he won by a distance. The following year he won for the last time, once again in fine style, at the age of 17. Another hero of the crowds, gallant old *Creggmore Boy*, veteran of several Grand Nationals, also had a final victory at 17, but carried on chasing until he was 22 and was a runner-up in 1961 at Ludlow, aged 21.

National Hunt aside, sprinters on the Flat have an impressive record of defying Anno Domini. For example, *Le Garcon d'Or* in 1972, aged 14, won the Joppa Handicap at Edinburgh. Moreover, he was made a confident favourite to do so and in achieving the victory took his personal tally of successes to 34, thus equalling the record for the 20th century set up by *High Stakes* in 1950. *O.I. Oyston*, Jack Berry's well-loved performer, was 13 when making all the running at Ayr in 1989, and Ken Ivory's *Dawn's Delight* was also 13 when winning at Ayr in 1991. Another 13-y-o, and former Royal Ascot winner, made history in 2004. This was *Astrac* who, at Chepstow in June, completed the amazing record of having raced on every Flat course in the UK. Successful 12-y-o include the redoubtable sprinter *Densben* (still going strong in 1998), whose 1996 Haydock win was his nineteenth; also at 12, game old *Ballydurrow* won in 1989 at Carlisle over 1 m 4 f, but sadly lost his life on the gallops not long afterwards. *Hard To Figure*, another popular sprinter and past Ayr Gold Cup winner, won his seventeenth race at the age of 11 in 1997, and narrowly failed, aged 12, to capture the race named after him at Bath.

To return to jumping, a good chaser is usually not mature for this kind of racing until the age of eight or nine. *Red Rum* won the Grand National when he was eight, nine, and twelve; the triumphs of *Arkle* over fences were between the ages of seven and nine; and that most recent idol of the crowds, *Desert Orchid*, was within six days of his thirteenth birthday when in 1992, full of honour and achievement, he was finally retired. As seen above, there are many jumpers who stay around for a long time after that, too, and win good races. The oldest Grand National winner is *Peter Simple*, 15 years old in 1853. The Queen Mother's *Special Cargo* won the Whitbread Gold Cup, one of the most important chasing prizes, in 1984, when he was 11, and there is now a statue of him at Sandown; ten years earlier, *The Dikler* had won it at the same age – both horses were saddled by the late Fulke Walwyn. Meanwhile, that old and much applauded favourite of the Uttoxeter crowds, *Jimmy Miff*, was 18 when running his final race (see Chapter Seven). As a further reminder that horses, like human beings, are as young as they feel, it is worth noting that in 1994, the most senior horse in training was that game old chaser, *Vulrory's Clown*. At the age of 16, he was still happily leading Owen Brennan's string, and in 1993 had recorded his sixteenth victory (five of them at Doncaster where he has a race named after him).

While at stud, many horses are active at even greater ages than this. One of the greatest broodmares in the history of racing, *Pocahontas*, whose progeny had untold influence on the course of racing and bloodstock breeding in the 19th century, delivered her last foal when she was 25, and, after retirement to the Marquis of Exeter's paddocks, died in 1840 at the age of 33. And some horses flourish when racing days are over. *Red Rum* took up a new career as a celebrity, opening betting shops, gracing charity fetes, travelling everywhere in his personal Mercedes horse-box, and was capable even at the age of 26 of bringing Liverpool traffic to a halt when he paraded through the streets, while *Desert Orchid* is still much in demand for guest appearances.

All-weather   A somewhat misleading term referring to the racing on synthetic surfaces at Lingfield, Southwell and Wolverhampton. Although they are proof enough against frost, even these courses cannot race in foggy conditions (or hurricanes). When 'all-weather' racing began in late 1989 it was officially 'being introduced primarily to offset the financial losses caused to the levy (*q.v.*) by abandonment of race meetings during the winter period'. Despite early criticism and setbacks (such as the banning of hurdle races because of the number of horses killed), 'all-weather' racing has established its own following and betting public.

   Lingfield (which also stages racing on turf) has a surface known as Polytrack. This was installed in late 2001 and has proved a great success and a huge improvement on the course's original synthetic surface, which was called Equitrack. The newer surface has in effect revolutionised all-weather racing, for it now has more in common with the dynamics of turf racing and has resulted (together with higher prize-money) in a far better class of performer than used to be the case.

   Southwell and Wolverhampton have Fibresand surfaces, but Wolverhampton, following severe drainage problems and an outcry after race cancellations, is to have its surface ripped up and replaced with Polytrack in a £3 million project due to be completed by the autumn of 2004. Wolverhampton is the most recent 'all-weather' after a drastic transformation. Habitués of the old turf course, in a setting which suggested that the Industrial Revolution was only yesterday, used to have sidebets on how long a goods train would take to crawl across the nearest viaduct. The revamped course opened in late 1993 and introduced a new standard of amenity for its racegoers.

   Following Wolverhampton's latest improvements, all-weather racing has taken significant steps towards further expansion. Newmarket is to have a synthetic stretch alongside the Rowley Mile. It had been hoped that work on the new track would begin in 2004 so that it would be in action by 2005, but plans have been delayed because of a dispute over fixtures. Plans have also been approved for an all-weather track at Sedgefield, while at Great Leighs, Essex (for more details see under **Courses**), work has now begun on a brand-new all-weather track.

   Trainers to follow at Lingfield in particular are Gerard Butler, James Eustace, Jeremy Noseda, Jamie Osborne and Alan Jarvis, and for equine specialists on the All-Weather, headed by the remarkable *Tempering* (23 victories according to some records), see Chapter Seven.

Ante-post betting   Traditionally, this is betting that takes place before the day of a big race, often several weeks or even months beforehand, as distinguished from the usual betting immediately before any given race. The term has been given several derivations, the most likely being a connection with the 'post betting' that

SPORTING INTELLIGENCE.

MANCHESTER RACES.—Thursday.

Although this was to be looked upon in the light of a by
day, the card was a heavy one and there was manifold promise of excellent sport. The day was one of glorious bright
sunshine and summer like warmth, instead of the clouds
and cold winds to which we have been so long accustomed,
and as a consequence the attendance was enormous,
much larger than on any previous off day. Some
time was cut to waste when the horses were at the
post for the first race, the City Welter Plate, in consequence of the temper displayed by Acrobat, who, after a
false start, could not be induced to join his opponents until
Glover dismounted and led him up. They then left the
post in close o~`  and Reay, Eo` ~v, and `  `~De
` t~

..on easil,   .ck, .
others, and A Maiaen Plate was .   by a length, after a
good race, by the colt by The Palmer, beating the King-
craft filly and five others. There was some little betting
on the Royal Hunt Cup during the day, which we give
below.

BETTING ON THE COURSE.

ROYAL HUNT CUP.

12 to 1 agst Sir Joseph (t.)	100 to 6 agst Fiddlestring
100 — 8 —— Avontes (t.)	(taken)
100 — 8 —— Sidonia (t.)	20 — 1 —— Cradle (t.)
100 — 7 —— Lady Ronald	33 — 1 —— Flotsam (t.)
(taken)	33 — 1 —— Priscillian (t.)

ORDER OF RUNNING, THIS DAY.

	H. M.		H. M.
Beaufort Stakes ...	2 0	Gerard Selling Plate	4 0
Summer Plate ...	2 30	Optional Sale Plate ...	4 30
Wilton Welter ...	3 0	Selling Handicap ...	5 0
Salford Borough Cup	3 30		

occurred in earlier days. Bets used to be struck on Newmarket Heath, for
instance, round the betting posts which can be seen in contemporary
illustrations. To bet ante post, therefore, was to strike a bet, as today, before the
wagering which immediately preceded a race or match between two horses.

There are many big races, notably those comprising the Spring Double and
Autumn Double *(q.v.)*, as well as the Classics *(q.v.)*, the Grand National and
events at Royal Ascot, Goodwood, York, Cheltenham and elsewhere, on which
bookmakers advertise betting prices long before the event, and which can attract
a lot of business. In the case of the Guineas races and Derby (*see CLASSICS*)
bets are struck as much as a year or more before the actual date, usually at
considerably longer odds than are available nearer the day and on it. Despite the
fact that many big ante-post gambles have been successful (see Chapter Three)
the continued existence of this form of betting suggests that bookmakers find that
it, despite losses, is a worthwhile exercise. That it is a long-standing practice is
illustrated in the reproduction above of the prices available on the Royal Hunt
Cup at Royal Ascot 1879, and laid on other courses in the week before the race.

In the past few years, there has been an extension of ante-post betting. This takes the form of offering prices on the morning of the day on which certain bigger races are to be run. Advertised in the sporting press, and known under various names such as 'early prices', these, like the traditional form of ante-post wagering, offer the attraction of possible longer odds than those available immediately before the race or races in question that afternoon. This, particularly on Saturdays, has become a popular and lively feature of the betting scene, with, on occasions, some very successful bets being struck. In addition, another extension of ante-post betting, albeit short-range, has become highly popular in recent years. This concerns big races due to be run on a Saturday. Entries (*q.v.*) are published earlier in the week, bookmakers also publish prices and it is then often possible to secure a better price on the eventual winner than that at which it is eventually returned (*see ODDS and STARTING PRICE*) on the day.

Apprentice allowance   In order to compensate for inexperience, apprentice jockeys receive an allowance in terms of weight, according to the total number of winners they have ridden. This weight is subtracted from the weight their horse is set to carry in a race, except in races confined to apprentice riders only. The scale of allowance is as follows: 7 lb until the apprentice has ridden the winner of 20 Flat races under the rules of any recognised Turf authority; thereafter 5 lb until he or she has won 50 such Flat races; thereafter 3 lb up to a limit of 95 winning races. In all cases Apprentice races are excluded from these totals.

Similar allowances apply to National Hunt races, with a notable proviso that they cannot be claimed in the Grand National, nor in selling races. There are quite complicated rules concerning allowances to National Hunt riders such as conditional jockeys (*q.v.*) and amateur riders.

No apprentice jockeys are allowed under the age of 16 or over 24. In the days when Lester Piggott began his meteoric career there was, fortunately, no such lower limit. Lester was apprenticed to his father, Keith Piggott, who trained at Lambourn, Berkshire. He had his first winner at the age of 12 on *The Chase* at Haydock Park in August 1948. He lost his right to the 7 lb allowance the following May, to the 5 lb allowance in October 1950, and on 26 May 1951, still only 15 years of age, he lost entirely his right to claim when he rode *No Light* into the winner's enclosure at Hurst Park.

The value of a good claiming apprentice, particularly in a big handicap, cannot be over-emphasised, especially at their natural riding weight. If they are talented, their light weight and ability to make their allowance more than compensate for inexperience can be a winning factor, with the reservation that apprentices do not often do well in competition with senior jockeys on courses that require very skilful and experienced jockeyship, notably the Derby course at Epsom, the round course at Ascot, and the equivalent at the main Goodwood meeting.

At the post   Nothing to do with ante-*post* betting, not these days anyway. Horses when they have arrived at the point from which a race is to be started are said to be 'at the post'.

Auction race Auction races are specifically for 2-y-o horses which have never before won and were bought as yearlings at specified public auctions. Example: Pontefract, 7 June 1993. June Maiden Auction Stakes 5 furlongs...for 2-y-o only, maidens at starting (*q.v.*), which were sold as yearlings by public auction (under the hammer) at sales administered by Tattersalls Ltd, Tattersalls (Ireland) Ltd, Goffs Bloodstock Sales Ltd, Ascot Bloodstock Sales or Doncaster Bloodstock Sales Ltd, or as 2-y-o at any of the following 'Breeze-up' (*q.v.*) sales, Doncaster 25 & 26 March and Newmarket 14 & 15 April 1993, for 5,000 guineas or less...

Autumn Double   The Cambridgeshire Handicap (1 mile 1 furlong) and the Cesarewitch (2 miles 2 furlongs), both first run at Newmarket in 1839, take place at an interval of about a fortnight in October. Each race normally attracts big fields, in particular the Cambridgeshire; correspondingly the bookmakers offer big prices about some of the runners, and an attempt to nominate the winner of both races, especially in the ante-post market which precedes them, is known as the Autumn Double. In other words, the choice for each race is combined in one bet, a double (see Chapter Five for more about doubles in general and how winnings are calculated). The longest-priced Autumn Double of recent years, in terms of starting price, was in 1987, when *Private Audition* (returned at 50/1) won the Cesarewitch, and *Balthus* (also 50/1) the Cambridgeshire. A bet of £1 double on them would have returned £2,600 before (off-course) deduction of the now abolished betting tax, but even these long odds might have been bettered in the ante-post market.   The heyday of the Autumn Double, when some spectacular gambles were landed, has probably passed. Because there are so many other good races with valuable prize-money available, horses are not so often specially prepared for months beforehand with, in particular, the Cambridgeshire in view.   But it still does happen, and, as ever, with the traditional objective – a successful gamble as the afternoon sun goes down early and the mists gather on Newmarket Heath. Coupling the winner of the Lincoln Handicap with that of the Grand National is known as the Spring Double.

Bad legs   A more common condition among racehorses than the public generally realise. To understand it, and, indeed, to appreciate the whole process of racing and training horses to race, it is necessary to think of the horses as equine athletes, which indeed they are. Using this analogy, would, for example, Sebastian Coe have shone over 100 metres; would he have raced if he had jarred his legs badly; or would he have dreamt of taking part in a contest without first and last using a track suit? To translate these points into equine terms, horses also have ideal distances over which they should compete – a crucial factor when it comes to weighing up their chances in a race; they wear blankets and rugs in the paddock before a race, and afterwards, when perspiring, have a 'string vest' thrown over them and blankets again; and they, no less than their human counterparts, pull muscles when racing, strain tendons, and because of leg trouble, either chronic or temporary, may 'break down' altogether and be unable to race.

   The horse's forelegs, particularly when jumping fences, and to an extent when running on hard ground, come under great pressure, and it is the forelegs which give trainers the greatest anxiety. Bad legs as a chronic condition occur for a variety of reasons, including heredity. A protective measure consists of bandages, sometimes semi-permanent, on the forelegs. *Arkle*'s great rival over fences, *Mill House*, wore bandages. *Crepello*, the celebrated Guineas and Derby winner of 1957, had suspect tendons and, as described by Dick Francis in *Lester, the Official Biography*, wore strong supportive bandages on his forelegs, 'the sort called Newmarket Boots, which were made of doeskin and sewn on tightly, semi-permanent. They had to be turned round on the legs every day to dislodge any piece of grit which might have slipped inside.' It is noteworthy that trainers are extremely proud (see Chapter Nine) and rightly so, when they have managed a big success with horses who are unsound in their legs. Some examples are the Grand National winner *Aldaniti* (1981, trained by Josh Gifford), the Queen Mother's Whitbread and Grand Military winner *Special Cargo* (Fulke Walwyn), the 1966 Cesarewitch winner *Persian Lancer* (Ryan Price) and that great stayer *Le Moss* (Henry Cecil), winner of the long-distance 'triple crown' of Ascot Gold Cup, Goodwood Cup and Doncaster Cup two years running 1979–80. Sometimes tendon trouble is still treated by the banned techniques of blistering or firing, but the modern, approved remedy is by carbon-fibre implants.

The best guide to whether a horse has suspect legs, wears bandages, or has been blistered or fired is *Timeform* (see Chapter Four).

Betting Exchanges   These are relatively recent phenomena which have enabled punters to bypass the bookmaker. Via the Internet, they can choose to take a price or, alternatively, lay odds against a horse on one of the Betting Exchanges that now exist. Betfair (www.betfair.com) is the largest and most popular of them. Another is the Dublin-based Betdaq (www.betdaq.com). Betting Exchanges cut out bookmakers and the betting takes place on a person-to-person basis. Publicity for them claims that they trade at more generous odds than those that bookmakers offer. Commission is payable on winnings only; a small percentage of winnings is taken, nothing on stakes. It should however be made clear that while Betting Exchanges are undoubtedly popular, they have also been used unscrupulously by some to profit unfairly, for example, by laying horses to lose. This concerns only a minority but helps to give racing a bad name.

Betting on the rails   In the Members' enclosure on racecourses, bookmakers are not allowed to make a book. However, a high proportion of those people who are either annual members (i.e. pay an annual subscription for membership entitling them to a metal badge) or pay on the day for entrance to that enclosure frequently go to the racecourse with the prime intention of having a bet. To get over this difficulty, the leading bookmakers have pitches immediately next to the rails separating the Members' from Tattersalls' Ring; they actually stand in Tattersalls', display their personal boards on the rails, and conduct business over the rails, as well as on the Tattersalls' side. In addition, from time immemorial they were unable to display prices, but now that has all changed. As from 1 January 2001, after a long campaign to enable showing off prices, rails bookmakers at last were permitted to do so. This was no less than a revolution in on-course betting, and bookmakers whose pitches (*q.v.*) are in Tattersalls' were very displeased, to put it at its mildest. They claimed not only that their business would be adversely affected, but also that many had been 'conned' into paying inflated prices for pitches in the Tattersalls' Ring after assurances that the rails bookmakers would not be permitted to display prices 'in the foreseeable future'. Much of the business is done with credit customers, but some cash is taken, if in big enough amounts, on the Tattersalls' side, and big business is done with other bookmakers through their runners. Rails bookmakers have their own association, and they comprise the top end of the racecourse betting market, as well as being vital to the price shifts of that market. But no longer, as used to be the case, do they dictate those movements exclusively. This is because 90 per cent of betting today takes place off the course. Heavy support for a particular 'betting shop horse' will force the price down on the racecourse because the money for it finds its way to the racecourse, and, in particular, the rails, by telephone, walkie-talkie and tic-tac, and immediately the shorter price is relayed to the other betting rings on the course.

Betting ring   Racecourse betting rings are the enclosures where betting takes place – mainly Tattersalls' Ring (see previous entry), where admission charges also cover admission to the paddock (*q.v.*), and the lower-priced Silver Ring, so-called because originally bookmakers would take bets made with silver coinage. Some courses no longer have a separate Silver Ring. Betting also takes place on certain racecourses (e.g. Epsom) in areas where there is free admission, and this is known as 'betting on the course'.

Betting shop   (See also Chapters Two and Six.) The number of betting shops has shown a downward trend since the boom times of the 1960s just after they were legalised. At present in the UK there are about 8,500. In 1993 it was announced that between 1 April and 31 August betting shops would be able to remain open until 10 p.m. in order to cater for evening racing, thus correcting, at last, an anomaly which had existed since shops were originally legalised in the 'sixties. Technology has made big advances in recent years, with prices and commentaries from SIS (*q.v.*) on view on batteries of screens.

Black type   If a horse has been successful in a Pattern race (*q.v.*) or Listed race (*q.v.*), he or she is said to have 'achieved black type' – i.e. in order to draw attention to the horse's putative importance for breeding purposes, his or her name appears in bold black type in pedigrees featured by bloodstock sales catalogues. Horses who finished fourth in such races, however, are now no longer entitled to 'black type'.

Blinkers   A device consisting of a hood which fits over a horse's head, with shields at the eye-holes which restrict the horse's peripheral vision. The purpose is to concentrate the horse's attention ahead by cutting out what might have been seen on either side. The fitting of blinkers for the first time is indicated in the more informative racecards published in the morning papers and is always worth noting – although, while it sometimes secures a dramatic improvement in a horse's racecourse performance, it should not be regarded as a sovereign specific for poor form. Blinkers are used more frequently these days than they used to be and have lost their reputation for being the tell-tale sign for a horse of dodgy character. In other words, although there are still unreliable horses who invariably wear blinkers, there are also perfectly genuine animals whose performance is better when wearing them. *Timeform* gives good comments on whether a horse is genuine or not, and the effect of blinkers on performance. A converse hint to a horse's capabilities occurs when, after being tried in blinkers, he or she races next time without them. A **Visor** is a pair of blinkers modified with a slit cut in the eye-shields so that a horse is given some peripheral vision, allowing, for example, other horses alongside to be seen. A **Hood** leaves the eyes clear but covers the ears because some horses are adversely affected by noise. Use of both visor and hood, like blinkers, will be publicised on racecards.

Blow up   Nothing to do with 'went like a bomb', which, self-evidently, is something quite different. A horse which has 'blown up' or which 'blew up in the straight' is one which, without explosion of any kind whatsoever – rather the reverse in fact – suddenly loses its place in a race after going well up to that point. Also known as 'stopping to nothing'.

Bookmakers
These can be divided into:
1.   Those who make a book on the racecourse.
2.   Those who operate betting shops off-course (which group includes, for simplicity's sake, those operating betting shops on racecourses, as well).
3.   Those who operate a telephone credit service (where an account may be based on pure credit, or cash deposits in advance) or a postal betting service.
4.   Firms who operate on the Internet.
5.   Firms who operate spread-betting services (*see SPREAD BETTING*).

A number of big firm bookmakers combine two or even all of the first three activities. Some of 2. and 3. will settle bets at Tote prices, if the backer specifies these odds, otherwise the settlement is at starting price (*q.v.*) or at a price taken in a betting shop, or a price based on the latest 'show' of betting.

On the racecourse, bets are settled at the prices quoted, or, if agreed with the backer, starting price (SP). Some bookmakers put up signs on their joints (*q.v.*) that they will settle at SP if required. However they settle, their activities, on-course and off-course, are governed by what goes on in the market on the racecourse. A betting market is formed immediately before each race (but see also Chapter Six). The prices fluctuate according to the total of money known to be on a particular horse in the ring as a whole, amounts of significance being signalled by tic-tac from rails to Tattersalls and back, and to the Silver Ring and bookmakers 'outside' – i.e. on the course itself (or, for example, at Epsom on Derby Day in the great mêlée on the Downs). The amount a price will contract or go out in the market varies, also, according to whether the market is a weak or strong one (see below).

The prices originally on offer in the early stages of any betting market are not, however, based on money bet, but (usually) on how the bigger Tattersalls' boards operators think the market ought to go. The earliest prices chalked up are very often shorter than they realistically should be. In the days up to and beyond the great post-war betting boom the true market price was dictated by on-course money, largely by big backers (whether professionals, commission agents betting on behalf of others, including trainers and owners, or trainers and owners themselves). The huge growth of off-course betting since the 1960s has changed all that. Seldom do trainers walk up to the rails, get a price about their horse, and affect the market accordingly. Most money is wagered off the course, and is transmitted, or news of it is transmitted, by telephone to the tic-tacs acting for the big bookmakers. The entire market reacts accordingly within a few seconds. The money which causes this is called 'office money' and in the case of big amounts placed off-course which crucially affect the market, the horses are known in the ring as 'betting shop horses'. Going back briefly to the very opening of the market, some Tattersalls and other bookmakers in other rings and 'outside' subscribe to a marked card known usually as the 'house card', which gives an opinion on how the day's racing might turn out. This used to be operated by 'Jack the Judge', who charged a fee for the service, and his successor still operates. Basing their prices on the 'house card' and/or their own judgement, the Tattersalls boards bookmakers form the early market.

As the market gets under way, and money starts to reinforce the bookmakers' original opinions of the prices or causes them to alter prices on the general principle of supply and demand, a punter can learn a great deal from following the market – that is, seeing how the odds are altering. The market can give strong hints on what to back, and, even more important, what not to back. On the racecourse, this involves having a look at how the prices are going at successive stages in the ten minutes or so immediately before a race. In the betting shop, with the aid of successive prices marked on the board or shown on video, following the market is rather easier, and watching the television makes it equally simple. All the market moves can readily be seen on television, and, depending on the channel, are backed up with information about why the prices are going the way they are. In betting shops with television or video, a similar advantage is enjoyed by the punters. On the racecourse, following the market is rather harder work, because the bookmakers erase the prices successively as the odds change; but, in general, the punter who can take the time and trouble should reap the reward.

Weak Markets/Strong Markets. Royal Ascot provides one of the strongest betting markets of the year on the Flat, and the Cheltenham Festival does so in National Hunt racing. The weakest markets are at small, under-patronised courses where the racing is poor. Here, a few hundred pounds can cause prices to tumble several points whereas in a strong market the same amount multiplied several times over would cause no price change. A fitting postscript to this entry is provided by an illuminating interview which Richard Evans, then Racing Correspondent of *The Times*, had in January 1999. It was with Victor Chandler, the leading bookmaker, who later started a betting revolution by going to Gibraltar and offering tax-free bets. He was shortly followed by other bookmakers and, as a consequence, betting tax in the UK was abolished by the Chancellor of the Exchequer, no less, in his 2001 Budget. Victor Chandler, at the time of the interview, had some fascinating observations on some of the changes that have overtaken the betting scene:

'The racecourse punter has never had it so good, according to Victor Chandler, who sponsors today's weather-threatened card at Ascot. As one of the leading rails bookmakers, who does not blink at laying five-figure bets, he should know because last year his on-course business barely broke even.

His analysis of why the on-course bookmaker is suffering and the professional backer is king is simple. There has been a dramatic change in the kind of person going racing, with far fewer people prepared to have a decent bet – and the influx of new bookmakers who are offering generous prices and betting to tiny margins. "To be a punter now is heaven. With no expenses, being a professional punter compared to a bookmaker has to be the better choice," he said yesterday.

Chandler explained: "At Cheltenham's last Sunday meeting, we did a survey and asked people whether they bet with bookmakers. Only 37 per cent said yes. The rest either don't bet or bet in small sums with the Tote.

"That confirms just how the culture of racing has changed. My on-course business has been decimated in the last two years. For example, three or four years ago at the Eclipse meeting at Sandown, I took around £200,000 on the big race. Last year, we took £8,000 on it. On Sundays, you see an enormous number of prams – they are not our punters.

"Every on-course bookmaker is doing less and less business, which makes it even more surprising the prices paid for pitches at the recent auctions. One of the reasons for the change has to do with the young professional.

"The City boys used to go racing and sometimes take a day off during the week but the Germans and Americans have taken over in the City, working a six-day week starting at 5am, and they don't get a Thursday off to go to Sandown. We don't see the young people during the week who were prepared to have a £50, £100, £500 or £1,000 bet. Added to which they are more interested in football."'

Box-walker Term for a horse who will not settle in his loose-box and persistently walks round and round it, thus losing weight and being difficult to train. The cure is often to give the horse a companion, such as a goat. This worked very well in the case of *Bonidon*, the very first winner Jenny Pitman had as a professional trainer. *Oath*, the 1999 Derby winner, was another reformed box-walker.

Breeze-up A form of bloodstock sale taking place at a racecourse, such as Newmarket, where instead of the usual practice of lots on offer merely being led round the sale-ring, they are put through their paces on the course in front of prospective buyers. This consists of them being cantered or 'breezed along' over two or three furlongs.

British Horseracing Board Commonly abbreviated to BHB, this is the governing and administrative body for racing which came into being in June 1993, thereby taking over effective overall control from the Jockey Club (*q.v.*). This in itself was the most radical shake-up of racing's power structure for more than 200 years and marked a watershed in British racing history. For the first time racing has, as its governing authority, a representative, accountable and democratic body which gives the industry an executive role in shaping its future.

The BHB's principal responsibilities include strategic planning and policy for racing; improving the financial position of racing; representing racing in dealings with government; the fixture list; race planning, including the supervision of race programmes and the employment of handicappers (*q.v.*); marketing and promotion of racing; nominating racing's representatives on the Horserace Betting Levy Board (*q.v.*); liaison with the betting industry; encouraging and fostering the breeding of bloodstock; collection and control of funds required for the administration of racing, including those required by the Jockey Club for the protection of the sport's integrity; the development and maintenance of programmes of training and education within racing; and the contract under which Weatherbys (*q.v.*) supply administrative services to racing.

The principal aim of the BHB is to give the leadership needed to put racing in Britain on a sound financial footing. This means ensuring that racing is making the best use of its resources, is maximising income from outside the sport and has a clear single voice with which to air its views in Parliament and elsewhere.

Among the BHB members are representatives of the Racecourse Association, Jockey Club (*q.v.*), Racehorse Owners Association, Thoroughbred Breeders' Association, and Industry Committee. The Chairman from 1 July 2004 is Martin Broughton. Greg Nichols is Chief Executive and Tristram Ricketts is Secretary-General and Company Secretary. Offices are at 42 Portman Square, London W1H 0EN, and there is now an attractive website full of information on the Internet at http://www.britishhorseracing.com

Bumping and boring Sometimes, in the final stages of a race, a horse may be tiring, and the jockey is unable to prevent him or her veering off a straight line, bumping an opponent, and 'boring' that opponent off its intended course. This may affect the opponent's chances, and in certain instances may cost him the race, in which case there will almost certainly be an objection by the losing rider; equally certain, in any case, is that when bumping and boring occurs there is a strong possibility of a stewards' inquiry, during which the evidence of the film from the camera patrol (*q.v.*)and a video re-run will be examined.

'By' and 'Out of' Expressions indicating the parentage of a horse. He or she is described as being BY a Sire (stallion) OUT OF the Dam (broodmare), whose origin will often be indicated in turn by brackets giving the name of her sire.
  e.g. *Commander-in-Chief* by *Dancing Brave* out of *Slightly Dangerous (Roberto)*
  or simply *Commander-in-Chief: Dancing Brave – Slightly Dangerous (Roberto)*

The Calendar Term for the Racing Calendar (*q.v.*).

Came again A phrase used in the form book to indicate a horse that has renewed its effort after dropping back in a race.

Camera patrol First officially used at Newmarket on 30 June 1960. Cameras originally photographed the closing stages of a race from different angles, including head-on, and later the coverage was extended to provide, by means of a mobile camera, a complete visual record of a race. The prime aim is to provide evidence when an objection is lodged or there is a stewards' inquiry. With widespread use of closed-circuit television on racecourses, the video re-run reinforces the evidence of the camera patrol. Together, their use has discouraged the skulduggery and malpractice in race-riding that often occurred in days gone by.

Card Abbreviation for racecard, the official programme of runners on sale on racecourses (see also Chapter Four). Also appears in newspaper headings such as 'Chepstow Card' or 'Card for Uttoxeter'. Used in phrases such as 'The best bet on the card is...', also 'Going through the card'. This means, specifically, selection or association with every winner on the card. Sir Gordon Richards almost went through the card on two successive days long before he was knighted. At Chepstow, on 4 October 1933, he rode all six winners, and, the following day, rode the first five winners, then, sadly, in the last race on the card, on *Eagle Ray*, was beaten into third place by a neck and a head. More recently, on 28 September 1996, Frankie Dettori went through a seven-race card at Ascot and earned his 'Magnificent Seven' title.

Carpet Anyone bemused by Channel 4's presentation of betting with John McCririck's slow-motion tic-tac and use of strange betting terms may be interested to know that 'carpet', one of his favourites, derives from criminal slang for a three-month 'stretch' in prison. Hence 'carpet' is 3/1 in the betting. The late John O'Neill had a far wider grasp of esoteric betting terminology, however, and his return of the starting prices in the press room of northern racecourses is much missed. Apart from communicating in a marvellous Cockney rhyming slang delivered in a broad Manchester accent, John used to announce the starting prices in the following code (still used today) compounded from rhyming slang, back-slang, bingo, and other sources, including the aforesaid criminal usage.

Straight up	Even money	Bundle (of sticks)	6/1
Bits against/on	11/10	Nevis (back-slang)	7/1
Nevis to rouf	7/4	Garden (Garden Gate)	8/1
Bottle (of glue)	2/1	Chinese odds	9/1
Carpet	3/1	Cock and hen (or Cockle)	10/1
Burlington (Bertie)	100/30	Macaroni (rhymes with pony)	25/1
Rouf	4/1	Double carpet	33/1
Jacks (alive)	5/1		

Tic-tac signals also give rise to the following: Wrist 5/4, Half arm 6/4, Shoulder 7/4, Top of the Nut 9/4, and Between the Eyes 5/2.

Cast in his/her box Horses which have lain down in their stable loose-box, or travelling horse-box, and have difficulty in getting up again off the straw are said to be cast in their box; not a welcome happening on the day of a race. According to the late Lord Rosebery, *Sir Visto*, one of his father's three Derby winners, was cast in his box on the morning before he went on to win the St. Leger in 1895.

Chalk jockey Also 'chalkie'. A phrase used to describe a rider who is not successful enough, or, in the case of apprentices, a rider who has not yet ridden enough winners to justify having his or her name painted on one of the jockeys' and riders' boards which fit into the numbers board on the racecourse. Instead, the name is chalked or whitewashed on a blank board.

Championships Jockeys' and Trainers' Championships are decided, respectively, by the greatest number of winners ridden and the largest amount of win prize-money earned in a season. Moreover, these are titles simply by tradition. There is no official recognition of championships whatsoever, although the jockeys' championships used to generate plenty of betting on the outcome. Some notable achievements have been Gordon Richards's 26 times top of the list between 1925 and 1953, George Fordham's (including one shared) 14 (1855–70), Fred Archer's 13 (1874–86), Lester Piggott's 11 (1960–82) and Pat Eddery's – youngest post-war champion at the age of 22 in 1974 – 11 up to 1996. Outstanding feats among trainers who led the field have been Alec Taylor, 12 titles between 1907 and 1925, Henry Cecil, 10 (1976–93), and Sir Noel Murless, 9 (1948–73). These were all on the Flat while Martin Pipe's record over the jumps is quite incredible: 16 championships in succession since 1988–89.

Chase Common abbreviation for steeplechase, which term, in turn, is derived from the fact that in Ireland in 1752, Mr Edmund Blake was challenged by Mr O'Callaghan to race their hunters four and a half miles across country from Buttevant church to that at St. Leger, the steeple of the latter being the winning post. From that event evolved National Hunt racing, the cornerstone of which is the steeplechase, but without the steeples. A chase, these days, is a race over fences (as distinct from hurdles), at a distance from two miles to four miles plus, but most commonly three miles. The fences, constructed of birch, consist of plain fences, open ditches (a ditch 6 ft wide is on the take-off side of the fence), and a water-jump, which is spectacular but considered by many an unnecessarily dangerous obstacle which has cost the lives of chasers in the past, including that of the 1957 Grand National winner *Sundew* when he was racing the following season at Haydock Park. Except for the water-jump (at least 12 ft wide and not more than 3 ft high) all fences must be not less than 4 ft 6 ins in height.

In general, how stiff an obstacle any given fence on a racecourse is depends to an extent on how tightly packed with birch it is, and this varies a good deal from course to course. The fences at Kempton Park and Newbury, for example, may look fairly innocent to the spectator, but they are stiff fences, and it is no good picking a doubtful jumper on these courses. By contrast, to my eye at least, at Aintree, The Chair these days seems to be more loosely packed at the top than it used to be. After the field has charged over and partly through the top of it in the National, the somewhat tattered remains of The Chair look as if a giant vegetarian rat has been giving the evergreen his close attention.

The headquarters of National Hunt *(q.v.)* racing in general and chasing in particular is Cheltenham (see Chapter Eight), which features the Gold Cup during its great Festival meeting every March, but the sport flourishes throughout the country.

Under the Rules of Racing, horses cannot be put to fences until at least July of the year in which they are four years old. In practice, it is common for chasers not to appear in public until they are five or six, often after they have had a hurdling career.

Claiming race Also known as 'a claimer'. This is a race in which any runner may be claimed after the race for an advertised sum or more. If the owner of any runner wishes it to carry less than the maximum weight, the price at which it may be claimed is reduced accordingly. The Rules of Racing stipulate that the minimum price for which a horse may be claimed out of a claiming race is the figure published next to its name on the racecard. Since the weight actually carried by the horse in the race depends on this minimum amount for which it can be claimed, the trainer handicaps his own horse. After the race, any claims must be made in writing. Any claim must be higher or equal to the racecard figure. A 'friendly' claim may be made by connections of a runner in the race. It is an attempt to retain their charge by making a bid higher than any competing claim.

All claims must be sealed and placed in the claims box on the Clerk of the Scales' table, not later than ten minutes after the 'All Right' (weighed-in) signal has been authorised by the stewards. Claims may not be withdrawn or altered.

The horse goes to the person submitting the highest claim above the minimum price. Lots are drawn in the event of a tie. The owner receives 15 per cent of any surplus above the published minimum claiming price as well as 90 per cent of that minimum. The racecourse receives the remaining 85 per cent of the surplus, plus 10 per cent of the published minimum. Connections submitting a friendly claim must therefore pay 85 per cent of the surplus and 10 per cent of the minimum in order to keep their horse if their bid is successful.

Example: Windsor, 19 July 1993. Iron Blue Claiming Stakes 1 m 67 yds...for 3-y-o and up which, at starting, have not won more than two claiming races since 24 March 1993, each claimable at or above their specified price...Allowances: For each £1,000 below the maximum published price of £20,000 1 lb (Minimum published price £3,000)...the claiming price and weight MUST be stated. Only one such claiming price can be accepted.

Class A etc. Races on the Flat are classified in terms of prize-money from Class A down to Class H. This classification is often used in framing Conditions races *(q.v.)*.

Classics As pointed out by Peter Willett in his book *The Classic Racehorse*, '...Classic is not found in the list of Definitions in the British Rules of Racing or in the corresponding French rules, the Code des Courses'. He also draws attention to the anomaly that in the *Pattern Race Book*, published jointly by the racing authorities of Great Britain and France, there is a section giving advance notice of the dates and conditions of 'The Classic Races in England, Ireland and France'.

'Classic' when applied to a race, therefore, is a term consecrated by long usage, and, to quote Peter Willett once again, 'Classic races...are races of long standing which habitually attract the best horses and are regarded as the criteria of excellence'. More specifically, the Classics are open only to three-year-olds, and are five in number in England:

Course & Distance	Time	Race	Open to	First Run
Newmarket				
Rowley Mile Course	Spring	2000 Guineas	Colts & Fillies	1809
Newmarket				
Rowley Mile Course	Spring	1000 Guineas	Fillies only	1814
Epsom $1^1/_2$ miles	Summer	Derby	Colts & Fillies	1780
Epsom $1^1/_2$ miles	Summer	Oaks	Fillies only	1779
Doncaster $1^3/_4$ miles	Autumn	St. Leger	Colts & Fillies	1776

Before the early years of the 20th century, the Classics now open only to colts and fillies were also open to geldings. They were excluded from the 2000 Guineas (whose title, like that of the 1000 Guineas, no longer bears any relationship to the actual prize on offer) from 1904 onwards, and from the Derby and St. Leger two years later. The only record of a gelding being placed in the Derby seems to be that of *Curzon*, runner-up to *Sir Visto* in 1895, while *Courlan*, third to HRH The Prince of Wales's *Diamond Jubilee* in 1900, appears to be the only gelding placed in the history of the St. Leger.

As far as fillies are concerned, it is rare these days for them to contest either the 2000 Guineas or the Derby, owners and trainers preferring to run them in the equivalent Classics open to fillies only: the 1000 Guineas and Oaks. The last filly to win the 2000 Guineas was *Garden Path* in 1944, although Jack Gerber's *Bebe Grande* was runner-up in 1953 to the northern-trained colt *Nearula* after leading for much of the race. The only other filly in the 20th century to win the 2000 Guineas was *Sceptre* (see Chapter Nine).

The last filly to win the Derby was *Fifinella* in 1916, and she also won the Oaks, a double achieved only eight years previously by *Signorinetta*. A rather charming story concerns the eventual Classic successes of *Signorinetta*. She was bred, owned and trained by the Chevalier Ginistrelli, a racing enthusiast who came to England from Italy and settled in Newmarket, where he was a popular figure. One of the mares he brought with him was mated with the great *St. Simon* and produced *Signorina*. She was unbeaten in nine races as a 2-y-o and came second in the Oaks. But when she retired she was barren for ten consecutive seasons. Eventually she seemed to take a fancy to a horse of no great racing ability called *Chaleureux*. The Chevalier was convinced they were in love and so they were mated. He may well, of course, have been right. The love-child was *Signorinetta*, whose Derby success was at 100/1, although two days later she was a more realistic 3/1 when capturing the Oaks as well. More recently, *Nobiliary* was second to *Grundy* in the 1975 Derby, while in 1998, another filly, Godolphin's 1000

Guineas winner *Cape Verdi*, also ran in the Derby. In this sporting gesture she was made favourite, but after a rough run was unplaced.

By contrast, the record of fillies in the St. Leger in recent times is much more consistently impressive. In 1985 *Oh So Sharp* won this oldest Classic, having previously taken the 1000 Guineas and Oaks, a feat in which she was emulating, in the 20th century, those great fillies of Edwardian times, *Sceptre* (1902) and *Pretty Polly* (1904), as well as *Meld* (1955) and *Sun Chariot* ridden by Gordon Richards in the colours of HM King George VI in 1942.

In 1977 there was another Royal success when HM The Queen's filly *Dunfermline* won both the Oaks and St. Leger. Sir Michael Sobell's *Sun Princess* did the same in 1983, and in 1992 Mr Bill Gredley's *User Friendly*, one of the best fillies of recent times, won the Oaks, Irish Oaks and St. Leger (and, after a tremendous run and looking like the winner, was caught by *Subotica* and beaten only by a neck in the Prix de l'Arc de Triomphe).

It is important to realise that, originally, there was no set intent to establish a pattern of Classic races. It simply evolved, and had become recognised as a pattern probably by about the middle of the 19th century. Classic winners have profoundly influenced the development of the thoroughbred, as well as achieving great prestige because in general they have proved themselves the best of their age and breed.

As a medium for betting, the Classics generally provide excellent opportunities. Well-advertised form mostly works out, except in a poor all-round year; well-backed horses tend to win, and, in strong ante-post markets, there are opportunities for long prices. For example, for those who took the opportunity with months to spare, *Nashwan* (SP for the 1989 Derby 5/4 Favourite) could have been backed at 40/1; and *Zafonic* (5/6 Favourite when winning the 1993 2000 Guineas) was at one time 33/1 and well taken at that price.

Some Classic statistics
Greatest winning margin in a Classic: 20 lengths, *Mayonaise*, 1859 1000 Guineas; longest winning odds: 200/1, *Theodore*, 1822 St. Leger; shortest winning odds: 8/100, *Pretty Polly*, 1904 Oaks; warmest losing favourite: 1/7, *Caesar*, 2nd 1839 2000 Guineas; longest-priced place horse: 500/1, *Terimon*, 2nd 1989 Derby; most Classic victories: *Formosa*, four in 1868, including dead-heat in 2000 Guineas, and *Sceptre*, four in 1902; most successful Classic jockey: Lester Piggott, 30 winners, 1954 (*Never Say Die*, Derby) – 1992 (*Rodrigo de Triano*, 2000 Guineas). Trainers: with *Love Divine* in 2000 providing a remarkable seventh Oaks success for Henry Cecil, he moved level with John Porter (1868–1900) in the trainers' Classic list. He is far ahead of his contemporaries with a total of 23 Classic victories since 1975, and is joint-fourth in the all-time list behind John Scott 40 (1827–63), Robert Robson 34 (1793–1827), and Mat Dawson 28 (1853–95).

Cleverly A horse which wins more easily than the winning distance suggests is said to have won 'cleverly'. He or she may equally be said to have won 'with something in hand'. It happens often on the Flat where a jockey has let the horse do only enough in order to win. The full amount of distance by which he or she might have won is therefore unknown both to the public, and, more important, to the handicapper who can only guess at the horse's true capability. Such horses are worth noting for the future on this sort of evidence, which will be given in the form books and amplified in the comments of *Raceform* and *Chaseform*, in the Analysis following results in the *Racing Post*, and in *Superform* and *Timeform*. Other phrases in the same connection are when a winner is noted as 'not extended' and 'won with his head in his chest'.

Colt Male thoroughbred from the age of two up to and including the age of four.

Conditions races All races other than handicaps. The conditions of a race determine the weight each runner will be set to carry: they may be based on age, sex, value and status of previous races won, and other factors, with weight allowances being made, for example, for not having won a race at all.

The most important category consists of Weight-for-Age *(q.v.)* races. The weight an older horse has to concede to a younger one varies throughout the Flat season and National Hunt season, becoming less and less as the season progresses. The precise weights are determined by application of the Weight-for-Age Scale *(q.v.)*. But there are many other kinds of Conditions race.

Examples:
Nottingham, 19 April 1993. Slip Anchor Conditions Stakes 1 m 54 yds...for 4-y-o and up which, at starting, have not won a Pattern race *(q.v.)*...Wts: Colts and geldings 8 st 10 lb; fillies 8 st 5 lb. Penalties: after 18 April 1991, for each Class E *(see CLASS A ETC.)* race won 2 lb. For each Class D race won 4 lb. For each Class C race won 6 lb. For each Class A or B race won 8 lb (Penalties halved for races won before 19 April 1992) (Penalties cumulative and maximum 18 lb)...
Royal Ascot, June. Queen Anne Stakes 1 m...for 3-y-o which, at starting, have not won a Group One race *(see PATTERN RACES)* and for 4-y-o and up...Wts: 3-y-o colts and geldings 8 st 5 lb; fillies 8 st 2 lb. 4-y-o and up colts and geldings 9 st 2 lb; fillies 8 st 13 lb. Penalties: a winner of a Group Two race 3 lb. Of a Group One race 6 lb (Races won at 2-y-o not to count for penalties for 4-y-o and up)...
Newbury, August. Washington Singer Stakes 7 f...for 2-y-o only, sired by stallions which won a race of one and a half miles or over...Wts: Colts and geldings 8 st 11 lb; fillies 8 st 6 lb. Penalties: a winner of a Class C race 3 lb. Of a Listed race *(q.v.)* or Class B race 5 lb. Of a Pattern race 7 lb...

Weight-for-Age
Cheltenham, March. Smurfit Champion Hurdle Challenge Trophy 2 m $1/2$ f...for 4-y-o and up...Wts: 4-y-o 11 st 6 lb; 5-y-o and up 12 st. Fillies and mares allowed 5 lb...
Ascot, July. King George VI and Queen Elizabeth Diamond Stakes 1 m 4 f...for 3-y-o and up...Wts: 3-y-o colts and geldings 8 st 9 lb; fillies 8 st 6 lb. 4-y-o and up colts and geldings 9 st 7 lb; fillies 9 st 4 lb...

Some other kinds of Conditions race
Ascot, March. Golden Eagle Novices Chase 2 m 3 f...for 5-y-o and up which, at the start of the current season, have not won a chase...Wts: 5-y-o 10 st 10 lb;

6-y-o and up 11 st 4 lb; mares allowed 5 lb. Penalties: a winner of a chase value £5,000 4 lb. Of a chase worth £10,000 7 lb...

Ascot, April 1993. Mahonia Hunters Chase...for 5-y-o and up which, at starting, have not won a chase since 1 January 1991, other than a Hunters' Chase...Wts: 5-y-o 11 st 7 lb; 6-y-o and up 12 st; mares allowed 5 lb. Penalties: after 1991, a winner of a Hunters' Chase 4 lb. Of two Hunters' Chases 8 lb. To be ridden by Amateur Riders...

Newmarket, April. The Wood Ditton Stakes 1 m...for 3-y-o maidens (*q.v.*) only which, at starting, have never run. Wts: colts and geldings 9 st; fillies 8 st 9 lb...

Thus, as with apprentice jockeys, inexperience is allowed for in horses, and previous success makes further success harder. A higher proportion of favourites and well-backed horses win in Conditions races, especially 2-y-o races, than in handicaps; but beware placing too much reliance on a literal interpretation of form shown in a Conditions race if a horse subsequently runs in a handicap, because it does not necessarily, for various reasons, translate lb for lb. Equally, it is well worth studying the conditions of races and particularly the amount of penalty incurred for previous success which may not be enough to stop further victory.

Conditional jockey An inexperienced National Hunt rider who must be under the age of 26 and may claim allowances (except in the Grand National and certain valuable Weight-for-Age [*q.v.*] races) as follows: 7 lb until he or she has won 15 races; then 5 lb up to a total of 30 races; thereafter 3 lb up to 65 races won.

Courses One of the outstanding features of racing in Great Britain is the huge variety of the 59 racecourses providing differing tests of ability for horses both on the Flat and over jumps, as well as pleasure in this very variety for racing enthusiasts. On turf, 15 courses stage both Flat racing and jumping; 17 are devoted to the Flat only, while no fewer than 24 cater for jumping only. In addition (*see* ALL-WEATHER) Lingfield and Southwell stage racing on turf and artificial surfaces and Wolverhampton on artificial only. Fuller details of the principal courses are given in Chapter Eight, while the *Racing Post* daily gives a description of relevant courses with plans and statistics; the *Sun* Annuals contain similar information and a recommended comprehensive guide to them all, as well as hotel and leisure facilities in the vicinity, is *Travelling the Turf*, published by Kensington West Productions.

Most of the jumps-only courses are anything but principal racecourses, but that does not make them any the less important in the pattern of variety. Many of them are small, friendly country courses, as different in atmosphere from the National Hunt 'Mecca' at Cheltenham as Royal Ascot is from, say, the little course staging Flat racing only on the downs above Bath. They range from Perth and Kelso in Scotland to Bangor-on-Dee in Wales, from Sedgefield in Co Durham to Plumpton in Sussex, from Market Rasen in Lincolnshire to Newton Abbot and Exeter in Devon, and others in the West Country.

Some courses are right-handed, some (a slight majority) left-handed, and although many are approximately oval, there is a huge variety of differing shapes: Ascot, triangular; Windsor and Fontwell, figures-of-eight; Chester, circular; Brighton, like a big U with a kink in the lower part; Epsom, fittingly, like a great horseshoe with one straight side; Goodwood, like a bent hairpin, and Salisbury, like a straightened one; Carlisle, pear-shaped; and Hereford, almost square. This is all in great contrast to, say, the United States where, although there is racing on turf, more takes place on dirt, and the tracks are fairly uniform, with a standard distance of $1^1/4$ miles. Also unlike the States, where, because of the climate, race-meetings last for weeks, the majority of meetings in the UK last for only one, two, or three days. The longest continuous racing in Britain, in fact, takes place at Ascot in June and Goodwood at the main July/August meeting, both meetings lasting for five days.

Two items of unwelcome news during the winter of 1998–99 were that both Nottingham and Windsor (after 130 years) discontinued National Hunt racing, giving 'financial reasons' as a disgraceful, lame excuse. As some sort of counterbalance, there are plans for a new course at Fairlop Waters in Essex. If they come to fruition, Fairlop would be the first racecourse in the London area since the much-lamented and popular 'Ally Pally' (or more formally, Alexandra Park, Muswell Hill) closed in 1970. The original Fairlop scheme, after public objections and a turned-down planning application, has been scaled down to a much smaller floodlit all-weather track which, if plans come to fruition, is being aimed at starting racing in 2006. Another course in the planning stage is in Wales, on the site of the former Ffos Las opencast site near Llanelli. This would combine turf and all-weather and has already been granted ten turf fixtures by the British Horseracing Board. However, over and above all the planning hopes, a positive step forward towards expanding British racing has already taken place: the £40 million all-weather project at Great Leighs in Essex is now under construction. On the site of the Essex County Showground near Chelmsford, it is to have a left-handed mile Polytrack surface. The bulldozers moved on site in early 2004 and work is scheduled to be complete by mid-2005. Great Leighs will then be Britain's first new racetrack since Taunton opened in 1927.

Meanwhile, there is further encouraging news: Manchester will have its own racecourse again if plans to build a £100 million track at Salford Forest Park win approval. Peel Holdings, which owns the Manchester Ship Canal, hopes to revive the Manchester Cup, last run when the former racecourse at Castle Irwell held its last meeting in November 1963, ending 87 years of racing. The New Manchester Racecourse would combine Flat racing on turf with a floodlit all-weather track and accommodate 6,000 spectators.

Finally, the ownership and control of racecourses has been undergoing significant change recently. While the Jockey Club's Racecourse Holdings Trust owns 13 courses, including several of the most important (for details see under **RHT**), there have been an increasing number of closely fought takeover battles and buy-outs concerning racecourses in the past few years. The most determined and acquisitive force in this Turf version of Monopoly played for real has been Sir Stanley Clarke with Northern Racing, in which company he has a majority shareholding. Having started with Newcastle, Uttoxeter, Chepstow and Brighton, Northern Racing and other Stan Clarke subsidiaries have now also taken over Hereford and Bath, while a bitter legal battle over Sedgefield has gone in their favour. At the same time, Arena Leisure have steadily been accumulating tracks and now own half a dozen: Folkestone, Lingfield, Southwell, Windsor, Wolverhampton and Worcester.

Dead-heat This occurs when, even with the aid of the photo-finish, a judge is unable to declare an outright winner of a race. Before the advent of the photo-finish there was frequent uproar when the judge declared a dead-heat when it seemed plain to everyone else that there had been a definite winner. The angle of the actual finishing line is difficult to assess on some racecourses and in many cases the uproar was not justified; in other instances it was. Owners, trainers and outraged punters would have been correct in their assessment that they had been robbed by the judge's eyesight, or lack of it, because in a dead-heat the owners of horses concerned share the prize-money and bets on the winners are settled to a reduced stake (for full details see Chapter Five). The first dead-heat decided by photo-finish occurred at Doncaster in October 1947, the horses being *Phantom Bridge* and *Resistance*. Sprint handicaps tend to result in more dead-heats than other events, when several horses may be within inches of winning in what is sometimes called a 'blanket finish' (the horses are so close they could all be covered by a blanket). There have been many multiple dead-heats in the fairly distant past. The abbreviation used in the form book for dead-heat is 'd-h'.

Declarations *See ENTRIES.*

Distance
1. The distance is a point 240 yards from the winning post. There is no mark on the racecourse to indicate it, but it is frequently referred to in form summaries and the form book – e.g., 'Led at the distance, soon went clear'. However, courses *are* marked out along the straight with prominent signs indicating how many furlongs from the winning post. The distance is thus 20 yards before the one-furlong marker is reached.
2. Horses are sometimes judged (rarely on the Flat, but quite often at jumping meetings) to have won 'by a distance' (see *De Pluvinel* under **Aged**). This, technically, is also 240 yards, but usually means that the winner and runner-up are separated by such a margin that the judge cannot make an accurate estimation by eye. But this official margin may be consigned to the history books if talks within the Jockey Club's judging department conclude that punters would be better served by having access to more precise figures. An obstacle to this at present is that the software associated with the photo-finish is currently incapable of assessing distances in excess of 30 lengths.
3. The distance of a race. No race on the Flat can be less than 5 furlongs. There is no limit on how long a Flat race can be, but in practice there are not many races beyond 2 miles. The longest race in the Calendar is the Queen Alexandra Stakes at Royal Ascot over 2 3/4 miles.

In National Hunt *(q.v.)* racing, no chase or hurdle can be less than 2 miles. There used to be $1^1/2$-mile hurdles, but these were abolished, to the relief of all concerned, some years ago. The longest jumping race is the Grand National: about 4 miles 856 yards.

4. Winning distance. The shortest winning distance is a short-head (in practice, sometimes not much more than a cigarette-paper, judged on the photo-finish film), then a head, then a neck, then half-a-length, and so on. The French also have an intermediate winning distance translated as a 'short-neck' (see Chapter Twelve). Here are the distances which were added to in 1994, with their usual abbreviations:

Short-head	sh	One length and three quarters	$1^3/4$l
Head	hd	Two lengths	2l
Neck	nk	Two and a half lengths	$2^1/2$l
Half a length	$1/2$l	Three lengths	3l
Three-quarters of a length	$3/4$l	Three and a half lengths	$3^1/2$l
A length	1l	Four lengths	4l
One and a quarter lengths	$1^1/4$l	A distance	Dist.
One and a half lengths	$1^1/2$l		

There is a further term used in the case of a horse placed third, but so far back as to make accurate estimation of distance an irrelevance. In this case, the horse is judged to be a 'bad third', which appears in the form book, say, where the distance between first and second is three lengths, as '3l, Bad'. This occurs most commonly in chases. But see above concerning the margin of 'a distance'. If this were to be amended, presumably the 'bad third' margin would also be replaced by a more precise assessment.

Doll   Hurdles singly used to mark direction in National Hunt racing, usually when part of the course is waterlogged or unusable for some other reason, when that part of the course will be said to be 'dolled off'.

Draw   The draw for which position a horse shall occupy in the stalls at the start of a Flat race is made on the day before the race at the overnight declarations office (*see* WEATHERBYS), and is drawn by lot. There is no draw for places in National Hunt racing. Number one in the draw occupies the extreme left-hand position (in stall number one – the number being indicated over the front of the stall), the horse drawn two goes into stall number two, and so on. On certain courses (see Chapter Eight) a low number in the draw – or high number – over certain distances and sometimes depending on the going may give advantage in running, so it is important to study what effect the draw may have, especially with big fields, and how horses are drawn. The draw is published in the newspapers (and on the racecourse appears both on the racecard and numbers board [*q.v.*]), but it took a long and hard campaign to secure this advantage to those off the course wanting a bet, as well as to trainers and jockeys wishing to plan in advance how their horse should be run. Until the late 1960s, the draw was not made until shortly before a race, and sometimes backing a favourite ante

3.45 **Sagitta 1000 Guineas Stakes**
[OFF 3.46] **Showcase Race (Class A) (Group 1)**
1m July
For: 3-y-o 1st **£128,500** 2nd £47,500 3rd £22,750 4th £9,250 5th £3,625 6th £1,375

1   **WINCE** (19) 3 9-0......................................(106) **K Fallon**
b f by Selkirk (USA)–Flit (USA) (Lyphard (USA))
(H R A Cecil) *raced stand side, held up, headway over 2f out, led over 1f out, hung left, ridden out* [bets of £6,000-£1,000, £10,000-£1,800, £5,000-£900, £50,000-£10,000, £25,000-£5,000, £5,000-£1,000(x6), £4,000-£800, £3,000-£600, £2,500-£500(x2), £2,000-£400 £2,250-£500(x3), £8,000-£2,000, £4,000-£1,000(x2) and including office money]
[op 11/2 tchd 6/1 in a plac] **4/1F**

2   ¹/₂ **WANNABE GRAND (IRE)** (13) 3 9-0 ....(112) Pat Eddery
b f by Danehill (USA)–Wannabe (Shirley Heights)
(J Noseda) *raced stand side, held up, headway and switched right over 1f out, hung left, ran on well* [bets of £20,000-£1,200 each-way, £16,000-£1,000]   [tchd 20/1 in places.] **16/1**

3   *shd* **VALENTINE WALTZ (IRE)** (1) 3 9-0....(115) R Cochrane
b f by Be My Guest (USA)–Save Me The Waltz (King's Lake (USA))

post which ultimately received a bad draw was so much money thrown away (the Lincolnshire Handicap used to be an important case in point with an often enormous field, and the draw crucially affecting a horse's chance). That particular extreme situation has not substantially been altered today, but at least the overnight draw gives time for reconsideration, and the benefit in ordinary day-to-day Flat racing is striking as far as off-course punters are concerned, in particular. There is one anomaly to be noted, however. For example, in 1981 *Great Eastern* won the Wokingham Stakes at Royal Ascot, drawn 30 in a field of 29. This has a logical explanation, despite the seeming illogicality. Overnight there were 30 runners, but on the morning of the race one horse was withdrawn, leaving only 29. In cases such as this, the remainder of the field still occupy their original allotted draw positions at the start. A useful book is *The Effects of the Draw* by Graham Weldon (Raceform).

Drifter A horse whose price lengthens appreciably, or 'drifts', in the betting before a race, say from 3/1 out to 8/1. It means that the bookmakers expected it to be backed, possibly by stable connections, but there is little money for it, and so, after prudently quoting a shortish price when the market opens, the price is gradually lengthened. Not, usually, a hopeful sign for the punter, although it sometimes happens that a horse from a stable which does not bet in big amounts is 'put in' at a short price when the market opens, drifts, and wins. The opposite to a drifter is a 'springer', a horse whose price tumbles dramatically, say from 7/1 or 8/1 or even longer, perhaps to be returned 6/4 favourite. This is a hopeful, if not infallible, sign for the punter able to watch price movements on television or in the betting shop, if not on the course. Springers to watch for particularly are those in two-year-old races, especially when they concern previously unraced two-year-olds. Springers to treat with caution, however, occur with poor and/or small fields and a consequently weak betting market where quite small amounts of money on a horse can cause dramatic fluctuations in prices. Also, even in a reasonably strong betting market, the fact that a horse's price tumbles does not automatically mean that it will win; but at least it usually means that it is fancied by those who know most about its chances, and the money is down.   The modern buzzword for a particular kind of springer, specifically one backed down from generous early morning prices, is a 'steamer'.   A good example of a 'steamer' is afforded by *Wince*, winner of the 1000 Guineas in 1999.   The graphic opposite shows how she came down in the market on the course, and in the morning at least one leading bookmaker was offering 8/1.

Dwelt   A horse that does not immediately get away when the stalls open is said to have 'dwelt at the start', abbreviated to 'dwlt' in the form book.   It also happens in National Hunt *(q.v.)* racing where there are no starting stalls, but the longer the race the less important this becomes in its effect on the outcome of the race, or the horse's performance in it.

Each-way bet   To bet each way (*not* both ways) is to stake equal amounts for a win and for a place (see Chapter Five for definitions of *placed* horses according to the number of runners and type of race).   On the racecourse it used to be difficult for the ordinary punter to get a bookmaker to lay an each-way bet except in big events such as the Derby and Grand National.   It is much easier nowadays: many bookmakers will take each-way in certain races, and put a notice on their boards 'Each-way taken' with the odds they are offering.   Credit bookmakers on and off the course, betting shops, and the Tote, on and off the course, all take each-way bets.

EBF   Initials of the European Breeders' Fund. This originated in June 1983, when breeders in Great Britain, Ireland and France signed an agreement to create a fund into which stallion owners would pay an annual contribution equal to the average covering fee for each sire being nominated to the scheme, and from which only the progeny of those participating stallions would be eligible to benefit.
    The proceeds of the fund in the British part of the scheme are channelled into prize-money, breeders' prizes for horses sired by British-based stallions, owners' premiums for selected Pattern and Listed races on the Flat, and veterinary research.
    The EBF, which was introduced in the wake of Levy Board *(q.v.)* prize-money cuts, was modelled on the similarly funded American Breeders Cup Scheme, to which a cross-registration agreement was negotiated.   Each of the three countries involved in the EBF agreed that from 1984 half their two-year-old maiden races would be restricted to the progeny of EBF-nominated stallions, and in Britain this amounted to approximately 220 races.   The EBF is a sponsor of races, all of which have the initials in the title of the event.

Entire   A male horse that has not been gelded (castrated) (*see GELDING*).

Entries   Entries for nearly all races are made five days beforehand to Weatherbys *(q.v.)*.   Weights for such races are allocated the following day according to the published conditions of the race or, if the event is a handicap, by the official handicapper. The entry may be withdrawn at any time ('scratched') up to the day before the race, at which time, if it is intended to compete, it must be 'declared' to run. This is the overnight declaration stage and trainers these days can telex or fax Weatherbys with 'odecs'.

Entries for the most important races, including the Classics, Royal Ascot, Cheltenham Festival, Grand National etc., are more complicated in that they close early – i.e. weeks or months before the event – and can include a forfeit stage or forfeit stages in between entry and the date of the race at which owners have to pay extra if they wish their horses to stay in the race. In addition, a new plan provides for a 48-hour Declaration stage for Group One races (*see PATTERN RACES*).

Acceptors. 'Big Race Acceptors' is a heading sometimes seen in the newspapers. Below it will be a list of horses remaining in a big race after a forfeit stage.

Even money *See ODDS.*

Favourite The horse or horses at the shortest price in the betting. When there are two at equal shortest prices they become joint-favourites. When there are more than two they become co-favourites. Several methods of betting depend on backing the favourite, either by name or simply nominated as 'favourite'. The horse next in the betting is known as the second-favourite, and so on.

Field
1. In general, this refers to the total number of runners for a particular race. Hence 'The field for this year's Derby will be the smallest since *Nijinsky* beat ten opponents in 1970' does not mean that an unusually cramped alternative to Epsom racecourse has been found.
2. In betting terms it means the shortest-priced horse in any given field, so, effectively, that is the price of the favourite, as in the bookmakers' shouts of 'Six to four the field...' (*see ODDS*).
3. The field book is a bookmaker's record of bets taken on a race, kept by the bookmaker's clerk on specially ruled paper on a large clip-board, or in a bookmaker's central office in the case of ante-post betting (*q.v.*). The field book records bets taken, prices laid and to whom (either by name or ticket number) and the total liability should any given horse win (called the 'take out'). No doubt, however, impending computerisation will have its effect on all this. (See Chapter Six.)
4. Field money is the bookmakers' term for the total amount staked on a race out of which must come take out and profit.
5. Fielding against the favourite means that bookmakers are laying the favourite excessively (in the expectation of it not winning).

Filly A female thoroughbred from the age of two up to and including four years. At five she officially becomes a mare (*q.v.*). Game fillies and mares exert a powerful influence on the affections of racegoers, and none more so than those heroines of Edwardian times *Sceptre* and *Pretty Polly*. The career of *Sceptre* with her record four Classic successes in 1902 is dealt with in detail in Chapter Nine. Very soon afterwards came *Pretty Polly* and her extraordinary success, on which is based the contention that she was the best ever filly in Turf history. In 1903–04 she won off the reel the first 15 races of her career and now shares with later contestants *Bayardo* (1909–10) and *Brigadier Gerard* (1970–72) the record for the longest winning sequence by a Flat horse trained in Britain since 1900. She triumphed nine times as a two-year-old, then her first six victories the following season included the 1000 Guineas, Oaks, Coronation Stakes and St. Leger. Eventually, she won no fewer than 23 races including the 1905 Coronation Cup when, with a quite phenomenal performance, she easily beat the older, previous season's champion, *Zinfandel*, and created a record for the Derby course which stood for many years. No wonder they called her 'Peerless' *Pretty Polly*. In the book *A Century of Champions*, John Randall and Tony Morris firmly rate her worldwide top of the fillies and mares since 1900 on a mark of 137. Farther back in time, *Beeswing* (see Chapter Eight under **Newcastle**), between 1835 and 1842, won 51 of her 64 races including four Doncaster Cups and the Ascot Gold Cup; another stayer, *Alice Hawthorn*, won over 50 races in the 1840s; and *Catherina* won the astonishing total of 79 out of 174 races between 1833 and 1841. There was no cotton wool and whisking quickly off to stud in those days.

In more recent times there have been some marvellous fillies and racemares including Prince Aly Khan's flying grey *Petite Etoile* (1959 1000 Guineas; Oaks; Sussex Stakes; Champion Stakes etc.; 1960 and 1961 Coronation Cup); *Aunt Edith* (1966), *Park Top* (1969) and the French-trained *Dahlia* (1973 and 1974), all of whom won the King George VI and Queen Elizabeth Diamond Stakes in the years bracketed. *Dahlia*, in fact, was the first horse ever to win consecutive runnings of the King George and Queen Elizabeth Stakes. She retired with then record earnings for a mare of nearly $1.5 million, after 15 victories in France, England, Ireland, Canada and the USA. She was 31 when she died in 2001. Also based across the Channel, well-named *Allez France* inherited blinding acceleration from her sire, *Sea Bird II*, and, like him, counted (in 1974) the Prix de l'Arc de Triomphe among her 13 victories but sadly was never at her best when competing in England. However, *Triptych*, trained at one time in Ireland where she beat the colts in their 2000 Guineas in 1985, later returned to France but regularly came over to race in this country, where she became a great favourite of the crowds. Her impressive record was that she contested no fewer than 14 Group One races (*see PATTERN RACES*) in England between 1985 and 1988 when she was six years of age and was never out of the first three, her victories consisting of both the Champion Stakes and Coronation Cup twice each and the Matchmaker International (now the Juddmonte International) at York. Tragically, she was killed in a bizarre accident not long after she had gone to the United States to become a broodmare. Fortunately, her name continues to shine on as the topmost equine female since the Pattern began. *Pebbles* captured the Breeders Cup Turf (see Chapter Twelve) in 1985 as well as the Champion Stakes and Eclipse. The same season saw the brilliance of *Oh So Sharp* with her fillies' Triple Crown (*q.v.*) to her credit, while among other outstanding fillies of the 1980s must be mentioned *Indian Skimmer*, unbeaten as a 3-y-o and at 4-y-o winner of both English and Irish Champion Stakes and third in the Breeders Cup Turf; also *Sonic*

Lady, whose brilliant career at 3-y-o took in Group One wins in the Irish 1000 Guineas, Coronation Stakes, Sussex Stakes and Prix du Moulin. Last but not least is a more recent heroine adored by the public, the sprinter *Lochsong* (see Chapters Ten and Twelve).

Form   The form of any given horse is the sum total of its achievements or otherwise on the racecourse as recorded in the form book (see Chapter Four), or extracted from the form book at length in the sporting press, and in a rather more compressed presentation in other newspapers. A horse which has 'no chance on the book' is one whose form, on close examination, does not give it a winning chance in a future race. Just as music can be seen as merely a series of notes written on paper for a musician to play, so the form book provides only facts. Equally, musicians are capable of varying performances from the same set of notes, and the facts in the form book are similarly open to differing interpretations.

The word 'form' is often related to a particular race, as in the phrase 'The Coventry Stakes form is working out rather well,' meaning that horses beaten in the Coventry Stakes have been running consistently with the form shown in that race, and several of them, perhaps, have subsequently won. They will then be said to have 'advertised' the Coventry Stakes form. The converse is to 'let the form down' – for example, in the spring of 1999, when various Guineas hopes who had done well the previous autumn in the Dewhurst Stakes were beaten in the various trials, it was said: 'The Dewhurst form is in tatters'.

Front runner   A horse who likes to go out in front and stay there, or 'cut out the running'. *Timeform* and the form book give plenty of hints on this preference. Conversely, many horses have to be 'covered up' until the last minute because once in front they tend to idle, thinking they have done enough. Again, *Timeform* and the form book give the clues. Tracks on which front-running tactics often pay off are Chester and Sandown Park. Notable front runners were that idol of the crowds, *Desert Orchid*, and the 1987 Derby and St. Leger winner, *Reference Point*. Many of Martin Pipe's horses, also, like to go off and 'make all'. But beware races where there are two or more known front runners, particularly over the jumps. They may go tearing off in front together, have a prolonged tussle for the lead and, in the end, as racecourse jargon has it, 'cut each other's throats'.

Full brother, Full sister   A full brother (also known as an own-brother) or full sister (also known as an own-sister) refers to horses who share the same sire and the same dam. Such coincidence does not guarantee comparable ability on the racecourse, for example HM The Queen's *Aureole* (foaled 1950), runner-up to *Pinza* in the Coronation Year Derby and winner of the King George VI and Queen Elizabeth Stakes the following season, was by that great sire *Hyperion* out of an Oaks runner-up, *Angelola*. *Angel Bright* (foaled 1951) shared the same parents and was thus *Aureole*'s full sister, and he her full brother. But the best *Angel Bright*, who also carried the royal colours, could manage was to win the Lingfield Oaks Trial. In the Oaks itself she led briefly in the straight but finished unplaced.

A half-brother or half-sister refers specifically to horses who share the same dam, but NOT to horses who are out of differing dams though sharing the same sire. Hence the Jockey Club Stakes winner *Unfuwain* (foaled 1985) was by *Northern Dancer* out of *Height of Fashion* and thus a half-brother to the outstanding colt of 1989, *Nashwan* (foaled 1986), who was by *Blushing Groom* out of *Height of Fashion*.

Gelding A colt (*q.v.*) or male horse which has been gelded (castrated). There are several reasons why it may be thought wise to have a racehorse 'cut' or gelded. Ungelded older horses which remain in racing often become temperamental and difficult to deal with; gelding them would have normally made them more amenable, partly through taking their minds off sex, and through the change in temperament caused by a shift in hormonal balance common to all neutered animals, human beings included. Thus a gelded horse is more likely to concentrate on racing, and is certainly easier to train when older. In National Hunt racing there is a further practical reason for gelding horses, and that is the discomfort, to put it at its mildest, suffered by entire horses in brushing through or over fences made of birch. All but a small minority of chasers are geldings. In Ireland it is customary to geld intended future chasers at a very early age. The last entire (i.e. not gelded) winner of the Grand National was *Battleship* in 1938, ridden by Bruce Hobbs. The last entire Cheltenham Gold Cup winner was *Fortina* in 1947. He subsequently proved his worth, for good measure, at stud, and for a long time his progeny put him among the top half dozen National Hunt sires.

On the Flat, many races, including the Classics, are not open to geldings, although several important races have now been opened to them. These include the semi-classic Eclipse Stakes over $1^1/4$ m at Sandown Park in early July, and the Ascot Gold Cup, the premier race for stayers (*q.v.*) in the Calendar. The logic of opening the Ascot Gold Cup to geldings rested partly, it seems, on the lamentable decline (see Chapter Ten) of interest on the part of breeders (with one or two notable exceptions) in producing out-and-out stayers, against which it was argued that the admission of geldings to the race might reduce the status of Ascot Gold Cup winners. The reason for this was based on the nonsensical assumption that if a valuable (in future stud terms) colt is beaten by a gelding, then devaluation instantly sets in. This, in turn, rests on the fact that a gelding is worthless in stud terms, whereas a colt can win the Derby or Prix de l'Arc de Triomphe and is instantly worth millions of pounds to a stud syndicate; yet a king among horses such as *Arkle*, because he was a gelding, was worth no more the day after he won the Cheltenham Gold Cup than the day before. Nonetheless, the prejudice of breeders will not cloud the vision of those race-goers who admire the exploits of geldings without whom National Hunt racing would not tick and gallant deeds on the Flat such as those of *Teleprompter*, an international flag-bearer for English racing, owned by Lord Derby and trained by Bill Watts, and winner in 1985 of the Budweiser-Arlington Million in the USA.

Indeed, it is noteworthy that in 1998, on cumulative merit in the most important races, the two top horses in the land were both geldings: the 6-y-o *Decorated Hero* and 5-y-o stayer *Persian Punch* each won three Pattern races (*q.v.*), a unique record since the Pattern began nearly 30 years ago. The only other geldings during that time to achieve pre-eminence in a season have been the French-trained sprinter *Nuclear Debate*, who in the year 2000 came over and won the Gr1 Nunthorpe Stakes and Gr2 King's Stand Stakes, and in France the Gr2 Prix du Gros-Chene, and *Boldboy* (see Chapter Ten), who in 1977 also achieved three Group victories, but had to share his title with four colts and a filly.

In the light of future events, by far the most celebrated escapee from gelding was *March Past*. Ken Cundell, his trainer, was going to have him cut but relented for the sake of the owner, Mrs Trimmer-Thompson, whose first horse this was.

That single decision considerably changed the recent history of racing. *March Past*, foaled in 1950, became, after a distinguished career which included winning the Wokingham, an even more distinguished sire. His great asset was that he was able to transmit the sterling quality of genuineness to his progeny, and among his winners were *Major Rose* (Cesarewitch and placed in the Champion Hurdle), *Marcher* (Wokingham), *Smartie* and *My Hussar* (both Royal Hunt Cup), the sprinter *Constans* (King George Stakes and Prix St. George three times between age 7 and 9), *Scots Fusilier* (Newbury Spring Cup), *Dawn Review* (Esher Cup), *In Command, Marchakin, Christmas Review* and many others; but above all *Queen's Hussar* (Sussex Stakes and Lockinge Stakes). *Queen's Hussar* inherited *March Past*'s best characteristics and sired one of the most brilliant horses of the century in *Brigadier Gerard* as well as HM The Queen's outstanding filly *Highclere*, winner of the 1000 Guineas and Prix de Diane in 1974. *Highclere*, when retired to the stud, became the dam of *Height of Fashion*. She, in turn, became the dam of *Nashwan*, winner of the 2000 Guineas, Derby, Eclipse and King George VI and Queen Elizabeth Diamond Stakes. Since then, *Nashwan* has sired *Swain*, twice a winner of the King George VI and Queen Elizabeth Diamond Stakes in 1997 and 1998, while his half-brother *Unfuwain* has sired, among others, the Irish Oaks successes *Bolas* and the brilliant *Petrushka* as well as the 1000 Guineas winner in 2000, *Lahan*. Who knows, even this may not be the end of *March Past*'s influence on the stud-book.

Going The state of the ground for a race meeting. The following official categories appear in the form book and are given in advance forecasts in the newspapers: hard; firm; good to firm; good; good to soft; soft; heavy. In muddy conditions, the form book may also note 'Soft with heavy patches' or will differentiate between the going on different parts of the course as, for example, 'Going: round course, soft. Straight course, good to soft'.

The state of the going is perhaps *the* most important random factor in determining the outcome of a race. Some horses prefer soft going, or go better on it ('likes some cut in the ground' or 'likes some give underfoot'). Others give of their best only when the mud is flying and will be noted in the reference books and elsewhere as a 'confirmed mudlark'. Some horses dislike soft conditions and need good going ('needs the top of the ground'), while a few actually prefer firm going ('likes to hear his hooves rattle').

Clerks of the Course, who are responsible for defining the state of the going, come in for occasional heavy wiggings from press and trainers when their assessment does not appear to be all that it might be. Science seemed to have come to their aid with an instrument with the rather sinister title of 'Penetrometer', in popular use in France; in this country a device called a GoingStick was introduced not long ago at Sandown. Its readings range from 1.0–2.9 (Heavy) through 7.0–8.9 (Good) to 13.0–15.0 (Hard). It is anticipated that it will in time be in general use but until that happens the time-honoured method of testing the going by prodding with a walking stick seems likely to remain.

A change in the going can occur overnight after a heavy downpour, so not only is it necessary to note a horse's preference, if any, for a particular kind of going, but an eye should be kept on the weather forecast for a meeting. The going as advertised in all good faith in the newspapers in the morning may be 'good'; but in actual fact rain may have changed it, after the newspapers have been printed, to soft, or worse. This, at one extreme, causes last-minute withdrawals of horses whose chances have been knocked out by the rain; conversely, it may transform a near certain loser into a possible winner.

Apart from *Timeform*, the newspapers also publish plenty of information on the subject of going, illustrating how vital it is in determining trainers' intentions for their horses. Look out for, 'He'll only run if it's soft,' or conversely, 'He's no good on anything but good ground, and we'll only run if we get that.' One last word: there are some courses which are affected by rain more than others. At Newmarket, for instance, it very rarely becomes worse than soft. Good ground or good to soft in the spring and autumn on the Rowley Mile are usually the prevailing states of going, however much rain has fallen. Liverpool, where the turf is old and springy, is another course where it does not often become heavy – 1980 was an exceptional year for the National with only four finishers because of the demanding conditions.

Good walker A horse that walks well will usually gallop well. Something to watch for in a pre-race paddock inspection, and particularly worth noting is whether the hind hoof coincides or overlaps where the front hoof has been. However, here is a cautionary tale told about a noted and blunt Yorkshire trainer. His son had bought a horse, brought him back to the yard, unboxed him and nervously waited for the verdict of the father after inspection with a critical eye. Nothing at first was said. Then, said son, even more nervously: 'He's a good walker, Dad.' Said Dad, uncompromisingly: 'They don't have walking races.'

Greys All thoroughbred grey horses trace back to the Alcock Arabian, foaled in 1704 and imported to England via Constantinople by a Sir Robert Sutton. They represent only about three per cent of the entire horseracing population, but that proportion is no indication of their popularity, particularly in the National Hunt (*q.v.*) field. The bold, front-running *Desert Orchid* became a famous and much-loved public hero with his prodigious feats between 1983 and 1991. He quite dominated the jumps scene with 34 wins, including the King George VI Chase four times, Cheltenham Gold Cup, Whitbread Gold Cup, Irish National, and was unplaced only 17 times in 70 outings. Another grey chaser with a firm place in popular affection was *One Man*, who sadly died on the racecourse in 1998 following two King George VI victories and other successes. In 1998–99, the charismatic *Teeton Mill* was another grey who was rapidly recruiting a fan club after spectacular victories, but was injured in the Cheltenham Gold Cup. Meanwhile, two greys are members of an elite club, who, admittedly on handicap *(q.v.)* terms, defeated the greatest chaser of the last century, *Arkle*. These were *Flying Wild* and *Stalbridge Colonist* who, respectively, beat him in the 1964 Massey-Ferguson Gold Cup and the 1966 Hennessy Gold Cup. Only two greys have ever won the Grand National, *The Lamb* in 1868 and 1871 and, the most recent, *Nicolaus Silver* in 1961.

On the Flat, the most recent grey to have become a great favourite of the crowds was *Further Flight* (for details of his astonishing career, before retirement in 1998, see Chapter Ten). His colour came from his dam's side, tracing back to a very successful grey sprinter, *Vilmorin*. Among other greys on the Flat in recent years must be mentioned two stayers *(q.v.)*: *Grey Shot* (1997 Goodwood Cup; 1998 Jockey Club Cup; later a leading hurdler) and *Silver Patriarch* (1997 St. Leger; 1998 Coronation Cup) as well as the versatile and brilliant *Daylami* (1997 French 2000 Guineas; 1998 Eclipse Stakes and Gr 1 Man O'War Stakes USA; 1999 Coronation Cup, King George VI and Queen Elizabeth Diamond Stakes, Champion Stakes and Breeders Cup Turf). Two popular grey sprinters who were still winning when they were 11 years old are *Young Inca* (14 victories up to 1989, including five at Ascot) and *Hard To Figure* (17 wins up to 1997; but see also under **Aged**). Going somewhat farther back in time, no list of eye-catching grey performers in post-war years would be complete without the following: the Aly Khan's flying filly *Petite Etoile* (1000 Guineas and Oaks among a string of top-class successes in 1959, and Coronation Cup the following year); *Abernant* (one of the fastest horses of the 20th century and champion sprinter of 1949 and 1950); and *Airborne* (winner of the Derby and St. Leger in 1946). *Airborne* was the fourth and most recent grey to capture the Derby, the others being *Gustavus* (1821), *Tagalie* (1912, also the only grey filly ever to have won the Derby), and *Mahmoud* (1936). Another grey who recently began to build up his own faithful following was *Rooster Booster*, winner of the Champion Hurdle in 2003 at the age of nine and beaten only once in half a dozen outings that season. In addition, mention must be made of the 11-y-o grey gelding *Palacegate Touch*. When scoring at Southwell in April 2001, this sprint handicapper was recording his 32nd success: a tremendous feat in itself, but also only two short of the post-war record for wins on the Flat in this country held by (see under **Aged**) *Le Garcon d'Or* and *High Stakes*. Finally, it is welcome recognition of the public regard for much-loved greys that in 2003 Newmarket decided to stage a race, the first of its kind, exclusively for them. The £10,000 SportingOdds.com Grey Horse Handicap over six furlongs was run on the July Course in August. It drew a field of 13 greys and was won by *Smart Predator* who eventually finished the season with five victories to his name. As Lisa Hancock, managing director of Newmarket racecourse, commented: 'People love to see grey horses and we thought it would be really interesting to put on a race where they're all grey.'

Group races *See PATTERN RACES.*

Handicap A handicap is a race in which horses are allotted different weights in order to give each of them, theoretically, an equal chance of winning. Like George Orwell's animals, however, some horses are more equal than others, and the fact that handicap races almost always produce a clear-cut winner is a lasting tribute to the fact that horses, while usually producing the form of which the handicapper thinks them capable, do vary slightly (if for no other reason than that, like human beings, they are not always feeling on top of the world).

The basis of handicapping is that horses are 'allowed' weight one to another according to Weight-for-Age (*q.v.*) and according to the distance by which one beats the other in a race, with due allowance made for the state of the going and other factors, such as the overall pace at which the race was run.

A rough scale of assessing weight according to finishing distances is as follows: on the Flat, from five furlongs to seven furlongs, 3 lb per length (there is a school of thought which allows as much as 4 lb per length at the minimum distance); from one mile to 11 furlongs, 2 lb per length; from one and a half miles to two miles, 1^1/$_2$ lb per length; more than two miles, 1 lb per length. National Hunt races: 1 lb per length.

Thus, over a sprint distance, horse A carrying 9 st beats horse B carrying the same weight ('at level weights' in other words) by a length; horse B is therefore 3 lb 'inferior' to horse A. In a subsequent race, the handicap therefore should read: horse A 9 st, horse B 8 st 11 lb. In a National Hunt three mile chase (*q.v.*), horse A carrying 11 st beats horse B carrying 10 st 12 lb by four lengths. The handicapper may then adjust the weights for the next time they meet so that horse A carried 11 st 4 lb and horse B carried 10 st 12 lb, thus, in theory, equalising their chances.

Handicapping is carried out by official (BHB) handicappers whose handicap for any particular race is based on central information contained and regularly up-dated on computer. This provides a handicap 'rating' (*q.v.*) for every horse in training qualified to run in a handicap (in the case of 2-y-o they are not rated until July of their first season's racing and no horse can be handicapped until it has run three times). These ratings are the basis, on a scale from 0 upwards, for the graded handicaps introduced in recent years, which are designed to give fairer opportunities for handicap horses all round.

At the lower end of the scale a handicap may be restricted to horses rated 0-70. Horses rated above this mark are not eligible to compete. There are many handicaps such as this, designed to give winning chances to the more moderate animals. At the top end of the scale, big handicaps such as the Ebor and the Cambridgeshire are open to horses rated 0-115.

The ratings are revised every week and a list of horses whose handicap mark has changed appreciably is published in the sporting press. These lists are well worth keeping an eye on. The handicap range in a Flat race in general is from 7 st 7 lb to not less than 10 st; in National Hunt races, from 10 st to 12 st except in handicaps of three miles and over where the top-weight is 11 st 10 lb. Despite the restricted range, when the handicapper deals with the entries for a given race, he will allot weights below the permitted bottom-weight (this is known as the 'long handicap'), because frequently the top-weight is withdrawn, and the weights have to be raised accordingly.

Thus:

Original handicap: top-weight   horse A   10 st
                   next in weights   horse B   9 st 8 lb
                   two bottom-weights horse C   7 st 7 lb
                                        horse D   7 st 7 lb

But in actual fact, the handicapper has given C and D a 'long handicap' assessment of 7 st 6 lb and 7 st 2 lb respectively. Before the declaration stage horse A is withdrawn. The weights are raised by 6 lb all round, thus the two bottom-weights, which were 'out of the handicap' and stood little chance, now have a proper mark and a chance to compete at proper handicap terms:

New handicap, as run: top-weight   horse B   10 st
                      horse C   7 st 12 lb
                      horse D   7 st 8 lb

Throughout the season there are a number of 'limited' handicaps in which the weight range is narrower than in a normal handicap. These events are meant to attract the better-class horses.

Admiral Rous was the first Jockey Club handicapper and is acknowledged to have been one of the finest that ever lived. After laying down his pen after completing work on a particularly difficult handicap he is said to have remarked: 'There, now none of them can win!' More recently, Dick Whitford was a well-known and uncannily accurate 'private' handicapper – i.e. he produced his own ratings, and once wrote: 'A good handicap is like a work of art; a painting by Picasso or a symphony by Beethoven. It is not the produce of a statistician or an accountant or a computer with its peripheral equipment. A good handicap, in fact, is the creative act of a good handicapper; a balancing of fine judgements; an appraisal of will o' the wisps; an array of intelligent guesses.' And it is thus that 'private' handicaps, including those published in newspapers as 'ratings' as well as publications such as *Raceform Private Handicap*, are devised, showing how the 'private' handicapper differs from the official assessment of a horse's ability and relative chance in a race.

Handicappers   A two-fold definition, first meaning the official BHB team who *frame* handicaps. The second use of the word refers to horses who run in handicaps, sometimes in a sniffy sort of way as in: 'Oh, he's only a handicapper'.

At Lingfield, in November 1998, *Soaked* joined a select band by equalling the then 20th century record for the most handicap wins in a Flat season. This was his ninth handicap success and he thus joined *Sihafi* (1998), *Vindaloo* (1995), *Star Rage* (1994), *Glencroft* (1988) and *Chaplin's Club* (1988 and 1985) who all achieved nine handicap victories in a season. *Soaked*, *Glencroft*, and *Chaplin's Club* were all trained in Yorkshire by David Chapman.

Yet even these doughty deeds were shortly to be eclipsed. In 2001, that redoubtable 6-y-o mare, *Madame Jones*, scored no fewer that 11 victories in handicaps. She, therefore, captured the 21st century record for the number of handicap wins in a season and in so doing equalled the totals of *Misty Morn* in 1858 and *Honesty* in 1869 for the all-time record of handicap wins in a season.

Head lad Not a lad at all, but usually a very mature second-in-command of a racing stable on whom much reponsibility for organisation, feeding the horses, and running the yard devolves. A good head lad can make a stable, and a bad one break it. There is also the travelling head lad, who is chiefly responsible for accompanying horses on their journeys to and from the stable and racecourse. An example of a highly successful trainer who was once a head lad (to Sir Noel Murless) is Clive Brittain, while another top trainer is Barry Hills, once travelling head lad to John Oxley.

Hanging Not as drastic as it may sound. Tired horses in a finish sometimes 'hang' in either towards the rails, or more seriously towards an opponent. Should be corrected by a jockey showing them the whip.

Hobdayed Having had a Hobday operation on the larynx: for horses which are unsound in wind. *Timeform* will say whether a horse has been hobdayed. The operation was pioneered by the eminent veterinary surgeon Sir Frederick Hobday (1870–1939).

Homebred A homebred horse is one which has been bred at its owner's stud, as against one bought, most usually, at public auction.

Hunter-chases These are races confined to horses which have been regularly hunted during the season in which they compete in hunter-chases, and a certificate has to be signed by a Master of Foxhounds to that effect. There have been some famous hunter-chasers in the past, notably *Baulking Green*, who won no fewer than 22 hunter-chases, including the United Hunts Challenge Cup at the Cheltenham Festival four times in the 1960s; he was runner-up at the age of 15 and had his own faithful fan club.

Hurdles Horses beginning their careers on the National Hunt (*q.v.*) scene often begin over hurdles, even though the ultimate intention is usually to put them to fences. (A proportion of chasers, including ex-hunters and point-to-point horses, never jump a hurdle in their lives and, correspondingly, a few hurdlers remain hurdlers for the rest of their racing careers.) No horse can race over hurdles until the July of the year in which he or she is three years old, but, in practice, the majority of hurdlers of this age, and also many at four years old, are bought out of a Flat racing stable in the autumn or winter following the decision not to run them any longer on the Flat. Ability to stay a long distance on the Flat is not a prerequisite for making a successful hurdler, although the minimum and usual distance is two miles and a fair proportion of races are even longer.

The three-year-old may start in races once called juvenile hurdles and confined to that age group or in novice hurdles, for which the qualification is never having won a hurdle by the start of the current season. The Rules lay down the specification for hurdles: that they must be not less than 3 ft 6 ins in height from the bottom bar to the top bar; that they consist of bars of wood, such as willow or oak interspersed with birch, broom or gorse, and are driven in sections across the hurdles course (which is separate from the steeplechase course) at an angle sloped from the take-off side.

The top bar of a hurdle these days is padded so that horses do not rap themselves badly when striking the hurdle; this has slightly reduced the clatter which used to be heard like successive cracks of rapid riflefire round the racecourse during a hurdle race. But there is still plenty of noise, as well as danger in the often furious pace. One danger occurs when a hurdle has been nearly but not quite kicked flat, and it swings back. Falls in a hurdle race, though less frequent than in a chase, can be more dangerous with a tighter bunched field and at a faster pace. The Rules of Racing also lay down that there must be at least eight flights of hurdles in a two mile race, with an additional flight for every complete quarter of a mile beyond that distance.

At present, there is a move afoot to modify the traditional British hurdle of the kind described above. Ferdy Murphy is one trainer who has described them as 'barbaric' and others are also supporting a campaign to introduce French-style 'brush' hurdles. These resemble mini-fences, and it is thought that they would reduce the risk of injury. Kempton has already held a demonstration of the brush-type hurdle while Worcester is installing them, and Henrietta Knight was reported to be having one installed at her Wantage training grounds for other trainers to try it out.

Famous hurdle races include the Champion Hurdle, the Triumph Hurdle (for four-year-olds) and the Ladbrokes World Hurdle at the Cheltenham Festival, the Tote Gold Trophy (Handicap) at Newbury, and the Imperial Cup at Sandown, while there are many other valuable sponsored prizes for hurdlers (see Chapter Eight).

Hurdlers as well as chasers in the past have become public favourites and they include: *Sir Ken*, three times winner of the Champion Hurdle (1952–54), ridden by Tim Molony; the well-loved *Persian War*, game little winner of the same race three times (1968–70) and runner-up in 1971 in the colours of Mr Henry Alper, which intentionally resembled those of West Ham United FC; and the dual Champion Hurdle winner *National Spirit* (after winning in 1947 and 1948, he blundered at the last flight in 1949, leaving *Hatton's Grace* clear for the first of his three victories – achieved between the age of nine years old and 11 years old). More recent public favourites in the Champion Hurdle have been *Night Nurse*, winner 1976 and 1977, third the following year; *Monksfield*, winner 1978 and 1979, runner-up in 1977 and 1980; *Sea Pigeon*, winner 1980 and 1981 (when he was 11 years old) and runner-up the two previous years; *Dawn Run*, the mare that captured the affections of the Cheltenham crowd; the triple winner from 1985 to 1987, *See You Then*; and, most recently, the barnstorming Irish-trained *Istabraq*, who seized the champion crown in a quite outstanding and impressive manner in 1998, 1999 and 2000.

Finally, on the subject of public favourites, another remarkable old hurdler and mud-loving Cheltenham specialist must be mentioned: *Willie Wumpkins*. Between the ages of 11 and 13 he won the Coral Golden Hurdle Final three times. He has since died, but at age 26, in 1994, proudly paraded before the event.

In the frame This term means that a horse has won or been placed – in other words, it has had its number hoisted in the winning frame on the racecourse numbers board.

Irons A term for stirrups, most commonly in the phrase 'He lost his irons', used when, during running, a jockey's riding boots become parted from the stirrups.

Jockey Club The oldest Turf Authority in the world, which had its origins at the Star and Garter, Pall Mall, in 1752, was incorporated in 1970 by Royal Charter, and until recently was the sole governing body of horseracing in Britain, both on the Flat and over jumps. Formerly, jumping meetings were administered by the National Hunt Committee, but in 1968 this body was amalgamated with the Jockey Club.

In turn, in June 1993, the absolute rule of the Jockey Club, which had lasted for over two centuries, was superseded by that of the British Horseracing Board (*q.v.*), although the Jockey Club, within the BHB, retained certain of its original powers. Of most importance, these were: disciplinary matters; security and anti-doping measures; the regulation of horseraces and race meetings; the licensing of racecourses, Clerks of the Course, trainers and riders; the registration of stable employees; and the approval and registration of individual owners and companies. There are currently 123 ordinary and 17 honorary members, from whom the six Stewards and members of the various committees and external bodies are appointed. The present Senior Steward is Julian Richmond-Watson.

To those who abhor self-perpetuating, self-elected autocracy in any form, the Jockey Club is still, nevertheless, anathema. Such prejudice is not only blind to the early work of, particularly, Sir Charles Bunbury, Lord George Bentinck and Admiral Rous (see Chapter Two) in shaping racing into a form recognisable today, but also ignores the reforms wrought within the club in the past two or three decades. These have effectively taken the membership away from domination by a landed aristocracy and crusty horse-owning backwoodsmen and considerably broadened its base. Men with commercial experience, in particular, have been recruited, and the club, in 1977, admitted women, of whom in 1999 there were 13.

The Jockey Club has its premises at the Jockey Club Rooms in the High Street, Newmarket, where it owns approximately 4,500 acres of land, including the Heath where the racing takes place, as well as 2,800 acres of training gallops and other freehold property in the town. There are also large modern offices in Portman Square, London. Racecourse Holdings Trust is a subsidiary of the Jockey Club which owns/manages nine racecourses. The day-to-day administration of racing is in the hands of Messrs Weatherbys (*q.v.*), now under contract to the BHB.

Also, the Jockey Club has an informative website on the Internet at http://www.thejockeyclub.co.uk It (see graphic on following page) gives details of current news stories concerning Jockey Club decisions, a history of the Club and its present activities, how day-to-day racing is conducted, the safety and welfare side of affairs, and a run-down on discipline and licensing.

Joint This is the name given to the bookmaker's temporary 'establishment' on the racecourse.

Lads, Lasses Stable lads and, more than ever these days, stable lasses constitute the workforce without whom the entire business of racing would fall apart. They are not well rewarded, at least in financial terms, for a pretty tough life at what modern jargon is pleased to call unsocial hours. For a maximum basic of about £181.85 a week they muck out, ride out and tend to their (usually these days) three horses. Without a massive increase in prize-money and/or a major readjustment in how that prize-money is distributed, their wages seem destined to remain below what they should be. Sure, there are prizes for best turned-out horses – the Rules of Racing specifically stipulate these days percentages of prize-money that have to go to stable staff – but, altogether, it is a very depressing scenario, which was graphically analysed once by Sue Montgomery in the *Racing Post*: 'One of the problems of working with horses is that very few people do it unless they want to. And it has always been the vocations – nursing, the cloth, teaching, working with animals – that have been lowest in the pecking order for conditions and money. With horses, employers have traditionally taken advantage of, firstly, their employees' desire to do the job and, secondly, their love for individual horses under their care...Human nature being what it is, there are good stable lads and bad stable lads. There are trainers who are good employers, with good senior staff, and trainers who are rotten bosses, with vindictive, small-minded head lads bent on squashing any display of talent or initiative in the ranks below. Overall, ours is an industry with labour force problems, and no-one is more aware of it than the lads.'

Leg Term with several meanings as in 1) 'He's done a leg', meaning suffered a leg injury (*see BAD LEGS*); 2) phrase indicating the stages of a multiple bet, as in the Lincoln Handicap being the first 'leg' of the Spring Double and the Grand National the second; 3) a term for the 'blacklegs', or disreputable forerunners of modern bookmakers, known as 'legs' (see Chapter Two).

Levy Board The commonly used abbreviation for the Horserace Betting Levy Board. This statutory body was established in 1961, the same year in which betting shops were made legal. The prime object of the Levy Board was and is to siphon back some of the money that annually goes into betting in order to apply it in various directions for the good of racing. However, following the new arrangements for taxing bookmakers originally allowed for in the 2001 Budget, a date has now been announced for the closure of the Levy Board. This will take place in September 2006.

Limited stakes A race restricted to horses which have been awarded handicap ratings (*q.v.*) at or below a figure specified in the race conditions.

Listed race A Listed race is one whose importance ranks immediately after the Group races (*see PATTERN RACES*) on the Flat.

Maiden Nothing to do with the sex of a horse – a maiden is a horse, either colt (*q.v.*), filly (*q.v.*), or gelding (*q.v.*) which has not won a race. There are an enormous number of races throughout the Flat season confined to maidens, and an equivalent number during the jumping season for horses that, up to a specified time, have not won a hurdle, or have not won a chase. These are called, respectively, novice hurdles and novice chases. On the Flat, most maiden races are open only to 'maidens at starting', horses that, up to the day of the race, have not won. These are normally run at weight-for-age (*q.v.*) with allowance for fillies against colts and geldings. There is sometimes a weight allowance for horses who have never run before. Maiden races may be confined to two-year-olds, or three-year olds (these are the most usual categories), but there are also maiden events for three-year-olds and older.

Maiden handicap A handicap restricted to maidens at starting which have run at least four times in Britain.

Makes a noise A horse who has respiratory trouble 'makes a noise'. Also known as a 'roarer'. This may be alleviated either by a Hobday operation, or by 'tubing' – by-passing of obstruction in the larynx by insertion of a tube.

Mare Female thoroughbred of five years of age and older. If she has been retired to the paddocks for breeding purposes she becomes a broodmare (see Chapter Ten). It is fairly usual these days not to give fillies (*q.v.*) a long racing career. In most well-bred cases, provided they have won a race of some sort, if possible they will be retired before they are four years old to be mated with a stallion standing at stud. In the bloodstock industry, fees are charged for a stallion's services, usually on a no-foal-no-fee basis, and the foal is the property of the owner of the mare.

Match A match is a race between two horses, the property of two different owners, on terms agreed by them. In the early days of the Turf they were a common form of competition, but gave place to the form of racing we know today. There have, however, been matches in the not too distant past, mostly for charity and, in the earlier days of women jockeys, for the publicity afforded by the participation of well-known personalities. For example, *Mill Reef*'s faithful old companion, *Aldie*, in 1977 when he was aged 11, won two matches, one against *Star Performance*, ridden by Angela Rippon. Also trained by Ian Balding, *Morris Dancer*, when aged 12 in 1973 won a match at Haydock Park, which was his final race. And in May 1985, the season after which Lester Piggott went into his first retirement from the saddle, he took part in a match in which the opposing rider was the brilliant National Hunt champion John Francome, himself only just retired (though unlike Lester, sadly, never to return, at least on a permanent basis). Lester on *The Liquidator* (at 2/1 on), trained by Martin Pipe, won, as the form book put it, 'cleverly' by two lengths. But the interesting point is that the roads to Warwick racecourse that evening, despite desperate weather, were jammed, the car parks had to be closed and the stands were packed. Perhaps matches of this kind deserve a revival?

Monkey Betting term for £500. Hence the bookmaker's shout of, for example, 'I'll take two monkeys', meaning he will take £1,000 to return £500 plus stake back, if the favourite at 2/1 on wins (*see* ODDS).

Morning glory A horse which shiningly produces marvellous work in his home gallops of a morning, but utterly fails to reproduce the same sort of performance on the racecourse.

Museums A welcome and enlightened development in the past few years has been the emergence of museums devoted to the rich and fascinating history of racing. The National Horseracing Museum, in Newmarket High Street, next to the Jockey Club Rooms, was opened in 1983 by HM The Queen. Like most museums these days, it is not a dead place of solemn glass cases. For example, there is a reconstruction of a weighing room from the time of Fred Archer. There are videos of famous races up to the present. They back up a quite superb collection of paintings and marvellously mounted photographs which, with every kind of memento, bring to life this great sport and the horses who, with their trainers, jockeys and owners, have helped to make it so. York had a museum long before Newmarket, which befits the role of this major European racecourse. The museum is on a smaller scale than the one at Newmarket but is on a par for interest. Witness the original Matchbook, billed as 'probably the earliest official record of British racing', two of the feet, mounted in gold, of the incomparable *St. Simon*, and an engraved glass goblet which shows the finish of the match between *Mrs Thornton* and *Captain Flint* in 1805, not many weeks before the Battle of Trafalgar. Cheltenham, meanwhile, amply does justice to the National Hunt scene with its quite outstanding Hall of Fame, which concentrates in its memorabilia and thrilling video replays on the history of the Festival and the course's role in the making of jump racing. Epsom, too, opened a Hall of Fame in 1994.

Names Rule 40 of the Rules of Racing requires some explanation. It states: 'No owners shall make use of an assumed name for the purpose of entering or running horses'. The penalty, should a horse be so run, is disqualification. The reason behind the rule is the prevention of the use of a *nom-de-course* in order to disguise the true identity of an owner. This used to be quite common practice. Thus, records give the winner of the 1000 Guineas in 1854 as 'Mr Howard's *Virago*'. This conceals the identity of Henry Padwick, a notorious and rapacious moneylender of the time. The owner of the 1879 Derby winner, *Sir Bevys*, appears as one Mr Acton. This, in fact, was Leopold de Rothschild, who took his 'name' from the place near London where he had a stud, and which, in its present suburban incarnation, hardly leaps to the mind as a place where a racing stud might be found. Several Classic winners, including *Lemburg, Bayardo*, and *Gay Crusader*, the Triple Crown winner of 1917 (who was sired by *Bayardo*), are down in the ownership of a certain 'Mr Fairie'. This was the *nom-de-course* of Mr A.W. Cox, a taciturn Australian who had made an enormous fortune in the Broken Hill silver mines. Sir George Chetwynd, meanwhile, whose malpractice on the Turf led to one of the greatest of all Victorian racing scandals, was 'Mr Mortimer' in his early days. In more recent times, that great and immensely likeable owner-breeder, Sir Victor Sassoon, used a *nom-de-course* (though in racing in India, China and Hong Kong, not in the UK). It was formed from his initials so he became 'Mr Eves'. Hence he called his stud the Eve Stud; similarly his villa in the Bahamas. And the reason why Lester and Susan Piggott's stables at Newmarket were called 'Eve Lodge' is that the name was a tribute to the warm friendship between the former champion jockey and his family and Sir Victor and Lady Sassoon.

Not only do owners these days have to identify themselves accurately, but horses also must be named before they can race. The 1797 Derby winner is still only vaguely recorded as the 'Duke of Bedford's brown colt by *Fidget* out of sister to *Pharamond*'. There were several other early Classic winners who were unnamed at the time they won. *Bay Middleton*, who became a pervasive influence in the stud-book through his progeny, had been named by the time he won the 1836 Derby, but not when he took the 2000 Guineas earlier in the season. The rules now forbid this practice, although when a horse first goes to a stable yard, he or she may not have a name, and will simply be known, at first, as 'the *Nijinsky* colt', say, or 'the *Warning* filly', after his or her sire.

The art of naming a racehorse lies in making, if possible, an apt play on the names of its sire and dam. *Whistler*, foaled in 1950, for example, was well named, in view of the lawsuits the artist of the same name was involved in. He (the colt that is) was by *Panorama* out of *Farthing Damages*, and a glance at the dam's side of his pedigree shows that he was by no means the first in his family to have a witty name:

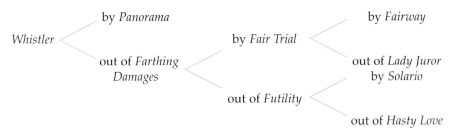

Which brings to mind a jumper of some years ago called *Abdul the Bul Bul*. Those familiar with the rugby player's hymnal will best appreciate how accurately named he was, being by *Gigantic* out of *Turkish Tourist*. The late John Hislop chose an inspired name for his brilliant colt *Brigadier Gerard*, who was Conan Doyle's swashbuckling hero of Napoleonic times. The equine brigadier was by *Queen's Hussar* out of *La Paiva* – the name of a famous Parisian courtesan. Others with great appeal are *Mr Dormouse* (*Comedy Star* – *Teapot*), *Swiss Affair* (*Private Account* – *Ten Cents a Kiss*), while HM The Queen exercised her well-known talent for naming her horses when she called one of her colts *Sharp Prod*. He was by *Sharpo* out of *Gentle Persuasion*. There are other owners, meanwhile, with certain principles in naming their horses. The late Lady Beaverbrook used to go for a lucky seven letters in her choice – for example, *Bustino*, *Niniski* and *Boldboy* (see Chapter Seven); Mrs Arpad Plesch was fond of botanical titles for the horses she and her husband bred, hence, for example, *Thymus* (1959 French 2000 Guineas), *Sassafras* (1970 French Derby; 'Arc'), and one of her purchases, *Henbit* (1980 Derby). Also, striking a somewhat more bizarre note, Mr Steven Astaire favoured for his horses the names of characters played by Groucho Marx. Thus, *Wolf J. Flywheel*, *Rufus T. Firefly* and *J. Cheever Loophole*, among others.

An instruction bars names consisting of more than 18 letters or spaces and letters. Thus the amazing and appalling name of the chaser at St Albans in 1869, *Neurasthenipponskalesterizo*, would have been disallowed these days (and quite rightly so). Nevertheless, some rather more comprehensible and ingenious contractions do get legally by, such as *Tuwhittuwhittuwhoo*, *Kissinthebackrow*, *Shewhomustbeobeyed*, and *Letsbeonestaboutit*.

A thick book published biennially by Weatherbys (*q.v.*) lists all the registered names, more than 20,000 of them, which by definition are not available for use. The names of celebrated winners, including those of the Classics, the Ascot Gold

Cup, King George VI and Queen Elizabeth Diamond Stakes and Grand National, are marked with an asterisk and are not available in perpetuity. So, too, are those of certain outstanding horses marked with a double asterisk appearing in the International List of Protected Names. These include, for example, the colossus of post-war jumping, *Arkle*; the wonderful American champion of 1919–20, *Man o'War*; and the Australian hero of the late 1880s and early 'nineties, *Carbine*.

National Hunt   This embraces all steeplechases and all hurdling, and is descriptive of courses which exclusively stage these events and those that are devoted to Flat racing during the summer but stage such events in the winter. There used to be a separate governing body called the National Hunt Committee (*see JOCKEY CLUB*). Previously it was the Grand National Hunt Committee, which gave rise to the official name of the Grand National Steeplechase (see under **Liverpool** in Chapter Eight).

National Hunt Flat race   This may seem to be a contradiction in terms. In fact, it represents the revival in recent years in this country of a type of race popular in Ireland, namely the 'Bumper' – an unflattering reference to the style of the amateurs who were often the sole contestants. The idea of running potential jumpers on the Flat is to give them experience of racing without actually having to clear an obstacle. The Champion Hurdler *Morley Street* and the Grand National winner *Royal Athlete* are among successful graduates from this form of racing.

Non-trier   A horse which does not give its best running. This used to happen a great deal, and there are innumerable instances of horses being 'pulled' by their jockeys, often in order to attempt to bamboozle the handicappers, get a lower weight than the horse merited on its true capabilities, and thus have something 'in hand' in a race if the ploy succeeded – which it often did. It is now strictly dealt with under Rule 151, with fines for offending trainers, one recently being £2,500. Horses often used to be run at the beginning of the season to get them fit; this was known as 'training on the racecourse' and has also effectively been fined out of existence by the stewards.

In the days of the barrier start in big fields, a famous Clerk of the Course (Malcolm Hancock) used to tell the jockeys to line up in two lines: 'Non-triers at the back'. Jockey Club fines apart, the camera patrol (*q.v.*) and video re-runs have been instrumental in diminishing the incidence of non-triers, which were sometimes a figment of a losing punter's imagination. 'Not off a yard', 'Not wanted today' would be the comments to rationalise any failure on the part of the judgement of the punter; that, at least, still happens today. A genuine example of non-trying that happened decades ago is illustrated in another story told to me, this time by the late Jack Topham, senior race reader and the power in the field behind *Raceform* for many years. He told me of a race at Windsor, the figure-of-eight course by the Thames (the strong Yorkshire accent of this big man who looked as if hewn from the Pennines, and was known as Heathcliff, has to be imagined): 'I was at Windsor one day when a jockey – you'll know who I mean, he's training now and he won an Imperial Cup – well, at the bottom turn he was third and by the time they'd got to the junction he was nowhere. I said to him afterwards: "You'd have been quicker coming up by river!" There's one that wasn't wanted. All together, now, with the Salvation Army Psalter...'

Numbers board A mine of information for those who bother to read it on racecourses that still have one. Essentially a metal frame about 20 ft high, usually situated opposite the stand on the course beyond the far running rails and worked by a system of pulleys and counter-weights. It gives the name of each jockey taking part in the race (*see CHALK JOCKEY*). The numbers carried on the saddlecloth of each horse, corresponding to the numbers on the racecard (and in the morning papers), appear on the left of the name of the jockey who is riding the horse, black on white except in the case of claiming apprentices, whose numbers appear as follows: 7 lb allowance – red number on white; 4 lb allowance (steeplechases and hurdle races, and National Hunt Flat races) *or* 5 lb allowance (Flat races) – black number on orange; 3 lb allowance – white number on blue. On the right of the jockey's name appears the draw for places at the start. Underneath the jockey's names are separate boards which give the state of the going, details of overweight, and colour changes, as for example when an owner is running more than one horse and the jockeys are distinguishable by different-coloured caps. All this information is hauled down when the race starts. After the race, the numbers of the winner and placed horses go up in a small, separate frame to one side of the main board; in the case of a photo-finish the letter 'P' appears 'in the frame' (*q.v.*). When the jockeys have been weighed in after the race and found to be carrying the correct weight corresponding to the one they weighed out with before the race, the 'all right' signal is displayed on the numbers board. This is done by hoisting a blue flag. Bookmakers pay out winning bets when the 'all right' signal is shown. If there is an objection or/and stewards' inquiry, a red flag is hoisted. When the inquiry is completed, and placings are unaltered, the red flag is replaced with a white flag; inquiry completed and placings altered is indicated by a green flag and the hoisting of the correct placings in the frame. All this is backed up by the public address system. If there has been an inquiry, bookmakers pay out winning bets when the result is made known.

Nursery handicap A handicap (*q.v.*) confined to two-year-olds . It used to be the rule that no nursery could be run before September, but now they are commonly run in August, and some even in July.

Odds Prices at which a bookmaker lays bets. Prices are odds against, even money, or odds on:

Even money is when an equal amount is laid by a bookmaker to the amount put on by a backer. 'Evens this favourite', 'Even money the field' are the shouts in the ring. In other words, for every £1 staked £1 is returned.

Odds against are when the bookmaker offers more money than the amount staked, fractional though it may be.

Odds on is the term used when bookmakers offer less money against the amount staked, also frequently in fractions. Thus a successful bet at odds of 2/1 against (two to one against) wins *twice* the amount staked. At odds of 2/1 on (two to one on) it will win only *half* the amount staked. So, for every £1 wagered at 2/1 against, £2 is returned plus stake back and for every £1 wagered at 2/1 on, 50p is returned plus stake back. Similarly, a successful bet at 6/4 (six-to-four) against wins 1½ *times* the amount staked and at 6/4 on yields *four-sixths* (*i.e. two-thirds*) only. So, for every £1 wagered at 6/4 against, £1.50 is returned plus stake back and for every £1 wagered at 6/4 on, only 66p is returned plus stake back. Or, in a more usual racecourse version of such bets, £4 on at 6/4 against would return £6, while £6 on at 6/4 on would yield £4.

In shouting the odds on the racecourse when *laying* odds, bookmakers can be heard as follows: 'Two to one the field', 'I'll go two's this favourite', both meaning 2/1 against. But 'I'll *take* two to one', '*Take* six to four', 'Seven to four on this favourite', all mean that the prices quoted are odds on, and that the bookmakers are *taking* odds.

Bar one. In the fruity hubbub of Tatteralls' Ring before a race can often be heard 'Five to one bar one', or 'Four's Bar', yielding the impression that bar one and/or bar are ever present runners in every race, an impression the pre-race presentation on television does little to dispel, although they do quite frequently say something on the lines of 'Ten to one bar these four', having listed the prices of the first four horses in the betting market. The shouts can be interpreted as follows: 'Five to one bar one' = five to one against, or better, all the rest of the field *except* the favourite. 'Four's bar' = four to one, or better, all the rest of the field *except* the horses already quoted, including the favourite, at odds of less than 4/1 against.

Longer odds, shorter odds. 10/1 is longer or a longer price than, say, 5/1 (and much longer, say, than even money, or an odds on price). Conversely, an odds on 'chance' (as the phrase goes) is said to be shorter in the betting, or in the market, than a horse quoted at odds against. 'Henry Cecil's Derby candidate is bound to start at a short price this afternoon' means that the horse trained by Henry Cecil, which is a Derby entry, is bound to start at about even money or odds on, though it might be quoted in the market (at least to begin with) at slightly ('a shade of') odds against. On the other hand, 'Long odds can still be had about this quietly fancied Grand National candidate' refers to prices usually in excess of 15/1.

When a horse's price contracts in the market, it is said to shorten, or come in. When the odds on offer become larger, it is said to lengthen, or go out; and if it goes out appreciably, say, from odds on to 2/1 against or from 4/1 to 10/1, it will be said to have 'taken a walk in the market' (*see* DRIFTER), or 'gone badly in the market'. Short odds are said to be 'cramped'; long odds, if 20/1 or above, lead to the horses to which the prices refer being described as not only 'outsiders' at 'any price you like' but 'rags' or 'out with the washing'.

Fractions. There is a very ancient racing chestnut about the bookmaker teaching his child to count. The lesson goes: 'Evens, 11 to ten, six to five, five to four, 11 to eight...' and so on. At least this superannuated joke possesses the merit of illustrating some of the bizarre fractions used in the Ring which have more logic in them than might appear at first acquaintance. Below is a full list of the odds in smaller fractions, which will be more readily understood when it is realised that they are based on the English currency in use before decimalisation in 1971. To convey why the fractions are as they are, totally unchanged since before that date, it is unnecessary to explain the details of the old currency (of which only a very few aged under 40 can have much more than a vague recollection), except to say that, essentially, as far as betting was concerned there were eight half-crowns (8 x 2 shillings and sixpence) to the pound, or sovereign as it used to be even earlier in the century. Also, but of minor significance, there were ten florins (or two-shilling pieces) to the pound. There were also ten-shilling notes (half-sovereign coins earlier) worth half the value of a pound. The abbreviation for pence was 'd'.

The frequent occurrence of 4s and 8s in the list may therefore be seen in this light.

Present Odds	Actual Fraction	Amount won in pre-decimalisation currency to the given stake: £1	£10	10 shillings (£½)
Evens				
11/10	One and 1/10	£1 and 1 Florin	£11	11 shillings
6/5	One and 1/5	£1 and 2 Florins	£12	12 shillings
5/4	One and a quarter	£1 and 2 Half-Crowns	£12.10s	12s 6d
11/8	One and 3/8	£1 and 3 Half-Crowns	£13.15s	13s 9d
6/4	One and a half	£1 and 4 Half-Crowns or 10 Shillings	£15	15s
13/8	One and 5/8	£1 and 5 Half-Crowns	£16.5s	16s 3d
7/4	One and three-quarters	£1 and 6 Half-Crowns	£17.10s	17s 6d
15/8	One and 7/8	£1 and 7 Half-Crowns	£18.15s	18s 9d
2/1				

The list then goes on: 9/4, 5/2, 11/4, 3/1, 100/30, 7/2, 4/1 and up to 9/1 in halves and whole numbers; thereafter up to 12/1 in single whole numbers; then up to 20/1 two 'points' at a time.

The settling of bets at these odds in the old currency (except for small bets under ten shillings) can therefore be seen to have been a good deal easier than it is today, if a comparison is made between the table above and the late 20th century ready reckoner published below. However, decimalisation has made some bets, notably multiple bets, easier to calculate. The one figure that stands out from the table as seemingly anomalous is 100/30. Why, suddenly, a hundred to thirty? This may be understood by translating it back to 100 shillings to 30 shillings, in other words, £5 to a £1.10s stake.

Settling apart, the change to new pence has had only one effect on the odds, and that is the sweeping away of the old and now nostalgic sounding figures of 100/8, 100/7, and 100/6. These have been rounded to 12/1, 14/1 and 16/1, which are obviously easier to settle in new currency.

Odds ready reckoner Winnings shown include return of stake.

SP	10p	20p	25p	50p	£1.00	£5.00
1/3	13½	26½	33½	67	1.33½	6.67
2/5	14	28	35	70	1.40	7.00
4/9	14½	29	36	72½	1.44½	7.22
1/2	15	30	37½	75	1.50	7.50
4/7	16	31½	39	79	1.57½	7.86
8/13	16½	32½	40½	81	1.61½	8.08
4/6	17	33½	42	83½	1.67	8.33
8/11	17½	35	43½	86½	1.73	8.64
4/5	18	36	45	90	1.80	9.00
5/6	18½	37	46	92	1.83½	9.17
10/11	19	38½	48	95½	1.91	9.54½
Evens	20	40	50	1.00	2.00	10.00
11/10	21	42	52½	1.05	2.10	10.50
6/5	22	44	55	1.10	2.20	11.00
5/4	22½	45	56½	1.12½	2.25	11.25
11/8	24	47½	59½	1.19	2.37½	11.87½
6/4	25	50	62½	1.25	2.50	12.50
13/8	26½	52½	66	1.31½	2.62½	13.12½
7/4	27½	55	69	1.37½	2.75	13.75
15/8	29	57½	72	1.44	2.87½	14.37½
2/1	30	60	75	1.50	3.00	15.00
9/4	32½	65	81½	1.62½	3.25	16.25
5/2	35	70	87½	1.75	3.50	17.50
11/4	37½	75	94	1.87½	3.75	18.75
3/1	40	80	1.00	2.00	4.00	20.00
10/3	43½	87	1.08½	2.17	4.33½	21.67
7/2	45	90	1.12½	2.25	4.50	22.50
4/1	50	1.00	1.25	2.50	5.00	25.00
9/2	55	1.10	1.37½	2.75	5.50	27.50
5/1	60	1.20	1.50	3.00	6.00	30.00
11/2	65	1.30	1.62½	3.25	6.50	32.50
6/1	70	1.40	1.75	3.50	7.00	35.00
13/2	75	1.50	1.87½	3.75	7.50	37.50
7/1	80	1.60	2.00	4.00	8.00	40.00
15/2	85	1.70	2.12½	4.25	8.50	42.50
8/1	90	1.80	2.25	4.50	9.00	45.00
17/2	95	1.90	2.37½	4.75	9.50	47.50
9/1	1.00	2.00	2.50	5.00	10.00	50.00
10/1	1.10	2.20	2.75	5.50	11.00	55.00
11/1	1.20	2.40	3.00	6.00	12.00	60.00
12/1	1.30	2.60	3.25	6.50	13.00	65.00
14/1	1.50	3.00	3.75	7.50	15.00	75.00
16/1	1.70	3.40	4.25	8.50	17.00	85.00

20/1	2.10	4.20	5.25	10.50	21.00	105.00
25/1	2.60	5.20	6.50	13.00	26.00	130.00
33/1	3.40	6.80	8.50	17.00	34.00	170.00

Off The off is the start of the race, officially timed, as in betting shop commentaries: 'They're off Warwick. Off Brighton. Off at all meetings.' Off-course bookmakers will not take bets after this time. However, on the course it is often possible to have a bet in the very early stages of longer races, particularly steeplechases.

Off the bit Also 'off the bridle'. When horses, in the earlier stages of a race, are hard held by the jockey and travelling smoothly, they are said to be 'on the bit' or 'on the bridle'. Some horses pull harder than others and may be difficult to settle at this stage. When given their head, or 'let down', and urged for an effort they are said to be 'off the bit' or 'off the bridle'.

On Betting term meaning that a bet or sidebet has been struck: '60 to 40 the favourite falls.' 'You're on.' Or 'What did you back?' 'I couldn't get on.'

Overweight When a jockey cannot, physically, get down to the weight due to be carried, the difference between that weight and what the weighing room scales show is called 'overweight'. It is yet another piece of information given on the numbers board, e.g. when a horse in a handicap is weighted at 8 st, and the jockey cannot turn the scales, with the saddle and saddlecloth and other equipment included, at less than 8 st 2 lb, he has to declare 2 lb overweight.

Paddock Before a race, horses are led round the parade ring in the paddock area. This is a good opportunity to assess them for looks, temperament and fitness. As far as looks are concerned, Henry Cecil's views are quoted in Chapter Nine. Good walkers have already been dealt with in this chapter. Unfortunately it is not always possible fully to assess how fit a horse is looking until the rugs come off, but good signs are the indented lines on its quarters (the muscular upper part of the hind legs), indicating the horse has done plenty of work, and a coat with a bloom on it demonstrates good health. Other good signs are for a horse to appear alert and on his toes. By contrast, sweating up in the paddock is sometimes a sign (particularly froth on face and neck) that a horse is unnecessarily worked up and nervous. But some horses (*Mr Frisk*, the immensely popular Grand National and Whitbread Gold Cup winner of 1990 is a good example) invariably get into a lather, and dampness around the neck is not necessarily a bad sign. *Timeform* (see Chapter Four) usually refers to this characteristic. Fillies (*q.v.*), in particular, feel the cold, and will look 'all tucked up' on a bleak day early in the season.

In the autumn, horses may also begin to 'go in their coats' – i.e. there are signs of them growing their winter coats, which is often accompanied by them losing their form. At this time, too, horses go 'over the top' after doing enough racing for the year and may have 'run up light' – i.e. appear lean and ribby behind the saddle. It is worth paying attention to the paddock comments in *Raceform* (see Chapter Four) which will say if a horse looks well or is backward, etc.

Pattern races The most important Flat races in Europe have been formed into a coherent 'pattern' throughout the season to give suitably spaced opportunities for the best horses according to age, sex and racing distance. The concept of the Pattern originated in the Duke of Norfolk's Pattern of Racing Committee appointed in 1965 to make recommendations on the general programme of races, with special attention to the needs of top-class horses. From its original findings and via a further committee chaired by Lord Porchester was evolved the European Pattern system, which got underway in 1971 and included the United Kingdom, France and Ireland; in 1979 it was joined by Germany and Italy.

Intrinsically it consists of races throughout the season of three Groups. Group One consists of Classic and other races of championship standard having major international importance. They are run without penalties (*q.v.*), on a weight-for-age (*q.v.*) and weight-for-sex basis. Group Two is a category of races immediately below championship standard and also significant in an international context. Group Three completes the series of tests for the best horses. These are mainly of domestic importance in the member countries.

In Groups Two and Three, penalties are based on success in previous Pattern races. Beyond the Group events, the next most important are called Listed races. The most successful Pattern race winners are *Brigadier Gerard* (beaten only once in his career), the outstanding Cup horse, *Ardross*, the German star, *Acatenango*, and, most recently, that wonderful and immensely popular but now sadly deceased old campaigner, *Persian Punch*. They each have a record 13 Pattern victories to their credit. Of these, *Persian Punch*'s achievement was perhaps the most remarkable. In 2003, at the age of ten, he brilliantly scored no fewer than three Group victories, including his third Jockey Club Cup and both the Goodwood and Doncaster Cups, as well as, for good measure, being runner-up in the Ascot Gold Cup. *Triptych* (see under **Filly**) is topmost equine female with ten Group successes. *Further Flight* (see Chapter Ten) is next in the overall Pattern table with his stirring nine wins, while *Daylami* (1997–99) had seven Group victories in Europe plus two Grade One in the USA.

Under National Hunt Rules, there is similarly a Pattern spread evenly throughout the season as to chase or hurdle, distance, and whether or not for novices and juveniles. It is also distributed evenly on a geographical basis throughout the United Kingdom.

The events are graded One to Three. Grade One and Two are Conditions (*q.v.*) or Weight-for-Age (*q.v.*) races, and Grade Three, important handicaps (*q.v.*).

Penalty The term given to the extra weight added to a horse's original weight in a race as a consequence of having won in between being entered for that race and actually running in it, where the handicapper has not been able to re-assess the original weight allotted. It is worth studying the conditions of a race to see what the penalty values are: some are simply 'straight' penalties for winning any race, some are 'graded' penalties according to the value of race won. The better the class of race, the better the penalised winner. Penalised horses, especially if they have won easily, are often worth following up for another win.

Photo-finish   A camera is installed in line with the winning post which photographs the finish of a race, and, in the instance (very frequent on the Flat) of several horses being closely involved at the finishing line, the judge (*see RACECOURSE OFFICIALS*) calls for a photograph to decide the winner and / or other placings (*see DEAD-HEAT*). The photograph shows the horses, a scribed-in finishing line, and a mirror image of the horses (to circumvent parallax error).

The photo-finish was first used at Epsom in April 1947, when *Parhelion* was judged to have beaten *Salubrious* in the Great Metropolitan Handicap. In the early days of the photo-finish, the professional backer Alex Bird was extremely successful in beating the bookmakers in the market which was formed as soon as a photograph was announced. This was during the days when the film took rather longer than it does today to be processed. Alex Bird used to stand in exact line with the finish, close one eye, and not move his head as the horses passed the post. On certain courses – e.g. Cheltenham, and also at Ascot and on the Rowley Mile at Newmarket, where the horses often race wide apart – it is quite difficult to judge a finish correctly from a distant angle, and bookmakers in those days frequently selected the wrong horse to make favourite in a photo-finish, laying odds against the other(s). Alex Bird, who tells his full story in *The Life and Secrets of A Professional Punter*, took a fortune out of the ring by using his techniques.

Pitch   The precise place in the betting ring where a bookmaker bets at his joint (*q.v.*). The best pitches on a racecourse are in the front rank of Tattersalls' Ring and diminish in desirability the further back they are towards the racecourse running rails – rather like the graduation from orchestra stalls to pit, and based on the fact that the front row are likely to attract more customers because they are situated nearest the stands.

Pitches used to be allocated in order of seniority and length of service by a committee under the auspices of the National Association of Bookmakers. Promotion to the front rank occurred only on a principal's retirement or death. Temporary moves, to fill vacant pitches on a daily basis, were dealt with in order of personal seniority. In the attempt to modernise on-course betting facilities, these arrangements (dating from 1958) no longer exist, and a body called the National Joint Pitch Council, appointed by the Levy Board (*q.v.*) is in charge.

Under the new rules, permanently allocated pitches have been scrapped and replaced by a system of 'picks' according to a single list of bookmakers drawn up for each racecourse. Bookmakers turn up one hour before racing and choose their site in order of their place on the list, which will have been decided on the basis of 'commensurate seniority' – an amalgam of previous personal and inherited seniority. This has proved a contentious issue and one of the reasons why there has been discontent among some bookmakers who have found they are lower down the list than others more recently established in business. An even more fundamental change has been the auction of pitches, starting in 1998. One auction (at York) yielded almost £2.5 million. At another, a single bookmaker spent more than £200,000 on fresh pitches. And Irish bookmakers have predictably and notably been successful in buying up prominent pitches at Cheltenham. This and other aspects of the upheaval in the betting ring have caused several well-known bookmakers to quit and a good deal of head-shaking among others (see Victor Chandler's comments under **Betting on the rails** earlier in the chapter).

Place A horse that wins, is second, third, or frequently these days, finishes fourth in a race (and sometimes even fifth and sixth). These are placings according to which the prize-money for the race is awarded, and they differ, particularly in the case of most fourth and all lower placed horses, from the placings a bookmaker or the Tote will pay out on for a place. As far as betting is concerned, in small fields of five to seven runners commonly only the first two are 'placed', and in most of the remainder of races places are paid on the first, second and third, with the exception of certain big handicaps (*q.v.*) and sometimes the Derby, where a fourth place may qualify for pay-out. (For details see Chapter Five.)

Point to point Point to points are amateur races run over fences under the auspices of individual Hunts. Known also as racing 'between the flags', this is an immensely popular sport and has its own form book. In recent years, point to points have become a greatly successful nursery for horses graduating to chasing under National Hunt Rules. Among the graduates have been *Cool Dawn* (1998 Cheltenham Gold Cup); *See More Business* (1997 King George VI Chase; 1999 Cheltenham Gold Cup); *Coome Hill* (1996 Hennessy Gold Cup); *Harwell Lad* (1997 Whitbread Gold Cup); and *Teeton Mill* (1998 Hennessy Gold Cup; King George VI Chase). Not everyone is in favour of this process.

Pony Term commonly used to mean not a small version of a horse but the sum of £25 staked. Similar to monkey (*q.v.*) in ring usage.

Pressure A horse which, 'off the bit' (*q.v.*), has to be driven to keep his place in a race or to make further effort is said to have come 'under pressure'.

Prize-money This is made up of the sum total of the fees paid in entries, forfeits and declaration by the owners, and a sum added by the racecourse executive and/or, increasingly, commercial or other sponsors. National Hunt racing, in particular, in recent years has greatly benefited from commercial sponsorship. Once the Grand National used to be the only big prize worth going for. Today there are many substantial prizes over the jumps, although none that can match the hundreds of thousands of pounds for races such as the Derby on the Flat. The prize-money, not all that long ago, was simply divided up between the winning owner and those who had taken second and third places with their horses. A percentage of this, by unwritten agreement, went to trainer and jockey, but that, except for a cup or plate in addition, was that. Today, there are two entire closely printed pages in the Rules of Racing devoted to the distribution of prize-money, with percentages calculated to two decimal places affecting not only owners, jockeys and trainers but stables (i.e. lads and lasses), the apprentice training scheme, jockeys' valets, and Jockeys' Association Pension Fund, and so on. It is interesting, while on the subject, to realise that pleas for greater prize-money are not without foundation. A comparison between the value of prize-money for the winners of the Classics in 1893 and that in 1993 is instructive. Allowing for inflation, the value of the 1893 money in real terms of a century later is given in brackets:

	1893		1993	
1000 Guineas	*Siffleuse*	£3,750 (£211,237)	*Sayyedati*	£107,063
2000 Guineas	*Isinglass*	£4,250 (£239,403)	*Zafonic*	£110,871
Derby	*Isinglass*	£5,515 (£310,660)	*Commander-in-Chief*	£447,580
Oaks	*Mrs Butterwick*	£5,180 (£291,789)	*Intrepidity*	£147,500
St. Leger	*Isinglass*	£5,300 (£298,549)	*Bob's Return*	£194,720
		(£1,351,638)		£1,007,734

Europe's Top Flat Races listed by Prize Money
Values are for the year 2003.

	Race	Value (£)
1.	Derby	1,470,000
2.	Prix de l'Arc de Triomphe	1,038,960
3.	Irish Derby	799,375
4.	Derby Italiano	780,195
5.	King George VI and Queen Elizabeth Diamond Stakes	750,000
6.	Prix du Jockey-Club	714,287
7.	Irish Champion Stakes	600,000
8.	Grosser Preis von Baden	496,104
9.	Juddmonte International	460,000
10.	Oaks	415,000
11.	Champion Stakes	400,000
12.	St. Leger	400,000

Racecourse officials All are licensed annually by the Jockey Club (*q.v.*).

The Clerk of the Course makes or breaks a racecourse. It is on his or her enterprise in attracting sponsorship and ingenuity in framing races that will attract fields to bring in the crowds that the success of a racecourse depends. But apart from running the course in a strategic sense, he or she is also responsible for all the routine and smaller details, from checking out the racecard to the printers to seeing the racecourse stables are properly disinfected. A busy individual, and not only on race-days.

The Clerk of the Scales is responsible for weighing jockeys and their equipment according to the rules, as well as promulgating information on the numbers board and furnishing the starter with a list of runners.

The Starter is responsible for starting the race from starting stalls (on the Flat only). He or she is responsible for 'calling the roll' of jockeys at the start, seeing the horses are either loaded into the stalls or lined up properly for the start. When all is ready, the field will come 'under starter's orders', after which even if a horse fails to start he is deemed a runner. If there is a false start, through malfunction of starting stall or any other reason, the field may be recalled by a flag operated down the course by a starter's assistant. The 1993 Grand National, declared void, is the most spectacular example in living memory of how this system can go wrong. When the field has arrived at the start, they are said to be 'at the post'.

Stewards. Three stewards for each race meeting are appointed by the racecourse executive and approved by the stewards of the Jockey Club. The stewards are in overall control of a race meeting, including disciplinary matters – they may order stewards' enquiries or hear evidence on objections. They may impose fines or suspensions, or if they feel that it is warranted, refer a matter to the stewards of the Jockey Club. If they consider a jockey has made a frivolous objection they may fine him. The stewards are also responsible for deciding, in bad weather, to abandon a race meeting, and during frosty weather in winter they will hold inspections of the course the previous day, or earlier, as well as on the morning of racing to decide whether or not it is possible to race.

Racing Calendar Name of the official and expensive weekly publication which gives entries in full for future races, weights allocated in handicaps, as well as other information such as details of the official findings of inquiries, fines imposed, list of unpaid forfeits and other notices. Published by Weatherbys (*q.v.*).

Racing plates Lightweight horseshoes specially fitted for racing.

Rails
1. The white posts and rails which mark out a racecourse on either side, and known in full as running rails. When it is reported that 'his jockey found an opening on the rails...' it does not mean that quite literally but that during the running of a race, a gap has opened alongside horse A running next to the rails, and the jockey on horse B, just behind, has seized the opportunity and taken his horse through it, passing between horse A and the rails.
2. Rails which separate different betting rings (*see BETTING ON THE RAILS*).

Rated stakes A handicap for which the range of weights shall be limited to not more than 14 lb.

Ratings Ratings are the expression in figures of a horse's ability (see under **Handicap**). Every year there is an international meeting of handicappers which includes in its findings the seasonal order of merit in Europe on the Flat. *Dancing Brave* in 1986 (141) is the highest rated of recent years, closely followed by *Alleged* in 1978 (140) and *Shergar* in 1981 (140). Over the jumps, the French-trained *First Gold*, rated 176 in 2000–01, comes out as top steeplechaser, followed by

Best Mate, rated 175 in 2002–03. *Baracouda*, also French-trained, tops the hurdlers' list with 170.

Record sequences Most prolific winner among British-trained fillies and mares since the war was the late *Branston Abby*, trained by Mark Johnston, who broke the existing record with her twenty-third victory in a sprint in Munich in 1996. Previously, *Laurel Queen*, trained by Jack Berry, had held the record since 1993. The record number of wins by a British-bred horse is the astonishing 79 achieved by the mare *Catherina* between 1832 and 1841. More recently, Britain's topmost and most versatile winning horse since 1900 is *Crudwell*, who won no fewer than 50 races between 1950 and 1960: seven on the Flat, four over hurdles and 39 over fences, most notably the Welsh Grand National in 1956.

In 1990, *Timeless Times* with his sixteenth victory equalled the record total for a 2-y-o, and in 1998, the game 3-y-o filly *Lady Rockstar* achieved an amazing progression of eight wins in succession while her handicap rating rose from 41 to 89.

A less enviable sequence has been that of *Quixall Crossett*, who, just short of the venerable age for a racehorse of 18, was retired in December 2002 after racing 103 times without getting his head in front. Nevertheless, this gentle creature, quite rightly, had his own fan club and a great measure of popularity. He also had his own website, a race named after him at Wetherby and, although never winning, was twice runner-up and six times third.

A comprehensive list of racing sequences can be found in Tony Morris and John Randall's admirable *Horse Racing Records* (published by Guinness Books).

Result   The result is, obviously, the outcome of a race. But it has a particular meaning for bookmakers. When they say: 'We got a result', they mean that an unbacked or very lightly backed outsider has won, with resulting profit for the layers.

RHT   Initials of the Racecourse Holdings Trust. Formed in 1964, this is a non-profit-making company whose directors receive no fees, and is a wholly owned subsidiary of the Jockey Club (*q.v.*) with the prime object of preserving racecourses for horseracing.   Each of its racecourses is run as an individual commercial enterprise, with RHT acting to ensure the highest possible standards of operation. Courses belonging to RHT are: Aintree, Carlisle, Cheltenham, Epsom, Haydock, Huntingdon, Kempton, Market Rasen, Newmarket, Nottingham, Sandown, Warwick and Wincanton.

Ringer   Name given to an older horse illegally running in a race in the name of a younger one.   Because of more mature development, a four-year-old, for example, early in the season, has a tremendous pull in the weights if he can masquerade in a race confined to three-year-olds.   The object of ringing is to hoodwink authority and land a gamble. Two of the best-known cases which did not succeed are those of *Running Rein*, a four-year-old who finished first in the 1844 Derby, and *Francasal,* who was involved in a celebrated attempted coup in 1953 at Bath (see Chapter Three). Who knows how many did succeed?

Selling race   This is a race after which the winner must be offered for sale at auction on the racecourse, and is sometimes abbreviated to (S) Race in the title. A reserve price has to be specified.   If the winner's owner and trainer wish to keep the horse after a bid has been made, they must bid a better price. If they are eventually successful the horse is said to have been 'bought in'. The standard of racing is not generally high in 'sellers' as they are usually called (which once gave rise to a notable mistake in the *Evening Standard* when a horse was said to have been 'bought out of a cellar at Warwick'). Altogether, the selling race constitutes a long-outmoded method of buying racehorses (a century ago it was commonplace for horses to be bought in this way and some big prices changed hands), but they are often the medium of a gamble, particularly 2-y-o sellers.

Spread a plate   The expression used when a horse has damaged or lost a racing plate (*q.v.*) before the start, which is delayed while the farrier is summoned to re-shoe him or her.

Spread betting   Spread betting is a form of betting which deals with every kind of sporting activity – football, cricket, golf, tennis and so on – but also very much includes horseracing. It was started by Sporting Index in 1992 and they remain the leaders, although there are other firms now specialising in this expanding field. As far as racing is concerned, spread betting differs significantly from the traditional form of betting, which restricts the backer to wagering on a specific horse to win or be placed, or have forecasts, placepots, jackpots etc. which also demand the choice of specific horses to succeed.

SPORTING INDEX-
FIRST PAST THE POST FOR RACING

tote
SPORTING INDEX

MARTELL CUP
3 miles 1 furlong Chase, Aintree 2.35pm, live on BBC TV

Majadou	26 - 29	Escartefigue	8 - 11
Go Ballistic	22 - 25	Macgeorge	6 - 8
Dr Leunt	8 - 11		

Win = 50pts; 2nd = 25pts; 3rd = 10pts. All quoted

HOW DOES THIS WORK?

If you fancy MAJADOU to run well then you <u>BUY</u> (go high) at 29.
If you want to oppose MAJADOU then you <u>SELL</u> (go low) at 26 and have every other horse in the race running for you!

SPORTING'S MATCH OF THE DAY

MAJADOU is favourite to beat GO BALLISTIC by 0.5 - 2.0 lengths
(Maximum Make-Up of 15 lengths)

HOW DOES THIS WORK?

To back MAJADOU you <u>BUY</u> (go high) at 2.0 giving Go Ballistic a 2.0 length start.
To back GO BALLISTIC you <u>SELL</u> (go low) getting 0.5 length start.

FOR EVERY LENGTH YOU ARE RIGHT OR WRONG YOU WIN OR LOSE A MULTIPLE OF YOUR STAKE.

Our Full Racing Menu will be available every day at Aintree.
Including Favourites, Winning SP's, Double Cards, Winning Lengths and Jockey Indices.
For More Details see Channel 4 Text p.604

At the core of spread betting is a 'spread' of numbers representing the firm's idea of the outcome of an event. Backers can 'buy' if they think the result will be a higher number than the one quoted, or 'sell' if they consider the result will be represented by a lower number than the one quoted. The graphic above illustrates the general idea.

Thus, with spread betting it is possible to oppose the favourite in a race without having to nominate the winner.

In addition, every day for each main race meeting Sporting Index quote a Favourites Index spread with their idea of the prospects of all the favourites. A backer may differ in his or her opinion and 'buy' or 'sell' accordingly. Beyond that, there is a wide range of bets concerning, for example, the fate of every No. 1 on the racecard, the aggregate of SPs, the aggregate of winning racecard numbers, winning distances and jockeys' performances.

More details may be had from: Sporting Index, Gateway House, Milverton Street, Kennington, London SE11 4AP, and Internet: www.sportingindex.com

Sprinter The term given to horses which specialise at racing at the minimum distances on the Flat – i.e. five or six furlongs. See Chapter Ten, where *Hever Golf Rose* is mentioned. Trained at Epsom, by T.J. Naughton, *Hever Golf Rose* is the proud holder of the record for the biggest total of prize-money ever won by an English-based sprinter, but she did not get the recognition she deserved because nearly all her important successes were abroad. Her win and place total in 65 outings between 1993 and 1998 was £659,789, just ahead of that amassed by *Sheikh Albadou*, the 1991 Breeders Cup Sprint winner, in his illustrious career. *Hever Golf Rose*'s sole Group (*see PATTERN RACES*) triumph in Britain was the King George Stakes in 1995, but overseas she won three times both at Longchamp and in Stockholm and once each at Chantilly, Rome, Hamburg, Baden-Baden, Bremen, and Gelsenkirchen: a profitable globetrotter indeed.

By contrast, a little earlier, another filly (*q.v.*) and later mare (*q.v.*), *Lochsong*, owned by Jeff Smith, trained by Ian Balding, and justly named the 'Queen of Speed', had far less racing but from 28 runs between 1991 and 1994 won 15 times, was placed ten times, and earned £600,866 in prize-money. In her earlier career, *Lochsong*'s progress up the ratings (*q.v.*) as a handicapper was truly remarkable, and in 1992 she won off the reel the topmost sprint handicaps (only horse ever to have won the Stewards' Cup, Portland Handicap and Ayr Gold Cup in succession). She then rose above handicap company and captured no fewer than eight Group races in the top sprinting bracket, including the Prix de l'Abbaye and King George Stakes twice each, the Nunthorpe, the Temple Stakes and the Palace House Stakes, which provided yet one more illustration of her liking for making all the running.

Starting price Usually abbreviated to SP. Starting prices are the odds which appear in the newspaper results columns, are broadcast on television and radio, and form the basis for the pay-out in betting shops and by credit bookmakers. They used to be determined on the racecourse by a representative of Mirror Group Newspapers and one from the Press Association, supplemented by freelances, who, before each race, noted the varying prices on the rails and in Tattersalls', and, after consultation at the 'off', reached a consensus on what they considered the fairest majority version of how each horse was quoted when the race was started. This system was superseded in 2004 by the use of a computer to determine SPs. This has replaced the reporters. Nevertheless, there is still a Press Association employee, now called a validator, overseeing the computerised version. The problem is still, however, the very fact that a 'market' means varying prices, and although a favourite may be quoted by most bookmakers at 11/8, others will be marking at 6/4, and yet others at 5/4. At longer prices there may be even greater variations, so, understandably, since the difference between, say, 4/1 and 5/1 could make a great difference in the amount paid in the SP offices and betting shops, not every bookmaker agrees that the SP returned is the correct one. SP is now clearly defined as 'the price generally available at the off to good money'.

Stayer The term given to a horse which specialises at racing over the longest distances on the Flat – that is two miles plus. See Chapter Ten. Two notable stayers of recent times are not, however, mentioned in that chapter and deserve notice. They are *Trelawny*, the most popular stayer since *Brown Jack* (for his details, see Chapter Seven), and another public hero, *Grey of Falloden*:

Trelawny was exceptional at extreme distances, and though as a gelding (*q.v.*) he was barred from the Ascot Gold Cup, he achieved the Ascot Stakes–Queen Alexandra Stakes double in both 1962 and 1963. His second victory in the Queen Alexandra, the longest Flat race in Britain, was greeted by an ovation which rivalled the one for *Brown Jack* after his last win in the same race 29 years earlier.

Trelawny also won the Chester Cup, Brown Jack Handicap and Goodwood Cup, plus the Spa (now Stayers') Hurdle at Cheltenham. In his peak years he was trained by George Todd.

Grey of Falloden, second to *Trelawny* in the 1963 Queen Alexandra Stakes, was in the same mould as that relentless stayer. Indeed, both were bred by the Astor Studs. Trained by Dick Hern, he won the Queen's Prize in 1963, and the Doncaster Cup and Cesarewitch in 1964; he beat the weight-carrying record for that handicap by defying top weight of 9 st 6 lb. *Timeform* commented: '*Grey of Falloden* is as tough and game as they come [and] evidently thrives on hard work.'

The following year he won the Henry II and Queen Alexandra Stakes, and set an earnings record for a gelding on the Flat.

Stuffy horse   A horse that needs a lot of work to keep his breathing clear. Opposite to a 'clean-winded' horse.

Tic-tac   The system of tic-tac on a racecourse represents what flags were to Nelson and what satellite communications are to the Fleet today. Betting moves, money put on, who has put it on – all are signalled by the white-gloved representatives of bookmaker firms, and read by their own tic-tac men. Tic-tac is one of the strange and abiding features of the English and Scottish racecourse scene, lending a tremendous air of secrecy and big money changing hands, and all beyond the range of the average racegoer, who, even if he could read tic-tac sign language, with the waving arms and lightning Swedish drill bends, would find it of no use, because like Fleet signalling again, the signs are not transmitted in 'plain language' – they are further encoded by reference to what is known as the twist card. Thus on the racecard the numbers of horses in an eight-horse race run in sequence from one to eight. But on the twist card, which again differs from firm to firm of tic-tacs, they are jumbled so that one may be seven, seven may be six, and so on.

Sadly, tic-tac is gradually being replaced by the use of walkie-talkies, which more and more boards bookmakers are using.

The Tote   The usual abbreviation for the Horserace Totalisator Board. The Tote is also more popularly known as 'The Nanny' – abbreviated rhyming slang ('Nanny Goat'). It provides an alternative means of betting to the bookmakers, and was instituted by Act of Parliament in 1928. One of its stated aims at the time was to generate money to support racing, and this it does today by making substantial payments to racecourses based on a percentage of turnover, sponsorship and levy payments.

Following the establishment of the on-course Tote in 1928 an off-course subsidiary, Tote Investors Ltd, was set up for the purpose of accepting off-course

Tote credit bets which were transmitted to the racecourse pools. At this time bookmakers operated on all racecourses and could also accept credit bets by telephone off the racecourse. But off-course cash betting remained illegal by Tote or bookmaker. The law was frequently broken, however, by the bookmakers, who operated a network of illegal betting through factory and street runners. This structure continued from 1929 until 1960, and during this period the Tote was able to make contributions to racing of nearly £9 million, while the bookmakers gave virtually nothing.

In 1960 the Betting and Gaming Act legalised off-course cash betting, but the opportunity to establish an off-course Tote monopoly was missed. Bookmakers were given licences to bet by local magistrates. A year later a new organisation was established by statute, the Horserace Betting Levy Board (*q.v.*), empowered to levy money from both bookmakers and Tote for the benefit of racing.

Betting shops spread throughout the country and reached a peak of 15,780 in 1968 (but today number not many more than half that). The Tote was unable to take part in this off-course betting boom. Although allowed to run betting shops like the bookmakers, they were not allowed to offer starting price betting. And this is what the public were used to, for they had traded illegally at starting prices for many years. The proliferation of starting price betting shops had an adverse effect on the Tote's financial position and in 1972, in order to restore their competitive position, the Tote was empowered by Act of Parliament to accept bets at starting price as well as Tote odds.

Today the Tote in Britain is organised into several sections. First there is pool betting on the racecourse – the Tote's original function. The Tote operates at every racecourse in Britain throughout the year. Computerised win, place and dual forecast pools are run at all meetings. There are daily jackpot, placepot and quadpot bets (see Chapter Five).

The next section is Tote Credit, formerly known as Tote Investors. It is the largest credit betting business in Britain with a high-tech headquarters at Wigan, plus at least one office on every racecourse. The Tote Credit offers its customers credit facilities at Tote odds and starting price. Tote bets are placed in the racecourse pools.

Tote Bookmakers is responsible for 435 betting shops. Like Tote Credit they accept bets at Tote odds (except on-course) and starting price, but in cash not credit.

Tote Direct was established in 1992. With Tote betting terminals installed in bookmakers' shops for onward transmission of Tote bets into the pool, it now operates the largest UK network of on-line gaming terminals after the National Lottery. It offers the full range of Tote pool bets on horseracing through a network of more than 5,000 terminals in licensed betting shops throughout Britain.

The Tote's latest figures show that the profit before contribution to racing in 2002–03 rose by 14.6 per cent to £96.7 million, with £10.7 million being its contribution to the racing industry.

A major part of the Tote's support of racing is through sponsorship. In the current year that will amount to a sum of £2 million, making the Tote racing's largest commercial sponsor. The Tote name will feature on over 200 races during the 12-month period. These include the Totesport Cheltenham Gold Cup, the

Totesport Ebor Handicap at York, the Totesport International Handicap at Ascot, the Totesport Gold Trophy at Newbury, and the Totesport Cambridgeshire and Totesport Cesarewitch Handicaps at Newmarket.

It was announced in May 1999 that the Tote is to be privatised, after an Act has been passed enabling this transfer from public ownership. In its manifesto, the Government pledged to sell the Tote to a racing trust. The following is quoted from the *Sunday Telegraph*:

'Even though the Tote has a monopoly on pool betting, it was decided that breaking up the Tote to encourage competition would be unworkable because betting pools would diminish. This would deter punters because potential prizes would also dwindle.

'The Government now needs an Act of Parliament to allow the Tote to be sold, putting additional pressure on an already crammed Parliamentary timetable. Observers believe that the Act will not be put forward until after the next General Election. Even the Act could be preceded by a legal challenge over the actual ownership of the Tote.

'The British Horseracing Board believes the Government has only thin claims on ownership of the Tote and the BHB would be willing to challenge them in court. A previous Government review of the Tote also concluded that ownership was in question. While the Treasury would like to see any privatisation proceeds swell its coffers, the BHB believes the Tote belongs to the racing industry or even that the company owns itself.

'Ownership will have to be sorted out before the Government can push ahead with a decision on how best to privatise the Tote, which could come through a management buyout, trade sale or possibly a flotation.

'Analysts believe the sale could be carried out within a year once the parliamentary go-ahead has been given....'

Triple Crown Winning the 2000 Guineas, Derby and St. Leger constitutes the English 'Triple Crown'. *West Australian*, in 1853, was the first to accomplish this feat, and *Nijinsky*, in 1970, the latest of 15 colts to do so. As far as fillies are concerned, that splendid and much-admired performer *Oh So Sharp* captured their corresponding Triple Crown by handsomely winning the 1000 Guineas, Oaks and St. Leger in 1985. In this achievement, she thus followed, in the 20th century, *Sceptre* (1902), *Pretty Polly* (1904), *Sun Chariot* (1942) and *Meld* (1955). The equivalent for stayers consists of the Ascot Gold Cup, Goodwood Cup and Doncaster Cup.

Turn of foot A commonly used expression meaning a horse's capability for speed and/or acceleration which also is sometimes referred to as 'toe'.

Virus Omnibus term for a number of highly infectious 'flu-like ailments which can spread quickly through a stable and virtually put it out of action. Symptoms of the worst form are a dry cough, temperature and nasal discharge. Horses take some time to recover their best form after such attacks.

Weatherbys Weatherbys date from 1770, when James Weatherby, an attorney from Northumberland, was invited by the Jockey Club to move to Newmarket and become Keeper of the Match Book, Stake Holder, and Secretary to the Jockey Club. Until recently, Weatherbys were frequently referred to as 'racing's civil service', but they are in fact much more than that.

For over two hundred years the position of Secretary to the Jockey Club was filled by successive members of the Weatherby family – nine of them in all. With this, the firm also supplied the London secretariat for the Jockey Club, for the National Hunt Committee (during its existence), and briefly for the BHB. In 1995 Weatherbys finally withdrew from this function, transferring it to the BHB and to the Club.

Today Weatherbys, under a contract with the BHB, continue to supply the complex administration required for racing in Great Britain. This they do from their headquarters in Wellingborough, Northamptonshire. Here, some 70 of Weatherbys' 280 staff are directly engaged on racing administration, using automated office systems based upon the latest computer technology. Among a multiplicity of tasks, they maintain all of racing's records, grant names for horses, approve 'colours', issue passports for horses, take all entries and declarations and the majority of jockey bookings. The last two operations are centred on the Racing Operations Department, where the unpopular balloting out and eliminations take place, races are divided, re-opened and re-offered as necessary, weights raised and the draw made for starting stalls.

Following the actual races the official returns arrive at Wellingborough for recording, and from these a financial account is produced for each race and the monies collected and distributed under the Orders and Rules of Racing. Weatherbys is also an authorised bank, and offers owners, trainers and others a broad range of banking services through which they can organise all of their racing finances.

As part of racing administration the *Racing Calendar* and the programme books are produced and published at Wellingborough.

Weatherbys' proprietorship of the *General Stud Book* started in 1791 when another James Weatherby, nephew of the above, published the first volume.

In 1983, Weatherbys introduced the world's first computer system for the automated production of pedigrees for the sales catalogues of Tattersalls and Goffs. Major breeders and bloodstock agents are now able to interrogate the computer at Wellingborough for pedigree and statistical information.

Wellingborough's computer systems provide essential statistics for racing and breeding. The most prominent examples of these are the *Statistical Record*, which is published four times a year; *The Stallion Book*, an annual which presents extensive details on stallions; and the *Bloodstock Sales Review*, which focuses on information relevant to the bloodstock sales. All of these are published by Weatherbys, with much of the data, and other racing information, now also made available on subscription on-line or through the Internet (website address: www.weatherbys-group.com). Similar technology is used to provide racecard services to many racecourses, and data and editorial services for other organisations at home and abroad.

Weatherbys also run Turf Newspapers, whose kiosks are on all main racecourses and who operate a mail-order book service from:
(e-mail) turfnews@weatherbys-group.com
or by post from:
Weatherbys Turf Newspapers Ltd, Sanders Road, Wellingborough, Northants NN8 4BX.
(This article kindly supplied by John Gallimore, Company Secretary, Weatherbys.)

Weight-for-Age This is the scale, originally devised by Admiral Rous, which lays down how horses of differing ages improve month by month throughout a season, the differences being expressed in terms of weight. The Weight-for-Age scale provides the basis for the weights carried by horses in Conditions races (*q.v.*), as well as a bedrock for handicappers.

Nevertheless, the *Racing Post* disagree with the figures given in this time-honoured scale, saying that it is over-generous to 2-y-o early in the season, and gives too much allowance to 3-y-o running in distance races. Consequently, they are producing their own *Racing Post* weight-for-age scale for use with their ratings service. This new scale will provide an alternative to the official figures quoted in the table below.

Weight-for-Age Table

Allowance assessed in lb, which 3-y-o will receive from 4-y-o, and 2-y-o will receive from 3-y-o

		April (Mar+) 1–15	April 16–30	May 1–15	May 16–31	June 1–15	June 16–30	July 1–15	July 16–31	Aug 1–15	Aug 16–31	Sept 1–15	Sept 16–30	Oct 1–15	Oct 16–31	Nov
5 furlongs	2	32	31	29	27	26	25	25	23	21	20	19	18	17	16	15
	3	13	12	11	10	9	8	7	6	5	4	3	2	1	–	–
6 furlongs	2	–	–	30	29	29	28	27	26	26	24	22	21	21	20	18
	3	15	14	13	12	11	10	9	8	7	6	5	4	3	2	1
7 furlongs	2	–	–	–	–	–	–	–	–	–	–	24	23	23	22	21
	3	16	15	14	13	12	11	10	9	8	7	6	5	4	3	2
1 mile	2	–	–	–	–	–	–	–	–	–	–	27	27	26	25	24
	3	18	17	16	15	14	13	12	11	10	9	8	7	6	5	4
9 furlongs	3	18	17	16	15	14	13	12	11	10	9	8	7	6	5	4

1¼ miles	3	19	18	17 16	15 14	13 12	11 10	9 8	7 6	5
11 furlongs	3	20	19	18 17	16 15	14 13	12 11	10 9	8 7	6
1½ miles	3	20	19	18 17	16 15	14 13	12 11	10 9	8 7	6
13 furlongs	3	21	20	19 18	17 16	15 14	12 12	11 10	9 8	7
1¾ miles	3	21	20	19 18	17 16	15 14	13 12	11 10	9 8	7
15 furlongs	3	22	21	20 19	18 17	16 15	14 13	12 11	10 9	8
2 miles	3	22	21	20 19	18 17	16 15	14 13	12 11	10 9	8
2¼ miles	3	23	22	21 20	19 18	17 16	15 14	13 12	11 10	9
2½ miles	3	25	24	23 22	21 20	19 18	17 16	15 14	13 12	11

Jumping Weight-for-Age Scale

The hurdles chart below shows the number of pounds 3-y-o should receive from 4-y-o, and 4-y-o from older horses. The chase chart shows the number of pounds 4-y-o should receive from 5-y-o, and 5-y-o from older horses. This revised scale has been used since 1 January 1985.

Distance	Age	Jan	Feb	Mar	Apr	May	Jun	Jul	Aug	Sep	Oct	Nov	Dec
2 m	3	–	–	–	–	–	–	17	17	16	16	16	14
Hurdle	4	12	10	8	6	5	5	3	3	2	1	–	–
2 m 4 f	3	–	–	–	–	–	–	18	18	17	17	17	15
Hurdle	4	13	11	9	7	6	6	3	3	2	1	–	–
3 m	3	–	–	–	–	–	–	19	19	18	17	17	16
Hurdle	4	14	12	10	8	7	7	4	4	3	2	1	–
2 m	4	–	–	–	–	–	–	12	12	12	12	12	11
Chase	5	10	9	8	7	6	6	3	3	2	1	–	–
2 m 4 f	4	–	–	–	–	–	–	12	12	12	12	12	12
Chase	5	11	10	9	8	7	7	4	4	3	2	1	–
3 m	4	–	–	–	–	–	–	12	12	12	12	12	12
Chase	5	12	11	10	9	8	8	5	5	4	3	2	1

CHAPTER TWO

How It All Began: A Brief Chronology of the History of the Turf and Betting

Racing has always been, and will always be, a gambling speculation.

Admiral Rous

It is generally accepted that there was racing of a kind in England at the time of the Romans, but the first documented evidence dates from the 16th century. Henry VIII kept a training establishment at Greenwich and a stud at Eltham. Racing is recorded at York as far back as 1530; Chester had the first racecourse as such by 1540; Queen Elizabeth I visited Salisbury and Croydon for the races; and two racecourses appeared on a map of Doncaster in 1595.

James I noted Newmarket as an ideal place for sport and Charles I spent much time there, but not until the Restoration (1660), and Charles II, did Newmarket begin to flourish and become the centre for organised racing, among other sports, notably hunting and hare-coursing. The King, an outstanding horseman, founder of the Newmarket Town Plate, which is still run today, assisted in framing conditions for races which were run over long distances with heats and a final all on the same day. Betting was heavy among courtiers and royal guests, as well as among attendant grooms, footmen and other servants as 'debt of honour transactions' with no cash changing hands until settlement afterwards, and certainly no bookmakers (who did not appear for another 150 years). Old Rowley was the name of Charles's much-loved hack; the King, in turn, was so nicknamed, and hence the title for the Rowley Mile racecourse at Newmarket.

Tregonwell Frampton (1641–1727), who became known as the 'Father of the Turf', was another influential figure of the time – an arbiter, like Charles II, in racing disputes, and, as Keeper of the Running Horses first to William III, then to Queen Anne (who founded Ascot racecourse in 1711), an early, if not the earliest 'trainer', despite being an appalling man who was an obsessive gambler and cruel to horses in his continual wagering.

However, the foundation of racing as we know it stems from the importation of stallions from the Near East in the late 17th and early 18th centuries, most significantly the so-called Byerley Turk (1689), the Darley Arabian (*c*1704) and the Godolphin Arabian (1730). They founded sire lines through, respectively, *King Herod* (usually abbreviated to *Herod*), *Eclipse* and *Matchem,* to which virtually all thoroughbreds of the world today trace their ancestry, *Eclipse* having by far the greatest influence. Following this, and up to the first quarter of the 19th century, there was 'a period of intensive evolution...which resulted in the emergence of the thoroughbred as he is known today...[when]...the average height of the racehorse increased by about a hand and a half, or six inches, and there were corresponding increases in overall size and physical scope, strength, length of stride and speed.' (Peter Willett, *Introduction to the Thoroughbred*.) The site of the Godolphin Arabian's grave has recently been identified at West House at Wandlebury Ring just outside Cambridge. A £20 note was touchingly left not long ago on his grave by an Australian horse-breeder for the purpose of keeping the stone well scrubbed. The Godolphin Arabian's most recent notable progeny, many decades later, are *Airborne* and *Santa Claus*, who each won the Derby, in 1946 and 1964 respectively. Before that his other Derby winners include *West Australian* (1853), *Blink Bonny* (1857), *Sir Visto* (1895), *Signorinetta* (1908) (see Chapter One under **Classics**) and *Call Boy* (1927).

1715 *Flying Childers* foaled – the first great racehorse, sired by the Darley Arabian, capable of speeds not much less than those of today, subject of much legend and hearsay, and still commemorated on pub signs and in a race at Doncaster.

1750s The Jockey Club was founded in 1751 by racing enthusiasts. The term 'Jockey' included them, and did not then possess only today's narrower and more specialised meaning. The Star and Garter in Pall Mall, London, was one of the original meeting places. Later in the century, at Newmarket, their social headquarters were the Red Lion and the Coffee Room, leased in 1771 for a 50-year period. The Rules of the Jockey Club, which began to evolve, originally applied only to racing at Newmarket, but, in time, the jurisdiction and authority of the club grew and were accepted elsewhere, so that it became the sole Turf authority in the land.

John Pond's *Sporting Kalendar* was first published in 1751, containing regulations which helped to form the Rules of Racing. 1752 saw the earliest recorded steeplechase in Ireland.

In 1758 the Jockey Club passed its first resolution requiring all riders to weigh in after a race; those who did not declare overweight beforehand were disqualified. By 1759 they had opened races to public participation, but betting remained a matter between private individuals.

1760s Racing colours were first registered at Newmarket in 1762. Richard Tattersall began to organise bloodstock sales in London at Hyde Park Corner. He was an experienced dealer specialising in 'thro-bred' horses; that is, those tracing pedigree from the best known imported Arab stallions. Tattersall also used the Turf Tavern close by for his business. This was frequented by racing men who did not wish only to inspect the horses for sale but also wanted to bet. Thus, the Turf Tavern became the first centre of off-course betting. This was all conducted, still, 'on the nod'. Meanwhile, at the races themselves, and on Newmarket Heath in particular, betting was conducted round the betting posts in a jostle of men on horseback and a throng of gambling 'legs', touts, grooms, nobility and non-entities, and tradesmen from the town. This was also all 'on the nod', while some of those who had struck a bet, galloped off after the horses taking part and had a better view than from the rudimentary building which then served as 'grandstand'.

In 1768 Sir Charles Bunbury was elected steward of the Jockey Club. Eventually he became, in effect, perpetual president, and was for more than 40 years the first of the three so-called 'Dictators of the Turf'. Bunbury's influence was far-reaching, and was felt almost immediately on his taking office.

Previously, horses which raced were mostly four years old or upwards, carrying ten stone and more in punishing heats, commonly of four miles or so. Bunbury was instrumental in introducing racing for younger horses, in age groups, with less weight on their backs, and over not such extreme distances. He can thus be said to have recognised the possibility of developing speed in the thoroughbred at the expense of stamina.

Eclipse was the horse of the decade, and, in respect of his subsequent influence at stud, the stallion of every other decade since. Not raced until he was five, *Eclipse* was unbeaten in 18 races, giving rise to the much-repeated utterance of '*Eclipse* first, and the rest nowhere', although this originated in a remark of O'Kelly, his owner, when he bet that he could place the runners in a heat in correct order. Since *Eclipse* won the heat, and the rest were all more than a distance behind (i.e. nowhere), O'Kelly, a former sedan-chairman who had made a fortune out of betting, had wagered correctly.

1770s Run simply as 'a sweepstakes', the race which two years later became the St. Leger took place in 1776 at Doncaster. This was the first Classic, although the term was not in use until the following century. The fact of the race being for three-year-olds is further testimony to Bunbury's ideas; but the distance was two miles and remained so until 1812.

Highflyer was foaled in 1774. Bred by Bunbury (and a descendant through *Herod* of the Byerley Turk), sold to Lord Bolingbroke, and later bought by Richard Tattersall, *Highflyer* was unbeaten in a dozen races, and when he retired to stud (Fee 50 guineas) his progeny made him the greatest sire of his time (see **1790s**) and earned a fortune for Tattersall, which he acknowledged in an affectionate epitaph when *Highflyer* died. The Highflyer sales are still held by Tattersalls today.

A second Classic was inaugurated in 1779: the Oaks (then the Oakes Stakes), run at Epsom for fillies only and won by Lord Derby's *Bridget*. The following year Sir Charles Bunbury's *Diomed* won the first running of the Derby, for colts and fillies (unlike the Oaks, which was always over a mile and a half, the first four runnings of the Derby were over a dog-leg mile before becoming the same distance as the Oaks in 1784).

Tattersall's London premises at 'The Corner', as it was known by now, were much expanded. Two rooms were set aside, eventually, for the sole use of members of the Jockey Club, an astute move which ensured a seal of approval for Tattersall from the men who controlled racing. Equally important for backers, Tattersall also established his subscription rooms. This ensured that those who seriously wanted to have a wager on, or lay a bet against, a horse, could do so with other 'Members of Tattersalls', knowing that settlement would be prompt and that bets could be struck up to tens of thousands of pounds. The subscription rooms became known simply as 'The Room'. From this stage it was only a step to the origin of the term which still exists on every racecourse two centuries later: Tattersalls' Ring. This evolved because those in 'The Room' who wanted to bet gathered round a large, six-sided, hollow-centred table and quoted prices, argued about them, and struck bets accordingly, and in the way that commodity dealers might arrange a market. Tattersall, anticipating the force of Admiral Rous's later remark (quoted at the head of this chapter) to the effect that racing and gambling were inseparable, undoubtedly realised that by attracting the betting element to 'The Corner', he was sure to promote his bloodstock sales more effectively.

1780s In 1786 the Derby was won by *Sir Thomas*, owned by the Prince of Wales, later King George IV, who kept fairly fast company at Newmarket, and was infatuated with the sporting life there. But a scandal early in the following decade involving his horse *Escape* and his jockey Sam Chifney caused the Prince to sell his racing interests and quit Newmarket, never to return.

1790s A handicap involving 14 runners had already been run at Newmarket in 1785, but it was not until 1791, with the Oatlands Stakes at Ascot, the first public handicap with weights ranging from 5 st 3 lb to 9 st 10 lb, that 'the full fascination of racegoers eager to bet on a public cavalry charge became evident', as Dick Whitford (see p.42) once wrote in *The Sporting Life*. The Oatlands Stakes, won by the Prince of Wales's *Baronet*, drew an estimated crowd of 40,000, who were said to have gambled nearly one million pounds on the race: an event of prime significance for racing, and the forerunner of today's big handicaps such as The Wokingham, Stewards' Cup, and Cambridgeshire. Richard Tattersall died in 1795, but the firm founded by him continued to flourish and dominate the bloodstock sales market.

Highflyer in 1796 was champion sire for the twelfth consecutive time, and for a thirteenth time in 1798. Both records still stand today. Other champion stallions of the late 18th century were *Highflyer*'s sire, *Herod* (eight championships 1777–84), and one of his progeny, the Derby winner of 1787, *Sir Peter Teazle* (ten championships between 1799 and 1809).

1800–1825 The early years of the 19th century saw the foundation of the remaining Classic races, and in 1807 the first running of the Ascot Gold Cup, which came to be the outstanding race for stayers. In 1816, the year after the Battle of Waterloo, a horse-drawn trailer was first used to convey a horse to the races. Before horse-boxes, horses walked to the races, a fact which must have contributed to the toughness of the breed in those days.

In the early years of the 19th century, too, there appeared corrupt, violent and ruthless men who were the disreputable originators of what came to be known as bookmaking. As Roger Longrigg wrote in *The History of Horse-Racing*: 'About 1804 the "legs" appeared: the blacklegs, the fielders. They invented the principle of laying bets at various prices about every horse in a race. This was called "betting-round", and later "making a book". The leg became known as a penciller, metallist or bookmaker. If a leg laid heavily against a fancied horse he climbed out of his risk by hedging, but this reduced the margin of profit. It was better to allow a clear favourite to be established by weight of public money, and then stop the horse winning.

'The first notorious examples of this were in 1809–11. A trough at Doncaster was poisoned, then one at Newmarket...two horses died, others were damaged and "the stable cat ran about like a maniac". In 1811 Richard Prince's trough at Newmarket was poisoned with arsenic. Four horses died...

'The first appearance of the legs in numbers was at Brighton...'

As often seems to occur after a war, there was a betting boom after Waterloo. One of its features was the appearance of the list houses, an early form of betting shop. Lists of runners and prices based on those quoted at 'The Corner' began to appear in all sorts of places – shops, clubs, even private houses. They opened up betting opportunities to a wider public than hitherto, but still on credit. New subscription rooms had also been opened at 'The Corner', and with them came a new and less rough and ready betting man to replace the old-style leg. One of these was Richard Crockford, who already had much experience of London gambling hells. He was said to have fake teeth and eyes that were 'coffin-cold', but it is to this man, one of the first bookmakers in the proper sense of the word, that we owe today the existence of the Yankee, the Patent and other multiple bets. Crockford was the first to see the immense mathematical probability of profit for a layer in such bets, and he invented the double, treble, and four-timer, even though these terms had yet to be coined. At the betting posts at Newmarket he stood up and laid these bets by the score, so appealing were they to the big-profit-for-small-outlay mentality. As he took the wagers, he could calculate in a twinkling his liabilities, even though he laid half a dozen bets in as many seconds, and knew that after the last race he would be a richer man than ever. When he died, in 1844, he had built, out of the profits, a Newmarket house, gaming rooms in the High Street, and owned a farm and training stables.

In 1821, Sir Charles Bunbury died, having wrought changes in racing which set the pattern that would inevitably evolve towards the one we know today. So the scene was set for the next 'Dictator of the Turf', Lord George Bentinck, son of the Duke of Portland, through which connection the Jockey Club was to acquire its wealth, thousands of acres, and further influence at Newmarket. Alan Ross (in *The Turf*) wrote: 'Bentinck was an unscrupulous gambler on a vast scale, an arrogant and successful owner who won seven Classics...an MP who led the Protectionist Party, and an outstanding turf reformer, especially in his concern for ordinary racegoers and his war on crooks. He invented the flag start, developed Goodwood as a racecourse, and died on the verge of a great political career.' Among his other reforms were the practice of parading runners in the paddock before a race, and numbering them.

1826–1850   The first St Albans Steeplechase took place in 1830, organised by Thomas Coleman. This led to a proliferation of steeplechasing, and Coleman is regarded as the 'father' of the sport in the form we know it today. He had been a stableman, a trainer, and later an hotelier. He bought the lease of the old Chequers Hotel in St Albans, rebuilt it, renamed it the Turf Hotel, and it quickly became the equivalent of Tattersalls' rooms for chasing. It continued to attract year after year for a decade, bringing great trade to the town, and spectators from all over the country to see riders such as the redoubtable Captain Becher, and horses such as *Moonraker* and *Grimaldi*. By the time the popularity of the St Albans Steeplechase had begun to wane, the sport was well established with a fixture list for just the month of March 1838 that contained 26 meetings at places as far apart as Ashby-de-la-Zouch and Abergavenny, and Cheltenham (racing had begun at Prestbury Park in 1831) and Chatham Garrison.

At Liverpool, meanwhile, steeplechasing had begun, and the race now known as the Grand National was first run at Aintree in 1839. It did not take this title until 1847, its first official name being 'The Great Liverpool Steeplechase'. (Nevertheless there is strong evidence for the unofficial title of the race being what it eventually became. *Bell's Life of London*, later incorporated into *The Sporting Life*, for 24 February 1839, quite clearly heads a paragraph: 'Grand National Steeple Chace'.)

The present title stems from the Grand National Steeplechase Committee, which was formed to run the race and eventually evolved into the National Hunt Committee, chasing's equivalent of the Jockey Club until the two bodies were amalgamated in 1968. A report of the first running of this unique and, as it became, world famous event reveals that, as a crowd puller, it started much as it continued: 'as early as nine o'clock the road leading to Aintree was crowded with pie-men, chimney sweeps, cigar sellers, thimble riggers and all the small fry of gaming-table keepers...Not a vehicle of any description that could by any means be made to go was left in the town, not a coach or a cab was to be had for love or money...the grandstand had not accommodation for more than three-quarters of the people who presented themselves.' There was heavy betting among the 40,000 or so estimated to have turned up; the original ante-post favourite, *The Nun* at 8/1, was displaced in the market by *Lottery* at 5/1, who, as the sporting sheets of the time would have had it, 'duly obliged' ridden by Jem Mason, beating 16 opponents over the punishing cross-country course, which included ploughed fields and a stone wall opposite the stands (and during the course of which Captain Becher fell from *Conrad* into the famous brook). The crowd hemmed in the main Irish hope, *Rust*, baulked him, and effectively put him out of the race.

In 1831, on the Flat, the Jockey Club refused to resolve any further disputes arising at meetings where its rules were not in force. In 1842, it took a further major step and divorced itself entirely from settling betting disputes. Both these measures came into force under Bentinck. In practical terms, it meant henceforth a more rarefied role for the Jockey Club, as well as the permanent connection between Tattersalls and betting disputes. A later Richard Tattersall, who now ran the firm, was invited by the Jockey Club to oversee a committee which they would license for the purpose of arbitration of betting disputes. This was the origin of Tattersalls' Committee, and the rules it evolved, reproduced in an appendix to this book, still govern betting just as the committee still settles major betting disputes to this day. In a striking echo of previous usage, just as 'The Room' ruled earlier betting, so today when anyone is summoned to Tattersalls'

Committee to answer a case of offence against betting rules, they are said to have been 'In the Rooms'. In 1846 Bentinck sold his racing interests for £10,000 and retired from the Turf to pursue his political career, but died only two years later. Admiral Rous succeeded him as the third and last 'Dictator of the Turf.'

One further event during this period has to be noted, which had the most far-reaching significance for horserace betting. A man called William Davies appeared on the scene and became known as 'Leviathan' Davies, such were the size of the bets he laid and paid. His significance was that he took and handed out cash, being the first bookmaker to do so. Davies started his cash revolution in the 1840s, but its effect was in the following decade and after. Meanwhile, the list houses continued to flourish, in barber's shops, in stalls selling snuff, in warehouses, in back streets. Some were reputable, others not; some paid out, and others greeted the hopes of winning clients with the shutters up and evidence of a moonlight flit – so much so that a House of Commons Select Committee began to sit in 1844 and its findings were to have a great effect after 1850.

By 1850, in fact, racing was in a form which would be recognisable to a racegoer today. In only a century, the Jockey Club, with its 'Dictators of the Turf', had quite revolutionised the sport from a rough and ready affair into one which could be seen as a basis for the highly organised industry-cum-sport of today. From 1850, too, the various changes on the Turf were refinements of what had gone before, and the chronology from this point to the present day therefore takes a more abbreviated form:

1850   'Leviathan' Davies loses £50,000 on *Voltigeur's* Derby.

1853   *West Australian* is the first winner of the Triple Crown. New Betting and Gaming Act makes cash betting off-course illegal. It is another century before it is made legal; in between the two dates there is much hounding of small bookmakers and backers who offend the new law.

1855   The Jockey Club appoints Admiral Rous, the third 'Dictator of the Turf' and a man of great probity and shrewdness in assessing horses' abilities, as their official handicapper. He invents the weight-for-age scale which is, with only minor adjustments, still in use today (see p.58).

George Fordham, known as 'The Terror', 'The Demon' or 'The Kid' (because he kidded other jockeys into losing races), was the jockey of this and the next decade.

1859   Jockey Club forbids racing of yearlings.

1865   *Gladiateur* becomes the first French-bred colt to win the Derby and becomes known in France as 'the Avenger of Waterloo'.

1870   The Jockey Club rules that no meeting should start before the week including 25 March or continue beyond the week including 15 November.

1875   Sandown Park, first enclosed racecourse in England, is opened.

1877   Admiral Rous dies.

Draw for places at the start is made subject of a Jockey Club rule for the first time. The Jockey Club also declares that it will not recognise any meeting not under its rules.

1879   Jockeys have to be licensed.

Photography reveals the true action of a horse when galloping, thus proving past painters mistaken in their portrayals.

Fred Archer is at the height of his prowess as champion jockey and becomes the first widely known and popular jockey, whom the public would back irrespective of what he was riding.

1886   Archer commits suicide, and the entire racing world is stunned at the tragedy and loss. He was 29.

1895   The origin of the present day crouching (as against upright) seat for Flat racing is introduced with American jockeys coming to England and riding 'monkey-on-a-stick' winners.

1896   *St. Simon* becomes champion sire for the seventh season in a row, following *Hermit*'s seven consecutive championships (1880–86).

1897   First Derby recorded on film.

Starting gate introduced.

Edwardian Turf era at its height with 'plungers' winning and losing thousands in a single race, led by HRH The Prince of Wales.

1900   Horses owned by the Prince of Wales win both the Derby and Grand National (*Diamond Jubilee* and *Ambush*).

1902   *Sceptre* runs in every Classic and wins all but the Derby.

1903   Doping banned by the Jockey Club. *Hackler's Pride* wins the Cambridgeshire, backed down from 33/1 to favouritism, and takes a reputed quarter of a million pounds out of the ring for the Druid's Lodge syndicate – or more than £10 million in today's terms.

1910s   The Jockey Club decrees that no race on the Flat should be shorter than five furlongs.

National Hunt headquarters established at Cheltenham.

Steve Donoghue is the reigning champion jockey on the Flat (ten times 1914–23).

1920s   Number cloths carried for the first time.

1924 sees the first running of the Cheltenham Gold Cup.

The great era of Gordon Richards begins – he was champion 26 times between 1925 and 1953 and rode a record 4,870 winners.

Protective headgear made compulsory under National Hunt Rules.

Sporting press agree that only one amalgamated version of the starting price will be published as a basis for settling bets throughout the country.

New type of starting gate introduced at Lingfield.

1930s   Dead-heats no longer run off.

The Derby is televised for the first time in 1932.

Miss Dorothy Paget's *Golden Miller* is the outstanding steeplechaser of the decade and favourite of the crowds, winning no fewer than five Gold Cups (1932–36) as well as the 1934 Grand National.

Another public hero, the diminutive *Hyperion* (Derby and St. Leger winner of 1933, bred and owned by Lord Derby) starts his stud career at Newmarket in 1935 and becomes an outstanding success. He was champion sire six times between 1940 and 1954.

1940s   National Hunt racing suspended for two seasons because of the War.

Photo-finish is introduced.

Americans pioneer air travel for horses.

Post-war times bring tremendous crowds to racecourses and a great boom in betting. At the same time the French, notably Marcel Boussac, the textile millionaire, have great success in the Classics and other important races in England.

In 1947 the first evening meeting is held at Hamilton Park.

1950s   First running of the race now known as The King George VI and Queen Elizabeth Diamond Stakes.

Electrical timing introduced at Newmarket.

Later in the decade the first sponsored National Hunt races take place, beginning a great increase in prize-money for the winter game.

Sir Gordon Richards retires in 1954, the season after winning the Derby in Coronation Year on Sir Victor Sassoon's *Pinza*.

Lester Piggott wins the Derby for the first time on *Never Say Die* in 1954. He eventually rides a record-breaking nine Derby winners among 30 Classic winners (up to 1992), also a record.

1960s   The camera patrol comes into use as well as overnight declarations.

Lester Piggott is champion jockey for the first time in 1960. He is eventually 11 times champion, finally in 1982.

Starting stalls are introduced at Newmarket in July 1965.

Arkle, owned by the late Anne, Duchess of Westminster, and trained by Tom Dreaper in Ireland, overshadows all other steeplechasers in the mid-sixties. Among his feats are three Gold Cups in succession (1964–66), which would surely have been more had he not had to retire through injury. Another feat of this charismatic hero was forcing the construction of two handicaps in England: one if he ran, another if he did not!

Jockey Club is forced to grant trainers' licences to women.

James Callaghan re-introduces betting tax.

Betting shops legalised.

1970s   Jockey Club permits races for women riders.

Computer-assisted handicapping introduced, and graded handicaps on the Flat.

More and more sponsorship of racing, and many more horses competing internationally from the UK.

Pat Eddery champion jockey for the first time in 1974. He is eventually champion 11 times.

1980s   'All-weather' racing introduced on artificial surfaces at Lingfield (Equitrack) and Southwell (Fibresand).

Arab owners begin to dominate British racing.

Lester Piggott retires in 1985 but makes a successful comeback in 1990, then retires again in 1995. Total winners on the Flat in the UK: 4,493, making him second in the all-time list behind Sir Gordon Richards.

John Francome, seven times National Hunt champion jockey 1976–1985, retires.

Desert Orchid is the National Hunt idol of the crowds from the mid-eighties to retirement in 1992.

1990s   Control of racing taken over by the new British Horseracing Board.

Sunday racing proves popular with the crowds but not with the bookmakers, who complain of lack of business.

Advent of racing under floodlights at new 'all-weather' track at Wolverhampton.

Peter Scudamore, record-breaking National Hunt rider, eight times champion 1982–92, retires. His record of eight consecutive seasonal centuries, however, is beaten by Richard Dunwoody with a ninth in 1997–98, and Dunwoody also, in 1999, passes Scudamore's career total of 1,678 successes, which had been a National Hunt record. Dunwoody, in turn, retires later that year. Tony McCoy in 1997–98 also beats a Scudamore record (of 221 winners in a season) by riding no fewer than 253 NH winners.

Grand National declared void in 1993 after false starts.

Red Rum, record-breaking National hero (three times a winner and twice placed 1973–77), dies in 1995, aged 30, and is buried by the Aintree winning-post.

There is great controversy towards the end of the decade over jockeys' use of the whip. Stricter rules result in many suspensions, and races are foreshadowed in which the whip may be carried but not used.

2000s   HM The Queen Mother, that tremendous enthusiast and ambassador for National Hunt racing, dies, greatly mourned by the entire racing world, in March 2002. She was leading owner over the jumps five times between 1961–62 and 1974–75 and had well over 400 winners between *Monaveen* in 1949 and *First Love* on 8 March 2002. Among her best-remembered horses were *Manicou* (winner King George VI Chase 1950), *Game Spirit* (winner 21 times between 1971 and 1976), *Tammuz* (winner Schweppes Gold Trophy 1975), *Laffy* (winner Ulster Harp National 1962) and *Makaldar* (15 victories, including Black and White Gold Cup 1967).

Martin Pipe continues to demolish training records. On 4 February 2000, he beats Arthur Stephenson's previous record of most winners trained in Britain (2,988). By the end of the 2003–04 season, Pipe has sent out 3,814 winners since 1975. At the same time, he also beats his own records for most wins in a season: 243 (beginning in 1987–88 when, with 129, he took over from the pre-eminent Victorian, Arthur Yates, whose record of 124 had lasted since 1892).

By the end of the 2003 Flat season, *Sadler's Wells* (see Chapter Ten) is champion sire for the twelfth successive year and the thirteenth time in 14 seasons. He thereby well exceeds the achievement of *St. Simon* (eight championships between 1887 and 1901), surpasses the record of *Sir Peter Teazle* around the beginning of the 19th century and stands alongside *Sir Peter Teazle*'s sire, *Highflyer* (13 titles in 14 years), on the all-time list.

Initiated by Victor Chandler (see Chapter One under **Betting on the rails**) and his operation in Gibraltar, there is a strong move by other book-makers towards offshore betting which gets round the UK Betting Tax.

One result is that the Betting Tax is abolished in the 2001 Budget as from 1 January 2002 and replaced by 15 per cent taxation of bookmakers' gross profits. This means that there will no longer be deductions from winnings in betting shops.

Also in 2001, Foot and Mouth Disease disastrously disrupts racing, causing the loss of many meetings, including the Cheltenham Festival, and the abandonment of point-to-pointing.

Pat Eddery's glittering career comes to an end when he retires at the end of the 2003 season. Since 1969 he had amassed a phenomenal total of 4,632 winners, and finished second in the all-time list only to Sir Gordon Richards, who remains at the top with 4,870. Eddery was 11 times champion jockey and had 14 domestic Classic wins, including the Derby three times, on *Grundy* (1975), *Golden Fleece* (1982) and *Quest For Fame* (1990), as well as the Oaks three times and the St. Leger on four occasions. In addition, he rode four winners of the Prix de l'Arc de Triomphe, *Detroit* (1980), *Rainbow Quest* (1985), *Dancing Brave* (1986) and *Trempolino* (1987).

Tony McCoy continues to dominate the jumping scene like a titan, in an unstoppable, spectacular way the like of which has never before been witnessed under National Hunt Rules. In 2004 this riding genius took his total of winners past the 2,000 mark, achieved in only eight seasons since 1994. This was an amazing 300-plus ahead of the previous all-time best (1,699) scored by Richard Dunwoody in 17 seasons between 1983 and 1999. In addition, in 2001–02, McCoy completed his best-ever season with the phenomenal total of 289 winners.

CHAPTER THREE

Frauds, Coups, Plungers, Ringers and Tipsters

'...It is thought that Gates, Drake and the rest of them took something like £2,000,000 out of the ring between 1897 and 1901. Most of their horses were ridden by the brothers Lester and Johnny Reiff. In their knickerbockers and Eton collars they looked as innocent as choirboys, but the fact of the matter was that either of them would stop any horse if it suited the gang who employed them.'

(*Headquarters* Richard Onslow)

Because of the inter-dependence of betting and racing, and in the consequent pursuit of money through horses via the need to outwit the bookmakers, secrecy, deception, and outright villainy have frequently played their part in Turf history; as has the winning and losing in a single race of more money in individual bets than most people see in an entire lifetime. The following stories are a random selection of such manipulations, successful and otherwise, which, despite the immense cleaning up of racing during the past few decades, are still evident – and not only in racing novels.

Running Rein's Derby

First past the post in the 1844 Derby was *Running Rein*. After a long investigation, however, Lord George Bentinck was instrumental in proving that *Running Rein* was really *Maccabeus*, aged 4-y-o. When a 2-y-o, *Maccabeus* had been secretly exchanged for the real *Running Rein*, a yearling at the time. This was the first notable exposure of a 'ringer'. The men responsible fled to France and the race was awarded to *Orlando*, the original runner-up.

A more recent celebrated ringer was *Francasal,* who was the centre of a long-running press sensation after winning the Spa Selling Plate at 10/1 at Bath in July 1953. Bets of several thousand pounds at SP had been placed all over the country on *Francasal,*who would almost certainly have started favourite had the money been laid off on the course. But this was impossible because just before the race all telephone communication between Bath racecourse and the outside world went dead. A gang with lorry and ladders had cut the wires. This proved the undoing of the men who had engineered an audacious plot to take a £60,000 reward at a false SP. Four were jailed after an Old Bailey trial lasting nearly two months, during which *Francasal* was established to have been, in reality, an older horse called *Santa Amaro*. Nonetheless, *Francasal* came out of it best in the end as he had a race at Bath named after him.

Even more recently, *Flockton Grey*, supposedly a 2-y-o, won the Knighton Maiden Auction Stakes at Leicester by a suspiciously easy 20 lengths in March 1983, also at 10/1, and, after lengthy inquiries, he was alleged to be a 3-y-o called *Good Hand*. Here again, there had been organised backing at SP. At the trial which followed, three men were convicted of conspiracy to defraud, while

Flockton Grey's trainer was declared a disqualified person by the Jockey Club. But there is a happy ending to the story. After several years of well-fed idleness in police custody, doubtless helping them with their enquiries, *Flockton Grey* was bought in 1988 by the trainer Robin Bastiman. He was then sold on to the golf professional Patrick Tallack and the TV presenter Michael Aspel. Bastiman schooled *Flockton Grey* over fences, but just before he was about to run in a chase at Edinburgh he backed into a wall and injured himself. His next owner was Sharon Dick, the northern amateur rider, who adored him, and when last heard of at 12, and nearly white, *Flockton Grey* had been placed in several hunter trials.

The Trodmore Hunt

A quite inspired and astonishing plot to take both the sporting press and the bookmakers for a ride occurred on 1 August 1898. The editor of *The Sportsman* was asked to print the card for the Trodmore Hunt race meeting on that day, and the runners and riders duly appeared in the paper. Bets were placed with several bookmakers in the London area, and on the next day the results were also printed in *The Sportsman*. Some bookmakers paid out on these printed returns, but others said they would wait for *The Sporting Life* to publish the results. It so happened that when *The Sporting Life* did publish, they made the SP of one winner 5/2, whereas *The Sportsman* had returned it at 5/1. As a result there was an inquiry, and it was found that no such place as Trodmore existed, let alone a Trodmore Hunt, complete with race meeting. Thus an ingenious coup was foiled, but the extremely practical jokers were never traced.

The Hermits of Salisbury Plain

Around the turn of the century, the biggest ring of professional backers were the so-called 'Hermits of Salisbury Plain'. They were a syndicate of five, led by the 20-stone, 6-foot figure of Etonian Percy Cunliffe, city financier and mastermind of operations. In the Transvaal, where he made a fortune in gold, he had met Wilfred Purefoy, Irish stud owner and shareholder in Romano's restaurant and the Gaiety Theatre. It was Purefoy's task, unsmiling behind his pince-nez, to see to the smooth and secret running of the Druid's Lodge stables on Salisbury Plain and work the undercover commissions. The others financially involved included the best vet of his time, Holmer Peard, who founded Phoenix Park racecourse in Dublin and was responsible for Robert Sievier buying *Sceptre*; while another Irishman, Jack Fallon, trained the horses to the minute. In little more than a decade they took millions of pounds out of the ring. A single famous coup, when *Hackler's Pride* won the 1903 Cambridgeshire (ridden as a 6 st 10 lb apprentice by the future famous trainer Jack Jarvis), netted them £250,000 (£10 million in today's terms), while *Ypsilanti*, backed from 25/1 to 7/2 favourite for the Great Jubilee at Kempton earlier the same season, earned them the equivalent of £4 million in bets alone, plus prize-money equivalent to more than £130,000 (the race, in those days, was one of the richest handicaps in the Calendar). Scores of other successful coups were launched from the remote Druid's Lodge, where secrecy was paramount, no touts were ever seen, all stable lads' mail was opened, and where all that could be heard from the gallops of a horse's chance was the silence of Stonehenge itself.

Charlie Hannam was another great backer of that time and later, and was known as 'Old England' because of the then influx of corrupt American gamblers. Once asked how much betting money had gone through his hands, he said, 'I couldn't tell you. Perhaps 25 or 30 millions.' 'Boyo' Beattie was a stable commissioner who not only won substantially for those he put on for, but profited enormously himself and managed to hold on to the money. He kept £30,000 for himself when *Verdict* had a lucky neck win in the 1923 Cambridgeshire, and when he died he left £180,000. The Marquis of Hastings was £120,000 out of pocket when *Hermit* won the 1867 Derby (he had backed the runner-up, beaten by a neck), but another great plunger, Captain Machell, was very much in pocket, as he was when his horse *Disturbance* won the Grand National six years later. His first bet alone on the horse had been £200 at 500/1. The bookmaker William Chandler, turned backer, is said to have cleared £120,000 from fellow layers when *Ocean Swell* won the wartime substitute Derby at Newmarket in 1944.

The late Geoffrey Hamlyn, who for many years was the senior SP man for *The Sporting Life*, had many stories of major gambles both before and after the 1939–45 war, the biggest of which occurred in 1947, when the French-trained *Monsieur l'Amiral*, the previous season's Cesarewitch winner, was successfully backed from 100/8 down to 7/2 in a very strong market for the Queen Alexandra Stakes at Royal Ascot. Hamlyn recalled that one commission agent told him that he had been given £42,000 to stake on the eventual winner: 'And he got it all on, too. He wouldn't get half that on today.' The late Graham Rock, who had worked for Phil Bull, the late founder of *Timeform*, who was known as 'the sage of Halifax', once wrote an extremely engaging tribute in *The Times* to his former employer in which he estimated that in 20 years after the war, and before betting tax put an end to his bonanza, Bull took half a million pounds out of the ring. But 'Not every arrow hit the target'. In the summer of 1967, Bull had a staying 3-y-o called *Philoctetes* in training with Teddy Lambton at Newmarket. He decided that the potentially useful colt should be prepared for a starting-price coup on a race at Yarmouth, using the nation's network of betting shops:

'*Timeform* staff, their wives, girlfriends, ex-employees and friends were recruited, briefed with military precision and despatched to the corners of the nation, armed with town street maps marked with betting shop locations and bundles of the folding stuff. Women were told to wear headscarves, carry shopping baskets and to mispronounce deliberately the name of the horse in order to persuade betting office staff that they were mug punters. But the bookmakers' delicate network unearthed the plot. *Philoctetes* opened at 5/1, was supported down to 5/2 and compounded the disaster by finishing only third.'

More recently, as well as more successfully, the Irish-born pub and club owner Tony Gleeson landed a huge coup with his horse *Rotherfield Greys* in the 1988 Stewards' Cup at Goodwood. He himself cleared a quarter of a million and other members of his family a similar amount. The horse started at 14/1, but they were 'on' at 33/1 and 40/1 the previous week. Then, in 1992, Gleeson and family struck again for a further half a million pounds. It was garnered in a massive gamble from 14/1 down to 4/1 joint-favourite on *Father Hayes* in a handicap at Sandown in June.

The American dopers
The quotation at the head of the chapter is taken from Richard Onslow's description of the effect of American gamblers on the English Turf at the turn of the last century. Gates and Drake were heavy gamblers. They employed a trainer called Enoch Wishard, also American, whose speciality was the use of dope. Their technique was 'to buy a moderate horse that was fully exposed, run it way above its class, fill it with dope, and back it off the boards'. The coups that resulted eventually grew into a public scandal, but it was not until 1903, and following demonstrations by the trainer the Hon. George Lambton, that the Jockey Club made doping an offence, which led eventually to the stringent security and other precautions which exist today.

'I gotta horse'
This was the racecourse cry of the flamboyant, befeathered tipster of the 1930s and immediate post-war era who called himself Ras Prince Monolulu. Born in Abyssinia in 1880, Monolulu had a favourite ditty which might not stand the political correctness test today: 'God made the bees, the bees made the honey. The public back the favourites and the bookies take the money. Hooray for the roast beef, two veg, and Yorkshire pudding of Old England. White man for pluck. Black man for luck!' He always took care to be within camera shot when big race winners were led in, and perhaps his biggest tipping success occurred when *Spion Kop* won the 1920 Derby at 100/6 and Monolulu himself reputedly took home £3,000. He died in 1965, but his reputation lived on, because there was a London pub named after him. He, and other tipsters of the time, added greatly to the colour of the racecourse scene. One used to dress as a jockey; another, calling herself Mae Marsh, claimed to be the only woman tipster on the course: 'Only this mornin', ladies and gents, 'is Majesty comes up and says "'Ello Mae, wot are you tippin' for the big 'un today?" I says, "Your 'orse, your Majesty," and 'e says, "Quite right. That's the one. No danger." And it went in, didn't it, could 'ave won pullin' a cart, and at twenty to one...them's the kind of prices you can expect from old Mae...' Sadly, the only on-course tipsters left today seem to be the furtive figures peddling dubious brown envelopes in the racecourse car parks. Only once in my life have I ever fallen for the brown envelope trick, when years ago at Market Rasen I paid ten bob to a rather anxious-looking lad by the gate. On opening the brown envelope, I found, rather surprisingly, there was not a blank slip, but the names of four horses. All of them were trained by Lionel Elwell, and all of them, even more surprisingly, won. But now the bad news. I backed only two of them, *D'Artagnan* and *Matkah*. Somewhere there's a moral in all of this.

*** Since *The Punter's Friend* was first published, a brilliant, intriguing and exhaustive account of the Hermits' activities has been written by Paul Mathieu (*The Druid's Lodge Confederacy*, J.A. Allen 1990). Richard Onslow has also edited a series of fascinating anthologies entitled *Great Racing Gambles & Frauds*. Published by Marlborough Books from 1991 onwards, four volumes have now appeared. All highly recommended reading.

CHAPTER FOUR
Form at the Fingertips:
How to Look for Winners

Time spent in Reconnaissance is seldom wasted.

(Military adage)

There is no doubt that the public has never been better informed about racing, with an extraordinary number of daily, weekly, monthly and annual publications to choose from. Also, television, quite apart from its specialised services, has meant that there is excellent live coverage of racing and the preliminaries, including last minute hints and betting, as well as programmes such as 'The Morning Line' on Channel 4, on Saturdays; and, on occasions such as Royal Ascot, Clare Balding, for the BBC, fronts a first-class preview daily. Meanwhile, Radio Five Live is essential listening. To serve a more demanding armchair punter, therefore, newspapers have sharpened up their presentation of racecards. Added to all that, under pressure to recognise the needs of the popular racegoer and stay-at-home backer, the Jockey Club brought in several reforms, including the overnight draw. The introduction, in the 1960s, of an overnight declaration system, while not specifically designed to ease the clairvoyant requirements of off-course enthusiasts, did so nonetheless. So, altogether, the daily newspaper's presentation of the card is now improved out of all recognition. Only a matter of 30-odd years ago, this is what a typical racecard as published by *The Times* looked like (compare the version from a modern broadsheet for the same race, on p.94):

3.15.—The CHAMPION HURDLE CHALLENGE CUP.
with £3,000 added (2m.).
200 **Plainsman** (Mr. Joseph Bennett) Maund,
6-12-0 J. Lindley
030 **Quita Que** (Mrs. L. Brand) Ireland,
8-12-0 Mr. J. R. Cox
111 **Caesar's Helm** (Mr. A. C. Bryce-Smith) Ireland,
6-12-0 C. Finnegan
213 **Solatium** (Mr. C. G. Crawley) Crawley,
7-12-0 M. McCourt
213 **Flame Royal** (Mr. L. H. Dowling, sen.) A. Thomas,
7-12-0 T. Molony
210 **Ivy Green** (Mr. J. G. Duggan) Ireland,
7-12-0 W. J. Brennan
444 **Peggy Jones** (Gp.-Capt. H. I. Hanmer) S. Palmer,
7-12-0 D. Leslie
303 **Strait-Jacket** (Mr. D. Hickey) Ireland,
8-12-0 A. Brabazon
312 **Merry Deal** (Mr. Arthur Jones) A. Jones,
7-12-0 G. Underwood
111 **Clair Soleil** (Mr. G. C. Judd) H. Price, 8-12-0 F. Winter
330 **Curling Iron** (Mr. E. G. Ketteringham) Goodwill,
6-12-0 J. Fitzgerald
111 **Stroller** (Mr. H. Lane) Ireland, 9-12-0 —
110 **Straight Lad** (Miss D. Paget) H. Nicholson,
7-12-0 D. V. Dick
000 **Francette** (Mr. E. Morris) H. T. Cross,
7-12-0 H. T. Cross
100 **Winning Hit** (Mrs. H. J. Rice-Stringer)
Rice-Stringer, 6-12-0 A. Dennis
012 **Nankula** (Mr. O. G. M. Williams) O. Williams,
7-12-0 P. Morrissey
121 **Rosati** (Mrs. T. Hanbury) Walwyn, 5-11-12 J. Gilbert
Tout ou Rien (Comte ie Monteynard) France,
5-11-12 R. Emery

15 to 8 Clair Soleil, 9 to 2 Rosati, 7 to 1 Flame Royal, 8 to 1 Quita Que, 10 to 1 Tout ou Rien, 100 to 7 Peggy Jones, 100 to 6 Straight Lad and Strait-Jacket, 20 to 1 Ivy Green, 33 to 1 Merry Deal, 50 to 1 others

Racecards, too, have taken a similar turn for the better. The modern card from the Ascot Festival (see pp.91–92) can be favourably compared – with its form summary, betting forecast, and many other details, including a guide to the conformation of the horse and a glossary of racing terms – with the cards reproduced below and on p.90, both of them historic in that they show the details as presented on the cards of the time for one of *Arkle*'s Gold Cup successes at Cheltenham and *Pinza*'s memorable victory in Coronation Year. As far as these cards are concerned, not much more than some rudimentary form figures embellish the usual details of breeding and owners' colours, the Derby card being the more primitive. Marks across the horses' numbers can be seen as well as figures also written in. These were the days long before declarations and an overnight draw. The practice then, on the racecourse, was to mark off the actual runners from the 'probables' which had been printed (some non-runners can be seen) and to take the draw off the numbers board. An addition to the Epsom programme, unusual for those days, was the printing of jockeys' names.

THE 40ᵀᴴ YEAR OF THE CHELTENHAM GOLD CUP

with £11,000 added (to include a Cup value £300, and also £5,000 given by the Horserace Betting Levy Board); a Sweepstakes of £15 each, £15 extra unless forfeit be declared by Tuesday, February 23rd, £15 in addition if declared to run by Monday, March 8th, and £15 in addition unless such declaration be cancelled by Wednesday, March 10th; the second to receive 20% and the third 10% of the whole stakes; a steeplechase for five-yrs-old and upwards; five-yrs-old 11st 5℔, six and aged 12st; three miles, two furlongs and about 76 yards (13 entries, viz. 4 at £60, 2 at £45, 4 at £30 and 3 at £15).—Closed January 27th, 1965.

VALUE TO THE WINNER £7,986 10s.; TO THE SECOND £2,239;

TO THE THIRD £1,089 10s.

Rider/Form		Trainer	Age	st	℔	Owner
.... **2** 411	MILL HOUSE .... *b g King Hal—Nas Na Riogh* F. Walwyn		8	12	0	Mr W. H. Gollings Black, white slvs and cross-belts, scarlet cap
.... **4** 033/	CADUVAL .... *br g Lacaduv—La Francaise* G. Balding		10	12	0	Mrs A. R. B. Owen Green and white stripes, white slvs
.... **5** —	STONEY CROSSING .... *br g North Riding—Sunlit Stream* W. Roycroft		7	12	0	Mr W. Roycroft Green, gold "V" back and front, gold stripe on sleeves, gold cap
.... **6** 131	ARKLE .... *b g Archive—Bright Cherry* T. W. Dreaper in Ireland		8	12	0	Anne Duchess of Westminster Yellow, narrow black belt and cap with gold tassel

4 DECLARED RUNNERS

3.30—THE 174th DERBY STAKES (RENEWAL) of 100 sov. each, 50 sov. forfeit if declared by the Tuesday in the week before running, or 10 sov. only if declared by the first Tuesday in July, 1952, with 4250 sov. added (including a trophy value 250 sov.), *for entire colts and fillies foaled in* 1950 ; colts, 9st, fillies, 8st 9lb : the second to receive 10% and the third 5% of the whole stakes ; one mile and a half (446 entries, 50 sov. forfeit declared for 271, and 10 sov. for 141).—Closed November 6th, 1951. Declaration of forfeit to Messrs Weatherby and Sons only.

VALUES : WINNER £19,118 10s.; SECOND £2,261 : THIRD £1,130 10s.

	Owner and Name		st	lb	Trainer	Jockey
1	The Queen ....19...AUREOLE		9	0	C. Boyd-Rochfort	W. H. Carr
	Ch c Hyperion—Angelola Purple, Gold braid, Scarlet sleeves, Black Velvet cap with Gold fringe					
2	Ld Antrim ....11..CITY SCANDAL		9	0	H. Smyth	A. P. Taylor
	B c Rockefella—Milady Rose Blue, Gold facings & cuffs, Black cap					
3	M. Marcel Boussac ....10.....PHAREL		9	0	C. Semblat (France)	J. Doyasbere
	B c Djebel—Pharelle (foaled in France) Orange, Grey cap					

	Owner and Name		st	lb	Trainer	Jockey
16	Mr L. Lipton .....6....PRINCE CHARLEMAGNE		9	0	T. Carey	L. Piggott
	Ch c Prince Chevalier—Swift Gold Flame, Silver sleeves & stripe, Flame cap					
17	Mr J. McGrath .21..............NOVARULLAH		9	0	W. Stephenson	C. Spares
	B c Nasrullah—Nova Puppis Green, Red seams & cap					
18	Ld Milford .25.........EMPIRE HONEY		9	0	J. Jarvis	W. Rickaby
	B c Honeyway—Brave Empress Black, White sash & sleeves, Gold cap					
19	Mr J. Olding .13.........VICTORY ROLL		9	0	H. Persse	
	B c Nasrullah—Chinese Puzzle Yellow, Black hooped sleeves, Black cap					
20	The late Mr James V. Rank ....CRITICISM		9	0	J. Dines	T. Masterson
	Ch c Orthodox—Superior Black, Grey sleeves, Green & Red quartered cap					
21	Mr J. G. Morrison...23.........FELLERMELAD		9	0	N. Cannon	A. Breasley
	Br c Scottish Union—Jollification Dark Green, White cap					
22	Mr Chas. H. Rodwell .18.......PETER-SO-GAY		9	0	T. Griffiths	P. Evans
	B or br c Blue Peter—Soga Scarlet, White " V," Yellow cap					
23	Sir Victor Sassoon ......5................PINZA		9	0	N. Bertie	Gordon Richards
	B c Chanteur II.—Pasqua Peacock Blue, Old Gold hoops & sleeves					
24	Prince Said Toussoun .15.........PINK HORSE		9	0	J. Cunnington (France)	W. R. Johnstone
	B c Admiral Drake—Khora (foaled in France) Red & White stripes, Red cap					

By comparison, here is how the best modern cards appear, with colours printed in colour:

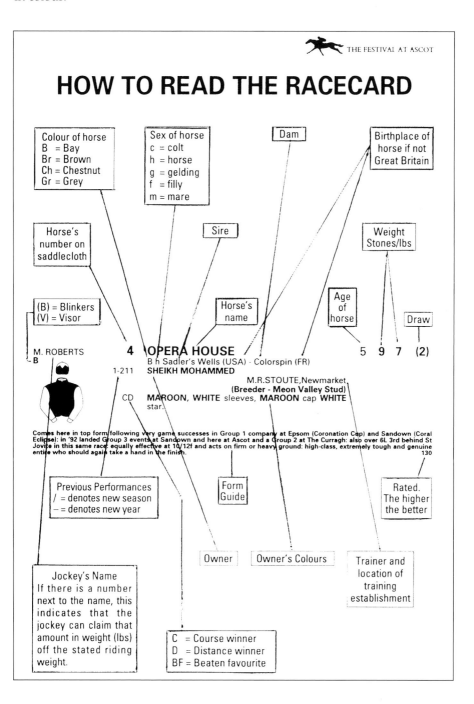

THE DIADEM STAKES (CLASS A)-continued

RIDER	FORM	OWNER	TRAINER	AGE	ST	LB	DRAW

J. REID **3 MONTENDRE**   **6   9   0   (9)**

34325 B g Longleat (USA) - La Lutine
MR DAVID MORT
MRS D. C. MORT
M.McCORMACK,Wantage
(Breeder - A. B. Phipps)
LIGHT BLUE, RED disc, **DARK BLUE** sleeves, **RED** cap.

Below best when over 5L 5th behind Stack Rock in a Newmarket listed event 4 weeks ago: usually the epitome of consistency, in '92 scored at Newbury (listed) and Chepstow and 3rd to Wolfhound in this same race: 6f specialist, likes some cut in the ground: could sneak into the frame.   **133**

M. ROBERTS **4 CATRAIL (USA)**   **3   8 11   (1)**

15112 B c Storm Cat (USA) - Tough As Nails (USA)
SHEIKH MOHAMMED
J.H.M.GOSDEN,Newmarket
(Breeder - Calumet Farm)
MAROON, WHITE sleeves, **MAROON** cap, **WHITE** star.

Found stablemate Wolfhound 1L too good in Group 1 Hazelwood Sprint Cup at Haydock 3 weeks ago: won 3 of 4 previous starts in the campaign at Leicester, Haydock and Newbury (listed): juvenile Newmarket scorer: very effective at 6/7f: has raced mainly on a sound surface, but not disgraced on yielding in Queen Anne stakes at the Royal meeting here and will prove hard to beat.   **137**

PAT EDDERY **5 EUROLINK THUNDER**   **3   8 11   (4)**

31412 B c Fairy King (USA) - Prosperous Lady
EUROLINK GROUP PLC
J.L.DUNLOP,Arundel
(Breeder - Genesis Green Stud)
YELLOW, GREY sleeves, **GREY** and **YELLOW** quartered cap.

Runner-up to Asema in a Group 3 over 1m at The Curragh on latest start: earlier successful at Kempton, Newmarket (listed) and Newcastle (Group 3): juvenile scorer at Newbury and Wolverhampton: smart colt who does handle an easy surface, but the drop back to 6f is the chief cause for concern.   **124**

C. ASMUSSEN **6 LOOK WHO'S HERE (IRE)**   **3   8 11   (5)**

14106 B g Heraldiste (USA) - House Call
MR S. L. EDWARDS
B.A.McMAHON,Tamworth
(Breeder - Hollyhill Stud)
ROYAL BLUE, YELLOW stars, **YELLOW** sleeves, **ROYAL BLUE** stars.

Far from disgraced when under 6L 6th behind Inchinor in Group 3 Hungerford Stakes over an extended 7f at Newbury on latest start 6 weeks ago: earlier landed a couple of handicaps: tough and genuine gelding, but probably not quite up to this class.   **116**

M. HILLS **7 SPLICE**   **4   8 11   (3)**

11454 Ch f Sharpo - Soluce
CHEVELEY PARK STUD
J.R.FANSHAWE,Newmarket
(Breeder - Cheveley Park Stud Ltd)
RED, WHITE sash, **ROYAL BLUE** cap.

Close-up 4th of 9 behind Stack Rock in a listed contest at Newmarket late last month: won first 2 starts this term at Newmarket (listed and handicap): in '92 scored twice, both times again at Newmarket: suited by waiting tactics over a stiff 6f, but best form at Newmarket on good or faster ground.   **122**

Seemingly light years away, but in reality not much more than a century ago, this is how *The Times* was printing details of future racing on a day in June 1879:

> Wednesday is perhaps the most pleasant day of the races, as the contest for the Hunt Cup with its large field streaming up the straight mile is one of the prettiest sights of the meeting. The Cup is a piece of plate value 300 sovs., added to a handicap sweepstakes, and there are 66 entries, out of which a field of 20 runners may come to the post. Isonomy is top weight with 9st., but he has too much weight to carry and will probably be reserved for other races at the meeting. Belphœbe · 8st. 9lb., is a good mare over the course, but both she and Rylstone, 8st. 5lb., may be withdrawn in favour of Lady Ronald, 7st. 2lb., who is well handicapped if she can only stay the course. Placida, 8st. 6lb., is fairly treated if in her best form, as she has considerably less to carry than the ordinary weight-for-age impost ; but she seems to have gone off since she was a three-year-old. Mandarin, 8st. 4lb. ; Master Kildare, 8st. 3lb. ; Spendthrift, 7st. 5lb. ; and Leghorn, 6st. 1lb., are trained by Cannon, and whichever is the selected one of the stable is sure to be heavily backed at the post and will probably run well. The same may be said of Bonnie Scotland and La Merveille, each 7st. 10lb.; Visconti, 7st. 9lb. ; Morier, 7st. ; Bute, 6st. 5lb., who ran very fast in the Two Thousand Guineas, and Chocolate, 5st. 12lb., all trained by Peck. Avontes, 8st. 3lb., and Broad Corrie, 6st. 5lb., are in Taylor's stable. and of these the first-named on

How far the presentation of racing information has progressed in daily papers (*Racing Post* included but dealt with later) can be judged by the enormously informative and stylish modern racecard for the 1999 Champion Hurdle from *The Times* printed on page 94.

SP forecasts in daily papers

Facts to remember when looking at an SP Forecast are that it cannot accurately gauge the amount of money that may go on a favourite, or a well-backed horse, or the extent to which bookmakers will eventually push prices of outsiders out in order to attract some money with which to pay out on a 'good thing'. Therefore backers of favourites often complain when they find they have supported a horse at, say, 2/1 on when the papers judged it to be a 6/4 chance. Conversely, backers of outsiders, expecting 12/1, are sometimes pleasantly surprised by a return of 25/1 or 33/1.

Coverage

The tabloid revolution in Fleet Street, as well as the demise of the early editions of London evening papers, has had its effect in depriving racing followers of coverage of the sport – that is to say full reports of the previous day's racing, future news and plans, and in-depth analysis of the day's racing (but my friends, colleagues, and able practitioners on *The Sun, Express, Mail* etc. battle valiantly against the odds every day and always against an appalling lack of space).

Against this, their racecards these days contain far more information than they used to. The broadsheets, in particular *The Times* and *Daily Telegraph*, have an obvious advantage here:

THE BIG RACE FIELD (C4)

3.15 **SMURFIT CHAMPION HURDLE CHALLENGE TROPHY**
(Grade I: £138,000: 2m 110yd) (14 runners)

1 10-2554 **BELLATOR** 17 (D,G,S) Miss V Williams 6-12-0 ....N Williamson 133
Owner: P Richardson   Record: 3 wins from 13 starts, prize-money £38,230
Running on in sixth when brought down at the final flight in last year's race. His efforts this season seem to confirm he would prefer a much stiffer test of stamina.

2 1111-4F2 **BLOWING WIND** 17 (B,BF,C,D,G,S) M Pipe 6-12-0 ....R Dunwoody 136
Owner: P Deal   4 wins from 18 starts, prize-money £69,537
Landed some big bets when winning the County Hurdle 12 months ago. Has not progressed as anticipated, though, and has been rejected by stable jockey Tony McCoy.

3 12-4232 **CITY HALL** 31 (V,D,G,S) Mrs V Ward 5-12-0 ....R Thornton 144
Owner: Mrs R Key and Mrs V Ward   2 wins from 9 starts, prize-money £50,189
Front-running grey who found only Upgrade too strong in the Triumph Hurdle last year and ran a cracker in the Tote Gold Trophy at Newbury a month ago. Each-way claims.

4 11-P212 **FRENCH HOLLY** 51 (C,D,F,G,S) F Murphy 8-12-0 ....A Thornton 150
Owner: K Flood   6 wins from 14 starts, prize-money £130,485
The top novice last season and has progressed again. Flattered to finish within a length of Istabraq at Leopardstown in January but may again give him most to do.

5 1-11261 **GREY SHOT** 19 (CD,G,S) I Balding 7-12-0 ....J Osborne 143
Owner: R Hitchins   5 wins from 8 starts, prize-money £83,483
Smart stayer on the Flat. Has not always looked a natural over timber but he won over course and distance in December and will be suited by the drying ground.

6 12-1111 **ISTABRAQ** 51 (CD,F,G,S) A P O'Brien (Ire) 7-12-0 ....C F Swan 162
Owner: J P McManus   14 wins from 16 starts, £485,185
Emphatic winner last year and has looked even better this season. Will be the shock of the meeting if this outstanding champion fails to defend his title successfully.

7 11/3312 **MIDNIGHT LEGEND** 19 (D,F,G,S) D Nicholson 8-12-0 ....A Dobbin 119
Owner: Mrs H Clarke   4 wins from 8 runs, prize-money £68,051
Former stallion who has run with credit this season. Could not peg back Grey Shot at Wincanton last time, though, and that suggests he will be a supporting player.

8 06/11UU **MISTER MOROSE** 80 (D,G,S) N Twiston-Davies 9-12-0 ....C Llewellyn 145
Owner: Mrs J Mould   5 wins from 12 starts, prize-money £44,841
Reverts to hurdles after an unsuccessful spell over fences – something Beech Road did when winning in 1989. Goes well fresh so do not be put off by his lengthy absence.

9 -121251 **NOMADIC** 24 (D,S) N Meade (Ire) 5-12-0 ....P Carberry 118
Owner: D Sharkey   5 wins from 11 starts, £62,672
Finished a close third in the Triumph Hurdle last year and has trained on this campaign. Twice put firmly in his place by Istabraq, however, and would prefer softer ground.

10 320-443 **THEATREWORLD** 24 (BF,D,S) A P O'Brien (Ire) 7-12-0 ....T P Treacy 125
Owner: Mrs J Magnier   6 wins from 27 starts, prize-money £172,535
Runner-up for the past two years. Overhauled more positively ridden opponents late on last year, and similar tactics may not reap such a reward this time.

11 1-21F16 **TIUTCHEV** 31 (BF,CD,G,S) D Nicholson 6-12-0 ....M A Fitzgerald 122
Owner: Liars Poker Partnership   4 wins from 13 starts, prize-money £38,329
Travels strongly in his races but found little off the bridle when soundly beaten at Newbury last month. Needs things to go all his own way and easily passed over.

12 P-3F0F3 **UPGRADE** 19 (C,D,G,S) N Twiston-Davies 5-12-0 ....C Maude 123
Owner: M Archer and Mrs J Broadhurst   4 wins from 12 starts, £59,017
Made virtually all to win the Triumph Hurdle last year. Those exertions seem to have taken their toll this season, however, as he has not reproduced that form since.

13 41-1323 **ZAFARABAD** 51 (C,D,G,S) D Nicholson 5-12-0 ....R Johnson 143
Owner: Mrs E Bains   5 wins from 9 starts, prize-money £64,657
No match for Istabraq or French Holly at Leopardstown last month and no obvious reason why he will turn the tables. Would be better served by a longer distance.

14 0651-11 **LADY CRICKET** 22 (B,G,S) M Pipe 5-11-9 ....A P McCoy 103
Owner: D Johnson   6 wins from 13 starts, prize-money £108,179
Main hope of champion pair Pipe and McCoy. Ex-French mare looked an exciting prospect when winning on her British debut but was less convincing in a muddling race latest.

BETTING: Coral: 1-2 Istabraq, 5-1 French Holly, 12-1 Theatreworld, 16-1 Lady Cricket, 25-1 Grey Shot, 28-1 Blowing Wind, Nomadic, 33-1 Bellator, City Hall, 40-1 Midnight Legend, Tiutchev, Zafarabad, 66-1 Mister Morose, Upgrade.
Ladbrokes: 1-2 Istabraq, 9-2 French Holly, 10-1 Theatreworld, 18-1 Lady Cricket, 25-1 Blowing Wind, 33-1 Grey Shot, Nomadic, 40-1 Bellator, City Hall, Zafarabad, 50-1 Midnight Legend, Tiutchev, 66-1 Mister Morose, Upgrade.
Tote: 1-2 Istabraq, 9-2 French Holly, 12-1 Theatreworld, 16-1 Lady Cricket, 25-1 Grey Shot, 33-1 Blowing Wind, City Hall, Zafarabad, 40-1 Nomadic, Tiutchev, 50-1 Midnight Legend, Mister Morose, 66-1 Bellator, Upgrade.
William Hill: 1-2 Istabraq, 9-2 French Holly, 14-1 Theatreworld, 16-1 Lady Cricket, 25-1 Blowing Wind, 33-1 Bellator, City Hall, Grey Shot, Tiutchev, Zafarabad, 40-1 Midnight Legend, Nomadic, 66-1 Upgrade, 100-1 Mister Morose.
1998: ISTABRAQ 6-12-0 C F Swan (3-1 fav) A P O'Brien (Ire) 18 ran

The Sporting Life, which long ago incorporated the popular Victorian racing paper *Bell's Life of London,* closed down in 1998, although the title still exists on the Internet (see later in this chapter). Now, the sole daily 'trade' paper specialising in racing is the *Racing Post.* This is how its racecards look, with colours in colour:

SHOWCASE RACE

2.20 Pertemps King George VI Chase [CH4]
RACE 4 (Class A) (Showcase Race) (Grade 1)
Winner £64,360   3m

£100000 added **For** 5yo+ **Weights** 11st 10lb **Allowances** Mares 5lb **Entries** 12 pay £175pay £325 **Penalty value** 1st £64,360 2nd £24,363 3rd £11,931.50 4th £5,445.50

1 F47F-47 **CHALLENGER DU LUC** (FR) ²¹ [D]   b 8 11-10
   b g Chamberlin-Islande II   A P McCoy (172)
   M C Pipe D A Johnson

2 7/3P-1P **COOME HILL** (IRE) ²⁸ [D]   9 11-10
   b g Riot Helmet-Ballybrack   J Osborne (163)
   W W Dennis Mrs Jill Dennis

3 121-423 **ESCARTEFIGUE** (FR) ²¹ [D]   6 11-10
   b g Start Fast-Dona Clara   R Johnson (174)
   D Nicholson Darren C Mercer

4 18-1211 **IMPERIAL CALL** (IRE) ²⁰ [D]   9 11-10
   br g Callernish-Princess Menelek   M A FitzGerald (178)
   Raymond Hurley (IRE) Lisselan Farms Ltd

5 F6143-8 **MULLIGAN** (IRE) ¹⁴ [C]   8 11-10
   ch g Callernish-Anaglog's Pet   A Maguire (167)
   D Nicholson Lady Harris

6 111C-41 **SEE MORE BUSINESS** (IRE) ²¹ [CD]   8 11-10
   b g Seymour Hicks-Miss Redlands   J Tizzard (182)
   P F Nicholls Paul K Barber And Mr J A Keighley

7 462-322 **SIMPLY DASHING** (IRE) ¹⁴   v 7 11-10
   br g Simply Great-Qurrat Al Ain   L Wyer (179)
   T D Easterby Steve Hammond

8 U21-155 **SUPER TACTICS** (IRE) ³⁵ [CD]   10 11-10
   b g Furry Glen-Hilarys Pet   A Thornton (174)
   R H Alner H V Perry

9 1121-11 **TEETON MILL** ²⁸ [D]   9 11-10
   gr g Neltino-Celtic Well   N Williamson (174)
   Miss Venetia Williams The Winning Line

1997 (8 ran) **See More Business** P F Nicholls 7 11-10 10/1   A Thornton PM170

BETTING FORECAST: 5-2 See More Business, 11-4 Teeton Mill, 4 Imperial Call, 5 Simply Dashing, 8 Escartefigue, 12 Challenger Du Luc, 16 Super Tactics, 25 Coome Hill, 33 Mulligan.

The card is immediately followed by 'Spotlight', giving an appraisal of each horse in the race. Example (taken from the 1998 Racing Post Trophy at Doncaster) as below:

SPOTLIGHT

Commander Collins Sadler's Wells colt, closely related to 2,000 Guineas and Derby third Colonel Collins; looked good performer in the making when beating Chesham Stakes winner Rhapsodist at Newmarket in July on debut and confirmed that impression when failing by a head to overhaul Auction Hose (second in last week's Dewhurst) in 7f Champagne Stakes here next time; will be well suited by today's stiffer test of stamina; yet to race on soft but most of sire's stock handle it and likely to be hard to beat.

Housemaster Plenty to find at this level, fifth in the Chesham at Royal Ascot on soft and sixth of 26 in valuable sales race at Newmarket last time (did best of those drawn low).

Magno Ran out game all-the-way winner of 1m York maiden a fortnight ago by a neck from Lightning Arrow; had run creditably when third to Mukhalif on softer ground at Ascot on previous start but plenty of improvement needed at today's level.

Stormy Skye Battled on from the rear when third to 8l winner Daliapour in testing conditions for 1m Listed event at Ascot a fortnight ago; hard to see him taking a hand in the finish today.

The Exhibition Fox Well-beaten eighth of 10 behind Magno at York on his debut a fortnight ago and just making up the numbers today.

Timahs Brother to Derby winner Shaamit; supplemented for today's event following highly promising debut success in 1m good-ground Newmarket maiden a month ago; faces very different conditions today and much stiffer opposition, but represents powerful connections and clearly has to be respected.

Tumbleweed Quartet Looked bit unlucky when about 2l third to Auction House and Commander Collins in 7f Champagne Stakes here last month, staying on well after being hampered and losing place over 2f out; had won on soft on debut so should handle today's conditions and could give Commander Collins a bit more to do today.

| VERDICT | Hard to look beyond the trio who dominate the betting. |

Tumbleweed Quartet did not have the run of the race when third to Auction Hosue in the Champagne Stakes here last month and may be better than that bare form, but he still has something to find to turn the tables on **COMMANDER COLLINS** who should be well suited by this stiffer test of stamina. Newmarket maiden winner **Timahs**, who represents top connections, could be anything but is short of racing experience. [AC]

Form is fully given, and reports fully back up the statistical account giving all the details of running, betting and results:

How to read the form

1	**Diomed**	**9-12**
2–3–4	6-y-o (30 Mar) b g Royalty (11.5f) · Lady (Hyperion)	.... **5**
6	(4,200gns) third foal; dam won over 7f.	.... **7**
8	**T Rainer**	A Prentice (5) **9**
10	Placings: 0938RUP220/19-16	**Draw:** 10 .... **11**
12	OR**95** F**80** Starts 1st 2nd 3rd **Win & Pl**	

	Starts	1st	2nd	3rd	Win & Pl	
Turf	2	1	1	-	£3,821	.... **13**
14 .... All Flat races	6	1	1	2	£4,768	
15 .... 76 **10/88 Sthl** 1m E (0-90) Hcap good (AW)£5,020						
7/86 Sand 7f Mdn 2yo gd-fm £2,941						
Total win prize-money £7,961						

16 .... GF-HRD 1-2-5 GS-HVY 0-0-3	Course 1-3-5 Dist 1-3-5
17 .... 1 May Ayr (AW) 2m	E (0-90,85) Hdl Hcap £2,303
18 .... 13 ran FIRM 8hdls	Time 5m03.90s (slw8.10s)

19 .... 1 Coughlans Run 10 11-12 ..A Claimer (5)[12] 8/1 ....**20**
22 .... 2 Netherbridge 11 10-1ow2 ....J Ockey 7/1 ....**21**
24 .... 3 Grey Lad 12 10-3ex5 oh4 Mr C Amateur12/1 ....**23**
26 .... 7 **DIOMED** 5 10-0b[1] ....Ann Other 2/1F **25**
27 .... ridden over 2f out, btn 9 lengths
29 .... [PM75 TS76 0R77] [opened 6/4] **28**
31 .... Dist: 2-2-1-2-1 RACE PM 124/90/100 ....**30**
Racecheck: Wins 7 (2) Pl 2 Unpl 9

1 Horse's name (here Diomed) & weight to be carried (9-12).

2 Age, birthdate (2-y-o only) colour & sex (bay gelding)

3 Sire (Royalty)

4 Sire's stamina index (11.5f) - for 2+3yo, Flat only: average distance (to nearest tenth of furlong) of the Flat victories of the sire's offspring aged 3+ in GB & Ireland since 1988

5 Dam (Lady) & dam's sire (Hyperion)

6 Yearling sale price

7 Breeding comment for 2yo

8 Trainer (T Rainer)

9 Jockey (A Prentice) & claim (5lb)

10 Last 20 form figures under today's code (Flat or Jumps), most recent on right. Figures to left of hyphen are last season, to left of slash previous seasons; PTP & AW form in BOLD.

11 Draw (starting stall, Flat only)

12 Today's official handicap rating (bold if handicap), which determines weight for handicaps. In hurdle races, the latest official Flat rating (F) is added; in chases, the latest official hurdle rating (H).

13 Career record on turf or all-weather (jumps: chases, hurdles or NH Flat) as relevant.

14 Full career record under today's code.

15 Career WINS under today's code, showing handicap rating (76) month/year, course, distance to nearest ½f, class (A-H) race type, going & value.

16 Record (wins-places-runs) on fast and softish going, and course & distance.

17 LATEST OUTING: Date, course, distance to nearest ½f, class, type, value. 0-90 race is restricted to horses with maximum official rating of 90. 85 is highest-rated actual runner. AW=all-weather. PTP shows British

point-to-point races, which are excluded from career data.

18 Number of runners, going, number of fences or hurdles, time & comparison (fast or slow) with Racing Post standard time for the course & distance

19 First three, with age & weight carried

20 Jockey, weight claim for apprentice, conditional or amateur (5lb), draw (stall 12, Flat only)

21 ow2=2lb overweight (jockey unable to make intended weight)

22 ex5=5lb extra (handicaps only; penalty incurred for win since allocation of weights)

23 oh4=out of the handicap: horse merited 4lb less than the minimum weight.

24 t=tongue strap; b=blinkers, v=visor, h=hood, e=eyeshield, c=eyecover (b[1] or v[1]=first time under today's code)

25 Starting price (2/1), with F=favourite; J=joint fav of 2; C=co-fav of 3+

26 Comment, followed by distance beaten by winner if out of first six

27 PM-Postmark's assessment of the form; TS-Topspeed's assessment, based on time, OR-official BHB rating (for handicaps this figure is adjusted for any penalty, overweight or pounds out of handicap)

28 Odds fluctuations in betting market

29 Distances between first six

30 Race Postmark: Racing Post private handicapper's assessment of the first three (not to be confused with official handicap ratings, which measure the task rather than the achievement)

31 RACECHECK shows number of wins, places and unplaced runs from next two outings of all the runners. Figure in brackets is number of wins in same or better class.

CHELTENHAM

➪ *Continued from page 45*

2 **BELLATOR** 5 10-10 ....B Fenton 11/4
blundered 1st, chased winner, ridden along from 3 out, no chance when hit last
[PM146 TS101 OR155] [op 7/4]
3 Dreams End 10 10-8 ....N Williamson 9/1
Dist: 10-dist RACE PM: 154+/146
RACECHECK: Wins 1 Pl 1 Unpl 6

11 Feb 98 Ascot 2m½f D Nov Hdl £3,664
9 ran GOOD 9hdls Time 3m 58.30s (slw 0.10s)
1 **GREY SHOT** 6 11-7 ....R Dunwoody 8/11F
made all, mistakes 2 out and last, all out
[PM133 TS132] [op 4/6 tchd Evs]
2 King Kato 5 11-4 ....M A FitzGerald 12/1
3 Dawn Leader 7 11-7 ....C Llewellyn 9/4
Dist: hd-7-1¾-4-6 RACE PM: 133+/128/124
RACECHECK: Wins 2 (2) Pl 4 Unpl 6

Istabraq

b g Sadler's Wells - Betty's Secret (Secretariat)
Placings: 211111/111112-1111

A P O'Brien (IRE) 7 12-0

			Starts	1st	2nd	3rd	Win & Pl
F87			16	14	2	-	£486,102

1/99	Leop	2m Gd1 Hdl heavy	£37,250
12/98	Leop	2m Gd2 Hdl heavy	£13,750
11/98	Fair	2m4f Gd1 Hdl yld-sft	£26,000
11/98	Cork	2m Hdl sft-hvy	£38,850
3/98	Chel	2m½f A Gd1 Hdl good	£137,420
1/98	Leop	2m Gd1 Hdl yld-sft	£34,500
12/97	Leop	2m Gd2 Hdl heavy	£12,900
11/97	Fair	2m4f Gd1 Hdl yield	£26,000
10/97	Tipp	2m Hdl sft-hvy	£32,500
4/97	Punc	2m4f Nov Gd1 Hdl good	£18,600
3/97	Chel	2m5f A Nov Gd1 Hdl gd-fm	£49,585
2/97	Leop	2m2f Nov Gd2 Hdl gd-yld	£13,000
12/96	Leop	2m2f Nov Gd3 Hdl yield	£9,675
12/96	Fair	2m Nov Gd1 Hdl yield	£16,250

Total win prize-money £466,280

24 Jan Leopardstown 2m Gd1 Hdl £37,250
6 ran HEAVY 8hdls Time 4m 4.80s (slw 13.80s)
1 **ISTABRAQ** 7 11-10 ....C F Swan 8/15F
settled 2nd, challenged travelling easily after 2 out, led before last, eased clear flat, not extended, impressive
[PM176 TS161 OR164] [op 1/2]
2 **FRENCH HOLLY** 8 11-10 ....A Maguire 9/4
attempted to make all, headed before last, ridden and kept on flat, no chance with winner
[PM167 TS160] [op 2/1]
3 **ZAFARABAD** 5 11-6 ....R Johnson 16/1
2nd early, 3rd when slight mistake 4th, pushed along 3 out, ridden and kept on one paced from 2 out [PM156 TS149] [op 14/1]
4 **THEATREWORLD** 7 11-10 ......T P Treacy 16/1
wore tongue strap, held up in rear, 5th 3 out, ridden from 2 out, kept on one paced
[PM158 TS151 OR146]
5 **NOMADIC** 5 11-6 ....N Williamson 16/1
held up in touch, improved into 3rd briefly 3 out, 4th and ridden 2 out, no extra before last
[OR129] [op 12/1]
Dist: 1-7-2-dist-15 RACE PM: 176+/167/156
RACECHECK: Wins 1 Pl - Unpl 1

29 Dec 98 Leopardstown 2m Gd2 Hdl £13,750
3 ran HEAVY 8hdls Time 4m 30.40s (slw 39.40s)
1 **ISTABRAQ** 6 12-0 ....C F Swan 1/10F
tracked leader in 2nd, took closer order after 3 out, led travelling easily after 2 out, drew clear from last, not extended [PM162 OR164]
2 Shantarini 4 11-2 ....K P Gaule 10/1
3 Gazalani 6 12-0 ....T P Treacy 20/1
Dist: 8-15 RACE PM: 162+/130/127
RACECHECK: Wins 1 Pl - Unpl 3

29 Nov 98 Fairyhouse 2m4f Gd1 Hdl £26,000
6 ran YLD-SFT 11hdls Time 5m 4.20s (slw 12.90s)
1 **ISTABRAQ** 6 12-0 ....C F Swan 1/5F
tracked leaders in moderate 3rd, mistake 4th, headway after 4 out, led 3 out, edged clear before 2 out, eased from last, not extended

2 Master Beveled 8 11-8 ....T P Treacy 10/1
3 Padre Mio 10 11-5 ....K P Gaule 33/1
Dist: 4-5-3-shd-20 RACE PM: 152+/145/137
RACECHECK: Wins 2 Pl 1 Unpl 2

4 Apr 98 Aintree 2m4f A Gd1 Hdl £50,050
6 ran SOFT 11hdls Time 5m 31.00s (slw 33.90s)
1 Pridwell 8 11-7 ....A P McCoy 6/1
2 **ISTABRAQ** 6 11-7 ....C F Swan 4/7F
held up, headway 6th, challenged and hit 2 out, led last, hard ridden and headed near finish
[PM169 TS158] [op 4/9 tchd 4/6]
3 Kerawi 5 11-7 ....C Llewellyn 10/1
Dist: hd-26-3-dist RACE PM: 169/169/143
RACECHECK: Wins 2 Pl 1 Unpl 5

17 Mar 98 Cheltenham 2m½f A Gd1 Hdl £137,420
18 ran GOOD 8hdls Time 3m 49.10s (fst 12.20s)
1 **ISTABRAQ** 6 12-0 ....C F Swan 3/1F
always prominent, led 3 out, quickened clear after next, very easily
[PM174 TS171] [op 9/4 tchd 100/30]
2 **THEATREWORLD** 6 12-0 ....T P Treacy 20/1
held up, headway approaching 2 out, ran on well flat [PM159 TS155]
3 I'm Supposin 6 12-0 ....R Dunwoody 6/1
U **BELLATOR** 5 12-0 ....B Fenton 100/1
behind, headway from 3 out, staying on 6th when hampered and unseated rider last
[PM153]
Dist: 12-1-1¼-4-1¼ RACE PM: 174+/159/158
RACECHECK: Wins 7 (5) Pl 3 Unpl 13

Lady Cricket

ch m Cricket Ball - Lady Mariza (Dunbeath)
Placings: 1/118651-11

M C Pipe 5 11-9

			Starts	1st	2nd	3rd	Win & Pl
OR157			9	6	-	-	£100,211

	2/99	Font	2m2½f B Hdl good	£7,265
141	2/99	Newb	2m5f B Hdl Hcap gd-sft	£5,965
	4/98	Autl	2m3½f Hdl v soft	£35,354
	11/97	Autl	2m2f Hdl holding	£24,691
	11/97	Autl	1m7f Hdl 4yo soft	£13,468
	4/97	Autl	1m7f Hdl soft	£13,468

Total win prize-money £100,211

22 Feb Fontwell Park 2m2½f B Hdl £7,265
3 ran GOOD 9hdls Time 4m 44.00s (slw 22.10s)
1 **LADY CRICKET** 5 11-9 b ....A P McCoy 2/5F
set steady pace, made all, ridden and quickened 6th, driven along and held on from 3 out [PM146 TS99] [tchd 4/9 & 1/2]
2 Lord Of Love 4 10-7 ....B Clifford 16/1
3 Toto Toscato 5 12-0 ....A Maguire 9/4
Dist: 6-6 RACE PM: 146+/124/142+
RACECHECK: Wins - Pl - Unpl 1

12 Feb Newbury 2m5f B Hdl Hcap £5,965
9 ran GD-SFT 11hdls Time 5m 16.60s (slw 7.80s)
1 **LADY CRICKET** 5 12-0 b ....A P McCoy 4/1
held up and confidently ridden, steady headway from 7th, challenged from 4 out until led on bit 2 out, soon clear, pushed out run-in
[PM157 TS147 OR141] [op 3/1 tchd 9/2]
2 Scoring Pedigree 7 10-4 ....A Bates (3) 11/2
3 Ela Agapi Mou 6 11-2 b[1] ....R Dunwoody 8/1
Dist: 9-¾-6-14-18 RACE PM: 157+/125+/132
RACECHECK: Wins 1 (1) Pl 1 Unpl 4

25 Apr 98 Auteuil 2m3½f Hdl £35,354
6 ran V SOFT Time 4m 56.00s
1 **LADY CRICKET** 4 9-10 ....C Gombeau 12/1
raced in 5th, headway before 2 out, led flat, driven out
2 Raikabag Junction 4 9-13 ....D Vincent
3 Kimbi 4 10-6 ....J-Y Beaurain
Dist: ½-shd-4-10
RACECHECK: Wins 3 Pl - Unpl 2

29 Mar 98 Auteuil 2m2f Hdl 4yo Hcap £26,263
5 ran V SOFT Time 4m 29.00s

25 Nov 97 Enghien 2m1½f Hdl £33,670
10 ran V SOFT Time 4m 22.00s
1 Roboratif 3 9-11 ....J-P Godet
2 Lawful Find 3 9-11 ....X Hondier
3 Pontvallain 3 9-13 ....D Bressou
8 **LADY CRICKET** 3 9-11 b ....C Gombeau
always towards rear, ridden and beaten approaching 2 out (35/4) btn 17 lengths
Dist: ¾-1
RACECHECK: Wins 1 Pl - Unpl 1

Midnight Legend

b h Night Shift - Myth (Troy)
Placings: 4111/3312

D Nicholson 8 12-0

			Starts	1st	2nd	3rd	Win & Pl
OR154 F112			8	4	1	2	£67,572

2/99	Sand	2m½f B Hdl gd-sft	£8,208
4/97	Punc	2m Nov Gd2 Hdl good	£24,800
4/97	Aint	2m½f A Nov Gd2 Hdl good	£16,730
3/97	Winc	2m F Mdn Hdl gd-fm	£2,478

Total win prize-money £52,216

25 Feb Wincanton 2m A Gd2 Hdl £19,340
second, see **GREY SHOT**

6 Feb Sandown Park 2m½f B Hdl £8,208
5 ran GD-SFT 8hdls Time 4m 8.00s (slw 9.00s)
1 **MIDNIGHT LEGEND** 8 10-9 ....R Johnson 6/4F
made all, hard ridden approaching last, held on all out [PM143 TS146 OR147] [op 7/4 tchd 15/8]
2 Master Beveled 9 11-10 ....A P McCoy 9/4
3 Juyush 7 11-10 ....T J Murphy 7/2
Dist: shd-6-4-1¾ RACE PM: 143/159+/153+
RACECHECK: Wins - Pl 1 Unpl 2

12 Dec 98 Cheltenham 2m1f A Gd2 Hdl £21,665
third, see **GREY SHOT**

28 Nov 98 Newcastle 2m A Gd2 Hdl £21,770
third, see **FRENCH HOLLY**

22 Apr 97 Punchestown 2m Nov Gd2 Hdl £24,800
9 ran GOOD Time 3m 48.70s (slw 1.30s)
1 **MIDNIGHT LEGEND** 6 12-0 ....R Johnson 7/4F
made virtually all, ridden and quickened approaching last, ran on well [PM143 TS97]
2 Whats The Verdict 5 11-13 ....P Carberry 9/1
3 Gazalani 5 11-13 ....T P Treacy 14/1
Dist: 2½-½-½-7 RACE PM: 143+/139/135
RACECHECK: Wins 3 Pl 6 Unpl 7

3 Apr 97 Aintree 2m½f A Nov Gd2 Hdl £16,730
9 ran GOOD 9hdls Time 3m 56.30s (fst 8.40s)
1 **MIDNIGHT LEGEND** 6 11-0 .....R Johnson 11/2
chased leader, hit 5th, led 3 out, hung left flat, ridden and ran on well
[PM142 TS142] [op 7/2 tchd 6/1]
2 Sharpical 5 11-0 ....M A FitzGerald 100/30F
3 High In The Clouds 5 11-0 ....S Wynne 9/1
Dist: 2-3-10-2-dist RACE PM: 142/140/137
RACECHECK: Wins 1 Pl 5 Unpl 12

Mister Morose

b g Kings Ride - Girseach (Furry Glen)
Placings: 211F3/176/11UU

N A Twiston-Davies 9 12-0

			Starts	1st	2nd	3rd	Win & Pl
OR151			12	5	1	1	£45,120

	11/98	Chel	2m A Nov Gd2 Ch gd-sft	£12,440
141	11/98	Chep	2m4½f B Hdl Hcap gd-sft	£22,821
132	11/96	Newb	2m½f B (0-140) Hdl Hcap gd-sft	£4,900
	1/96	Winc	2m E Nov Hdl gd-sft	£2,758
	12/95	Ling	2m½f H Mdn NHF 4-6yo heavy	£1,371

Total win prize-money £44,290

26 Dec 98 Kempton Park 3m A Nov Gd1 Ch £22,715
7 ran GD-SFT 19fncs Time 6m 20.10s (slw 17.70s)
1 Lord Of The River 6 11-7 ....J Osborne 11/2

Among the regular contributions, Gerald Delamere's analysis for big-race meetings is penetrating, and also provides some long-priced winners from time to time. In addition there are daily boxes with trainer/jockey information for each meeting, a ratings service and other useful special features, plus results:

GRAND NATIONAL MEETING TOP JOCKEYS

Jumps 1998/99+ *WITH RIDES TODAY*

WINS-RIDES		JOCKEY — *TRAINER SUPPLYING RIDES TODAY* / GIVING BEST COURSE RECORD	WINS-RIDES	ALL RIDES	ALL RIDES £1 STAKE	COURSE RIDES SINCE WIN
9-40	23%	R Walsh [3] ....P F Nicholls	4-19	21%	+71.25	6
7-50	14%	A Dobbin [2] ....Jonjo O'Neill	2-4	50%	+29.00	11
7-73	10%	R Johnson [4] ....P J Hobbs	5-32	16%	−16.67	26
7-86	8%	A P McCoy [4] ....M C Pipe	7-79	9%	−32.47	8
6-30	20%	B J Geraghty [2] ......James Joseph Mangan	1-2	50%	+8.98	2
4-40	10%	J Culloty [2]	0-0	0%	+31.36	2
3-15	20%	L Cooper [3] ....Jonjo O'Neill	3-15	20%	+13.00	7
3-15	20%	T Doumen [2] ....F Doumen	3-14	21%	+5.50	4
3-21	14%	C O'Dwyer [1] ....C Roche	1-5	20%	−11.92	4
3-29	10%	P Carberry [2]	0-0	0%	−2.50	4
3-37	8%	C Llewellyn [3] ....N A Twiston-Davies	3-31	10%	+5.00	12
3-51	6%	T J Murphy [3] ....P F Nicholls	1-9	11%	−13.50	5
3-57	5%	M A FitzGerald [4] ....M Todhunter	1-1	100%	−35.75	11
2-12	17%	R McGrath [2] ....Miss Venetia Williams	0-2	0%	+8.50	0
2-20	10%	J A McCarthy [2] ....M C Pipe	0-1	0%	−0.50	14
2-27	7%	J Tizzard [1]	0-0	0%	−8.50	0
2-31	6%	T Scudamore [1] ....N A Twiston-Davies	0-2	0%	−2.25	16
2-33	6%	R Thornton [1] ....A King	1-12	8%	+2.00	3
1-1	100%	T Best [1] ....G B Balding	1-1	100%	+14.00	0
1-1	100%	Mr D Jewett [1]	0-0	0%	+5.50	0
1-7	14%	D N Russell [1]	0-0	0%	+27.00	6
1-22	5%	G Lee [3] ....D McCain	0-1	0%	−9.00	4
1-26	4%	D J Casey [2] ....W P Mullins	0-1	0%	−21.50	25
0-22	0%	R Greene [2] ....M C Pipe	0-21	0%	−22.00	22
0-20	0%	A Thornton [1]	0-0	0%	−20.00	20
0-19	0%	S Durack [1] ....C Roche	0-1	0%	−19.00	19
0-17	0%	N Fehily [2] ....C J Mann	0-11	0%	−17.00	17
0-15	0%	W Marston [2] ....Mrs S J Smith	0-3	0%	−15.00	15
0-13	0%	M Bradburne [2] ....H D Daly	0-2	0%	−13.00	13
0-11	0%	B Harding [1]	0-0	0%	−11.00	11
0-11	0%	J P McNamara [1] ....K C Bailey	0-2	0%	−11.00	11
0-10	0%	L Aspell [1]	0-0	0%	−10.00	10
0-9	0%	D Elsworth [2] ....Mrs S J Smith	0-7	0%	−9.00	9
0-6	0%	H Oliver [2] ....R C Guest	0-3	0%	−6.00	6
0-5	0%	R P McNally [1]	0-0	0%	−5.00	5
0-4	0%	Mr R Burton [1]	0-0	0%	−4.00	4
0-4	0%	James Davies [2] ......Miss Venetia Williams	0-1	0%	−4.00	4
0-4	0%	O McPhail [1] ....A G Juckes	0-1	0%	−4.00	4
0-4	0%	S Thomas [2] ....Miss Venetia Williams	0-2	0%	−4.00	4
0-3	0%	J R Barry [1]	0-0	0%	−3.00	3
0-3	0%	R Biddlecombe [1] ....Miss H C Knight	0-1	0%	−3.00	3
0-3	0%	Mr T Greenall [2] ....M W Easterby	0-1	0%	−3.00	3
0-3	0%	D J Howard [1] ....M C Pipe	0-3	0%	−3.00	3
0-3	0%	L McGrath [1] ....R C Guest	0-2	0%	−3.00	3
0-3	0%	P Moloney [1]	0-0	0%	−3.00	3
0-2	0%	G Carenza [1]	0-0	0%	−2.00	2
0-2	0%	F King [1]	0-0	0%	−2.00	2
0-2	0%	R M Power [1] ....P Mullins	0-1	0%	−2.00	2
0-2	0%	Dr P Pritchard [1] ....Dr P Pritchard	0-2	0%	−2.00	2
0-2	0%	Mr R Stephens [1] ....P J Hobbs	0-1	0%	−2.00	2
0-1	0%	Mr P Cashman [1]	0-0	0%	−1.00	1
0-1	0%	Mr J J Codd [1]	0-0	0%	−1.00	1
0-1	0%	Steven J Craine [2]	0-0	0%	−1.00	1
0-1	0%	Mr A P Crowe [1]	0-0	0%	−1.00	1
0-1	0%	Mr T J Malone [2] ....M C Pipe	0-1	0%	−1.00	1
0-1	0%	A Tinkler [2] ....N J Henderson	0-1	0%	−1.00	1
0-1	0%	L Vickers [1]	0-0	0%	−1.00	1
0-1	0%	Mr N Williams [1] ....P F Nicholls	0-1	0%	−1.00	1
0-0	0%	L Berridge [1]	0-0	0%	0.00	0

GRAND NATIONAL MEETING TOP TRAINERS

WITH RUNNERS TODAY 1998/99+	WINS-RUNS	£1 STAKE	NH FLAT & HURDLES WINS-RUNS		CHASES WINS-RUNS		COURSE RUNS SINCE WIN
Jonjo O'Neill [9]	10-37	27%	+90.48	6-25 24%	4-12	33%	10
M C Pipe [12]	10-187	5%	−94.72	6-100 6%	4-87	5%	23
P J Hobbs [6]	8-67	12%	+15.50	5-37 14%	3-30	10%	26
P F Nicholls [5]	8-87	9%	−20.50	2-20 10%	6-67	9%	10
Miss Venetia Williams [6]	5-59	8%	−22.17	3-29 10%	2-30	7%	1
N A Twiston-Davies [3]	4-44	9%	+19.00	3-22 14%	1-22	5%	12
F Doumen [1]	3-15	20%	+5.50	1-7 14%	2-8	25%	3
P R Webber [1]	3-23	13%	+2.50	0-8 0%	3-15	20%	1
E J O'Grady [1]	2-8	25%	+6.00	2-6 33%	0-2	0%	1
W P Mullins [2]	2-9	22%	+5.50	0-3 0%	2-6	33%	5
A J Martin [1]	2-12	17%	−4.00	1-1 100%	1-11	9%	8
S A Brookshaw [1]	2-13	15%	+36.00	0-8 0%	2-5	40%	0
C Roche [3]	2-17	12%	−10.00	2-11 18%	0-6	0%	12
J Howard Johnson [1]	2-24	8%	−17.12	0-7 0%	2-17	12%	19
Miss H C Knight [2]	2-32	6%	−15.64	1-16 6%	1-16	6%	14
N J Henderson [4]	2-73	3%	−59.00	0-42 0%	2-31	6%	5
James Joseph Mangan [1]	1-3	33%	+14.00	0-0 0%	1-3	33%	1
M Todhunter [3]	1-3	33%	+12.00	0-0 0%	1-3	33%	1
G B Balding [1]	1-4	25%	+11.00	1-3 33%	0-1	0%	0
E Bolger [1]	1-6	17%	−3.25	0-0 0%	1-6	17%	5
S E H Sherwood [1]	1-8	13%	+2.00	0-4 0%	1-4	25%	5
B Ellison [1]	1-9	11%	+4.00	1-4 25%	0-5	0%	0
C F Swan [1]	1-9	11%	+8.00	1-7 14%	0-2	0%	4
S Gollings [1]	1-10	10%	+16.00	1-10 10%	0-0	0%	0
Ferdy Murphy [1]	1-18	6%	−11.00	0-2 0%	1-16	6%	10
Mrs S J Smith [5]	1-22	5%	−14.50	0-10 0%	1-12	8%	1
A King [2]	1-25	4%	−16.00	1-16 6%	0-9	0%	11
M Pitman [2]	0-25	0%	−25.00	0-20 0%	0-5	0%	25
C J Mann [2]	0-20	0%	−20.00	0-10 0%	0-10	0%	20
Mrs M Reveley [2]	0-17	0%	−17.00	0-9 0%	0-8	0%	17
D McCain [1]	0-15	0%	−15.00	0-2 0%	0-13	0%	15
M F Morris [1]	0-12	0%	−12.00	0-8 0%	0-4	0%	12
Ian Williams [1]	0-12	0%	−12.00	0-6 0%	0-6	0%	12
Noel Meade [1]	0-11	0%	−11.00	0-8 0%	0-3	0%	11
K C Bailey [1]	0-10	0%	−10.00	0-1 0%	0-9	0%	10
H D Daly [1]	0-9	0%	−9.00	0-2 0%	0-7	0%	9
N G Richards [1]	0-9	0%	−9.00	0-5 0%	0-4	0%	9
M W Easterby [1]	0-7	0%	−7.00	0-4 0%	0-3	0%	7
R C Guest [4]	0-7	0%	−7.00	0-1 0%	0-6	0%	7
P Mullins [1]	0-5	0%	−5.00	0-4 0%	0-1	0%	5
J R Best [1]	0-4	0%	−4.00	0-2 0%	0-2	0%	4
N J Gifford [1]	0-3	0%	−3.00	0-0 0%	0-3	0%	3
Dr P Pritchard [1]	0-3	0%	−3.00	0-0 0%	0-3	0%	3
K A Ryan [1]	0-3	0%	−3.00	0-1 0%	0-2	0%	3
Mrs H Dalton [1]	0-2	0%	−2.00	0-0 0%	0-2	0%	2
H Morrison [1]	0-2	0%	−2.00	0-1 0%	0-1	0%	2
Mrs L B Normile [1]	0-2	0%	−2.00	0-2 0%	0-0	0%	2
A M Balding [2]	0-1	0%	−1.00	0-0 0%	0-1	0%	1
J I A Charlton [1]	0-1	0%	−1.00	0-0 0%	0-1	0%	1
A G Juckes [1]	0-1	0%	−1.00	0-0 0%	0-1	0%	1
Miss E C Lavelle [2]	0-1	0%	−1.00	0-1 0%	0-0	0%	1
C N Allen [1]	0-0	0%	0.00	0-0 0%	0-0	0%	0
John Berry [1]	0-0	0%	0.00	0-0 0%	0-0	0%	0
M Brittain [1]	0-0	0%	0.00	0-0 0%	0-0	0%	0
L A Dace [1]	0-0	0%	0.00	0-0 0%	0-0	0%	0
T Doumen [1]	0-0	0%	0.00	0-0 0%	0-0	0%	0
Mrs L C Jewell [1]	0-0	0%	0.00	0-0 0%	0-0	0%	0
J Mackie [1]	0-0	0%	0.00	0-0 0%	0-0	0%	0

TRAVELLERS' CHECK

THE following horses have travelled the farthest distance to Aintree

LINDEN'S LOTTO (IRE) (3.45) ....A J Martin, Kildalkey, Co Meath
RYHANE (IRE) (3.45) ....A L T Moore, Naas, Co Kildare
DARAPOUR (IRE) (4.50) ....A P O'Brien, Ballydoyle, Co Tipperary
BUDALUS (IRE) (4.50) ....C F Swan, Cloughjordan, Co Tipperary
SHANNON GALE (IRE) (4.20), KHAYRAWANI (IRE) (4.50) & KING WAH GLORY
(IRE) (5.20) ....C Roche, the Curragh, Co Kildare
OPERA HAT (IRE) (2.35)................................J R H Fowler, Summerhill, Co Meath
HIS SONG (IRE) (3.10)...M F Morris, Fethard, Co Tipperary
NATIVE STATUS (IRE) (3.45) ....Thomas Carberry, Ashbourne, Co Meath
EASTON GALE (2.00) & PEALINGS (IRE) (4.50) ....
....G A Hubbard, Worlingworth, Suffolk 232 miles
EVEN FLOW (IRE) (3.45) ....T Casey, Beare Green, Surrey 230 miles
AUETALER (GER) (2.00), CHALLENGER DU LUC (FR) (2.35), GRIS D'ESTRUVAL
(FR) (3.45), BALLYSICYOS (FR) (4.20), BLOWING WIND (FR) (4.50) & RAINBOW
FRONTIER (IRE) (4.50) ....M C Pipe, Nicholashayne, Devon 209 miles
THE LAND AGENT (5.20) ....J W Mullins, Wilsford-Cum-Lake, Wilts 206 miles
WAYWARD KING (3.45) ....R J Hodges, Charlton Adam, Somerset 200 miles
TAUFAN BOY (4.50).....................................G B Balding, Fyfield, Hants 198 miles
CALL EQUINAME (2.35), LINTON ROCKS (3.45), EXECUTIVE DECISION (IRE)
(4.50) & STORM DAMAGE (IRE) (5.20)P F Nicholls, Ditcheat, Somerset 194 miles
VILLAGE KING (IRE) (3.10), MUSICAL SLING (IRE) (4.20), SADLER'S REALM (4.50)
& ASHWELL BOY (IRE) (5.20) ....P J Hobbs, Bilbrook, Somerset 191 miles
BALLYLINE (IRE) (3.45) & DYSART O'DEA (IRE) (4.20) ....
....W T Kemp, Duns, Borders 191 miles
KING OF SPARTA (3.10) ....J G Portman, Compton, Berks 183 miles
BERLIN BLUE (4.20)....................................R M Stronge, Beedon, Berks 182 miles
RED BEAN (3.45) ....Simon Earle, East Kennett, Wilts 179 miles
MAKOUNJI (FR) (3.10), TEMPESTUOUS LADY (IRE) (4.20) & SERENUS (USA)
(4.50)...N J Henderson, Lambourn, Berks 177 miles
DOOR TO DOOR (IRE) (4.20) ....S E H Sherwood, Lambourn, Berks 177 miles
STORM OF GOLD (IRE) (4.20)........C J Mann, Upper Lambourn, Berks 176 miles
CLINTON (IRE) (5.20) ....K C Bailey, Upper Lambourn, Berks 176 miles
SANTABLESS (IRE) (4.20)................M Pitman, Upper Lambourn, Berks 176 miles
EVER BLESSED (IRE) (3.10), RICARDO (4.20) & YEOMAN SAILOR (IRE) (4.20) .
....Mrs J Pitman, Upper Lambourn, Berks 176 miles
ROYAL EVENT (5.20)................................D R Gandolfo, Wantage, Oxon 172 miles
LORD NOELIE (IRE) (4.20) ....Miss H C Knight, Wantage, Oxon 172 miles
IN THE ROUGH (IRE) (4.20) ....J A B Old, Barbury Castle, Wilts 171 miles

NEWMARKET RATINGS

POSTMARK is the Racing Post private handicapper's rating, adjusted to 10st (12st jumps), with allowance for weight-for-age; rating from last run (provided it was on today's surface within last 60 days Flat, 365 days jumps) and Master Rating are both shown, with pointer showing top-rated. The official scale is used (Flat 0-140, Jumps 0-175).

HANDICAPS: The figures on the left (chases & all-weather in bold) are the official handicap marks the horse ran off on its last six runs, adjusted for penalties, overweight and long handicap (jockeys' allowances are always added back). The superior figure shows finishing position. A dash indicates non-handicap, or a chase run for a hurdler, or vice-versa.
The TODAY figure is the official rating for this race, adjusted for penalties and long handicap. Its significance is in the comparison with past and future marks. The FUTURE figure highlights horses on a higher (+) or lower (-) mark for future handicaps. This column is usually significant for early-closing races – plus figures show horses well-treated here, but be wary of horses with minus figures, other than those caused by penalties.

NON-HANDICAPS: The adjusted official rating is the current BHB rating, adjusted to 10st (12st jumps), with allowance for weight-for-age. The top-rated has the best chance according to the official handicapper. Note that the highest published Flat rating before September is 120 (100 2-y-o). Beware that horses never entered for handicaps may not have a rating. Horses with neither Postmark nor official ratings are omitted.

IN THE FORM: the OR figure beneath the trainer's name is the horse's current official rating (bold for handicap). Compare this with the marks beneath for previous handicap wins.

2.05 HANDICAP

Last six outings (latest on right)	Horse	Today	Future	Latest	Master
100^9 — — — — —	Kumait	9-7 105	-1	111	116
— — 107^0 — 107^0 —	Tumbleweed Ridge	9-7 105		—	115
— — — — — —	Stanott	9-6 104		—	110
— — — — — 105^0	Daunting Lady	9-2 100		—	122
90^5 89^1 94^0 99^2 100^7	Granny's Pet	9-2 100		117◄	117
91^0 — — — 88^9	Astrac	9-1 99	-3	95	109
88^2 88^1 94^7 94^2 94^3	Al Muallim	9-0 98		—	119
92^2 96^2 97^0 96^0 95^2 95^6	Return Of Amin	8-13 97		—	122
— — — — — —	Daylight In Dubai	8-10 94		—	121
98^0 97^0 96^0 93^2 96^0 96^0	Emerging Market	8-10 94		—	117
94^4 94^3 94^5 97^7 95^4 93^3	Harmonic Way	8-9 93		—	124◄
— 83^2 84^4 86^5 85^1 88^2	Free Option	8-8 92		—	119
— 84^2 89^0 88^0 87^1 92^0	Epsom Cyclone	8-6 90		—	117
75^1 — 80^3 81^1 86^1 89^0	Salty Jack	8-5 89		—	121
92^4 — — 96^9 94^8 92^0	Omaha City	8-4 88		—	122
93^6 93^0 93^0 91^7 — 89^0	No Extras	8-3 88	-1	—	112
95^6 93^4 93^0 92^0 92^6 89^0	Showboat	8-2 88	-2	—	124◄
— 93^0 90^8 — 85^6 87^0	Temeraire	8-1 88	-3	91	117
88^7 85^0 85^0 83^0 72^8 83^8	Tertium	7-11 88	-7	101	111
— — — — — 85^0	Dushanbe	7-11 88	-7	80	112

3.10 HANDICAP

Last six outings (latest on right)	Horse	Today	Future	Latest	Master
— — — — — —	Bertolini	9-7 113		—	118◄
— — — — — —	Indiana Legend	9-6 112		—	113
— — — — — —	Undeterred	9-6 112		—	113
— — — — — —	Vision Of Night	9-5 111		—	118◄
— — — — — —	Kalidasa	9-1 107	-1	99◄	109
— — — — — —	Caballero	8-12 104		—	117

3.45 HANDICAP

Last six outings (latest on right)	Horse	Today	Future	Latest	Master
86^8 85^4 85^1 90^1 95^8 95^4	Hajr	10-0 95		91	103
— 85^4 — — 81^1 88^1	Rainbow Ways	9-10 92		—	97
— — — — 86^1 91^4	Alberich	9-8 90		—	105◄
— — — — — 89^P	Just In Time	9-7 89		—	100
70^1 77^1 80^0 80^0 85^0 75^0	Blurred	8-8 75	-5	73	99
75^2 — 78^1 — 80^0	First Master	8-7 75		—	99
— 78^3 77^3 77^6 — 76^2	Minivet	8-7 75		—	103
— — 77^9 74^0 72^3 74^4	St Lawrence	8-5 72		—	96
65^4 66^7 64^2 64^2 66^1 72^8	Lancer	8-5 72		92◄	103
— — — — — —	Wave Of Optimism	8-4 72		—	102
— — — — 84^9 —	Glory Of Grosvenor	8-4 72		—	93
67^1 74^4 74^5 74^3 75^5 60^0	Beaumont	8-2 69		—	103
83^9 86^6 80^6 73^0 68^7 65^7	General Assembly	7-12 65		—	87

RACING POST

POINTERS

MARK YOUR CARD

MARK YOUR CARD is our Tuesday column that highlights horses noted in running.
Featured horses engaged today are:
Macgeorge (IRE) ....Chel 3.55
Bosuns Mate ....Chel 5.05
Oriel Star ....Sthl 5.15

FIRST-TIME BLINKERS

HORSES wearing blinkers or visor the first time today (1st-time blinkered horse may previously have worn visor and visa-versa):
Makounji (FR) ....Chel 2.35
Aboo Hom ....Chel 5.05
Gold Drop ....Sedg 2.25
Guile Point ....Sedg 3.35
Stone Ridge (IRE) ....Sthl 4.05
Oriel Star ....Sthl 5.15
Selkirk Rose (IRE) ....Sthl 5.15

SEVEN-DAY WINNERS

WINNERS in the last seven days:
Carrie Pooter ....Sthl 2.15
won Sthl, 10 March
State Approval ....Sthl 4.40
won Sthl, 10 March

AHEAD OF THE HANDICAPPER

AHEAD OF THE HANDICAPPER shows horses Postmark considers well-handicapped on recent form:
Island Chief (IRE) ....Chel 3.55
Step On Eyre (IRE)....................Chel 3.55
Saguaro ....Sthl 3.25
Nifty Norman ....Sthl 5.15

TRAINER TRACE

HORSES having their first run today for a new trainer:
Hors La Loi III (FR) ....Chel 2.00
F Doumen→M C Pipe
Silence Reigns ....Chel 2.00
Sir Michael Stoute→P F Nicholls
Tell The Nipper (IRE) ....Chel 4.30
Michael Hourigan→M C Pipe
Ella Falls (IRE) ....Sedg 3.35
Miss J F Craze→J A Moore
Ironside Princess ....Sedg 3.35
R Simpson→G M Moore
Crashballoo (IRE) ....Sedg 4.50
P Cheesbrough→J Wade
Dromore Dream (IRE) ....Sedg 4.50
Mrs J Brown→G J Markham
Integrity Boy ....Sedg 4.50
N Tinkler→Miss A Armitage
Majic Rain ....Sedg 4.50
B Ellison→Allan Dickman
Mischievous Andy (IRE) ....Sedg 4.50
Francis Berry→A J Balmer
Polynth ....Sedg 4.50
W Brown→Mrs Lynne Ward
Ron's Pet ....Sthl 1.45
R Hannon→K R Burke
My Legal Eagle (IRE) ....Sthl 2.15
E G Bevan→R J Price
Smart (IRE) ....Sthl 2.15
Sir Mark Prescott→Andrew Reid
Genius (IRE) ....Sthl 3.25
S Dow→D W Chapman

NEWMARKET (JULY) FAVOURITES

1995+	NON-HANDICAPS WINS-RACES		£1 STAKE	HANDICAPS WINS-RACES		£1 STAKE
2yo	48-98	49%	+7.81	5-19	26%	−4.25
3yo+	45-119	38%	−8.68	51-175	29%	+14.23
Total	93-217	43%	−0.87	56-194	29%	+9.98

And this is how the *Racing Post* presents the results:

Ascot

GOING: GOOD TO FIRM (good in places); GOOD after first race.

Stalls: Straight Course - Stands' side; Round Course - Inside; Old Mile - Outside
Analysis: GRAHAM DENCH & BRUCE JACKSON
Betting details: BILL HOOKER
Comments: STEVE TAYLOR

2.00 Gardner Merchant Cumberland Lodge Stakes (Class A) (Group 3)
[OFF 2.00]
1m4f

For: 3-y-o and up **1st** £32,150 **2nd** £12,170 **3rd** £5,960 **4th** £2,720

1   **CAPRI** (5) 3 8-7 ow1 ....(110) **K Fallon**
ch c by Generous (IRE)–Island Jamboree (USA) (Explodent (USA))

(H R A Cecil) *prominent, keen hold early, tracked leader 3f out, driven to lead inside final, 2f, stayed on gamely when challenged throughout final furlong* bets of £3,000–£540, £10,000–£2,000, £5,000–£1,000, £3,500–£700, £2,500–£500(x3), £2,250–£500 and £1,800–£400   [op 5/1 tchd 11/2] **9/2**

2   ¾ **RABAH** (6) 3 8-9 ....(113) R Hills
b c by Nashwan (USA)–The Perfect Life (IRE) (Try My Best (USA))

(J L Dunlop) *led, ridden and headed inside final 2f, rallied gamely final furlong, no extra near finish* bets of £1,500–£500, £2,750–£1,000, £2,200–£800, £1,650–£600(x2), £1,100–£400(x4), £5,000–£2,000(x6), £2,500–£1,000(x4), £1,000–£400(x2), £1,125–£500, £900–£400 including office money   [op 11/4 tchd 3/1 in a place] **9/4F**

3   1¼ **SASURU** (7) 5 9-0 ....(114) R Cochrane
b c by Most Welcome–Sassalya (Sassafras (FR))

(G Wragg) *mid-division, driven and headway 3f out, stayed on to chase leaders final furlong, soon one pace* bet of £20,000–£1,000 each-way   [op 16/1] **20/1**

4   ½ **CLERKENWELL** (USA) (2) 5 9-0 ....(110) J Reid
(Sir Michael Stoute) *broke well, steadied, headway from 4f out, driven to chase leaders but hung badly right inside final 2f, not run on* bet of £20,000–£1,600 each-way   [op 10/1] **14/1**

5   3 **CRIMSON TIDE** (IRE) (3) 4 9-5 ....(114) M Hills
(J W Hills) *keen hold, held up in rear, headway 3f out, one pace final 2f* bet of £7,000–£700.   [op 8/1] **10/1**

6   ½ **STRATEGIC CHOICE** (USA) (8) 7 9-0 ....(115) T Quinn
(P F I Cole) *chased leaders, driven over 3f out, weakened 2f out*   [op 5/1] **7/1**

7   1¼ **SCORNED** (GER) (1) 3 8-6 ....(108) S Whitworth
(I A Balding) *held up in rear, driven along 3f out, not pace to reach leaders* bets of £2,750–£500, £5,000–£1,000   [op 9/2 tchd 7/1] **13/2**

8   2 **FRUITS OF LOVE** (USA) (9) 3 8-11 ....(114) D Holland
(M Johnston) *keen hold early, held up in rear, shaken up 4f out, hung right and no response 2f out* bet of £6,000–£600   [op 8/1 tchd 12/1 in places] **11/1**

9   1¼ **KINGFISHER MILL** (USA) (4) 4 9-5 ....(111) Pat Eddery
(Mrs J Cecil) *chased leader, ridden over 3f out, soon weakened*   [op 10/1 tchd 14/1 in places] **12/1**

9 ran   **TIME** 2m 31.69s (fast by 0.31s)   **SP TOTAL PERCENT** 111
1st OWNER: H R H Prince Fahd Salman BRED: Newgate Stud Co TRAINER: H R A Cecil at Newmarket, Suffolk
2nd OWNER: Hamdan Al Maktoum
3rd OWNER: A E Oppenheimer
TOTE WIN £4.70; PL £1.60, £1.30, £4.30; DF £4.00; CSF £12.91

ANALYSIS   **CAPRI** justified connections' decision to drop him back half a mile in distance when returning from 11 weeks off in most determined fashion.

Henry Cecil admitted afterwards that he had "made a mistake by running Capri over too long a trip".

He said: "We thought he would stay further than a mile and a half, but we got it wrong, so we gave him a break and brought him back a fresh horse."

A crack at next month's St Simon Stakes at Newbury is on the cards for the colt, who is likely to stay in training.

The rain held off long enough for **Rabah**, and he went down fighting, as ever. He is a tough horse to beat under these conditions. Suitable opportunities will be hard to find with the ground due to change, but Angus Gold, representing the owner, said he hopes the colt, who "never runs a bad race and was beaten by a better one", will stay in training.

Sasuru's problems have been well chronicled and this was much his best performance of the season-he looked for a moment as if he might trouble the first two. Geoff Wragg was understandably "delighted" and will run him in either the Champion Stakes ("the logical next race") or the Rothmans International at Woodbine.

Clerkenwell once again gave the impression that something may be hurting him. He travelled well through most of the race once again, but edged behind the principals inside the last 2f.

Crimson Tide won a weak race at Epsom and faced a tough task with a penalty. He was never going to trouble the first two.

Strategic Choice is not the force he was, **Scorned** might have found this too soon after Newbury and would have appreciated more give, and both **Fruits Of Love** and last year's winner **Kingfisher Mill** were disappointments.[GD]

Timeform

The late Phil Bull, a shrewd judge of a horse and its capabilities, an incisive and learned writer about them, and a vigorous campaigner for the good of racing, started *Timeform* in the 1940s preceded by his annual volumes of *Best Horses*. Using time figures to back up his inimitable comments and observation of individual horses, Bull eventually evolved a system whereby each horse with sufficient form was given a numerical rating representing its merit or otherwise. This remains as an essential and distinguishing feature of *Timeform* today, as well as the use of the letter 'p' in its evaluations in order to indicate that improvement is likely.

However, for a long time now, *Timeform* has been a considerable and prospering organisation at its headquarters in Halifax, Yorkshire. Led by its chairman, Reg Griffin, it is constantly improving and adding to its services for the racing enthusiast.

The weekly *Timeform Black Book*, both for the Flat and National Hunt, is a long-established feature. Thirty years ago, it used to be pocket-sized but has long outgrown that format. Here are samples of its contents, including the entry on *Desert Orchid* in 1986 before he won his first King George VI Chase and the comments on one of 1998's stars, *Swain*:

DESERT OF WIND 4 b.c. Lyphard–Polynesienne (Relko) leggy, sparely-made colt; fair performer on Flat, won 9f minor event in July but wandered under pressure and also looked none too genuine on final start; sold out of L. Cumani's stable 6,200 gns Newmarket Autumn Sales; jumped none too fluently but ran well until hanging and weakening approaching the last when remote fifth to Ghofar in Daily Express Triumph Hurdle Trial at Cheltenham in December; needs to brush up on his jumping, but should improve (16d Dec 6). R. Hollinshead. –p

DESERT ORCHID 8 gr.g. Grey Mirage–Flower Child (Brother) (1985/6 16f* c17g* c16f* c16m* c20g* c16d^w c16s² c16m² c20g² c20g) sturdy, useful-looking gelding; very smart hurdler; has developed into an equally good chaser, and at Ascot in December won valuable 8-runner Frogmore Handicap by 12 lengths from Charcoal Wally rallying from 2 out and forging clear; had won quite valuable 4-runner handicap at Sandown in October; very good fourth, beaten 5½ lengths, behind Church Warden in very valuable limited handicap at Ascot in between; stays 2½m but best form at 2m; acts on any going with possible exception of heavy; best form on a right-handed track (ran creditably at Cheltenham eighth start); sometimes sweats up; ran poorly when tried in blinkers; bold-jumping front runner, inclined to make the odd mistake; game and genuine; sure to win more races (c20d* c20g⁴ c16g* Dec 13). D. Elsworth. c158 ?

DESTINY BAY 9 b.g. Deep Run–Sweet Counter (Tanavar) (1985/ 86 c16f* c16s*(dis)) tall, close-coupled gelding; fairly useful chaser; first past post in handicaps at Ascot and Cheltenham (relegated to second in conditional jockeys races) in first half of last season; showed he retains all his ability when around 7 lengths fourth of 7 behind impressive Pearlyman in handicap at Cheltenham in December, travelling strongly until after 2 out; barely stays 2½m when the ground is on the soft side, but probably acts on any going; finds little off bridle and needs holding up as long as possible; takes a good hold and may prove best with strong handling; has the ability to win more races (c17d c16d⁴ Dec 6). N. Henderson. c131 –

DESTROY 8 b. or br.h. Annihilate 'Em–Nun Better (Bupers) (1985/6 16g 16s² 17s³ ⁴7s² 17d⁴ 16f*) neat horse; in frame in novice hurdles prior to winning one at Worcester last May; got home narrowly from Whither Goest Thou in 24-runner handicap 106

8v⁵ Oct 21] IR 2,000F: lengthy filly: first foal: dam Italian 2-y-o 6f and 7.5f winner: modest maiden: creditable effort in first-time blinkers latest start: stays 1m: acts on heavy ground. *J. Parkes* (47 Ha8g 31 No8g 30 Ri10m)

SUTTON BANK 2 b.c. (May 11) Clantime 101 – Saja (USA) 56 (Ferdinand (USA)) [1998 6m 6d 7d Nov 2] second foal: dam thrice-raced granddaughter of sister to Mill Reef: always behind in maidens at Catterick and Redcar. *J. L. Eyre* (39 Ct6m 36 Ct6d)   –

SVELTANA 6 b.m. Soviet Star (USA) 128 – Sally Brown 120 (Posse (USA) 130) [1997 NR :: 1998 NR] leggy, angular filly: shows knee action: fair handicapper: probably stayed 1¼m: sold 36,000 gns in 1996, 65,000 gns in 1997. *G. Wragg*   –

SWAFFHAM 2 ch.c. (Jan 19) Whittingham (IRE) 104 – Nellie O'Dowd (USA) (Diesis 133) [1998 5d 5v⁴ Mar 30] 5,000Y: leggy colt: third foal: half-brother to French 9f and 11f winner Irish Full (by Full Extent): dam ran once over hurdles: sire (by Fayruz) Italian sprinter: some promise when tenth of 17 to Charlene Lacy in minor event at Doncaster on debut, possibly unsuited by heavy ground (soon off bridle and no impression from halfway) in maiden auction at Hamilton 4 days later. *M. W. Easterby* (48 Do5d)   58

SWAGGER 2 ch.g. (Jan 28) Generous (IRE) 139 – Widows Walk (Habitat 134) [1998 6v Oct 21] 52,000Y: seventh foal: half-brother to 3 winners, including 1¼m winner Sadler's Walk (by Sadler's Wells) and 1¼m to 1½m winner Rainbow Walk (by Rainbow Quest), both fairly useful: dam once-raced daughter of 1000 Guineas winner On The House: 20/1, shaped with some promise when seventh of 12 in maiden at Newcastle, unable to quicken and showing inexperience at halfway then soon eased (trainer fined £1,000 under 'non-triers' rule and horse banned for 30 days): subsequently gelded: will be suited by 1¼m+: likely to improve. *Sir Mark Prescott*   –p

SWAIN (IRE) 6 b.h. Nashwan (USA) 135 – Love Smitten (CAN) (Key To The Mint (USA)) [1997 12g² 12s* 11g³ 12f :: 1998 a10f² 12g² 12d³ 12m* 10d* a10f³ Nov 7] robust, attractive horse: has a fluent, rather round action: top-class performer: placed in Dubai World Cup (strong-finishing short-head second to Silver Charm), Coronation Cup at Epsom and falsely-run Hardwicke Stakes at Royal Ascot on first 3 starts this season: returned to very best when gaining repeat win in King George VI And Queen Elizabeth Diamond Stakes at Ascot in July by length from High-Rise, leading over 1f out, then beat Alborada comfortably by a length in Esat Digifone Champion Stakes at Leopardstown: every chance, hung badly right under very strong pressure when length third to Awesome Again and Silver Charm in Breeders' Cup Classic at Churchill Downs last time: effective at 1¼m given truly-run race and stays 1¾m: acts on any going: tough, game and consistent, and a credit to his connections: to stud in Kentucky in 1999. *Saeed bin Suroor* (131 As12m 129′As12s 111 Ep12g)   135

SWALLOW FLIGHT (IRE) 2 b.c. (Apr 20) Bluebird (USA) 125 – Mirage 60 (Red Sunset 120) [1998 6m 6m² 7g³ 8d² Oct 19] IR 30,000F, IR 62,000Y: tall, attractive colt: has a moderate quick action: fourth foal: half-brother to a German 1996 2-y-o 6.5f winner by Thatching: dam, modest maiden here, later won listed sprints in Germany: useful performer: placed in maidens and listed event last 3 starts, best effort when length second of 7 to Three Green Leaves at Pontefract on last-named: stays 1m. *G. Wragg* (92 Po8d 82 Nm7g 80 Nm6m)   95

The *Timeform Racecards* are another popular service. Here is an abbreviated illustration from a Royal Ascot card in 1998:

SECOND RACE (TV BBC1)   TRW   127 117 127 120 122 (Average 123)

3.05	THE QUEEN MARY STAKES (A)	5f
	(Group 3)	
	£45,000 added 2yo fillies	

---

1 AMAZING DREAM (IRE) 2 b.f. (Feb 14) Thatching 131 – Aunty Eileen
1482   (Ahonoora 122) [1998 5.2m⁵ 5d⁴ May 26] IR 31,000Y: good-quartered filly: 5d 103+ L
sixth reported living foal: half-sister to several winners, including fairly useful   5m 80+ W
1995 2-y-o 6f winner (stayed 1m) Astuti (by Waajib): dam unraced half-sister
to smart sprinter Lugana Beach: 9/1, stepped up on debut form when under 7
lengths fourth of 7 to Bint Allayl in listed race at Sandown, disputing lead
until over 1f out: capable of better still. *R. HANNON* (94Sa5d 82Nb5m)

108 p

8-8 Drawn 17   Dane O'Neill
Black, red chevron hoop and sleeves, black armlets, hooped cap (Mrs P. & Mr P. Jubert)

2 ATLANTIC DESTINY (IRE) 2 b.f. (Apr 23) Royal Academy (USA)
1721   130 – Respectfully (USA) (The Minstrel (CAN) 135) [1998 6g² 6g² Jun 5]   6g 106+ L
26,000Y: tall, useful looking filly: has plenty of scope: half-sister to several   6g 100+ M
winners, including Irish 3-y-o Make No Mistake (by Darshaan), 7f winner at
2 yrs, and Irish 1¼m and 2m winner Limbo Lady (by Theatrical): dam, ran
once in France, from family of Be My Guest: won 7-runner maiden at York in
May by 1½ lengths from Guinea Hunter, shaken up to assert approaching final
1f: duly improved a good deal from that when 2½ lengths second of 7 to Lady
Angharad in listed race at Epsom following month, helping force strong pace
and a spent force inside final 1f (rated better than result): open to further
pressure on latter course: open to further improvement. *M. JOHNSTON*
(106Ep6g 94Yo6g)

113 p

8-8 Drawn 7   D. Holland
Aquamarine, black cap (Atlantic Racing Limited)

3 AUBRIETA (USA) 2 b.f. (Mar 4) Dayjur (USA) 137 – Fennel 97 (Slew O'
1223   Gold (USA)) [1998 5.2m⁶ May 15] leggy, quite good-topped filly: first reported   5m 75 W
foal: dam, 2-y-o 6f winner, later successful at up to 1¼m in USA: weak
10/1-shot and decidedly green, never on terms when sixth of 7 to Golden Silca
in minor event at Newbury: should do better. *C. E. BRITTAIN* (75Nb5m)

– p

8-8 Drawn 16   O. Peslier
Grey, maroon triple diamond, white sleeves, grey cap, maroon diamonds (Mr Ali Saeed)

4 BINT ALLAYL 2 b.f. (Jan 19) Green Desert (USA) 127 – Society Lady
1482   (USA) 75 (Mr Prospector (USA)) [1998 5g² 5d* May 26] good-topped filly: 5d 122+ L
second foal: dam, ran 4 times at 2 yrs and should have been as effective at 1m   5g 110 W
as 7f, daughter of champion Canadian filly Queenseau: promising debut
when neck second to more experienced Pipalong in novice event at York:
emphatic winner of 7-runner listed race at Sandown 2 weeks later, travelling
well and showing impressive burst of speed to go clear over 1f out, eased near
finish but still beating Speedy James by 3½ lengths: will stay 6f: capable of
better still, and will prove hard to beat, even in Group company. *M. R.
CHANNON* (120Sa5d 111Yo5g)

126 p

WON 2/1

8-8 Drawn 5   L. Dettori
Yellow, black epaulets (Sheikh Ahmed Al Maktoum)

14 PIPALONG (IRE) 2 b.f. (Jan 26) Pips Pride 117 – Limpopo 49 (Green
1173   Desert (USA) 127) [1998 5s* 5g* May 12] 7,000Y: neat filly: fourth foal: 5g 117+ W
half-sister to a winner in USA by Common Grounds: dam maiden daughter of   5s 103+ M
smart Irish miler Grey Goddess: successful in maiden at Ripon by 12 lengths
from College Music and novice event at York by neck from Bint Allayl: speedy:
a well above-average early-season 2-y-o, should do better again. *T. D.
EASTERBY* (118Yo5g 100Ri5s)

119 p

8-8 Drawn 4   K. Fallon
Light blue, green sleeves, white cap (Mr T. H. Bennett)

Thirteen previous winners suggests a competitive renewal of the Queen Mary, but two fillies stand out. Pipalong is unbeaten in two starts and is noted as "a well above-average early-season 2-y-o". Nevertheless, Bint Allayl looks the pick – "capable of better still, and will prove hard to beat, even in Group company." Rated 7 lb ahead of Pipalong, and 3 lb above the TRW for the race, she must not be missed!

**Result: BINT ALLAYL 2/1 and Pipalong land a
1-2 for Timeform Ratings.**

Timeform Perspective was introduced in order to present information race by race instead of horse by horse, but with the advantage of in-depth analysis. It comes out three times a week in loose-leaf parts. Here is the essence of the *Perspective* entry for the Champion Hurdle 1999:

3226 Smurfit Champion Hdle Challenge   2m110y (8)
       Trophy (Showcase) (A) (Gr 1) (4yo+)
       £138,000

*2515	ISTABRAQ (IRE) *APO'Brien,Ireland* 7-12-0 CFSwan 1/2 4/9f		1
³2881	THEATREWORLD (IRE) *APO'Brien,Ireland* 7-12-0 TPTreacy.. 14 16/1	3½	2
²2515	FRENCH HOLLY (USA) *FMurphy* 8-12-0 AThomton 9/2 11/2	2½	3
ᵘʳ2109	Mister Morose (IRE) *NATwiston-Davies* 9-12-0 CLlewellyn 100/1	1	4
*2881	Nomadic *NMeade,Ireland* 5-12-0 PCarberry 50/1	1¼	5
⁶2763	Tiutchev *DNicholson* 6-12-0 MAFitzgerald 40/1	2	6
⁴2963	Bellator *MissVenetiaWilliams* 6-12-0 NWilliamson 50/1	½	7
²2763	City Hall (IRE) *MrsVCWard* 5-12-0 (v) RThornton 33/1	13	8
*2900	Lady Cricket (FR) *MCPipe* 5-11-9 (b) APMcCoy 14 16/1	3	9
²2935	Midnight Legend *DNicholson* 5-12-0 ADobbin 50/1	4	10
*2935	Grey Shot *IABalding* 7-12-0 JOsborne....................................... 33/1	14	11
³2935	Upgrade *NATwiston-Davies* 5-12-0 CMaude........................... 66/1	17	12
³2515	Zafarabad (IRE) *DNicholson* 5-12-0 RJohnson........................... 40/1		f
²2963	Blowing Wind (FR) *MCPipe* 6-12-0 (b) RDunwoody 33/1		bd

3.15race Mr J. P. McManus 14ran 3m56.82

This looked a largely substandard renewal of the Champion Hurdle, with only Istabraq and French Holly having form anywhere near what is usually required to win the race, and only one or possibly 2 of the others open to improvement; the most notable absentee was Dato Star but several others who'd have had place claims on their form this season were also missing—Master Beveled, the Tote Gold Trophy winner Decoupage and the perennially-injured Relkeel among them; the market for the race had long been dominated by the 1998 winner Istabraq, and with the ground having dried up too much for French Holly to be at his best he was left with a straightforward task to follow up; however, the way in which he was pushed out and the proximity of the likes of Theatreworld, Mister Morose and Nomadic suggests the Champion was some way from his sparkling best; the pace was just a steady one to the second flight, and the time doesn't compare favourably with the opening novice hurdle. ISTABRAQ, who'd sweated up quite a bit by the start, won for the second year running despite being not quite at his best; waited with in touch, he was briefly niggled at to close up after the fifth then led on the bridle 2 out before quickening decisively to go clear into the straight, 6 lengths up on French Holly at the last but unable to extend that margin; he'd looked as good as ever in the Irish Champion and hopefully will be able to prove it at Punchestown; post-race quotes for next year's Champion Hurdle of less than 2/1 suggest as much as anything the lack of opposition around with few serious challengers on the horizon, and it's clear that at present the staying division is stronger than the 2m one. THEATREWORLD had suggested at Leopardstown that he retained all his ability and showed it by finishing second for the third Champion Hurdle running; in now characteristic fashion he was behind, had plenty to do still 3 out but stayed on well after the next to go second on the run-in; though a durable and genuine hurdler, he's fully exposed as very smart at best. FRENCH HOLLY didn't have the soft ground to make it enough of a test of stamina and was some way below his best; pushed along to lead after the fifth, he was headed 2 out and couldn't quicken, not fluent at the last; in prize money terms he's had a good campaign though it's arguable that this has been a second wasted season, following his second one in bumpers, and that might prove against him now he's set to go chasing (for which he looks an ideal type) at the relatively advanced age of 8.▪▪•• ▪ ━ ▪ ▪▪ MIDNIGHT LEGEND's form this season was not up to the standard needed for this race but even so he ran below form, niggled at by the fifth and weakening before the next. GREY SHOT looked really sour beforehand and his performance matched that, looking decidedly reluctant when taken on for the lead and dropping away from the fifth; this was totally out of character with his previous performances on the Flat and over hurdles and perhaps all wasn't well with him. UPGRADE, winner of last year's Triumph Hurdle, had done nothing this season to suggest he was worth his place in this field and, though he really took the eye beforehand, he made little impression after starting slowly, almost last and going nowhere when hampered at the fifth; a drop in class and a step up in trip are needed. ZAFARABAD had been niggled at from an early stage and was not well placed when falling at the fifth. BLOWING WIND, winner of the County Hurdle at this meeting last season, was niggled at from an early stage and had only a couple behind him when brought down at the fifth.

For further *Timeform* services, see also under **Selected Annuals** and **Computer Aid** at the end of the chapter. In addition, there is an informative and excellent *Timeform* website on the Internet at www.timeform.com. It has recently been up-dated and (see below) laudably has a no-nonsense dig at fancy graphics. For Internet users, the *Timeform* website is highly recommended.

Timeform Body Page

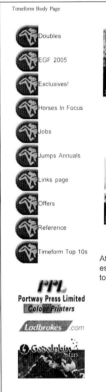

Doubles

EGF 2005

Exclusives!

Horses In Focus

Jobs

Jumps Annuals

Links page

Offers

Reference

Timeform Top 10s

PPL
Portway Press Limited
Colour Printers

Ladbrokes .com

Godolphin

2004 STALLION STATISTICAL REVIEW
OUT FOR THE DECEMBER SALES @ £25– IT'S A MUST

Packed with profitable pointers—and out now!

20/1 WINNER ON FRIDAY

Timeform's team of experts have identified fifty jumpers to follow this winter, and the winners are already flowing.

Tynedale **WON 20/1** made it a black Friday for the bookmakers, and you can be sure that there are plenty more winners to come.

£431 CLEAR PROFIT IN THE 2004 FLAT
to a £10 level stake on every start

At just **£5.95** (post free in UK) *Timeform Horses To Follow* is an essential purchase for any punter. Call **01422 330540** (24 hours) now to order your copy.

Stay ahead with Timeform Select   full story

Timeform Select, which costs **just 6 credits**, is the perfect complement to *Timeform Race Cards* and *Daily Form Guides*.
Every edition is packed with articles aimed at finding future winners.

......

Essential for the Jumps

'Chasers & Hurdlers 2003/04' is out now!

Four new Timeform annuals, including the renowned *Chasers & Hurdlers 2003/04*, are out now for the jumps. Click here for more details and for a **free twelve-page sample**.

Weekly papers
Racing Post Weekender and *Raceform Update* – these publications in their different ways provide excellent service in filling out the day-to-day racing details and supplying background material, much of it fascinating and of value in assessing the immediate past and future. There are, in weekly instalments, form records which can be collected together to give a permanent record. For those who cannot afford the more established form books, this is more than useful, but the format means that the record is essentially for study at home rather than pocket-size reference on the racecourse. They also give good resumés of what the betting market has shown in the way of likely future winners during the preceding week. The *Update* is the successor to the old established *Handicap Book* and also incorporates that old favourite *The Racehorse*, while the *Weekender* scores with some first-class interviews (accompanied by statistics) with trainers, particularly the smaller ones. Full coverage is given to the racing immediately ahead, with associated special features on big occasions, as well as sections on time figures and up-dating of handicap ratings.

Racing and Football Outlook – a relatively inexpensive paper in which, as the title suggests, football coverage in good detail shares the scene with racing. Until quite recently it was the only paper left where a back page column of tips, sometimes containing long-priced winners, retained an Edwardian vocabulary ('one to keep on the right side is...' and 'strong information concerns...') hinting of touts hidden with binoculars at the ready on the gallops. Sadly, that has now disappeared.

Selected magazines
Horse and Hound (weekly) – racing receives a certain amount of coverage, with Tim Richards reporting comprehensively and colourfully; Julian Muscat, Marcus Armytage and Tony Coleman contribute, as does Sue Montgomery with good features on breeding.

Pacemaker (monthly) – this is the official publication of the Thoroughbred Breeders' Association, incorporating what used to be *Weatherbys' Bulletin*. It is an extremely lively, smartly produced, attractive publication and a great pleasure to read, with excellent up-to-the-minute articles on the current racing scene, often with a refreshing thrust of controversy. These are balanced by specialised pieces concerning all aspects of breeding, with accompanying vital statistics, and the periodical is liberally illustrated by the sport's leading photographers. *Pacemaker*, indeed, is the thoroughbred of racing publications for professionals, written by experts and read by enthusiasts.

Selected annuals
The Sun Guide To The Flat 2004 (there is also an equivalent over the jumps) – 160 pages of close-packed and valuable information, including Horses to Follow, Interviews with Trainers, Jockey and Trainer Statistics for the past six seasons, Big Race Guides and Course Details. Highly recommended.

Racing & Football Outlook Racing Guide 2004 is another worthwhile annual, running to 250 pages, with a review of the 2003 season, a preview of 2004, comprehensive details and some fascinating statistics on ten top trainers and much else besides. Highly recommended.

The Racing Post Horses To Follow Flat 2004 is an essential guide to the Tote / *Racing Post* Ten To Follow competition. It contains in-depth profiles of all 500 horses in the contest. Special features include: Marten Julian's incomparable and essential dark horses; Craig Thake's summer of big race trends; the inside track from Ireland, France and the major training centres; the lowdown from leading jockeys and trainers; and Rachel Pagones highlights ten horses bred to excel in 2004.

100 Winners For 2004 (Raceform) and *Timeform Horses To Follow 2004 Flat Season* – both well worth buying for horses to watch during the season.

Ahead On The Flat – by Mark Howard. His opinion of the top Flat horses to follow in 2004 is contained in an excellent and attractively produced comparative newcomer to this competitive field. He features 40 top prospects with emphasis on lightly raced 3-y-o; stable interviews with 12 leading trainers; French horses to follow; top Irish horses; and 'Ahead of the Handicapper' plus a section on the Tote / *Racing Post* Ten To Follow competition. The NH equivalent, *One Jump Ahead*, is equally worthwhile.

Racehorses of 2003 and *Chasers and Hurdlers 2002–2003* – *Timeform*'s incomparable volumes running to more than 1,000 pages each and a total of about one million well-chosen words. These books, with their exhaustive, definitive essays on all horses in training, are the most eagerly awaited annuals of all. The relative costs may appear to be high but with close attention to the text can more than be recouped from the betting ring.

The Timeform Statistical Review – a valuable and detailed back-up to *Racehorses* (half-price if bought at the same time as that book). Contains analyses and statistics of more than 100 trainers, and with what type of horse they are most successful. For stallions, the average quality of their progeny is given, while leading trainers and stallions are minutely scrutinised by *Timeform* experts.

The Directory Of The Turf 2004 – comprehensive (552 pages) guide to owners, trainers, jockeys, studs, Turf Authorities, racecourses and every aspect of the racing and bloodstock scene, including very detailed international coverage and major Group One results from round the world.

Raceform Flat Annual 2004 and *Chaseform 2002–2003 Jumps Annual* – the bound versions of the form book (see later in chapter). The *Flat Annual* has a companion annual, *Racehorse Record Flat*, the first volume of which was published by *Raceform* in 1996. The latest is *Racehorse Record Flat 2004*, edited by Ashley Rumney. It is an A–Z statistical guide to horses that ran during the 2003 season. Running to 912 pages and generously illustrated, this, like its predecessors, makes a highly worthwhile and lasting informative record of the season.

Raceform Horses in Training – another book which has long been an automatic yearly addition to the shelf. It is pocket-sized (but quite fat these days), and the title is self-explanatory. The 2004 edition (over 650 pages) contains details of 17,000 horses, 612 trainers (some in France and Ireland), both Flat and National Hunt or both, as well as useful details about racecourses, jockeys' weights and retainers, excellent Turf statistics up to date, big-race results and fixtures, as well as bloodstock statistics – altogether a great expansion of information over the past ten years or so, making it a most valuable reference book. The illustration below from an earlier edition gives a sample of the detailed information about trainers which forms the main part of the annual:

256   MR B. W. HILLS, Lambourn

Postal: South Bank Stables, Lambourn, Newbury, Berks, RG16 7LL.

Phone: OFFICE LAMBOURN (0488) 71548 FAX LAMBOURN (0488) 72823

1 CASTING SHADOWS, 5, gr m Chief Singer—Six Ashes Mr S. Skelding
2 FURTHER FLIGHT, 8, gr g Pharly (FR)—Flying Nelly Mr S. Wingfield Digby
3 LAKE POOPO (IRE), 4, b f Persian Heights—Bolivia (GER) Mr R. E. Sangster
4 MARCO MAGNIFICO (USA), 4, b br g Bering—Viscosity (USA) Mrs Leonard Simpson
5 MONSIEUR DUPONT (IRE), 4, b g Alzao (USA)—Katie Koo Mr Wafic Said
6 NORTHERN BIRD, 4, ch f Interrex (CAN)—Partridge Brook Mr John E. Bradley
7 RINGLET (USA), 4, b f Secreto (USA)—Double Lock Sir Eric Parker
8 RITTO, 4, b c Arctic Tern (USA)—Melodrama Sheikh Mohammed
9 YAWL, 4, b f Rainbow Quest (USA)—Bireme Mr R. D. Hollingsworth

THREE-YEAR-OLDS

10 ARZINA (USA), ch f Zilzal (USA)—Agri Dagi (USA) Sheikh Mohammed
11 AS SHARP AS, ch f Hansome Sailor—As Sharp Mr D. O. Pickering
12 AVIRA, b f Dancing Brave (USA)—Sephira Mr K. Abdulla
13 BOLAS, br f Unfuwain (USA)—Three Stars Mr K. Abdulla
14 BRAARI (USA), b f Gulch (USA)—So Cozy (USA) Mr Hamdan Al-Maktoum
15 CLASSIC MODEL (IRE), b g High Line—Fast Car (FR) K. Al-Said
16 CLASSY, gr f Kalaglow—Julia Flyte Mrs J. M. Corbett
17 COMMENDATION DAY (IRE), b g Common Grounds—Sarah Siddons Mrs S. Brown
18 CURRENT SPEECH (IRE), b c Thatching—Lady Aladdin Mr J. Hanson
19 DELIVER (IRE), b f Rousillon (USA)—Livry (USA) Lucayan Stud Ltd, Mr K. Rawlings
20 DESIDERATA, b c Green Desert (USA)—Yildizlar Sheikh Mohammed
21 EQTESAAD (USA), br c Danzig (USA)—Last Feather (USA) Mr Hamdan Al-Maktoum
22 FIRE LILY, ch f Unfuwain (USA)—Indian Lily Sheikh Mohammed
23 GLIDINGONBY (IRE), b f Alzao (USA)—Tremulous (USA) Mr R. E. Sangster

48 TORCH ROUGE, b c Warning—Sistabelle Mr J. Hanson
49 TRES CHER (IRE), b f Be My Guest (USA)—Nancy Chere (USA) Mr R. E. Sangster
50 TRYST (IRE), b c Thatching—Finalist Mr K. Abdulla

TWO-YEAR-OLDS

51 B f 6/5 Known Fact (USA)—Abeer (USA) (Dewan (USA)) Mr K. Abdulla
52 B f 10/4 Dancing Brave (USA)—Ack's Secret (USA) (Ack Ack (USA)) Mr K. Abdulla
53 ASTROLABE, b c 6/2 Rainbow Quest (USA)—Sextant (Star Appeal) Mr R. D. Hollingsworth

97 SIERRA ESTRELLA, b f 12/4 Shareef Dancer (USA)—Asteroid Field (USA) (Forli (ARG)) Sheikh Mohammed
98 SPARROWHAWK (IRE), b f 14/3 Doyoun—Sparrow's Air (USA) (Assert) Mr R. E. Sangster
99 TAKLIF (IRE), b c 20/4 Sadler's Wells (USA)—Porphyrine (FR) (Habitat) Mr Hamdan Al-Maktoum
100 TEN PAST SIX, ch c 24/5 Kris—Tashinsky (USA) (Nijinsky (CAN)) Mr J. Hanson
101 TORCH VERT (IRE), b c 9/4 Law Society (USA)—Arctic Winter (CAN) (Briartic (CAN)) Mr J. Hanson
102 WARNING STAR, b f 5/4 Warning—Blade of Grass (Kris) Mr Stephen Crown
103 WICKEN WONDER (IRE), b f 5/5 Distant Relative—Blue Guitar (Cure The Blues (USA)) Mr William J. Heard
104 YACHT, ch c 7/6 Warning—Bireme (Grundy) Mr R. D. Hollingsworth
105 B c 20/5 Distant Relative—Yildizlar (Star Appeal) K. Al-Said
106 B f 25/2 Rainbow Quest (USA)—Zamayem (Sadler's Wells (USA)) K. Al-Said

Other Owners: Mr A. R. B. Aspinall, Mr T. Bailey, Mrs June Doyle, Lt. Cmdr. Per. A. Flaate, Mr B. W. Hills, Mrs Marjan Kindersley, Mr W. McDonald, Mr Paul McNamara, Lady Rose Musker, Mrs Jane Scrope, Mr Edward P. Winfield, Mr Christopher Wright.

Jockey (Flat): Pat Eddery (8-4).

Apprentice: S McCarthy (7-3).

Raceform Trainers Flat Statistics 2004 is another outstandingly fascinating 650-page reference book with details of every winning British trainer from J. Akehurst to Geoff Wragg (but also including the impressive record of Aidan O'Brien from Ireland). It gives every detail of their performances, broken down into age-groups, monthly figures, distances and all the details of their showing at the courses where they ran, their jockeys, winning horses and their owners. Incredibly useful and a definition of the word 'comprehensive'.

Form books

The bedrock of finding winners is the form book in whatever shape it takes. Today, *Raceform* (and its National Hunt equivalent, *Chaseform*) is the official record, published weekly in loose-leaf form, the parts being put into a pocket-sized cord-tied binder. This is how the form book (*McCall's Racing Chronicle*, price 1s 6d, the equivalent of 7p) looked on Derby Day in 1893:

---

405   EPSOM, MAY, 1993.   406

352 Coldwell 8-9......G.Chaloner -
8 to 1 on Glare, 3 to 1 agst School-
book. 10 Ladas, 12½ Mecca. Won a
length and a half; a head; School-
book a bad fourth.

Ashtend Plate (Selling) of 195l. 5 fur.
383*Huelva 3y 9-5 .... Calder 1
352*Blankney 5y 10-5 G.Chaloner 2
Batty 3y 9-5 ......Woodburn 3
816*Bog Myrtle 5y 10-5..T.Loates 4
392 Dulverton 5y 10-2 ....Warne -
849*Red Cent 4y 10-2......Pearce -
853 Miss Bendigo 4y 10-2
R.Chaloner -
849 Perilla 5y 10-2........J.Watts -
867 Odd Man 3y 9-8..S.Chandley -
Craig Maskeldie 3y 9-8
G.Barrett -
Won and Lost 3y 9-5 Rickaby -
816 Hecla 3y 9-5 ....F.Webb -
257 Virtus 3y 9-5 ......M.Cannon -
880*Iceni 3y 9-5 ....Barker -
6 to 1 agst Bog Myrtle. 6½ Virtus, 7
Craig Maskeldie. 100 to 8 each Huelva.
Won and Lost. 100 to 6 Blankney, 20
Perilla, 25 each Hecla, Iceni, Dulverton, 33 Batty, 40 each Red Cent, Odd
Man, Miss Bendigo. Won a head;
same each 2nd, 3rd and 4th. Winner
bought in 310gs.

Norbury Plate (Handicap) of 175l. 1 mi.
365 Halma 3y 8-5 ....G.Chaloner 1
296 Dazzle aged 10-4 S.Chandley 2
Anna 4y 8-12 ......M.Cannon 3
845*Ellerton 6y 10-0......J.Watts -
336 Rosellen 3y 8-8.......Finlay -
2 to 1 agst Anna, 3 Ellerton, 7 to 2
Dazzle, 4 Halma, 8 Rosellen. Won
four lengths; a length.

WEDNESDAY.—*Caterham Plate* of
195l. for 2y old. 5 fur.
366 Kiss 8-11..........T.Loates 1
822 Austral 8-8.........Wheeler 2
257 Magnus 8-11 ....White 3
820 Lady Carlton II. 8-8
R. Chaloner -
Assignee 8-8 ......G. Barrett -
Cataplasm 8-11..G. Chaloner -
204 New Zealand 8-8..M.Cannon -
FitzGalliard 9-0 ....F.Webb -
Sublimity 8-11 ......Rickaby -
11 to 8 agst Cataplasm, 2 Kiss. 10
Magnus. 14 Austral. Won two lengths;
four lengths; Lady Carlton fourth.

Epsom Town Plate (H'cap) of 100l.
5 fur.
337*Ejector 4y 8-4......G.Barrett 1
217 Lucky Devil 3y 7-10 Bradford 2

301 Bengaline 3y 6-10 P.Chaloner 3
Godwit 5y 8-7 ....Warne -
390 Sorcerer 4y 8-6....M.Cannon -
370 Bonnie Queen 3y 8-0
J. Woodburn -
272 Moonflower 3y 8-0 ....Calder -
382*Poppy 3y 7-10 ....Allsopp -
Hawkweed 3y 7-4 ..T.Loates -
849 Will o' the Wisp 3y 7-0 ..Joy -
258 Melbourne 3y 7-0 ....H.Town -
Miss Broadley 3y 6-12 ..Inge -
363 Lyrique 3y 6-9 ....Gough -
4 to 1 agst Hawkweed, 9 to 2 Ejector
5½ Sorcerer, 8 each Bengaline, Moonflower, 10 each Poppy, Lucky Devil,
12½ Lyrique. Won a neck; three-parts
of a length: Hawkweed 4th, Poppy
5th, Sorcerer 6th.

Derby Stakes of 5515l., for 3y old.
1 mi. 4 fur.
363*Isinglass 9-0........T.Loates 1
363 Ravensbury 9-0 ......Barker 2
318 Raeburn 9-0 ....J.Watts 3
865 Peppercorn 9-0......Rickaby 4
353 Son of a Gun 9-0....Calder -
352*Irish Wake 9-0....M.Cannon -
365 Quickly Wise 9-0 R.Chaloner -
317*William 9-0..T. Mullen -
317*William 9-0..........F.Webb -
321 DamePresident 8-9 G.Barrett -
318 Royal Harry 9-0....Bradford -
95 to 40 on Isinglass, 14 agst Irish
Wake, 16 William. 20 each Raeburn,
Dame President, 25 Ravensbury, 33
Son of a Gun, 100 each Quickly Wise.
Lord William, Peppercorn, 200 Royal
Harry. Won a length and a half; two
lengths: bad fourth; Quickly Wise 5th,
Royal Harry 6th. 2m. 43s.

Headley Plate (Selling) of 197l. 6 fur.
290 Pampero 4y 10-0 ....Rickaby 1
56 IndianBrave 4y10-3 M.Cannon 2
371 Semmel 3y 9-2 ......F. Webb 3
Primrose Way 4y 10-3
R. Chaloner -
11 to 8 agst Indian Brave, 2 Semmel
5 Pampero, 6 Primrose Way. Won half
a length; three lengths. Winner bought
in 430gs.

Stanley Stakes of 412l., for 2y old. 5 fur.
Letterewe 8-9 .... Finlay 1
393 Clatterfeet 8-9 ......G.Barrett 2
362*Simon's Bay 9-0 .... J.Watts 3
Bolton 8-12 ....M.Cannon -
256 Drosera 8-12 ....Rickaby -
Sir John Broad 8-9 Bradford -
F. by Foxhall—Nespola 3-6
A. White -

Some progress may be observed by comparison with the following extract from the modern *Raceform* (see Appendix B for meanings of abbreviations). Both *Raceform* (as can be seen from the example) and *Chaseform* now incorporate the *Notebook* comments which used to be recorded in separate loose-leaf binders:

Raceform

1778   VODAFONE DERBY STKS (Gp 1) (3-Y.O C & F) (Class A)
3-45 (3-47) 1m 4f 10y £598,690.00 (£223,210.00: £108,480.00: £45,900.00: £19,825.00: £9,395.00) Stalls: Centre
GOING minus 0.18 sec per fur (GF)

		SP	RR	SF
1125* High-Rise (IRE) (112) (LMCumani) 3-9-0 OPeslier(14) (in rr: 12th st: gd hdwy over 2f out: led 1f out: all out) .....—	1	20/1	122	89
1207² City Honours (USA) (118) (SbinSuroor) 3-9-0 JReid(1) (lw: hld up: 5th st: rdn over 2f out: ev ch fnl f: r.o wl) .....hd	2	12/1	122	89
1207³ Border Arrow (118) (IABalding) 3-9-0 RCochrane(11) (lw: in rr: last st: rdn over 2f out: gd hdwy over 1f out: r.o wl ins fnl f) 2½	3	25/1	119	86
1195a² Sunshine Street (USA) (NMeade,Ireland) 3-9-0 JPMurtagh(2) (leggy: unf: lw: led after 1f: rdn over 3f out: hdd 1f out: unable qckn) .....hd	4	150/1	118	85
1222* Greek Dance (IRE) (117) (MRStoute) 3-9-0 WRSwinburn(3) (lw: a.p: 3rd st: rdn over 3f out: wknd over 1f out: lame) 3	5	5/1³	114	81
1042² The Glow-Worm (IRE) (110) (BWHills) 3-9-0 DHolland(8) (swtg: 13th st: hrd rdn & hdwy 2f out: nvr nrr) 1	6	20/1	113	80
1125² Sadian (111) (HRACecil) 3-9-0 KFallon(7) (lw: chsd ldr 11f out tl over 1f out: sn wknd) 2½	7	25/1	110	77
1506a³ Second Empire (IRE) (APO'Brien,Ireland) 3-9-0 MJKinane(10) (str: scope: 10th st: rdn over 3f out: no hdwy fnl 2f) .....s.h	8	9/2²	110	77
993* Cape Verdi (IRE) (SbinSuroor) 3-8-9 LDettori(5) (lw: hld up: hmpd 5f out: bmpd & 6th st: wknd over 2f out).2½	9	11/4¹	101	68
1737a⁴ Saratoga Springs (CAN) (APO'Brien,Ireland) 3-9-0v WRyan(4) (hld up: rdn 4f out: 7th st: wknd 3f out) 2 10		20/1	104	71
1042* Gulland (113) (GWragg) 3-9-0 MHills(9) (b: b.hind: lw: led 1f: 4th st: rdn over 3f out: wknd over 2f out).....7 11		12/1	94	61
868* Courteous (112) (PFICole) 3-9-0 TQuinn(13) (plld hrd: hld up: slipped 4f out: 8th st: wknd 3f out).....½ 12		14/1	94	61
1325² Mutamam (113) (ACStewart) 3-9-0 MRoberts(15) (plld hrd: 11th & m wd st: bhd fnl 3f).....2½ 13		50/1	91	58
974⁵ Haami (USA) (116) (JLDunlop) 3-9-0 RHills(6) (lw: mid div whn rdn over 4f out: 9th st: bhd fnl 3f) 6 14		20/1	83	50
974* King Of Kings (IRE) (APO'Brien,Ireland) 3-9-0 PatEddery(12) (14th st: a bhd: lame).....7 15		11/2	73	40

(SP 128.3%) 15 Rn

2m 33.88 (-0.62) CSF £213.58 CT £5,428.19 TOTE £15.20: £2.70 £5.10 £6.20 (£102.10) Trio £723.90 OWNER Sheikh Mohammed Obaid Al Maktoum (NEWMARKET) BRED Sheikh Mohammed Obaid al Maktoum

STEWARDS' ENQUIRY Peslier susp. 15 & 19/6/98 (improper riding - failure to allow horse time to respond to whip). Interference to Cape Verdi (IRE) by Courteous 4f out. No action taken.

IN-FOCUS: This was one of the most open and fascinating Derbies in years, with the favourite tag flip-flopping from horse to horse over the last few weeks. It was certainly an extremely high-quality field and was run in the third fastest ever time.

1125* High-Rise (IRE) has followed the same route as Cumani's 1988 Derby winner Kahyasi and even occupies the same box at the stables. He looks a real champion and maintained his unbeaten record in the World's greatest race in an extremely fast time. He certainly had it all to do entering the straight, but he made up a tremendous amount of ground in a very short space of time and struck the front a furlong out. Engaged in a tremendous ding-dong battle with the runner-up, he responded gamely to stern pressure to just hold on. His jockey was later suspended for two days for his use of the whip. His fine turn of foot and battling qualities are sure to hold him in good stead this season and he is the one they all now have to fear in the Irish Derby. (20/1)

1207 City Honours (USA) lost absolutely nothing in defeat and ran a blinder. Throwing down the gauntlet from below the distance, he had a tremendous tussle with the winner in the final furlong and may even have got his head in front for a couple of strides before just losing out. This was a tremendous performance and a decent prize should not be long in coming his way. A rematch with the winner in the Irish Derby looks a mouth-watering prospect. (12/1)

1207 Border Arrow appreciated this trip. Out with the washing until the straight, he made giant strides in the last furlong and a half and came storming through to finish a highly creditable third. This was a tremendous performance and his jockey reported afterwards that he is only half a horse at present, but will make a lovely four-year-old. He will probably have a break and miss the Irish Derby. With some rain, he will have no problems winning a Group race. (25/1)

1195a Sunshine Street (USA) appeared to be here to make up the numbers, but he relished the step up in trip and ran the race of his life as he took the field along. With a useful advantage early in the straight, he certainly had his opponents worried but, collared a furlong out, failed to find another gear. (150/1)

1222* Greek Dance (IRE) looked in really good shape and was faced with the acid test after two wins in minor events so far this season. Never far away, he was bustled along early in the straight, but had run out of steam below the distance. Swinburn thought the colt was unsuited by the course and he is certainly up to winning a Group race. Unfortunately it transpired that he was badly lame on his near-hind. (5/1)

1042 The Glow-Worm (IRE), already successful over this course and distance this year, stayed on under stern pressure from the back of the field in the straight without ever threatening to play a serious role. (20/1)

1125 Sadian beaten just a neck by the winner in the Lingfield Derby Trial, was soon racing in second place but, collared for that position over a furlong out, soon had bellows to mend. Both his wins to date have been with cut in the ground and, given some rain, he can find a Group race. (25/1)

1506a Second Empire (IRE), who raised more than a few eyebrows with his performance in the Irish 2,000 Guineas, probably found this race coming too soon and was making no impression in the straight. Given time to really come to himself, connections should then be rewarded for their patience. (9/2)

993* Cape Verdi (IRE) was only the sixth filly to tackle the Derby since 1918. Reported to have been working really well at home since her 1000 Guineas demolition job, she looked extremely calm and relaxed in the paddock, but Dettori reported that she was not happy on the track and that she was interfered with running down the hill and was then given a bump rounding Tattenham Corner. However, the signs were already looking worrying and she gave up the ghost over two furlongs out. The trip appeared beyond her and, dropped down to a mile and a quarter and on a more conventional track, she can land another valuable prize. (11/4)

1737a Saratoga Springs (CAN) found his exertions from last Sunday's French Derby taking their toll and he was back-pedalling early in the straight. His unorthodox journey to Epsom - the three O'Brien runners were forced to re-route from Shannon airport and arrived late - can not have helped. (20/1)

1042* Gulland struggled to win over this trip in the Chester Vase, and this time, in this class, it certainly proved to be beyond him, as he stopped as if shot over two furlongs from home. (12/1)

868* Courteous would have preferred softer ground, but he completely failed to handle this notoriously difficult track and was all at sea running down the hill and Tattenham Corner. (14/1)

1325 Mutamam, who has not had an ideal preparation, refused to settle early and, not coming down the hill well, was getting left behind in the straight. He is much better than this. (50/1)

974 Haami (USA) ran no race at all and, not looking happy round Tattenham Corner, was then getting left behind. (20/1)

974* King Of Kings (IRE) looked in fine shape leaving the paddock, but he sweated up dreadfully in the parade and to say he ran no race at all would be something of an understatement. He has reportedly been retired to the Coolmore Stud after aggravating an old injury to his off-fore knee. (11/2: 10/1-5/1)

A further *Raceform* service is the *Private Handicap*. This gives the *Raceform* handicapper's assessment compared with the weights for any given race. Those at the top are considered to have the best winning chance:

By adjusting the Master Ratings in the Raceform index according to the weight carried in any future race, subscribers can compile a list of ratings for the runners in that race. However to save this rather laborious procedure the figures are published on a daily basis in **RACEFORM PRIVATE HANDICAP** with the entries for each race listed in order of their chances at the weights.

RACEFORM PRIVATE HANDICAP also carries the last three performance ratings for each runner and a Speed Figure as shown in the final column of each race in **RACEFORM**.

Other features of the **PRIVATE HANDICAP** are the distance and going for which each performance rating was achieved, the Raceform race number in which each horse ran, the number of days since he last ran and his last six form figures.

For all televised races, an expert comment has been compiled for each horse, giving his career details, his preference for distance and going and his prospects for the race in question.

0310 {S} GREAT NORTH EASTERN RAILWAY DONCASTER CUP STKS (GP 3) (3-Y.O+) (CLASS A) 2m 2f

RHR	LAST 6 HORSE-AGE-WEIGHT	LAST RF	LAST THREE OUTINGS	SF

129 45-682 .Double Trigger (IRE) (7-9-5) 42   3218   129¹⁶gs 127²⁰s 112¹⁶g 97
Very high-class horse, effective 16 to 20f, best at 16f, acts on sft to frm, best on gd, has worn blinkers, excels at Longchamp and Goodwood. Turf high 120 - 1st of 9 giving 3lb to Canon Can (30 Jly Goodwood RF 3218). This hugely popular stayer made a lot of the running on his reappearance at Newmarket, but slightly different tactics were tried at Sandown, unsuccessfully as it turned out. He reverted to his former front-running role in the Ascot Gold Cup and ran a blinder, only finding the progressive Kayf Tara too strong, but had that one behind when running out the emotional winner of the Goodwood Cup. Wonderfully game. *M Johnston [13-28] R W Huggins.

128 11-8434 Three Cheers (IRE) (4-9-3) 42   3218   126¹⁶gs 128²⁰s 127¹⁶g 94
High-class gelding, effective 15 to 20f, best at 16f, acts on sft to g-f, mostly wears blinkers (effectively), favours right handed tracks, and. Turf high 117 - 3rd of 16 to Kayf Tara (18 Jun Ascot 20f sft RF 2085) - also 1st of 9 from Bonapartiste (4 Oct Longchamp RF 4658a). He looked a progressive young stayer last season, winning three times including a Group Three at Longchamp in October. He has been getting it together gradually this season, running his best race to date to finish a close third in the Ascot Gold Cup. He has shown his share of temperament, but still has some scope as a stayer. *J H M Gosden [3-10] Sheikh Mohammed.

1103-21 Busy Flight (5-9-5) 119   1221   123¹⁴g 126¹⁶gs 120¹²gs 59
High-class horse, absent for 119 days , effective 12 to 16f, best at 12f, acts on g-s to frm, best on frm, prefers left handed tracks, does well at Newmarket and Doncaster and Newbury. Turf high 119 - also 1st of 5 giving 9lb to Moon rise (12 Spt Doncaster RF 4134). Consistent. Usually a front-runner, he won a listed race in '97 and was proved in better company. Showed that two miles holds no terrors for him when a good second at Newmarket on his return, and followed up by winning the Yorkshire Cup. Off the track since. *B W Hills [6-17] Exors of the late Wingfield Digby.

Raceform Private Handicap
LONG ODDS WINNERS
LAST FLAT
All top-rated by Raceform Private Handicap

OO EE BE	won 33-1	GREEN BOPPER	won 14-1
CARLY'S QUEST	won 33-1	LAW DANCER	won 14-1
LUCAYAN BEACH	won 33-1	SHAHTOUSH (JT)	won 12-1
FLAG FEN	won 33-1	SILVER HOPE	won 12-1
HAPPY MEDIUM	won 33-1	PEARTREE HOUSE	won 12-1
BEACH BOY (JT)	won 33-1	WOODY'S BOY	won 12-1
PRIMARY COLOURS	won 25-1	DANCING RIO	won 12-1
YOUNG BIGWIG	won 25-1	MAY QUEEN MEGAN	won 12-1
LEAR SPEAR	won 20-1	PEACEFUL SARAH	won 12-1
REFUSE TO LOSE	won 20-1	BREYDON	won 11-1
ABUHAIL	won 16-1	WELSH MOUNTAIN	won 11-1
ASCOT CYCLONE	won 16-1	ALMATY	won 10-1
CLASS WAN	won 16-1	LITTLE ACORN	won 10-1
HENRY THE PROUD	won 16-1	MONTAQUE TIGG	won 10-1
MELLORS	won 16-1	LONE PIPER (JT)	won 10-1
SAN SEBASTIAN (JT)	won 16-1	COASTGUARDS HERO	won 10-1
SEIGNORIAL	won 16-1	DISTANT KING	won 10-1
ERUPT (JT)	won 16-1	MUHIB	won 10-1
DOWER HOUSE	won 14-1	TULLULAH BELLE	won 10-1
Q FACTOR	won 14-1	JOLI'S SON	won 10-1
TOM PADDINGTON	won 14-1	TOUS LES JOURS (JT)	won 10-1
ROFFEY SPINNEY	won 14-1	SCENE (JT)	won 10-1

And many other winners all top-rated
on the Flat in 1998

Raceform Private Handicap ratings are issued on a daily basis at the four-day entry stage and are mailed first class at least two days prior to racing. They are also obtainable by Fax or On Line (for charges ring 01635 578080).

An alternative presentation of the form book with narrative comments is achieved by *Timeform Perspective* (see p.108) as well as, with some use of abbreviations, by *Superform*, from whose 1994 Annual the extract below is reproduced:

3093	**3.10 GR 1 KEENLAND NUNTHORPE STKS 2YO+ (A) 5f Good 41 +15 Fast**
	£87584 £32104 £15152 £5906 3yo rec 3lb

*2675 LOCHSONG 21 [5] I A Balding 5-9-3 L Dettori 10/1: 443111: 5 b m Song - Peckitts Well (Lochnager)   **121**
Broke well & made every yard, challenged 1f out, ran on gamely & won rdn out (nicely bckd, best time of after-
noon): prev won at Sandown (Listed) & Goodwood (Gr 3 King George Stks): in '92 won val h'caps here at York,
Goodwood (Stewards Cup), Doncaster (Portland H'cap) & Ayr Gold Cup: equally eff over 5/6f: loves to front run &
acts on fast & soft grnd: remarkably tough & genuine mare, much improved & has developed into a high class sprinter.

2675 PARIS HOUSE 21 [1] J Berry 4-9-6 J Carroll 4/1: -11322: 4 gr c Petong - Foudroyer (Artaius)   **1½ 120**
Sn prom, challenged halfway, ev ch 1f out till no extra c! home (hvly bckd): high-class sprinter, only a hd bhnd
Lochsong in 2675 (weighted to reverse that form today): deserves a Group 1 success: see 1347.

*2767 COLLEGE CHAPEL 18 [10] M V O'Brien Ireland 3-9-3 L Piggott 9/4 FAV: 111213: 3 b c Sharpo -   **¾ 118**
Scarcely Blessed (So Blessed) Slowly away & sn outpaced, hdwy over 1f out, strong run final 1f & nrst fin (hvly
bckd): fine run over a trip short of best & shld prove hard to beat back over 6f: see 2767.

2183 ELBIO 42 [3] P J Makin 6-9-6(vis) W R Swinburn 6/1: 35-104: Held up, weaved through over 1f out,   **1 115**
stayed on well final 1f, but not reach ldrs (6-wk abs): best 1736 (yldg).

2675 BLYTON LAD 21 [2] 7-9-6 S Webster 33/1: 21-P65: Chsd ldrs in centre, no extra final 1f: back to   **nk 114**
best here & one to watch out for back at favoured Newmarket: eff over 5/6f on fast & yldg grnd: see 1034.

2675 KEEN HUNTER 21 [4] 6-9-6 M Roberts 9/2: 2-2436: Chsd ldrs, faded final 1f (well bckd): handles   **1 111**
fast grnd, tho' best on yldg/soft: 10lbs below best here: see 2675, 1709.

2675 FREDDIE LLOYD 21 [8] 4-9-6 J Reid 80/1: 004007: Dwelt & nvr a factor: front-runner, missed the   **3½ 101**
break here: acts on fast & yldg grnd: failed to sparkle so far this term: btr 1736, see 861.

3672) BOLD N FLASHY [9] 4-9-6 A Munro 50/1: 223168: Front rank till wknd over 1f out: Canadian   **½ 100**
challenger, successful at Woodbine in June: won 4 times in '92: very speedy sort, reportedly best on firm grnd.

*1524 SEA GAZER 73 [6] 3-9-3 K Darley 50/1: 5-1019: Cl-up will wknd over 2f out (10-wk abs).   **2½ 93**

1347 MILLYANT 80 [7] 3-9-0 W Carson 100/1: 15-000: Chsd ldrs till halfway, sn outpaced (11-wk abs):   **1½ 86**
speedy sort, highly tried & no form this term: best on fast grnd: see 861 (reapp).

1736 LYRIC FANTASY 62 [11] 3-9-0 Pat Eddery 8/1: 2-6100: Hung right throughout & behind from halfway   **1½ 82**
(9-wk abs, looked magnificat): not the force of last term & possibly not trained on: see 1179.

11 ran   Time 58.12 (1.32)   (J C Smith)   I A Balding Kingsclere, Hants.

For *Superform*'s on-line service see below.

The Internet

When this book was last revised, the great revolution in communications which is the Internet was reported underway and flourishing after only a short period of time.   Racing, even then, already had scores of websites devoted to its various aspects.   But since then, Internet participation has, incredibly, expanded no less than fourfold with (in January 2001) 8.6 million homes in Britain having access to every conceivable facet of racing: from horses to courses; from its administration to betting; from the dissemination of information, including newspapers, agencies and magazines, to trainers (including Martin Pipe).   Some of the website addresses have been mentioned already, but here is a selected list of the addresses of useful sites to visit.

INFORMATION

The *Racing Post* is on-line at www.racingpost.co.uk

Meanwhile, although its old rival, *The Sporting Life*, no longer exists as a newspaper, it now has a big and very impressive presence on the Internet, incorporating the British Racing Centre site, and, while dealing with all sport, there is comprehensive coverage of racing by the Press Association at www.sportinglife.com/racing.

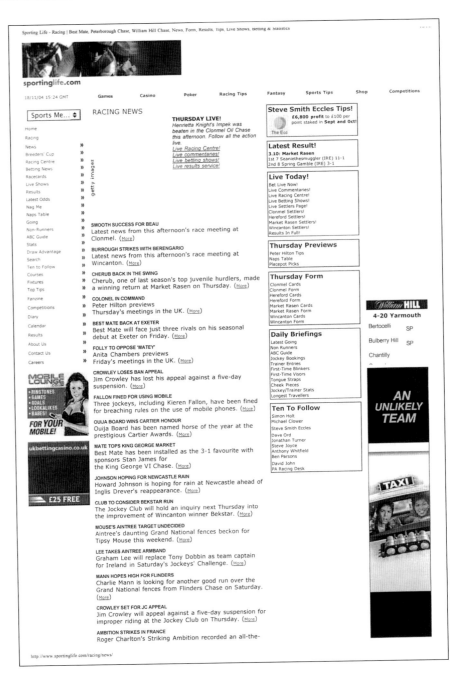

(<u>NB</u> A Java-enabled browser is required to view latest information.)

The Sporting Life website (see previous page) has been completely re-styled but its content remains basically similar. In addition, *The British Thoroughbred*, the quarterly bulletin of the British Horseracing Board, no longer appears on its own website. Instead, the British Horseracing Board's website is at www.britishhorseracing.com

britishhorseracing.com
The 1st place for British horseracing

BRITISH**HORSERACING**BOARD

◆ **GORACING**
racing
tickets
guide to betting

✚ **OWNING&BREEDING**
ownership
breeding

★ **INSIDE**HORSERACING
about BHB
racing industry
sponsorship
careers
media centre

The official website of the British Horseracing Board containing a wide range of information on British racecourses, online race tickets, major events, promotions, competitions, betting, race results, racehorse ownership, breeding, careers in racing, sponsorship, news and much more.

 Purchase Tickets

Purchase tickets for any racing event in Britain.

go »

Racenews, another comprehensive site, is at www.racenews.co.uk

Online Directory - Racenews Worldwide Racing Links

ABOUT RACENEWS   Services for Horseracing

THE RACENEWS WEBSITE	INTERNET CLIENTS
Newslink - is a free news service, providing twice daily news bulletins on all aspects of British and International thoroughbred horse racing. An Archive of past news is now being started.	Aintree
	Bangor
	Come Racing
	Cheltenham
	Epsom
Value Betting Column - the Racenews guide to Saturday's biggest betting heat - profiles the runners and highlights the value in the market. It is produced by a former professional gambler. It appears every Saturday morning.	Horsebooks
	Kempton
	Market Rasen
	Nottingham
	Robinski Bloodstock
	Racetech
Racing Around Britain - A tour of British racecourses and a guide to British racing online:	Racegoers Club
	RHT
Racing Around Britain highlights the best that the Internet has to offer to the follower of British racing.	Salisbury
	Sandown
	Stratford
	Tattersalls
Links -comprehensive Worldwide Racing Links.	Warwick
	Wincanton
	Windsor
Magazine - Fixtures - Archive - NetSearch	**CONTACT RACENEWS**
	e-mail

BEST OF THE REST			
Sports Results	**Business**	**UK Travel**	**Cricket**
BBC	Reuters	RAC	CricInfo
UK & World News	**Weather**	**Football**	
BBC	Met Office	Soccernet	

Racing Chronicle is a very attractive on-line magazine with quite outstanding photographs of racing action at major meetings at www.racing-chronicle.co.uk

HORSES AND COURSES

The majority of racecourses now have informative websites about fixtures, facilities and other relevant information. The list is too long to include in full, but the following are particularly recommended:

Aintree (www.aintree.co.uk);
Ascot (www.ascot.co.uk):
Cheltenham (www.cheltenham.co.uk).

ttree Racecourse - The Home of The Grand National

BOOKING HOTLINE: 0151 522 2929

| Racing | Racecourse Information | Ticketing & Online Buying | Entertaining & Hospitality | Sponsorship & Promotions | Conference & Banqueting | News & Press |

LATEST RESULTS
No results today

OUR NEXT EVENT
Festival of Horsepower - Friday 19th - Sunday 21st November

ENTER COMPETITION TO WIN VIP RACE DAY TICKETS
oddschecker
Grand National Odds

Aintree Audio Centre

Accessibility Site Map

SITE SEARCH
[   ] go

Booking Hotline
0151 522 2929

Hospitality Hotline
0151 522 2911

John Smith's to sponsor the Grand National

Aintree Racecourse announced today (Tuesday 9th November 2004) that the UK's number 1 selling ale, John Smith's, is to sponsor the Grand National meeting in a new three-year multi-million pound title sponsorship agreement. The very first John Smith's Grand National meeting will take place on Thursday 7th – Saturday 9th April 2005.

John Smith's, the Scottish & Newcastle owned brand will add the Grand National meeting, one of the 'Crown Jewels' in the British sporting calendar to its current portfolio of sponsorships within British horseracing. The Grand National race itself will become The John Smith's Grand National for the duration of the sponsorship agreement, 2005 – 2007 (inclusive), with an option to extend for a further three years.

Announcing the new sponsorship agreement, Managing Director of Aintree Racecourse, Charles Barnett said: "We are thrilled to have forged a relationship with such a powerful brand as John Smith's and are extremely excited about the prospect of working together to take the event to new levels over the next three years. Scottish & Newcastle plc is the UK's leading brewer and already has a successful track record in sports sponsorship, particularly with The Foster's British Grand Prix; Kronenbourg 1664 Official Beer of the Open Golf Tournament and Scrumpy Jack official drink of the English Cricket Team. We are confident that fresh ideas and this new association will help us to continue to build the Grand National meeting as the nation's favourite sporting occasion."

Tim Seager, Marketing Director of brand owners, Scottish & Newcastle added: "We are delighted to add the Grand National, a major world-wide sporting event, to our racing sponsorship programme

"The simple fact is that John Smith's drinkers love their racing and there's a perfect fit between the Grand National and the No Nonsense Pint. This agreement means so much more than simply attaching our logo to an event; we have made a long term commitment that will see the John Smith's Grand National, and racing in general, brought to life in pubs, clubs, supermarkets and off-licences, in a way that other brands have done with football. We are all very excited about the benefits this new partnership will bring to: racing; our business; our trade customers and John Smith's drinkers over the next three years."

Download the Official Grand National Brochure
Format: PDF / Size: 2.76Mb

betfair
SHARP MINDS BETFAIR

GRAND NATIONAL
BBC SPORT

BREAKING HEADLINES
LEE SET TO UNLEASH PROMISING ALMAYDAN AT AINTREE ON SATURDAY

Action on Ladies' Night

PROMOTIONS

Celebrate three days of horsepower at The Becher Meeting...
Friday 19th - Sunday 21st November 2004

Optimised for: 1024x768   Home   Contact Us   Register For Updates   Make This Home   Send To A Friend   Audio   Downloads

0In addition the following sites are well worth a visit:

Irish Racing – see below for the topics splendidly covered in this excellent guide to Irish racing at www.irish-racing.com

Irish Horses – fascinating, informative site and definitive database for the Irish horse industry. Topics include bloodstock, stud farms, the Irish National Stud, racing, trainers and jockeys at www.irish-horses.com/

Go Racing In Yorkshire – guide to the nine courses in the county, including York, at www.goracing.co.uk/index.htm

Northern Echo 'Go Racing' – articles on racing in the north of England with the emphasis on the north-east, in association with Go Racing In Yorkshire, at www.racing-north.co.uk/

ADMINISTRATION

The BHB site, already mentioned in Chapter One, contains a great deal of information and an offer well worth taking up of a useful free booklet on British racing, at www.britishhorseracing.com

The Jockey Club (see also Chapter One) is at www.thejockeyclub.co.uk

Weatherbys (see also Chapter One) has a user-friendly site explaining its functions at the nerve centre of British racing at www.weatherbys-group.com

FORM

Timeform's up-dated website at www.timeform.com has already been dealt with in this chapter, but *Raceform* is also on-line at www.raceform.co.uk

Superform, now in its thirtieth year (1974–2004), with an easy-to-use on-line method of computerising and presenting form (with an off-line facility for reading it) is available at www.superform.com

BETTING

At popular websites www.oddschecker.com and www.bestbetting.com you can view all of the bookmakers' odds for any selected event at a glance. These sites are very useful for punters and bookmakers alike.

Bets can be placed by bank debit cards using secure encryption supplied by Barclays Bank.

The major firms, including Sporting Index for spread betting (see page 63), and the Tote are also on-line, while Blue Square went live in May 1999. For a look at the facilities, the address is www.bluesq.com

Others include:

www.victorchandler.co.uk

www.williamhill.co.uk

www.ladbrokes.com

www.SportingOdds.com

www.betfred.com (backs up 385 shops run by Fred Done)

www.betdirect.net (run by Littlewoods)

www.skybet.com (Sky Sports)

www.stanleybet.com

www.betfair.com (biggest of the Betting Exchanges: see Chapter One)

www. betdaq.co.uk

www.sportingoptions.com

www.smartbet.co.uk

Computer Aid
Slightly preceding the astonishing growth of the Internet, it was inevitable in this age, when gazing at screens is more commonplace than wading through printed pages, that computer technology should come to the aid of the punter. *Computer Raceform*, which had its first full season in 1993, is one of the systems available, designed to run under the Windows package of database management for IBM-compatible PCs. It uses the speed and flexibility of the computer's retrieval system to provide a programme which effectively supersedes the 'steam' method of going through the form book. Enter the name of a horse, and there appears a list of all its previous starts. Examine a particular race, and the result appears in full detail with *Raceform* comments and ratings. These and several other advantages, including a search by trainer function and a facility for pulling out various race categories, come by subscription to *Raceform* which provides by post weekly up-dated disks which combine the official *Raceform* database, *Notebook* and *Private Handicap*.

In addition, *Timeform* also has a computer version with, at its heart, an encyclopaedic *Timeform* database which includes all the analysis and information found in *Timeform Perspective* and adds performance ratings and other features, including racecard commentaries for every runner. A demonstration version is free on request.

CHAPTER FIVE
A Compendium of Bets

Men not given to Guessing, piled on the Dibs in such a way as to make Settling Day seem a remote possibility...

Royal Ascot, the Derby, the Grand National are all occasions to quicken the pulse, if not the word-processor. They are looked forward to, written about *ad nauseam*, and slaved at, in varying degrees, by professional racing correspondents who all harbour yet a dread in their hearts: the extra-runners – not the racecard variety, but those who are, more or less, colleagues from the distant reality of what used to make up Fleet Street.

Royal Ascot produces the Hooray-Henries from gossip columns, and charming diary ladies. The Derby flushes out a corps of reporters eager to apply substance to any rumour. (The only good story I can recall on this marginal fringe concerns the occasion when the winning-post was pinched the night before the race. This resulted in a *Daily Mirror* scoop for John Godley, who was roaming around as a freelance.)

The Grand National also brings its own battalion of reporters seen out only once a year. Among them was always Bernard McIlwaine, taking a break with his racing *alter ego* from his usual role as a Mirror Group film critic. He shared with me a fondness for the lines which appear at the head of this page, a *Sporting Pink* quotation with an unmistakable echo of fearless plungers and the riches and ruin of the Turf in Edwardian days. When, at the bar of the Lord Nelson Hotel, Liverpool, late on the Friday night before the race, I heard it whispered into my ear in a gravelly, laughing, Canadian accent, I knew that Bernie's train had arrived at Lime Street, and that the Grand National could take place. It was a merry, annual, consecrated experience; now Bernie is dead, but this chapter is very much his sort of territory.

Before listing some of the bets it is possible to pile the 'Dibs' on, there are various contingencies and other matters to deal with and clarify, such as the definition of 'placed' horses and so on. The contingencies are covered by Tattersalls' Rules on Betting, which appear in full in Appendix A, but which may be summarised as follows:

Horses withdrawn without coming under starter's orders
Tattersalls' rule 4(c) deals with this. If there is insufficient time to form a new market excluding the withdrawn horse, winning returns on the remaining horses which take part in the race are subject to deductions which vary in ratio to the odds of the absent horse at the time of its withdrawal. If the current odds are:
   (a) 3/10 or longer odds on by 75p in the £.
   (b) 2/5 to 1/3 by 70p in the £.

(c) 8/15 to 4/9 by 65p in the £.
(d) 8/13 to 4/7 by 60p in the £.
(e) 4/5 to 4/6 by 55p in the £.
(f) 20/21 to 5/6 by 50p in the £.
(g) Evens to 6/5 by 45p in the £.
(h) 5/4 to 6/4 by 40p in the £.
(i) 13/8 to 7/4 by 35p in the £.
(j) 15/8 to 9/4 by 30p in the £.
(k) 5/2 to 3/1 by 25p in the £.
(l) 10/3 to 4/1 by 20p in the £.
(m) 9/2 to 11/2 by 15p in the £.
(n) 6/1 to 9/1 by 10p in the £.
(o) 10/1 to 14/1 by 5p in the £.
(p) If over 14/1 the liability would be unchanged.
(q) In the case of two or more horses being withdrawn before coming under starter's orders, the total reduction shall not exceed 75p in the £.

Bets on the withdrawn horse are void and stakes are returnable, or, in certain instances, transferred to another horse (as, for example, in bets concerning unnamed favourites; if the original favourite is withdrawn, the shortest priced remaining horse becomes 'favourite' for this purpose).

Horses withdrawn, but under starter's orders at the time of withdrawal
This is a losing bet, the horse being treated as if it had taken part. No deductions are made from winning bets on the remaining horses.

Non-runners
If a horse is declared as a runner overnight and is withdrawn before racing, or is withdrawn, not under orders, immediately before a race but in time for a new betting market to be formed, the bet becomes void, and stakes are returnable. Or, in certain circumstances, such as bets on unnamed mounts of jockeys, the bet may be transferred: e.g. K. Fallon appears in the morning papers as the rider of horse A. Horse A is withdrawn and Fallon, instead, has a chance ride on horse B. If horse A is withdrawn and Fallon has no other ride, the bet is then void. Any doubles on his unnamed mounts become singles, trebles become doubles, and so on. When two horses are nominated for a double and one of them does not run, the bet, to the same stake, becomes a single. When three horses are nominated for a treble, and one is a non-runner, the bet becomes a double to the same stake. If the remote chance occurs of two horses in the treble being non-runners, the stake becomes a single on the remaining horse. On the same principle, non-runners included in all other multiple bets, involving four, or five, or more runners, cause an automatic 'down-grading' of the bet. This, however, does NOT necessarily apply to ante-post bets, so bookmakers' rules, as ever, should be checked.

Dead-heats
In a dead-heat for first place, stake money on each of the horses concerned will be divided by the number of runners in the dead-heat and full odds paid on the

remaining stake. In a dead-heat for second, any place stakes are halved in races of six or seven runners. In a dead-heat for third, any place stakes are halved unless the first four home are being paid. In a dead-heat for fourth place, stakes are halved and full odds paid on the remaining stake.

Stakes wrongly calculated
If a wrong total is entered in the 'stakes' box of a betting slip and the betting shop clerk does not spot the error when accepting the slip, the bet, if a winner, will usually be settled on a proportional basis, although bookmakers independent of the big chain firms may operate their own different rules, so here, once again, is a good reason for studying bookmakers' rules.

Betting disputes
Tattersalls' Committee are the final arbiters in all betting disputes. In practice, only major disagreements (as well as cases of default) get as far as 'The Rooms' and all automated bookmakers now accept a decision from the IBAS (Independent Betting Arbitration Service) on disputes that are taken to it for settlement.

Place betting
The following are the general rules applied by bookmakers to determine the odds in place betting:

5–7 runners — $1/4$ odds, 1st or 2nd	All races
8–11 runners — $1/5$ odds, 1st, 2nd or 3rd	All races
12–15 runners — $1/4$ odds, 1st, 2nd or 3rd	Handicaps only
16+ runners — $1/4$ odds, 1st, 2nd, 3rd or 4th	Handicaps only

COMPENDIUM OF BETS
Where horses' names have been used in illustrations of how bets are settled, the names themselves are genuine enough. They have been chosen from both the recent and distant past history of the Turf, but no attempt whatsoever has been made to choose horses which in reality might have been included in the same bet, particularly with the more remote examples from the past.

One horse only involved

Single bets
Single bets offer by far the most reliable way of making betting pay.

Win only (Bookmaker or Tote)	£1 staked on *Rataplan* to win. Wins at SP of 10/1.	Return: £10 + £1 stake back. Return: £11
	£1 staked on *High-Rise* to win the 1998 Vodafone Derby, at Tote odds (some bookmakers will also settle at Tote odds off-course, if specified). *High-Rise* wins. Tote win dividend: £15.20.	Tote payout: £15.20 (including £1 stake back)
Place only (Tote odds only)	£1 staked on *Theatreworld* to be placed in the 1999 Smurfit Champion Hurdle. *Theatreworld* is second. Tote place dividend: £2.50.	Tote payout: £2.50 (including £1 stake back)
Each way An equal amount staked to win and for a place (Bookmaker or Tote, but see Chapter Six).	£1 e.w. (total £2) staked on *Opera House* to win or be placed in the 1993 Coral Eclipse Stakes (8 runners), with a bookmaker. *Opera House* wins. SP returned 9/2 and 1/5 those odds a place.	Bookmaker returns £4.50 + £0.90 + £2 stake back. Return: £7.40

£1 e.w. (total £2) staked on *Topsham Bay* to win or be placed in the 1993 Whitbread Gold Cup, with the Tote. *Topsham Bay* wins. Tote win dividend: £13.80. Place dividend: £3.10.

Tote payout: £13.80 + £3.10 (including £2 stake back). Return: £16.90

£1 e.w. (total £2) staked on *Jack Button* to win or be placed in the 1993 Ladbroke Chester Cup (18-runner handicap), with bookmaker. *Jack Button* is second at an SP of 12/1. Place odds are therefore $1/4$ x 12/1 = 3/1.

Bookmaker returns £3.00 + £1 place stake back, and keeps the losing £1 win stake. Return: £4.00

£1 e.w. (total £2) staked on *Blue Judge* to win or be placed in the 1993 Ever Ready Derby, with the Tote. *Blue Judge* is second. Tote place dividend: £18.60.

Tote payout: £18.60 (including £1 stake back, but the Tote keeps the losing £1 win stake). Return: £18.60

In 1999, in an enlightened move to help the once-a-year punter, Ladbrokes introduced the special slip overleaf.

THE
GRAND NATIONAL
QUICKSLIP Saturday 3rd April

MARK YOUR SELECTION(S) WITH AN 'X' IN BLACK PEN

1 select your horse(s)

Akarus	☐	Lord Atterbury	☐
Alcapone	☐	Lord Jack	☐
Alexander Banquet	☐	Mantles Prince	☐
Amberleigh House	☐	Maximize	☐
Ardent Scout	☐	Monty's Pass	☐
Artic Jack	☐	Moor Lane	☐
Ballybrophy	☐	Mr Bossman	☐
Bear On Board	☐	Puntal	☐
Bindaree	☐	Red Striker	☐
Blowing Wind	☐	Risk Accessor	☐
Bounce Back	☐	Royal Atalza	☐
Clan Royal	☐	Royal Predica	☐
Davids Lad	☐	Shardam	☐
Exit To Wave	☐	Simply Gifted	☐
First Gold	☐	Skycab	☐
Gunner Welburn	☐	Southern Star	☐
Hedgehunter	☐	Spot Thedifference	☐
Hermes III	☐	Takagi	☐
Iznogoud	☐	The Bunny Boiler	☐
Joss Naylor	☐	Timbera	☐
Jurancon II	☐	Tyneandthyneagain	☐
Just In Debt	☐	Wahiba Sands	☐
Kelami	☐	What's Up Boys	☐
Kingsmark	☐	Whereareyounow	☐
Le Coudray	☐	Wonder Weasel	☐

2 win or each-way?

WIN (1st) ☐   EACH-WAY (1st, 2nd, 3rd or 4th) ☐

Each-Way: If your horse finishes 2nd, 3rd or 4th you receive 1/4 of the full odds.

3 select your stake

If you bet 'Each-Way' your chosen stake will be doubled.
To select a stake which is not shown, mark boxes adding up to that amount.

50p ☐ £1 ☐ £2 ☐ £3 ☐ £4 ☐
£5 ☐ £10 ☐ £20 ☐ £25 ☐ £50 ☐

Mark this box to take the current odds for your horse, ☐
or leave it blank and get the Starting Price.

Please check your receipt carefully.

0396 **Ladbrokes**

(The Ladbrokes special Grand National slip has now been altered in appearance, but still fulfils its enlightened object.)

Two horses involved

Doubles
Bookmakers' rules should be carefully inspected to see that there are no time restrictions on multiple bets, e.g. 'There must be a minimum of 15 minutes between each race in a double, treble etc.'

Win double (Bookmaker or Tote) Off-course	£1 is staked on *Ormonde* and *Bendigo* to win two separate races on the same afternoon, with a bookmaker. Both win, *Ormonde* at 2/1 SP and *Bendigo* at 6/1.	The bookmaker settles as follows: £2 won on *Ormonde* plus the original stake of £1 go forward as a stake of £3 on *Bendigo*. When he wins, the profit is thus £3 at 6/1 = £18, plus £3 stake, less £1 original stake = £20 (i.e. a 20/1 double)

Simplified settling:
$$(2/1 + 1) \times (6/1 + 1)$$
$$= (3/1) \times (7/1) = £21$$
Profit therefore
$$= £21 \text{ less original £1 stake}$$

A double at Tote odds is similarly settled, the entire dividend from the winning first 'leg' going as stake on the second leg, and the winnings calculated according to the dividend on the winning second leg. For example, the winning dividend of the first part of the double is £4.20. This goes on to the second horse, the winning dividend for which is £5.40. The winning return is therefore £4.20 x £5.40 = £22.68, i.e. a win double at approximately 21 to 1. This kind of double is not possible on the Tote at the racecourse, only with Tote off-course facilities, and with those bookmakers who will settle at 'Tote prices'.

If, in the above example, *Ormonde* had won, and *Bendigo* had been beaten or vice-versa, the £1 stake would have been lost. Prudent punters would normally cover the two horses singly to stakes that would cover the entire bet should either *Bendigo* or *Ormonde* get beaten.

Win doubles are also possible nominating favourites, jockeys' mounts, trainers' runners, e.g. '£1 Win Double Favourite in the 2.30 at Bath with the Favourite in the 3.00 at Folkestone'. If there are joint-favourites the stakes are divided between the number of favourites which, effectively, at least halves the bet.

With jockeys and trainers, a permutation bet is often made:
e.g. Pat Eddery has four rides at Goodwood: A B C D. Six bets are required to cover them all in win doubles: A with B, C & D; B with C & D; C with D. With an outlay of £6 in win doubles, a 5/1 double at least is required to break even. In the event, let's say he has two winners at even money and 7/2, in which case

there is a profit of £3. The bet is written: 'Full perm all Pat Eddery's mounts at Goodwood in win doubles. Stake 6 x £1'.

The method of calculating winnings on a double, and hence all multiple bets, is very simple:

e.g.   £1 win double
First leg of the double wins at 4/1
Second leg of the double wins at 6/1

Add one 'point' each to the respective winning odds (one betting unit is a 'point', thus 4/1 is one point greater than 3/1, and 3/1 is one point less than 4/1). So the winning double becomes $(4/1 + 1) \times (6/1 + 1) \times £1 = 5/1 \times 7/1 = £35$ and the profit, therefore, having subtracted the original £1 stake, becomes £34. A 34/1 double in other words, or 34 points profit.

Should fractional odds be involved, say winners at 7/4 and 13/8, the principle remains the same, i.e. $(7/4 + 1) \times (13/8 + 1) \times £1$ etc.

$$= (2\,^3/_4 \times 2\,^5/_8) \times £1$$
$$= (2.75 \times 2.625) \times £1$$
$$= \text{approx. } £7.22$$

Profit is therefore £6.22, but a pocket calculator is recommended to arrive at this figure.

Each way double
Off-course only.
An equal amount staked in a win double and place double on two horses in separate races, e.g. '£1 Each Way Double [stake £2] on *Beeswing* and *Alice Hawthorn*'.

Result: (a) *Beeswing* (3/1) and *Alice Hawthorn* (5/1) both win
Profit as follows: Win double $£(3/1 + 1) \times (5/1 + 1) - £1 = £(4/1 \times 6/1) - £1 = £23$
Place double say at $^1/_4$ the win odds $£(^3/_4 + 1) \times (1^1/_4 + 1)$
$- £1 = £(1\,^3/_4 \times 2\,^1/_4) - £1 = £2.94$ **Total £25.94**

Results: (b) *Beeswing* wins and *Alice Hawthorn* is placed
Alice Hawthorn wins and *Beeswing* is placed
The win double is lost, the place double pays out:
(–£1) (+£2.94) **Profit £1.94**

(c) Neither filly wins, but both are placed. The win double is lost, the place double pays out, as calculated above.

(d) *Beeswing* wins or is placed, *Alice Hawthorn* is unplaced. *Alice Hawthorn* wins or is placed, *Beeswing* is unplaced. The entire double goes down, and stake all lost.

Ante-post doubles, win or each way
Off-course, credit, betting shop or Tote, or may be struck with bookmakers on the racecourse (see Chapter One for more about **Ante-post betting**).
Popular doubles are attempts to couple the winner of the 1000 and 2000 Guineas, Derby and Oaks, Spring Double and Autumn Double (see Chapter One). The doubles are settled as above at full multiplied odds.

Any to come
In this kind of bet at least two horses are nominated with the proviso 'any to come' or 'if win' or 'if cash'...so much on the next selection in the series. In other words, any cash from previous bets in the series (winnings plus stakes) is used as stake on the succeeding selections. Many bookmakers limit the any-to-come part of such bets to double the original stake. At its simplest it would be written '£1 win *Spree*, A-T-C (or If cash or If win) £1 *Nortia*. Stake £1'. *Spree* wins at 4/1, so £1 from the winnings goes onto *Nortia*.

Up and down double
This is an any-to-come bet in which the stake is carried forward, then back to give two win singles x 2. Also known as a Cross Bet, Vice-Versa, Stakes About, On and Off, or Reverse Bet. The cross symbol X between the horses on a betting slip indicates that up and down is required, but instructions should also be spelt out: e.g. '£1 up and down win *Lochsong* and *Drum Taps* – stake £2.'
   Lochsong wins at 2/1; *Drum Taps* wins at 10/1
   The bet is settled: £1 at 10/1 = £10; £1 at 2/1 = £2

Tote exacta
In races with more than two runners, two horses can be chosen to finish first and second in correct order. A bet called a Reverse Exacta can be made nominating two horses in either order. In other words, if *Edwina Black*, say, and *Baddesley Ensor* are nominated, the Reverse Exacta bet is a winner if *Edwina Black* wins with *Baddesley Ensor* second or if *Baddesley Ensor* finishes first and *Edwina Black* is runner-up.

Computer straight forecast
Off-course bookmakers only.
This bet is one in which the first and second in a race have to be forecast in the correct order: e.g. '£1 CSF *Opera House* to beat *White Muzzle* Ascot 3.20'. The bookmakers' 'computer straight forecast', unlike the Tote Dual Forecast pool, as far as declared dividend is concerned, bears no relation whatsoever to the amount of money staked or the number of winning punters. The pay-out is made according to a fixed scale 'computed' by a complicated formula on the basis, primarily, of the SP of the horses concerned in the forecast. Thus, in the example given above, the CSF dividend, including £1 stake, was £66.88 (compared with the Tote's £38.40 for naming the correct horses, but in either order).
   A usual practice, if this bet is indulged in, is to make a permutation covering a number of possible horses to finish first and second, also second and first (reversed forecasts). This can be done to stakes as low as 10p. Thus four horses – A, B, C, D – coupled in straight forecasts and reversed forecasts would involve 12 bets: AB AC AD BA BC BD CA CB CD DA DB DC.
   The bigger the odds of the horses involved in a computer straight forecast, the more likelihood there is of a Tote Dual Forecast proving better value. There are a fair number of examples throughout the season when it pays better to nominate two horses in either order than attempt the correct forecast, an extreme example

being in *Touch of Grey*'s astonishing Dual Forecast pay-out when coupled in either order with *Manimstar* in the Wokingham in 1986. As against the Tote's £3,414 for the Dual Forecast, the CSF for naming the two horses in correct order was only £509.96.

Three horses involved

Treble
Win or each way. Off-course only. Ante-post also.
A treble seeks to clean up on the winners of three separate races:
e.g. '£1 Win Treble *Hyperion, Dancing Brave, Sea Bird II.* Stake £1'.

If a winner, this is settled by the same method as for a double, i.e. a point is added to the winning SP of each of the horses, and the three multiplied, with the original stake deducted to give the winning treble odds. Say the winning odds are 4/1, 6/1 and 6/4, then the treble is settled: £(5/1 x 7/1 x 5/2) – £1 = £86.50. As explained above, each way trebles are similarly settled, either with the bookmaker or Tote. In order to succeed, all three horses must win; two winners and a loser are no good. Correspondingly, an each way treble will succeed only if all three horses are at least placed. The treble is a popular bet, but the mathematical
odds against winning are fairly high. In practice, an 'uncovered' treble is not a sensible bet. Rather better winning opportunities are offered by covering the treble either with doubles, or, even better, with singles and doubles, which, although the total stake is increased, give more chance of at least some success. Most common of these bets are the Trixie and the Patent.

Trixie
Win or each way. Off-course only.
Form of bet involving one treble and three doubles:
e.g. '£1 e.w. Trixie. *Desert Orchid, Aonoch, Barnbrook Again.* Stake £8' (Stake for a £1 win Trixie would be £4).

This bet is settled as for doubles and treble explained above. Two winners out of three at multiplied odds for one successful double of about 7/2 are required to break even on this bet.

Patent
Win or each way (as for Trixie).
Probably the most popular, as well as the safest, way of betting involving the treble. The bet is one treble, three doubles and three singles and is written:
e.g. '£1 Patent. *Orchardist, March Past, Young Inca.* Stake £7.'

One winner at 6/1 is enough to break even on this bet, or two winners at even money and 6/4 (paying two singles and one double).

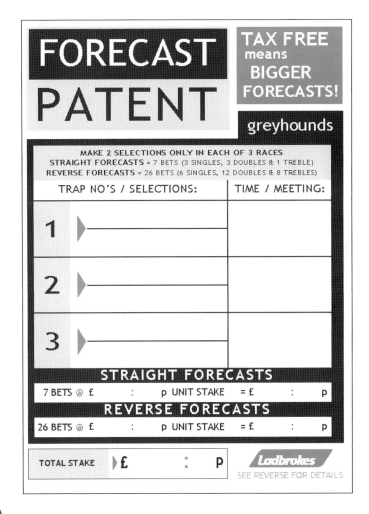

Tricast

Some off-course bookmakers only.

The Tricast is a bet in which winner, second and third in certain big races have to be forecast in correct order. The odds are computed in a similar way to the computer straight forecast. Bets can be made down to 10p units.

Tote Trifecta

The bet can be made with the Tote on-course, or in betting shops which operate Tote Direct.

The object of the Trifecta is to select 1-2-3 in correct order. It operates on big races only. The minimum stake is £1 but permutations are allowed to a minimum stake unit of 10p. The slips shown below give a full explanation of this bet, which was introduced in 1998 to replace the Tote Trio and provide a tempting alternative to the Tricast. In this it has already succeeded handsomely, beating Tricast dividends in a high percentage of cases. As someone once wrote,

'If you have a Tricast on a race offering the Tote Trifecta, declare yourself insane'. A new record for the Tote Trifecta was set in the Grand National 2001 when the dividend for forecasting *Red Marauder*, *Smarty* and *Blowing Wind* in the correct order was £25,681 – £3,000 more than the previous best which was declared at Newmarket in October 1998.

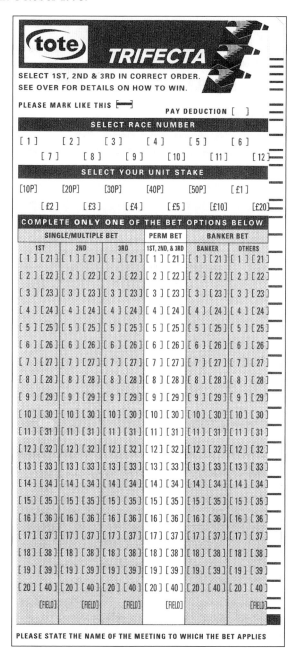

The Big Race Bet.

How to Win

* Select 1st, 2nd and 3rd in correct order.
* Mark entries with a Black/Blue ballpoint pen only.
* Use horizontal strokes to mark the card e.g. ⊢10⊣
* If you make a mistake, please start a new card.

1 Mark race number.

2 Mark your unit stake.

3 There are several ways to bet on Trifecta. Choose which bet option you require and complete **only one section, SINGLE/MULTIPLE, BANKER or PERM.**

*SINGLE/MULTIPLE BET - Mark Single or Multiple horse selections in each column to finish 1-2-3 in the **correct** order.*

*PERM BET - Select three or more horses in this column to obtain every combination of your selections - i.e they can finish 1-2-3 in **any** order.*

*BANKER BET - Select one horse you are sure will be in the first three. Mark it as a 'Banker' with any number of 'Others' to fill the remaining positions in **any** order. Alternatively, make two 'Banker' selections to be in the first three with any number of 'Others'.*

4 Calculate the cost of your bet by multiplying the number of combinations by your unit stake. *For details on calculating Multiple bets please ask a member of staff.*

5 Take this card to the cashier and state the name of the meeting to which it applies.

6 You will then be given a ticket which will contain all your bet details.

PLEASE CHECK YOUR TICKET CAREFULLY. YOU ARE RESPONSIBLE FOR MAKING SURE ALL THE DETAILS ARE CORRECT.
Please see Tote betting guides for more details about this bet.
All bets are subject to Tote rules.

How can I increase my chances of winning?

There are 3 ways you can cover more options and increase your chance of winning.

1. PERM TRIFECTA
(Complete within area B of the mark-sense card)

With a Perm bet you can pick 3 horses to finish first, second and third in **any** order.

You can in fact choose more than three horses, to give you a permutation of three to finish in the correct order.

A Perm Trifecta covers every combination of your selections and gives you more options for winning.

PERM BET	
1ST, 2ND, & 3RD	
[1]	[21]
⊢⊹⊣	[22]
[3]	[23]
⊢⊹⊣	[24]
[5]	[25]
⊢⊹⊣	[26]
[7]	[27]
[8]	[28]
[9]	[29]
[10]	[30]
[11]	[31]
[12]	[32]
[13]	[33]
[14]	[34]
[15]	[35]
[16]	[36]
[17]	[37]
[18]	[38]
[19]	[39]
[20]	[40]
[FIELD]	

This example shows a **Perm Trifecta** *with the numbers 2, 4, and 6 selected to finish first, second and third in* **any** *order.*

This bet would cost you **6 times** *your unit stake.*

2. BANKER TRIFECTA
(Complete within area C of the mark-sense card)

If you have a favourite horse which you think will finish in the first three places but aren't sure it will be the outright winner, try a Banker bet.

Here, your favourite horse can be selected as the "Banker" to finish first, second or third, and you can pick 2 or more other horses to fill the 2 remaining places in **any** order.

Choosing one horse as a "Banker" allows you to cover a wide range of the combinations you want as opposed to every combination covered with a Perm Trifecta.

BANKER BET			
BANKER		OTHERS	
[1]	[21]	[1]	[21]
[2]	[22]	[2]	[22]
[3]	[23]	[3]	[23]
[4]	[24]	[4]	[24]
⊢⊹⊣	[25]	[5]	[25]
[6]	[26]	[6]	[26]
[7]	[27]	[7]	[27]
[8]	[28]	[8]	[28]
[9]	[29]	⊢⊹⊣	[29]
[10]	[30]	⊢⊹⊣	[30]
[11]	[31]	[11]	[31]
[12]	[32]	⊢⊹⊣	[32]
[13]	[33]	⊢⊹⊣	[33]
[14]	[34]	[14]	[34]
[15]	[35]	[15]	[35]
[16]	[36]	[16]	[36]
[17]	[37]	[17]	[37]
[18]	[38]	[18]	[38]
[19]	[39]	[19]	[39]
[20]	[40]	[20]	[40]
		[FIELD]	

This example shows a **Banker Trifecta** *with number 5 selected as the "Banker" and numbers 9, 10, 12 and 13 to finish in the remaining places in* **any** *order.*

This bet has **36** *possible winning combinations and so your chances are greatly increased.*

To work out the cost of this bet simply multiply your unit stake by **36**.

3. MULTIPLE TRIFECTA
(Complete within area A of the mark-sense card)

This is the bet to place if you think you know the winner of the race and have several favoured horses for specific places.

A Multiple bet allows you to make several selections for each of the three placings, to cover **only** the winning options you want.

It is in effect like running several individual Trifectas on the same race.

SINGLE/MULTIPLE BET		
1ST	**2ND**	**3RD**
[1] [21]	[1] [21]	[1] [21]
[2] [22]	[2] [22]	[2] [22]
[3] [23]	[3] [23]	[3] [23]
▬ [24]	[4] [24]	[4] [24]
[5] [25]	[5] [25]	[5] [25]
[6] [26]	[6] [26]	[6] [26]
[7] [27]	[7] [27]	[7] [27]
[8] [28]	▬ [28]	▬ [28]
[9] [29]	[9] [29]	[9] [29]
[10] [30]	▬ [30]	▬ [30]
[11] [31]	[11] [31]	[11] [31]
[12] [32]	[12] [32]	[12] [32]
[13] [33]	[13] [33]	[13] [33]
[14] [34]	[14] [34]	[14] [34]
[15] [35]	[15] [35]	[15] [35]
[16] [36]	▬ [36]	▬ [36]
[17] [37]	[17] [37]	[17] [37]
[18] [38]	[18] [38]	[18] [38]
[19] [38]	[19] [38]	[19] [39]
[20] [40]	[20] [40]	[20] [40]
[FIELD]	[FIELD]	[FIELD]

This example of a **Multiple Trifecta** *shows number 4 to win, with 8, 10 and 16 to finish second or third.*

The cost of this bet would be 6 times your unit stake.

How much will it cost?

No matter which Trifecta bet you place working out the total cost is exactly the same.

You simply multiply the number of possible winning combinations by your unit stake.

With a Multiple Trifecta, depending on the selections made, calculating the number of winning combinations can be complex.

Should you need any help calculating the cost of your bet, please consult a member of staff.

How much can I win?

The Trifecta gives you the greatest chance of a big win for a small stake on a single race.

And on those occasions when there is no winner the pool is rolled over to the next Trifecta race.

Please note, all dividends are declared to a £1 unit stake.

What if one of my selections is a non-runner?

If any of your selected horses is declared a non-runner your money will be refunded on every combination which includes that horse.

What if I have any questions?

If you have a problem working out the total cost of your bet, or any other query, please ask one of our specially trained staff who are there to help you.

Union Jack
Off-course bookmakers only.
As the slip shows, with a full explanation, this bet, consisting of eight trebles, win or each way, or place only at Tote odds, follows the pattern of the red and white stripes in the British Union Flag. Anyone who has played noughts and crosses will see how it works, as well as appreciating that it is possible to achieve the not unremarkable feat of picking no fewer than six winners out of nine selections, and still lose the entire stake. If either diagonal contains three losers then a treble is not possible

Round Robin

The slip below explains what the bet is. It is settled as one treble, three doubles, six up and down singles.

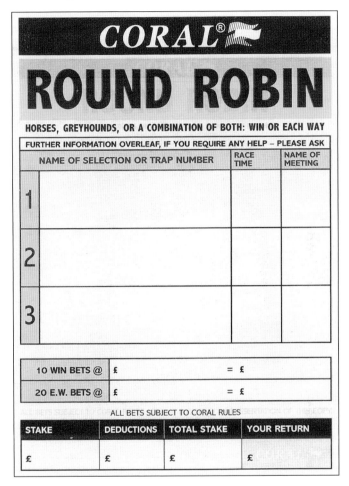

CORAL®

ROUND ROBIN

HORSES, GREYHOUNDS, OR A COMBINATION OF BOTH: WIN OR EACH WAY

FURTHER INFORMATION OVERLEAF, IF YOU REQUIRE ANY HELP – PLEASE ASK

	NAME OF SELECTION OR TRAP NUMBER	RACE TIME	NAME OF MEETING
1			
2			
3			

10 WIN BETS @	£	= £
20 E.W. BETS @	£	= £

ALL BETS SUBJECT TO CORAL RULES

STAKE	DEDUCTIONS	TOTAL STAKE	YOUR RETURN
£	£	£	£

Round the Clock

Involves at least three selections. Settled as follows:

Horse A   £1 Win
      Any to come £1 win B. Any to come £1 win C.
Horse B   £1 Win
      Any to come £1 win C. Any to come £1 win A.
Horse C   £1 Win
      Any to come £1 win A. Any to come £1 win B.

If all three selections win there will be three times as much going on to each winner as was originally staked. Some smaller firms stop this bet at a loser, so rules should be checked.

Four or more horses involved

Accumulator

Win or each way. Off-course bookmakers, or Tote.

A treble is technically an 'accumulator' involving the winnings from each horse successively going on to the next, but the term accumulator is more usually applied in cases of four horses or more. The specific term for a four-horse accumulator is a four-timer.

Four-timer

In practice, only the foolhardy would simply make a straight bet in the expectation of four winners, and this kind of accumulator is normally covered with a combination of singles, doubles, and trebles, as in the Yankee, perhaps the most popular Saturday betting shop wager.

We are now in the area where most off-course bookmakers make a good profit, and at the point where Captain Mainwaring in 'Dad's Army' would say Corporal Jones was 'getting into the realms of fantasy'. What Crockford invented more than a century and a half ago has been refined, embellished and honed to provide the ultimate in temptation of big profits for a very small outlay, the Achilles heel of all small gamblers (and some big ones, too). Today the betting scene in the high street offers a bewildering variety of Bullseyes, Lucky 15s, Sweet Sixteens, Dundee Shuffles, and so on, some of which are explained below. When there is a big pay-out on a multiple bet there is inevitably appropriate publicity as the cutting reproduced below demonstrates:

Ladbroke's sale boost punter

A Manchester punter won £47,019 with a 5p Heinz yesterday, despite picking a loser.

And, thanks to Ladbroke's Glorious Goodwood Sale, he received £11,525 more than if his bet had been settled at starting prices.

Ladbrokes increased the prices of Goodwood winners yesterday and plan to do the same today. They added one point to a horse priced 10-1 and over, two points to a 20-1 chance and over, and five points to outsiders chalked up at 30-1 and over.

The fortunate punter picked 33-1 winner Gemini Fire, settled at 38-1, Royal Loft (14-1 settled at 15-1), Murillo (10-1), Green Ruby (20-1 settled at 22-1), loser Mudisah and Star Cutter, who obliged at 7-2.

The bet was placed at Ladbroke's Miles Platting betting shop in north Manchester, and was 10p understaked at £3.25 since he also had a 25p each-way equally divided accumulator on the same horses.

The punter also lost out on another £5,000 or so as he did not pay the tax, but he probably will not be too worried when he collects his money.

Stop at a Winner
Another series bet. The first win in the sequence ends the bet with the total paid as a single to the winning odds:
e.g. '£1 each *Mailman, Sonic Lady, Reference Point, Pebbles*. Stop at a Winner. Possible Stake £4.'
They all win: 7/1, 6/4 on, even money, and 8/1. But the bet stops with *Mailman*'s gallant effort at 7/1.

Yankee
Win or each way.
Involves four selections and 11 bets. Written simply '£1 Yankee...and names of four horses involved (with racecourses + race-times also on the slip)...Stake £11.'
Involves six doubles, four trebles, one four-timer.

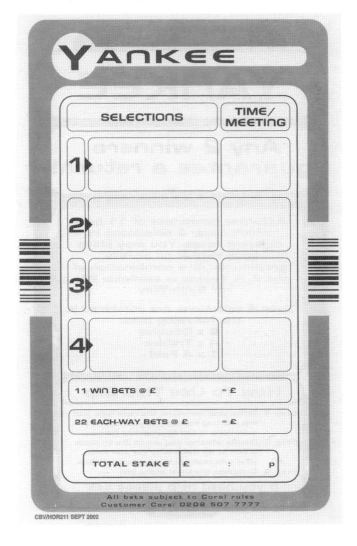

Lucky 15 or Yankee plus

LUCKY
15 • 31 • 63
horse racing

BONUS

ONLY ONE WINNER AND WE GIVE YOU DOUBLE THE ODDS!
(WIN PART ONLY IF EACH-WAY)
IF ALL YOUR SELECTIONS FINISH FIRST
WE WILL ADD A BONUS TO YOUR TOTAL.

SELECTIONS	TIME / MEETING
1 ⟩	
2 ⟩	
3 ⟩	
4 ⟩	
5 ⟩	
6 ⟩	

	BET TYPE	WIN		EACH-WAY	
4	LUCKY 15	15 BETS @	UNIT STAKE	30 BETS @	UNIT STAKE
5	LUCKY 31	31 BETS @	UNIT STAKE	62 BETS @	UNIT STAKE
6	LUCKY 63	63 BETS @	UNIT STAKE	126 BETS @	UNIT STAKE

BONUSES AND CONSOLATIONS APPLY ONLY TO SELECTED NON ANTE-POST
HORSE AND GREYHOUND BETS. PLEASE ASK STAFF FOR DETAILS.

TOTAL STAKE	⟩ £ : p	**Ladbrokes**

SEE REVERSE FOR DETAILS

Involves four selections and 15 bets. Same as Yankee but with the addition of four covering single bets. With the Ladbrokes bet of this kind, if you get all four single bets correct you get a 10% bonus added to the payout.

Canadian super Yankee
Involves five selections and 26 bets in ten doubles, ten trebles, five four-timers, one five-horse accumulator.

Heinz
Involves six selections, and, as the name implies, 57 bets. It was a Heinz that gave the Ladbrokes client in Miles Platting (see p.142) his big win. The bet is settled as:

  15 doubles,
  20 trebles,
  15 four-timers,
  6 five-horse accumulators,
  1 six-horse accumulator.
  Anyone who succeeds with a Heinz deserves the money, a remark which may be made with even greater force in the case of a Goliath (see p.147).

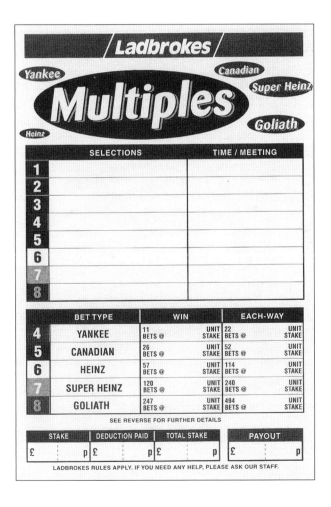

Goliath
Involves seven selections and 120 bets.
The set is settled as:
                    21 doubles,
                    35 trebles,
                    35 four-timers,
                    21 five-horse accumulators,
                    7 six-horse accumulators,
                    1 seven-horse accumulator.

Alphabet (Coral only)
Settled as two patents, one Yankee, one accumulator.

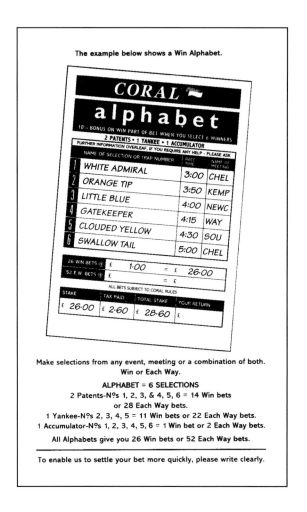

The example below shows a Win Alphabet.

Make selections from any event, meeting or a combination of both.
Win or Each Way.

ALPHABET = 6 SELECTIONS
2 Patents-Nºs 1, 2, 3, & 4, 5, 6 = 14 Win bets
or 28 Each Way bets.
1 Yankee-Nºs 2, 3, 4, 5 = 11 Win bets or 22 Each Way bets.
1 Accumulator-Nºs 1, 2, 3, 4, 5, 6 = 1 Win bet or 2 Each Way bets.

All Alphabets give you 26 Win bets or 52 Each Way bets.

To enable us to settle your bet more quickly, please write clearly.

Fivespot (Ladbrokes only)

Jackpot and Placepot

The Jackpot was launched at Royal Ascot in 1966, and the Placepot 11 years later. Since 1987 the pools have been based on a £1 unit stake system with part units down to 10p currently accepted both on- and off-course, although the minimum total wager is £1. The Jackpot has fluctuated in popularity, but a major innovation was made when 'marksense' coupons (as illustrated below) were introduced in 1988. The Placepot, in particular, has gained in popularity in recent years. The Tote Quadpot, a form of Placepot, is usually run on the last four of the first six Placepot races of any Placepot meeting. To win, a selection must be made of a placed horse in each of these four races. The Placepot and Jackpot, in particular, are now well-established features of the betting scene and there are even two books which expound the various strategies for success in the Placepot: *Winning the Place*, published by Winning Streak Publications, and *Win at the Tote Placepot* by Malcolm Boyle and published by Oldcastle Publications. All these bets are available with bookmakers operating Tote Direct as well as with the Tote on the racecourse and with Tote Bookmakers.

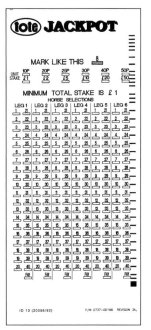

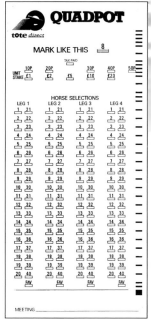

GUIDE TO BETTING ON THE TOTE JACKPOT AND PLACEPOT

The **Jackpot/Placepot** is usually run on races 1-6. In the Jackpot, you must select the winners of each race. In the Placepot, you select a horse for which a place dividend is normally declared in each race. Selections in races of four or less runners must win. There is only one Jackpot on any given day. The Placepot is usually available on all meetings covered by the S.I.S. Service.

Permutations are accepted for unit stakes of 10p and upwards. Minimum total outlay is £1. To calculate the cost of your permutation, you can simply multiply the number of selections in each race together and multiply this by your unit stake.

Favourite Un-named first favourites only are accepted. If you wish to select the SP Favourite, use the letters FAV at the foot of the appropriate race. When there are joint favourites, the one with the lowest racecard number will be taken as the selection.

Non-Runners If a non-runner is selected, the SP Favourite will be substituted. If there are joint or co-favourites, the lowest racecard number applies. Dividends are declared to a £1 stake. Part stake winners receive a return in proportion to their stake. Conditions covering acceptance and settlement can be found in the bookmakers rules as displayed in their betting offices.

How to Bet

* Use ball point pen (black or blue only) to mark entries.
* If you make a mistake, please start a new card.
* Use horizontal strokes to mark the card. e.g.
* 1. Please mark the bet type.
* 2. Mark your unit stake.
* 3. Mark your horse selections using racecard numbers. Use the first column for race one, the second for race two, etc.
* 4. Give your entry to the counterstaff. You will receive a ticket which will include all details of your bet.

PLEASE CHECK YOUR TICKETS CAREFULLY
YOU ARE RESPONSIBLE FOR ENSURING THEY
ARE CORRECT

Below is the sort of receipt for a Jackpot issued by a bookmaker operating Tote Direct:

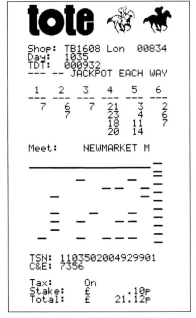

Scoop6

In 6 TV races specifically nominated by the Tote on a Saturday, a horse has to be picked in each race. The choices have to win or be placed for the bet to succeed. To boost the chance of success, more than one horse can be nominated in each of the races. A special Scoop6 betting coupon is required in order to place this bet with the Tote.

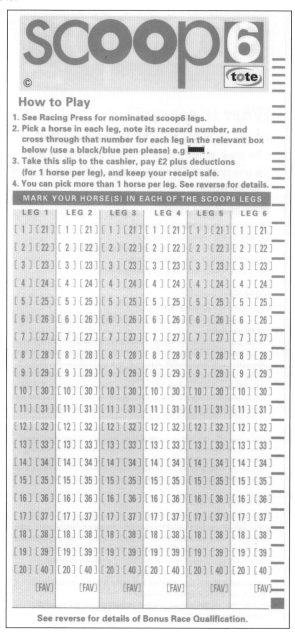

On Grand National day 2001, a small Sussex syndicate who had won Scoop6 before celebrated a £317,772 windfall. Their 324-line perm costing £648 got two lines through to the National on *Red Marauder* and *Smarty*, who had the race between them in the final stages. However, in April 2004, 51-year-old Ron Nicholson from Poole did even better than this. For a £4 stake he was the sole winner of Scoop6 and collected £878,939. This record amount also gave him another record. It made him the man who had won more in a betting shop than anyone else ever before.

CHAPTER SIX
How to Get 'On'

This section is especially for all those who are daunted by the notion of going into a betting shop, and for those who, on Grand National and Derby days, would so much like a bet, but have no idea how to go about it. Betting shops do, of course, vary, for some, they have never quite shaken off the image of the shops which flourished in the 'sixties and cashed in briefly on the amendment to the betting laws which permitted public betting in cash. Often these were unbelievably squalid back-street dumps, complete with a cast of derelicts, layabouts and drunks; and rip-off limits scrawled so high on the wall they could not be read, but if deciphered revealed that not much was allowed in the way of winnings.

Nowadays, all that has changed or is in the process of changing since Hill's, Ladbrokes, Coral's and the Tote between them dominate the betting shop operation up and down the country, with some good independent rivals. All but a few of the smaller gaffs have been bought out and refurbished with immense benefit to the off-course punter and betting has become an altogether much more pleasant experience. They do vary, but mostly it's between the carpeted establishment of the West End of London and other cities, complete with banks of videos, televisions, armchairs, no unreasonable limit on winnings and provision of almost every amenity except money to bet with, and the median grade of shop, which, without being exactly an annexe to the nearest Hall of Temperance or branch of the Chase Manhattan Bank, provides reasonably clean and tidy facilities, particularly before racing begins. Afterwards, depending on the area, things get a little more lively, though rarely unpleasant.

Here then is a step-by-step procedure for the betting shop, which may look long but is extremely simple:

1. First have an inspection of the local betting shops. There's often more than one to choose from, so find one which appears to have the best atmosphere, and which has the most favourable rules.
2. Next, if it's Grand National Day or Derby Day, weigh the possibilities up as early as possible, and prepare to make the bet *in the morning*, before the action, noise and queues start in the shop. On Grand National Day it can be like being in the Post Office when everybody in front is paying the telephone bill, water rates, *and* relicensing at least two cars. The morning, in fact, is a good time to bet anyway if you are not too worried about following the market changes, which are sometimes chalked up but, these days, more usually appear on the video screens.
3. Write out the intended bet beforehand on a slip of paper and take it to the betting shop.
4. Most important, take a ball-point pen. This is a most *vital* piece of kit, although most betting shops now provide pens.

5. Once in the betting shop, first have another careful look at the rules. With the big chains the rules are not desperately prohibitive, but it's worth a look in all cases to see what, if any, restrictions are placed on the amount that can be won in a single afternoon or single bet. And, most important, if there are special restrictions concerning ante-post bets.

   The newspapers, sporting or otherwise, are pinned round the walls, open at the various racecards for the day. This gives an opportunity for a final check that horses' names are correct (though, in practice, unless the name is wildly mis-spelt, the betting shop settler won't mind), as well as on the correct racecourse and time of race. Also on view, either marked up on big display boards, or now, more usually, on the video screens, will be the early prices available up to the time of the first show of betting from the racecourse. If a selection is considered to be better to back at early prices rather than trust to the SP (i.e. if it is considered the SP is likely to be shorter than the price on offer) this is the time to decide whether to take what it is hoped might turn out to be a bargain price, such as 8/1 on a horse that could well come in to 4/1 favourite. Judgement is required here, but then the whole business is concerned with judgement.

6. Next, take a betting slip. These are sometimes dispensed from machines, operated by the turn of a knob at the side, and situated above the ledges round the walls which are used for writing out bets. More usually, the slips may simply be contained in small racks in a similar position.

7. The kind of plain slip is illustrated overleaf. It will have a carbon attached, which, after the bet has been written and presented, will be returned as a copy.

8. Next, write the bet, following the slip of paper made earlier. Examples are given below, but write, or even better, print:
   (a) How much is to be staked on each bet.
   (b) What kind of bet, e.g. win only, each way (e.w.), double, treble etc. In the case of more complicated bets which the bookmaker will take immense delight in accepting, it is best to use one of the special slips usually provided, illustrated in Chapter Five.
   (c) Name(s) of horse(s).
   (d) Name of racecourse or, more usually, suitable abbreviation and time race is due to start.

9. The total amount to be staked should then be added and entered in the box at the bottom of the slip.

10. Take the completed betting slip and stake money to the counter, sometimes with a glass screen, and specifically to the part marked 'Bet Here' or a similar instruction.

11. (a) If the selections are intended to be paid out (if winners) at SP, simply hand the slip and cash under the glass. On the other side it will be checked through primarily to see that the bet is readily understood, and there are no obvious mistakes, and that the amount staked is correct (also to see that a second mortgage hasn't been raised, and an enormous bundle staked, in which case the boss may be called from the back-room to negotiate, depending on the locality of the shop and how well known

the punter is). These days in many cases the information is then collated from the slip onto a machine, (rather like the Lotto machines) which generates a detailed receipt.

(b) If an early price is required rather than SP, simply write the early price against the name of the horse on your slip and say, for example, 'I'll take *Rataplan* at 10/1', at which the early price of *Rataplan* will be checked and the 10/1 will be ringed and initialled. So, whatever the SP, 10/1 is the price at which the bet will be settled if *Rataplan* wins.

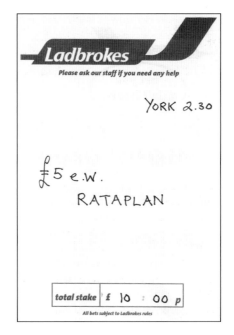

Nothing more need be done, except to tuck the receipt away in a safe place and wait for the results. Finally, assuming the happy circumstances of a winner, what to do then? Essentially, just present the receipt at the 'Payment Here' section of the betting shop counter, and the original transaction will be found and the cash remitted. Before collecting, however, it's as well to calculate what is expected from the winning bet. If the amount paid out doesn't tally with what is expected, point out that a mistake appears to have been made. Settlers *can* make mistakes; equally, so can punters, particularly when miscalculating the odds payable on a place bet, or, even more likely, on a complicated multiple bet.

One point about pay-out on big race-days such as the Grand National. Because of the likely amount of business, a notice may appear in the 'Bet Here' window saying something like: 'No winning bets on the Grand National paid until 5 o'clock'. This is not because the bookmaker is planning to hammer spikes into his shoes in the event of a big liability and leg it to the hills, but because the Grand National always generates more business than any other one day of the year (the Derby comes next; Cheltenham in March, and Ascot in June are also busy times). Particularly in the instance of a popular winner, depending on the size of the shop, and how many settlers are calculating the losses in the back-room and transferring them to individual winning slips, it may well be 5 o'clock before a pay-out is possible, by which time queues are forming. This is very much the case with small betting shops, though not the bigger ones. It may well be better to wait to be paid out until the next available day. Just because winnings are not collected on the day, it does not mean the money will not be paid out. Winning slips are put in dated racks if the cash has not been collected on the day. However in the case of the bigger groups the rush to get winnings paid out has been largely dissipated by the introduction of a facility whereby, for instance, a Ladbrokes winning slip can be paid out at any Ladbrokes shop

The obverse of this, of course, occurs on normal days when winnings can be collected soon after the 'weighed in' call has come over the loudspeaker.

Betting on the racecourse
1. *With a bookmaker*
   Many bookmakers operate 'minimum stake' limits. In Tattersalls at present these vary considerably. Some bookmakers also stipulate 'win only' or 'each way taken'. Some bookmakers are not interested in taking big amounts on an outsider, but will happily lay the favourite to the same sort of money. If it happens that a bet is refused or halved, there are always other bookmakers along the line, some of whom may not bat an eyelid at the amount. For the ordinary punter, however, there are no real problems about getting 'on'.

   If a bet on a horse running *at a different meeting* is wanted there are usually at least one or two bookmakers at the back or side specialising in this sort of bet. They will also, normally, bet at SP if stipulated. They can be located in Tattersalls by the time-honoured shout of 'AT the other meeting'. Also 'Nah then, who wants this favourite at Ponty...have you all done, now? They're off Ponty...yes, sir, which one do you want...?' Ted Murrell used to be a great specialist, a colourful figure in straw hat, making a book at the 'away' meetings. There is a story that Ted used to have a telephone on his joint (unconnected to anything but the floor of the ring) and in order to liven things up would get his clerk to make it ring, at which the following 'conversation' would take place – Ted: 'Yes, your Lordship...a pony on which one...oh a monkey...[aside to his clerk]...George, scrub off all that nine to two...yes, your Lordship, you've got 2,000 to five the favourite...' Another story, well documented, concerns his operations in shirt sleeves on hot sunny days at southern meetings when, say, he was making a book on the Warwick meeting. At some point Ted would say to his clerk, again to attract the business in: 'Put the umbrella up, George.' 'The umbrella, guv?' 'Yes, the umbrella. It's raining at Warwick.'

   It is also sometimes possible to get *a bet in running* on the course in the closing stages of a race when, say, the favourite looks as if he's not going to make it in the last furlong or so. From the bookmakers the shouts will go up 'I'll lay five hundred to one this favourite'. There also used to be a bookmaker at the smaller jumping meetings who would take bets up to the last fence, and was similarly able to spot a tiring or unwilling favourite approaching the final jump. He had a good line of patter: 'Come on now ladies and gents...up to the last fence...you can have anything you want, Green Shield Stamps, Omo Coupons, Savings Cerstificates, anything you like...here, six to one this favourite, sixes...up to the last fence...oh, that's done it...the favourite's down, yer money's on the floor...' As far as ordinary betting is concerned the procedure on the racecourse could hardly be simpler. All that has to be done is to go up to the bookmaker and say how much is wanted on any given horse at the price quoted on the board: e.g. if, say, *Rataplan* is quoted at 4/1, and a fiver is wanted on it, the exchange of words goes like this – Punter: 'Twenty pounds to five, *Rataplan*', or simply, 'A fiver, *Rataplan*'. Bookmaker: 'Twenty pounds to five, *Rataplan*, ticket number 998 [see above]'. The fiver is handed over in exchange for the ticket; the cash disappears into the satchel; the bookmaker's clerk notes the bet and ticket number in the field book; and you're on, not forgetting, however, to make a note of the exact odds and bet on the back of the ticket. Should *Rataplan* win, the bookmaker will pay out when the 'weighed in' signal is given on the public address. In the particular example above, when the ticket is given back to the bookmaker, he will pay out £20 winnings plus £5 stake returned. BUT, a word of warning. Under new rules, this time-honoured procedure is about to change. Already, as from October 1998, bookmakers are obliged to display a note of their maximum guaranteed liability to any individual punter. Notices must also be displayed about betting on forecasts, without the favourite, and on the winning distance. Bookmakers also must price up odds at least ten minutes before the off-time of a race. More drastically, and a step into the computer age, all bets are to be recorded by electronic voice-data equipment, and full indelible records maintained in a betting book or on computerised record. Furthermore, as from 31 December 1999, bookmakers were required to issue for each bet a ticket or slip showing name and contact address for payment and complaints; meeting code, date and race number; name and/or number of horse; stake; potential return, including stake; odds; type of bet. And finally, bookmakers must stay at their pitch for ten minutes after the 'weighed in' signal on any race in which they have unsettled cash claim.

2. *In the course betting shop*
    Many courses now have betting shops which offer similar facilities to those off-course.

3. *On the Tote*
    Close-circuit video is the usual method used now to give the approximate odds that may be expected if a bet is had 'on the machine'. In general, the Tote often pays out a longer price than the book on outsiders.

    The Tote operation has been computerised and the betting windows much simplified in recent years. The procedure again is very simple, and rather like buying a railway ticket, only quicker, even at the big Ascot and Cheltenham meetings. No horses' names are involved in betting with the Tote; everything is done by reference number on the racecard:

e.g. '£5 Win Number 8'   (Stake £5)
or '£5 each way Number 22 and £25 win Number 4'   (Stake £35)
or '£5 Forecast Number 6 and Number 10'   (Stake £5)
or '£10 Combination Forecast Numbers 2, 8 and 24'   (Stake £30)
    (This couples 2 and 8, 2 and 24, 8 and 24 in Dual Forecasts)
and so on.

Whatever the bet, the Tote operator behind the window will take the cash, press various buttons, and a ticket of the kind illustrated below will be issued. (Bookmakers' tickets also are similar computerised print-outs on flimsy paper. In this electronic age, their colourful card tickets of old have now, alas, been superseded.)

For Tote Jackpot, Placepot and Trifecta instructions see Chapter Five.

If the bet is a winning one, the pay-out takes place, after the 'weighed in' signal, at the windows. So, if £2 has been staked to win on a successful selection for which the win dividend declared is £6.20, the actual odds are £5.20 to £1, and the pay-out will be £12.40, which includes £2 stake returned.

The Tote also operates a Course to Course service.

CHAPTER SEVEN

Horses for Courses

When the straight was reached there were only two horses left with a chance, Brown Jack and Solatium. As they headed for home it sounded as if everyone on the course was cheering for Brown Jack...as he passed the post he was two lengths clear...in every enclosure hats were in the air but many who would have liked to cheer were rendered speechless by an inconvenient lump in the throat. Dignified individuals, whom one would never have suspected of displaying their feelings in public, unashamedly wept.

The above was written by the late Roger Mortimer (*Twenty Great Horses*) describing the final appearance at Ascot in 1934 of *Brown Jack*, then a ten-year-old, as he won the Queen Alexandra Stakes (originally the Alexandra Stakes), at over 2 m 6 f the longest race in the Calendar*, for the sixth year running. Altogether in his long career *Brown Jack* won 25 races, including the Goodwood Cup, Doncaster Cup, Chester Cup and the Champion Hurdle, but he reserved his most heroic feats for the Ascot crowds, who loved him. Altogether he ran there 11 times, winning seven times and being runner-up once. If ever a horse illustrated the saying about 'horses for courses', it was *Brown Jack*. His performances at Ascot captured the public's imagination and affection in a way that those of few horses have ever done. In more recent times *Arkle*, *Red Rum*, *Desert Orchid* and *Persian Punch* have been his equivalents.

Brown Jack, however, hated Newmarket, which was not the case with another great public favourite of the past, *Pretty Polly*. Of her 22 victories, ten were recorded at 'Headquarters'. Even farther back, the heroine of Northumberland in the 1830s, *Beeswing*, won a total of 51 races, many of them at Newcastle, including no fewer than six Newcastle Cups.

Historical perspective apart, there is plenty of contemporary evidence to back up the horses for courses theory. Whatever else may be said about 'all-weather' racing, it has helped to give the well-beaten old platitude a quite extraordinary fresh impetus. The well-bred *Tempering* (by *Kris* out of a *Nijinsky* mare) between 1990 and 1996, trained by David Chapman, won at least 21 times on the Fibresand at Southwell (some figures make the total an even more amazing 23). *Rapporteur*, by the time he was eight years old in the spring of 1994, had amassed an incredible 19 successes at Lingfield (14 on the Equitrack and 5 on the turf). Furthermore, he had no wins whatsoever on any other course. A similarly impressive tally of 18 was scored on the Fibresand at Southwell (mostly over hurdles, which have now been banned) by *Suluk*, who was a year older than *Rapporteur*. *Krystal Max*, meanwhile, triumphed 16 times on the All-Weather before he was retired through injury aged nine in 2002. He won on every all-weather course, including 13 times at Lingfield where, understandably, from the age of two to eight, he had a faithful following.

---

* In 1993, the Ascot Authority announced that the Queen Alexandra Stakes was to become a 1 m 2 f handicap. There was a huge outcry from the racing public, nearly 2,000 of whom signed a petition organised by John Livingstone-Learmonth. As a result, Ascot gracefully bowed to the pressure, and the decision was rescinded. Thus the Queen Alexandra Stakes still remains, at 2 m 6 f 34 yards, the longest race in the Calendar.

Additionally, there have been other all-weather stars, such as *Kingchip Boy*, another Southwell specialist with 13 victories there up to April 1999 when he was ten. A study of the *Racing Post* form figures will show up performers such as this and, for example, *Premier Dance*, who by the time he was 12 in 1999 had scored nine times at Wolverhampton in an all-weather total of 12.

On the Flat, on turf, there have been several quite exceptional course specialists in the past few years, foremost being gallant old *Rapid Lad* with 13 wins at Beverley 1980–89. Another veteran sprinter, *Touch Above*, recorded eight wins on the same course, including, in 1992, the Rapid Lad Handicap. *Turmeric*, a big, long-striding stayer who might have been thought to be unsuited to the sharp track, recorded eight wins at Catterick 1987–1990. On the same course, another consistent favourite of the crowds, the grey *God's Solution*, signed off aged ten in 1991 by winning for the sixth time the race at 6 f by then rightly named after him. At Lingfield, *Tauber* had an outstanding record, having won seven races on the turf plus a further four on the All-Weather before retiring in 1996 aged 12.

Meanwhile, National Hunt racing provides its own even more considerable contribution to the horses for courses theory. Too much, in fact, for a full list, but the following selection of some old favourites gives the general idea. *Desert Orchid* (1983–1991) was a specialist at no fewer than four circuits (all of them, significantly, right-handed): Sandown (9 wins), Ascot (8), Kempton (7) and Wincanton (6). Nevertheless, at the top of the entire list are *Manhattan Boy*, the selling hurdle star at Plumpton between 1986 and 1993 when he was 12 (he never won anywhere else), and *Certain Justice* at that other popular little Sussex course, Fontwell. They are the most prodigious course specialists of all in recent times, sharing the record of 14 course victories apiece; both, appropriately, had races named after them. In fact, Fontwell, in particular, seems to specialise in course specialists. It was here that *Stickler* recorded 12 of his 13 victories between 1968 and 1972 and *St. Athan's Lad* registered 11. Another more recent consistent performer was *Southernair* (9 wins and once disqualified after being first past the post). Also with 11 wins at a single course were *Kilbrittain Castle* (at Sandown), Peter Cazalet's Newton Abbot expert of the 1950s, *Diego Rubio,* and, a year or so later, the versatile *Domaru*, beaten only twice at Wincanton. Among those with a tally of ten were the 1951 Gold Cup winner, *Silver Fame* (Cheltenham), the game hunter-chaser of the 1960s, *Chaos* (Chepstow), *Ron's Nephew* (Newbury) and the evergreen, Scottish-trained *Peaty Sandy* (Newcastle), who also scored six times at Ayr. The Queen Mother's *Laffy*, meanwhile, long before the Equitrack, ruled at what was then truly Lovely Lingfield. He had nine successes there between 1961 and 1967, including the Sussex Handicap Chase three seasons running. *Potentate*, trained by Martin Pipe, won no fewer than nine times at Chepstow between 1995 and 1999, including the Welsh Champion Hurdle three times in succession, while that favourite old hunter-chaser *Teaplanter*, at the age of 14 in 1997, gained his ninth triumph at Towcester in a career total of 24 victories. At Aintree two names post-war stand out as specialists: *Freebooter*, winner of the Grand National and four other races over the stiff Liverpool fences, and *Red Rum*, National hero a record three times, twice runner-up – and an Aintree winner on the Flat as a two-year-old! Finally, two course specialists who also never failed to have the crowds cheering on their appearance: *Jimmy Miff* (see under **Aged** in Chapter One) who died aged 28 in 2000 but who had seven successes at Uttoxeter, including a Midlands Grand National in 1979; and *Lady Rebecca* with seven of her impressive haul of victories at Cheltenham, including the Grade 1 Cleeve Hill Hurdle three seasons in a row, 1999–2001.

There are many other names, some of them famous, which could be added to these lists, but sufficient has been written to underline the importance of the lines in newspaper racecards which indicate how many times a horse has won at a particular course and over what distance – for example, CD3 would indicate a runner who has won three times over course and distance of the particular race; C4D3 means that the horse has won four times at the track and three times over the distance of the race in question. The *Racing Post* gives in its form guide full details of where a horse has previously won, and course specialists show up very easily.

Now, having established the undoubted existence of a great number of horses for courses, an intriguing question remains. What gives horses a liking for a particular racecourse? Leaving aside what might be called the knock-on effect of connections tending to run their horses on tracks where they have been found to go conspicuously well, it is something that largely remains a mystery. Two trainers, both now retired, here give their views. The first is Bill Watts, who used to train the Edinburgh specialist *Show of Hands*, who in the later stages of his career was a pacemaker on the gallops for Lord Derby's popular gelding and winner of the 1985 Arlington Million, *Teleprompter*. But *Show of Hands* also had his own vociferous fan club, at the Musselburgh track. He won seven times 1981–84 at this very sharp course, where the turn into the straight is like a hair-pin, and he was adept at being first to the bend, or preferably bolting out of the stalls and making every yard of the running. His trainer explained: 'Seven furlongs on an easy track was just what he loved. He used to go a real gallop, get the rails and take that turn practically on one leg. It terrified the jockeys. But by the time he was into the straight, nothing could catch him. The crowd adored it. It was pure chance that I tried him first at Edinburgh and he won. Next time, at Pontefract, left-handed, it was hopeless.'

Next, I went to see John Benstead at Epsom. He used to train *Operatic Society*, a name which will bring back glowing memories to those who were racing in the 'sixties and were lucky enough to see in action this outstanding mile-and-a-half handicapper, with his striking white-blazed face, who was often partnered by 'Scobie' Breasley and sometimes Lester Piggott, wearing the cream colours with orange cap of Mr Ronald Agars-Walker. In a tremendous career lasting until he was 11 years of age (he is an inexplicable omission from current racing encyclopaedias), *Operatic Society* won no fewer than 30 races. More to the point, 14 of them were achieved at Brighton, Lewes or Epsom, all of them courses with a distinct switchback and roller-coaster element to their character. In particular, old '*Operatic*' was the popular hero of the holiday crowds at Brighton, where he was seven times successful.

His trainer from the age of four, John Benstead, had this to say about him: 'He was a very well-balanced horse who could handle the fast ground you invariably get at Brighton and Epsom; he was always set to carry a lot of weight which you can carry better at Brighton than, say, Newmarket and I think he loved all the ups and downs that went with it on that course.'

Some time later, John Benstead trained another course specialist: *Al Amead*. His particular liking was Lingfield. Not only that, he loathed practically everywhere else. He was a bundle of nerves, sweated up and was not a good traveller – except when going to Lingfield, where, unboxed, he was always cool, calm, and ready for battle. *Al Amead*'s 1985 record tells the story. He ran a dozen times, being unplaced in all his races except at Lingfield, where he ran six, won three and was never out of the first four. Later, he stretched his total of Lingfield successes to eight, including breaking the six furlong track record when leading from start to finish under 9 st 10 lb.

For this Jekyll and Hyde aspect of *Al Amead*'s character, Benstead's best explanation, given with a laugh, was: 'It was maybe because the canteen staff always made a tremendous fuss of him, I don't know. But whatever it was, he always *knew* when he was going to Lingfield. It was most odd and uncanny.' And he added categorically, 'Horses do know where they are and, just like human beings, they know where they like and can hate other places.'

This seems as good an explanation as we shall ever get, short of interviewing an articulate, genuine talking horse, although no less a trainer than John Dunlop disagrees. But there are, over and besides, several corollaries to the horses for courses idea, first of which is horses for races. Worth studying always at the bottom of the form guide is the result of the previous year's running of a particular race. It is quite surprising how many horses win the same race at least two years running. An extreme example is *God's Solution* (see above). *Willie Wumpkins* won three successive Coral Golden Hurdle Finals 1979–81. *Further Flight* (see Chapter Ten) captured a record five Jockey Club Cups, while *Sharpo* won the Nunthorpe (then the Sprint Championship) three times 1980–82, and the late Lady Beaverbrook's splendid sprinter *Boldboy* (for whom she made generous provision in her will and ensured a pleasant old age before he died in 1998) took the Abernant Stakes at Newmarket four times and was twice runner-up between 1974 and 1979. *Rambo's Hall* won the Cambridgeshire twice and in 1993 made the frame in a gallant further attempt under a big weight. In addition, *Manhattan Boy* won the Peacehaven Selling Hurdle at Plumpton five times between 1986 and 1993: a humble race, perhaps, but a feat by the course's favourite son not to be despised. See also above for *Laffy* in the Sussex Handicap Chase at Lingfield, and *Potentate* in the Welsh Champion Hurdle.

Another corollary is trainers for races. It is worth studying trainers' track records in this sort of direction. Here is a short list of such races and their main winners:

Flat

May Hill Stakes, Doncaster, September
   Since 1978, Henry Cecil has had 17 runners (up to 2001) of which **12** were winners, 3 runners-up and only 2 unplaced.

Dee Stakes, Chester, May
   Barry Hills: **11** winners 1970–2002.
Racing Post Trophy, Doncaster, October
   Henry Cecil: **10** winners 1969–1993.
Yorkshire Oaks, York, August
   Sir Michael Stoute: **8** winners 1978–2003.
Galtres Stakes, York, August
   Luca Cumani: **8** winners 1990–1999 (including 6 in succession 1990–1995).
Princess Royal Stakes, Ascot, October
   John Dunlop: **8** winners 1966–2001.
Craven Stakes, Newmarket, April
   Sir Michael Stoute: **7** winners 1985–2003.
Gordon Stakes, Goodwood, August
   John Dunlop: **6** winners 1968–2000.
Magnolia Stakes, Kempton, April
   John Dunlop: **6** winners 1991–2000 (including 3 in succession 1998–2000).
Cheshire Oaks, Chester, May
   Barry Hills: **6** winners 1974–1999.
Weatherbys Super Sprint (2-y-o), Newbury, July
   Richard Hannon has an amazing record in this race: **5** winners (1992–2003), runner-up 4 times and total places 10, including first and second in 1993 and first and third in 1992.

National Hunt

Weatherbys Champion Bumper (NH Flat Race), Cheltenham Festival, March
   Irish-trained horses have won **9** times and been placed a further 9 times since 1992.
Paddy Power Gold Cup, Cheltenham, November (renamed as from 2004, originally the Mackeson Gold Cup)
   Martin Pipe: **6** winners up to 2002.
William Hill Handicap Hurdle, Sandown, December
   Martin Pipe: **6** winners 1988–1997 plus 5 places up to 2002.
Coral Welsh National, Chepstow, December
   Martin Pipe: **5** winners since *Bonanza Boy* in 1988 and 1989 plus 4 places.

It is also important to study whether a horse has a liking for (or, perhaps more important, an aversion to) a left-handed or right-handed track (see *Desert Orchid* above). *Timeform* will often make a note on this point. There are countless examples, some of them notable horses, including Lester Piggott's first Derby winner, *Never Say Die*, who used to hang to the left. All sorts of ironmongery had been put on his bit to try and correct the tendency. At Lester's suggestion these were left off for the Derby, which, after all, takes place on a left-handed course, and *Never Say Die* was an easy winner. Unfortunately, *Never Say Die*'s next race was in the King Edward VII Stakes at Royal Ascot, a week or two later, Ascot being a right-handed course. It was this race which gave rise to Lester's most unjust suspension. He himself, in *Lester* by Dick Francis, says of *Never Say Die*'s tendency: 'He was perfectly all right on a left-handed course, but if you were going the other way he was inclined to come out. There are certain horses that don't go one way at all. You run them one way and they're useless, and the other way they're champions. You try to tell people it makes all that difference and they don't believe you, but it's a fact!'

Another significant factor in the relationship between horse and course is its stamina in relation to the particular track. A horse which barely lasts out a mile on an easy track, such as Kempton Park, will almost certainly not be able to get further than seven furlongs on a stiff, galloping course, such as Ascot or the Newmarket Rowley Mile. A horse's breeding may suggest that he should be able to get a mile, but if he fails to do so in a truly run race it will be said that 'he didn't get the trip'.

Finally, to conclude the observations on Horses for Courses, here is a moving poem written by the former jockey Anthony Webber after a final visit to his old friend *The Snipe*, a horse who tended to perform half a stone better at Cheltenham than anywhere else, and loved the course. With Webber in the saddle, he was a winner of the Massey-Ferguson Gold Cup at Cheltenham in 1978, beating *Zongalero* and *Bachelor's Hall*, and the following season was runner-up in both this race and the Mackeson Gold Cup.

Old Horse

With care the old horse steps across his field
On a caller from past ventures to attend;
A bear now shrouds his skin that was a seal's,
"It's been a while," a firm pat makes amends.
Here stands the link between two worlds,
An earth and water farm with the air of outdoor men
And the swelling roar as a steeplechase unfurls
With the surge of sinew up the hill at Cheltenham.
More than man can do for man so does the horse
Lift men to heights they never felt before,
Brings fire to warm their hearts upon the course
When asked for lasting effort, giving all.
Show me, as one such lifespan draws to end,
How to pay respect, saying fare well to a friend.

(© Anthony Webber. Reprinted with his kind permission)

A few days after Webber's final visit in 1998, *The Snipe*, aged 28 and increasingly troubled with diabetes, had to be put down.

CHAPTER EIGHT

Principal Courses and Records of Big Races

The figures for leading trainers and jockeys are based in general on the three seasons, both Flat and National Hunt, up to and including 2003.

ASCOT Right-hand Flat and National Hunt

> Draw: On the straight Royal Hunt Cup course, where there are big fields, both high and low numbers have an advantage over middle numbers. The side which has the ultimate advantage will be determined, if the field splits into two groups, by the pace on the stands side or opposite rails, which in turn may be affected by slight differences in going. Ascot has an artificial watering system which, though operated with expertise and the best will in the world, can produce this slight difference between stands side and far rails. When the going is soft, high numbers in any case hold a very slight advantage.

Ascot is the showcase of British racing. Despite persistent criticism, it has lost much of the starchiness of former days and the facilities are superb, with the prospect of entirely new stands (to replace the still handsome 1960s versions) by the year 2006. Work is scheduled to start on a £185-million project to realign the course, principally the present straight mile, in order to create space for the new stands. In addition, the long-term objective is to be able to stage up to 60 days' racing a year (double the present figure) and to establish Ascot as one of the top five racecourses in the world. As it is, at the five-day Royal meeting in mid-June with the best racing possible, Grandstand admission has now to be booked in advance for the wonderful programme (with no sponsorship), which includes no fewer than 15 Pattern races, among them, at Group One level, the St. James's Palace Stakes at a mile and the fillies' equivalent, the Coronation Stakes, as well as the stayers' championship event, the Ascot Gold Cup. Prize-money for winners alone is more than £3 million over the five days. This great event apart, Ascot also stages the following month, the King George VI and Queen Elizabeth Diamond Stakes (prize-money £750,000, including £435,000 to the winning owner). It is one of the two most important tests for 3-y-o and 4-y-o and upwards in Europe (the other being the Prix de l'Arc de Triomphe). Racing throughout the year, however, is of a consistently high standard and in the autumn there are some significant 2-y-o events, while September sees the Festival of British Racing, which offers superb racing with (in 2003) just over £840,000 winning prize-money and four Pattern races headed by the Group One Queen Elizabeth II Stakes, which settles the European mile championship, and the Group One Meon Valley Stud Fillies Mile.

National Hunt racing has taken place at Ascot since 1966, the hurdles and chase courses being laid out on the inside of the Flat courses. In the shadow of the huge stands it hardly possesses the intimacy of an afternoon's jumping at, shall we say, Plumpton, but it makes up for that in quality, and in early to mid-season there are many valuable prizes, including the Long Walk Hurdle (£40,000) and Ladbroke Hurdle (£58,000) and an entire day sponsored by Victor Chandler with prize-money totalling £90,000. The Ascot fences are quite stiff and provide good trials for both the Cheltenham Festival and Grand National. As might be expected with the overall high prizes for both Flat and National Hunt, the leading trainers in the country do best at Ascot. On the Flat the leaders are Mark Johnston (40 winners 1999–2003); Richard Hannon (26); Sir Michael Stoute (25); John Gosden (21); John Dunlop (15); A.P. O'Brien (Ireland; 12). Jockeys: Kieren Fallon (44 winners 1999–2003); L. Dettori (38); J.P. Murtagh (25); M.J. Kinane (23); Kevin Darley (22). The separate figures for Royal Ascot should, however, be noted. Henry Cecil leads the overall totals with 70 successes since *Parthenon* won the Queen Alexandra Stakes in 1970; Sir Michael Stoute comes next with 48. But here are the most up-to-date Royal Ascot totals 1995–2004 – Trainers: Saeed bin Suroor (26 winners); Mark Johnston and Sir Michael Stoute (21 each); John Gosden (13); A.P. O'Brien (Ire; 12); M.R. Channon (9). Jockeys: L. Dettori (31 winners); K. Fallon (23); M.J. Kinane (22); J.P. Murtagh (17); T. Quinn (15); R. Hughes (12).

Leading owners make an interesting Royal Ascot study over the past ten seasons: Godolphin (25 winners); Mrs John Magnier (in various partnerships) (14); Sheikh Mohammed (11); Maktoum al-Maktoum (10); Hamdan al-Maktoum (9); HH Aga Khan and Khaled Abdulla (8 each); Cheveley Park Stud (6); P.D. Savill (5). There could be few more telling illustrations of the rise of the Arabs in recent years. Compare, for example, the most successful owners at Royal Ascot a mere 30 years ago. The list, taken from 1969 to 1973, vividly depicts a racing scene that is now almost as submerged and vanished as Atlantis: Jim Joel (6 winners); the McCalmont family (4); David Robinson, Lord and Lady Rosebery, Sir Michael Sobell, Lord Howard de Walden, Jock Whitney (3 each); Lady Beaverbrook, Louis Freedman, Mrs John Hislop, Major Sir R. Macdonald-Buchanan, C.A.B. St. George, Dr C. Vittadini (2 each).

National Hunt figures, meanwhile, 1998–99 – 2002–03, are as follows – Trainers: Martin Pipe (44 winners); Nicky Henderson (17); Josh Gifford (11); P.F. Nicholls (10); P.J. Hobbs (9); Mark Pitman (8); F. Doumen (a French trainer to note at Ascot; 7); Miss Venetia Williams (6); J.J. O'Neill and Noel T. Chance (5 each). Jockeys: A.P. McCoy (50 winners); M.A. Fitzgerald (19); Richard Johnson (13); T. Doumen, Dean Gallagher and Carl Llewellyn (7 each).

Ascot is a triangular course of 1 mile and just over 6 furlongs: the first half of it is nearly all on the descent, and the last part, which is called the Old Mile, is exactly 1 mile and is uphill the greater part of the way. The Swinley Course is the last mile and a half. The comparatively short (2 $1/2$ furlongs) run-in from the sharp final bend to the winning-post puts a big premium on jockeyship on the Flat. If a horse is not in a good position at this final turn it is often goodbye to any chance (although Pat Eddery, in particular, disagrees with this long-held view, and that wonderful French filly *Dahlia* certainly disproved it in 1973 when coming from last to first!).

2 ¹/₂ miles   4-y-o+   The Ascot Gold Cup, Royal Ascot, mid-June

The Ascot Gold Cup is the most important stayers' event of the season, open to 4-y-o and upwards, colts, geldings and fillies at weight-for-age. In 2004, winning prize-money alone was £145,000. By contrast, when first run, in 1807, it was worth 100 guineas to Mr Durand, owner of *Master Jockey*; even so, a sizeable purse for those days, and in today's terms about £30,000. Some very famous 19th-century horses captured the Gold Cup, including *Beeswing*, *West Australian* (first winner of the Triple Crown the previous season), *Gladiateur* (the so-called 'Avenger of Waterloo' as the first French-bred to win the Derby, in 1865), *St. Simon* (who became one of the greatest stallions in the stud-book, and champion sire nine times between 1890 and 1901) as well as two further Triple Crown winners, *La Flèche* and *Isinglass* (who, when retired in 1895, held a record for stakes earned not surpassed until 1952, by *Tulyar*). The achievement of *Sagaro* in winning three times is unique in the history of the race, as is the record of his rider, Lester Piggott, who rode no fewer than 11 winners. A few years ago there was much criticism of the Gold Cup by a minority who considered that it was out of date, too long for the modern thoroughbred and unappealing to spectators. All this has been triumphantly answered by the race itself with a series of thrilling finishes in recent seasons, and by an increase in participants. Indeed, in 1999 it attracted its largest-ever field: 17 runners. Long may the Gold Cup continue as it is at present.

	Winner	Age	Owner	Trainer	Jockey	SP
1975	Sagaro	4	G.A.Oldham	F.Boutin (France)	L.Piggott	7/4 F
1976	Sagaro	5	G.A.Oldham	F.Boutin (France)	L.Piggott	8/15 F
1977	Sagaro	6	G.A.Oldham	F.Boutin (France)	L.Piggott	9/4
1978	Shangamuzzo	5	Mrs E.Charles	M.Stoute	G.Starkey	13/2
1979	Le Moss	4	C.d'Alessio	H.Cecil	L.Piggott	7/4
1980	Le Moss	5	C.d'Alessio	H.Cecil	J.Mercer	3/1
1981	Ardross	5	C.A.B.St.George	H.Cecil	L.Piggott	30/100 F
1982	Ardross	6	C.A.B.St.George	H.Cecil	L.Piggott	1/5 F
1983	Little Wolf	5	Lord Porchester	Major W.Hern	W.Carson	4/1
1984	Gildoran	4	R.Sangster	B.Hills	S.Cauthen	10/1
1985	Gildoran	5	R.Sangster	B.Hills	B.Thomson	5/2
1986	Longboat	5	R.Hollingsworth	Major W.Hern	W.Carson	Evens F
1987	Paean	4	Lord H.de Walden	H.Cecil	S.Cauthen	6/1
1988	Sadeem	5	Sheikh Mohammed	G.Harwood	G.Starkey	7/2
1989	Sadeem	6	Sheikh Mohammed	G.Harwood	G.Starkey	8/11 F
1990	Ashal	4	Hamdan al-Maktoum	H.Thomson Jones	R.Hills	14/1
1991	Indian Queen	6m	Sir G.Brunton	Lord Huntingdon	W.R.Swinburn	25/1
1992	Drum Taps	6	Y.Asakawa	Lord Huntingdon	L.Dettori	7/4 F
1993	Drum Taps	7	Y.Asakawa	Lord Huntington	L.Dettori	13/2
1994	Arcadian Heights	6	J.L.C.Pearce	G.Wragg	M.Hills	20/1
1995	Double Trigger	4	R.Huggins	M.Johnston	J.Weaver	9/4 2F
1996	Classic Cliche	4	Godolphin	Saeed bin Suroor	M.J.Kinane	3/1
1997	Celeric	5	C.Spence	D.Morley	Pat Eddery	11/2 2F
1998	Kayf Tara	4	Godolphin	Saeed bin Suroor	L.Dettori	11/1
1999	Enzeli	4	HH Aga Khan	J.Oxx(Ire)	J.P.Murtagh	20/1

2000	Kayf Tara	6	Godolphin	Saeed bin Suroor	M.J.Kinane	11/8 F
2001	Royal Rebel	5	P.D.Savill	M.Johnston	J.P.Murtagh	8/1
2002	Royal Rebel	6	P.D.Savill	M.Johnston	J.P.Murtagh	16/1
2003	Mr. Dinos	4	C.Shiacolos	P.F.I.Cole	K.Fallon	3/1 2F
2004	Papineau	4	Godolphin	Saeed bin Suroor	L.Dettori	5/1 2F

1 1/2 miles 3-y-o+   King George VI & Queen Elizabeth Diamond Stakes, Ascot, late July

First run in 1951 as the Festival of Britain Stakes, this event has become established as the most important mid-season test matching the 3-year-old generation against its elders for the first time over the distance at Group One level. It is a weight-for-age contest for colts, geldings and fillies and attracts a high-class and usually international field, although French interest has declined since the very early years. From *Tulyar* (1952) and *Pinza* (1953) onwards, 12 Derby winners have been successful in the same year, while among the older horses, one of the outstanding stars of the 20th century, *Ribot* (1956), must be mentioned, so too the French heroine *Dahlia*. She and *Swain* are the only dual winners of the race, while *Swain* in 1998 became the only 6-y-o ever to win. Sponsored by the De Beers Diamond Corporation, it was worth £435,000 to the winning owner in 2004, and no less than £165,000 to the runner-up.

	Winner	Age/Sex	Owner	Trainer	Jockey	SP
1970	Nijinsky	3c	C.Engelhard	M.V.O'Brien(Ireland)	L.Piggott	40/85 F
1971	Mill Reef	3c	Paul Mellon	I.A.Balding	G.Lewis	8/13 F
1972	Brigadier Gerard	4c	Mrs J.Hislop	Major W.R.Hern	J.Mercer	8/13 F
1973	Dahlia	3f	N.Bunker Hunt	M.Zilber(France)	W.Pyers	10/1
1974	Dahlia	4f	N.Bunker Hunt	M.Zilber(France)	L.Piggott	15/8 F
1975	Grundy	3c	Dr C.Vittadini	P.Walwyn	P.Eddery	4/5 F
1976	Pawneese	3f	D.Wildenstein	A.Penna(France)	Y.Saint-Martin	9/4 2F
1977	The Minstrel	3c	R.Sangster	M.V.O'Brien(Ireland)	L.Piggott	7/4 F
1978	Ile de Bourbon	3c	A.D.McCall	R.F.Johnson-Houghton	J.Reid	12/1
1979	Troy	3c	Sir M.Sobell	Major W.R.Hern	W.Carson	2/5 F
1980	Ela-Mana-Mou	4c	S.Weinstock	Major W.R.Hern	W.Carson	11/4 2F
1981	Shergar	3c	HH Aga Khan	M.Stoute	W.R.Swinburn	2/5 F
1982	Kalaglow	4c	A.Ward	G.Harwood	G.Starkey	13/2 3F
1983	Time Charter	4f	R.Barnett	H.Candy	J.Mercer	5/11 3F
1984	Teenoso	4c	E.B.Moller	G.Wragg	L.Piggott	13/2
1985	Petoski	4c	Lady Beaverbrook	Major W.R.Hern	W.Carson	12/1
1986	Dancing Brave	3c	Khaled Abdulla	G.Harwood	P.Eddery	6/4 F
1987	Reference Point	3c	L.Freedman	H.Cecil	S.Cauthen	11/10 F
1988	Mtoto	5h	Sheikh Ahmed al-Maktoum	A.C.Stewart	M.Roberts	4/1 2F
1989	Nashwan	3c	Sheikh Hamdan al-Maktoum	Major W.R.Hern	W.Carson	2/9 F
1990	Belmez	3c	Sheikh Mohammed	H.Cecil	M.J.Kinane	15/2
1991	Generous	3c	Fahd Salman	P.F.Cole	A.Munro	4/6 F
1992	St Jovite	3c	Mrs V.K.Payson	J.S.Bolger(Ireland)	S.Craine	4/5 F

1993	Opera House	5h	Sheikh Mohammed	M.Stoute	M.Roberts	8/1
1994	King's Theatre	3c	Sheikh Mohammed	H.Cecil	M.J.Kinane	12/1
1995	Lammtarra	3c	Saeed Maktoum al-Maktoum	Saeed bin Suroor	L. Dettori	9/4 F
1996	Pentire	4c	Moller Racing	G.Wragg	R.Hills	100/30 2F
1997	Swain	5h	Godolphin	Saeed bin Suroor	J.Reid	16/1
1998	Swain	6h	Godolphin	Saeed bin Suroor	L.Dettori	11/2
1999	Daylami	5h	Godolphin	Saeed bin Suroor	L.Dettori	3/1 2F
2000	Montjeu	4c	M.Tabor	J.E.Hammond(Fr)	M.J.Kinane	1/3 F
2001	Galileo	3c	Mrs J.Magnier/ M.Tabor	A.P.O'Brien(Ireland)	M.J.Kinane	1/2 F
2002	Golan	4c	exors. Lord Weinstock	Sir M.Stoute	K.Fallon	11/2
2003	Alamshar	3c	HH Aga Khan	J.Oxx(Ireland)	J.P.Murtagh	13/2
2004	Doyen	4c	Godolphin	Saeed bin Suroor	L.Dettori	11/10 F

c = colt f = filly h = horse

1 mile (Straight) Handicap   Royal Hunt Cup, Royal Ascot, June

	Winner(Draw)	Age	Wt	Trainer	Jockey	Ran	SP
1977	My Hussar(10)	5	8.10	J.Sutcliffe	W.Carson	15	10/1
1978	Fear Naught(19) f	4	8.0	J.Etherington	M.Wigham*3	19	12/1
1979	Pipedreamer(8)	4	8.5	H.Candy	P.Waldron	24	12/1
1980	Tender Heart(21)	4	9.0	J.Sutcliffe	J.Mercer	22	13/2 2F
1981	Teamwork(3)	4	8.6	G.Harwood	G.Starkey	20	8/1
1982	Buzzards Bay(14)	4	8.12	H.Collingridge	J.Mercer	20	14/1
1983	Mighty Fly(11) f	4	9.3	D.Elsworth	S.Cauthen	31	12/1
1984	Hawkley(13)	4	8.6	P.Haslam	T.Williams*5	18	10/1
1985	Come on the Blues(21)	6	8.2	C.Brittain	C.Rutter*5	27	14/1
1986	Patriarch(12)	4	7.12	J.Dunlop	T.Quinn	32	20/1
1987	Vague Shot(10)	4	9.5	R.F.Casey	S.Cauthen	25	10/1 2F
1988	Governorship(14)	4	9.6	C.R.Nelson	J.Reid	26	33/1
1989	True Panache(5)	4	9.4	J.Tree	P.Eddery	27	5/1 F
1990	Pontenuovo(4)	5	7.7	D.Elsworth	G.Bardwell	32	50/1
1991	Eurolink the Lad(30)	4	8.9	J.Dunlop	J.Reid	29	25/1
1992	Colour Sergeant(11)	4	7.8	Lord Huntingdon	D.Harrison*5	31	20/1
1993	Imperial Ballet(19)	4	8.12	H.Cecil	P.Eddery	30	20/1
1994	Face North(30)	6	8.3	R.Akehurst	A.Munro	32	25/1
1995	Realities(30)	5	9.0	G.Harwood	M.J.Kinane	32	11/1 2F
1996	Yeast(3)	4	8.6	W.J.Haggas	K.Fallon	31	8/1 F
1997	Red Robbo(17)	4	8.6	R.Akehurst	O.Peslier	32	16/1
1998	Refuse To Lose(6)	4	7.11	J.M.Eustace	J.Tate	32	20/1
1999	Showboat(30)	5	8.6	B.W.Hills	N.Pollard*3	32	14/1
2000	Caribbean Monarch(28)	5	8.10	Sir M.Stoute	K.Fallon	32	11/2 2F
2001	Surprise Encounter(29)	5	8.9	E.A.L.Dunlop	L.Dettori	30	8/1 2F
2002	Norton(10)	5	8.9	T.G.Mills	J.Fortune	30	25/1

| 2003 | Macadamia(6) | 4 | 8.13 | J.R.Fanshawe | D.O'Neill | 32 | 8/1 2F |
| 2004 | Mine(8) | 6 | 9.5 | J.D.Bethell | T.Quinn | 31 | 16/1 |

* Apprentice allowance claimed in lb.   f = filly

Favourites The Royal Hunt Cup is very much a prestige handicap and consistently attracts a good quality field, although gone are the days when Classic runners regularly competed. Two favourites and 6 second-favourites during the period under review may suggest it is a difficult race for backers, but this is not, historically, so. Despite a recent run of longer-priced winners, the race has most often been taken by a well-backed horse in the first 4 or so in the betting.

Trainers John Dunlop (Arundel): 3 winners; David Elsworth (Hampshire): 2 winners.

Age 4-y-o is the predominant age group and provides 58% of the average entry for the race, but 80% of the winners. Next is 5-y-o. 3-y-o do not do well.

Weights In the most recent 20 years, high weights have done particularly well, the bracket 9 st to 9 st 7 lb providing no fewer than 7 winners.

Draw The far side or the stands rails enjoy a marginal advantage.

6 furlong Handicap   The Wokingham Stakes, Royal Ascot, June

First run in 1813, but in its present form since 1874, this race is a feature of the final afternoon at Royal Ascot.

	Winner(Draw)	Age	Wt	Trainer	Jockey	Ran	SP
1975	Boone's Cabin(USA)(6)	5	10.0	M.V.O'Brien(Ire)	L.Piggott	20	6/1
1976	Import(1)	5	9.4	W.Wightman	M.L.Thomas	12	4/1 F
1977	Calibina(11) f	5	8.5	P.Cole	G.Baxter	13	14/1
1978	Equal Opportunity(3)	4	7.12	P.Arthur	R.Curant	24	20/1
1979	Lord Rochford(5)	4	8.8	B.Swift	S.Raymont*5	28	16/1
1980	Queen's Pride(19)	4	7.13	P.Cole	G.Baxter	29	28/1
1981	Great Eastern(30)	4	9.8	J.Dunlop	W.Carson	29	16/1
1982	Battle Hymn(2)	3	7.7	G.Harwood	A.Clark*3	24	14/1
1983	Melindra(22) f	4	7.5	D.Elsworth	A.McGlone*5	27	7/1 F
1984	Petong(18)	4	9.6	M.A.Jarvis	B.Raymond	28	11/1 JF
1985	Time Machine(2)	4	7.12	P.Hughes	W.Carson	30	10/1
1986	Touch of Grey(13)	3	8.8	D.Thom	M.L.Thomas	28	20/1
1987	Bel Byou(10)	3	8.3	P.Cole	T.Quinn	29	11/2 F
1988	Powder Blue(13) m	6	8.5	P.J.Makin	T.Ives	30	28/1
1989	Mac's Fighter(7)	4	9.12	W.A.O'Gorman	C.Asmussen	27	16/1
1990	Knight of Mercy(17)	4	8.6	R.Hannon	P.Eddery	28	16/1
1991	Amigo Menor(4)	5	8.7	D.Murray-Smith	C.Rutter	29	14/1
1992	Red Rosein(29) m	6	8.1	Capt J.Wilson	G.Carter	29	33/1
1993	Nagida(4) f	4	8.10	J.A.R.Toller	J.Weaver*3	30	11/1
1994	Venture Capitalist(30)	5	8.12	R.Hannon	J.Reid	30	20/1
1995	Astrac(16)	4	8.7	R.Akehurst	S. Sanders	30	14/1
1996	Emerging Market(7)	4	8.13	J.Dunlop	K.Darley	30	33/1

1997	Selhurstpark Flyer(5)	6	8.9	J.Berry	P.Roberts*5	30	25/1
1998	Selhurstpark Flyer(20)	7	9.7	J.Berry	C.Lowther	29	16/1
1999	Deep Space(3)	4	8.7	E.A.L.Dunlop	G.Carter	30	14/1
2000	Harmonic Way(28)	5	9.6	R.Charlton	R.Hughes	29	12/1
2001	Nice One Clare(4)	5	9.3	J.W.Payne	J.P.Murtagh	30	7/1 F
2002	Capricho(21)	5	8.11	J.Akehurst	T.Quinn	28	20/1
2003	Fayr Jig(13)/	4	9.6	T.D.Easterby	W.Supple	29	10/1
	Ratio(22) (dead-heat)	5	9.3	J.Hammond(France)	L.Dettori		14/1
2004	Lafi(30)	5	8.13	D.Nichols	E.Ahern	31	6/1 F

* Apprentice allowance claimed in lb.   f = filly, m = mare

Favourites The Wokingham is a highly competitive hell-for-leather dash over the tough Ascot 6 furlongs – the last 6 furlongs, in fact, of the straight Royal Hunt Cup course. This is no course for short runners and, run at a strong pace throughout, tests a sprinter to his or her limit. If a horse is not proven at the distance at Ascot or similar tough courses, a shown ability to get further on easier tracks is desirable.   Despite the attractive prices (because of big fields, normally) of the winners shown in the table, the Wokingham is *not* a race for outsiders. Well-backed horses usually win. As shown by the table, fillies and mares do particularly well.

Trainers Newmarket has sent out 9 winners since 1960, but mostly from smaller training establishments. Paul Cole should be noted as having saddled the winner 3 times; John Dunlop twice.

Jockeys Gary Carter: 2 successes.   Claiming apprentices (5 winners since 1979) have an excellent record.

Age Since 1974: 3-y-o 10% of winners; 4-y-o 48% of winners; 5-y-o 30% of winners. Four 6-y-o won in the 20th century: *Galleot* (1910), *Powder Blue* (1988), *Red Rosein* (1992) and *Selhurstpark Flyer* (1997), who completed a double in 1998 and so became the oldest-ever Wokingham winner.

Weight With the raising of the minimum handicap weight it is difficult to draw a useful conclusion.   In the entire post-war period since 1945 the 7 st 7 lb to 8 st 8 lb bracket has provided approximately 50% of all winners, but whereas it used to be the middle part of the handicap, it is now the lower.   One point of significance may be emerging, and that is the increased proportion, as already seen in the Royal Hunt Cup, of higher-weighted winners – 7 carrying 9 st 4 lb or more since 1975.

Draw The Wokingham is yet another race (see also the Cambridgeshire) where the draw is commonly supposed not to matter very much.   This is not so, as a look at the draw diagram opposite will show.   This is based on the draw expressed as a percentage of the total number of runners each year, which portrays the spread of the draw across the start, although a horse drawn 1 in a field of 20, for example, is expressed at 5%, and drawn 1 in a field of 30 becomes 3%.

From this it can be seen that 16 winners of the 35 runnings of the Wokingham since 1965 came from the 0–20% area, and a further 8 from the 80–100% sector: 65.7% of winners, therefore, drawn low-high. Winners' actual draw numbers were, 1–4: 13; within 4 of the highest draw: 7.

The main reason for the Wokingham draw being so oriented is, of course, that big fields invariably split, and, in a fast start, horses drawn in the middle lose ground getting over to either side. The positioning of the starting stalls must also be taken into account.

WOKINGHAM HANDICAP
Draw Diagram 1965–2000
(Draw as a percentage of no. of runners)

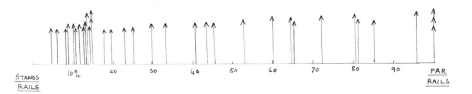

STANDS
RAILS

FAR
RAILS

AYR   Left-hand   Flat and National Hunt

Draw: Because of the long left-handed bend after the start, low numbers are favoured in races of 7 furlongs and 1 mile, particularly when there are big fields. Again, on the straight course in big fields when the going is soft, high numbers in contrast are preferable.

Ayr is one of the finest racecourses in Britain, and the best in Scotland. It is an oval of just over a mile and a half with easy turns, and the round course joins the 6 furlong course half a mile from the winning-post. Eleven-furlong races start on a chute joining the main course on the far side. There are minor undulations, but Ayr is essentially flat throughout. The biggest and most important Flat meeting, in September, is the Western Meeting which features the 6 furlong Ayr Gold Cup, sponsored by Ladbrokes up to 2000 and the Tote from 2001. This race invariably produces big fields and big starting prices for a gamble. It is an historic Scottish race, first run in 1804, won not long ago by *Lochsong* (see under **Sprinter** in Chapter One for her record). History was also made at Ayr in 1989, when the St. Leger was transferred here because the Doncaster course was unfit. Thus Ayr became the only course outside England to stage an English Classic. National Hunt racing at Ayr is also high-class, and among the races are the Scottish Grand National (whose winners include *Red Rum*, who followed up his second Grand National triumph in 1974, and now has his statue next to the paddock at both Ayr and Aintree) and Scottish Champion Hurdle. The course, like the Flat one, provides an excellent and fair test.

Leading trainers: *Flat*   Mark Johnston (18 winners); J.S. Goldie (10); Mick Channon (9); I. Semple (8); Miss L.A. Perratt (7).

National Hunt   L. Lungo (23 winners); N.G. Richards (14); P.F. Nicholls (8); Mrs. Reveley, A.C. Whillans, P. Monteith and Ferdy Murphy (7 each).

Leading jockeys: *Flat*   A. Culhane (14 winners); Kevin Darley (13); Kieren Fallon (9); W. Supple (8); K. Dalgleish (7); D. McGaffin (6); J. Carroll and Darryll Holland (5 each).

National Hunt   Tony Dobbin (31 winners); K. Fenwick (11); Richard Johnson (9); B. Harding (8); P. Robson, B. Storey and R. Walsh (7 each).

CHELTENHAM   Left-hand   National Hunt only

Cheltenham is the Mecca of National Hunt racing, the equivalent of Newmarket 'Headquarters' on the Flat, without the training – a place of pilgrimage for the hardy followers of the winter game. Its great Festival meeting in March is packed with wonderful racing in the spectacular setting below Cleeve Hill. Quite apart from the Gold Cup (sponsored by the Tote) and the Champion Hurdle (sponsored by Smurfit), there is not a race lacking top-class contestants and strong betting markets. Novice hurdlers and chasers, 2 mile chasers, long-distance hurdlers, hunter-chasers, amateur riders – all are catered for at this three-day (with four days in prospect) bonanza with, outside the Gold Cup and Champion Hurdle, the most valuable winning prizes (in 2004) including the 2 mile Queen Mother Champion Chase (£145,000); the Bonusprint Stayers Hurdle (3 m+, £81,200); the Irish Independent Arkle Challenge Trophy (2 m, £174,000); and JCB Triumph Hurdle for 4-y-o (originally rescued and revived in the 1960s by the *Daily Express* from its Hurst Park origins; worth £58,000). But the racing throughout the year at Cheltenham is superb, with prize-money to match. A recent innovation at Cheltenham has been cross-country racing, sponsored by Sporting Index (including in Nov: Sporting Index Cross Country Chase – 30 fences, £19,314 to the winner).

Cheltenham racecourse is, in fact, two racecourses. In the late 1950s a new course was added to the old one and both courses are now used, both approximately 1 1/2 mile ovals, with special chutes for the starts of races run over 2 1/2 miles, 3 1/4 miles and 4 miles. There used to be a chute, out of sight of the stands, for the start of the Gold Cup; also, 4 mile races used to disappear for a time somewhere beyond the stands and behind the car park. But that has all been changed. Quite unchanged, however, are the Cheltenham gradients including a severe uphill run-in from the last of the demanding fences, making this course a stiff test of both stamina and courage. One of the greatest heroes of Cheltenham is *Arkle*, a magnificent chaser, whose memory is now commemorated by a bronze statue. More recently, the Cheltenham crowd took to their hearts another Irish horse called *Dawn Run*. This outstanding mare is the only horse ever to win both the Champion Hurdle and the Gold Cup, a feat she achieved in 1984 and 1986, before cruelly meeting her death shortly afterwards while attempting to win the French Champion Hurdle for the second time. Her statue, unveiled in 1987, faces that of *Arkle*.

Leading trainers: Martin Pipe (36 winners); Philip Hobbs (18); Paul Nicholls (17); Nicky Henderson and Jonjo O'Neill (12 each); Miss Henrietta Knight (10); Ferdy Murphy and Miss Venetia Williams (6 each).

Leading jockeys: A.P. Mccoy (34 winners); Richard Johnson (19); Mick Fitzgerald (16); R. Walsh (13); Jim Culloty (10); B.J. Geraghty (9).

As with Royal Ascot, it is worth looking at the details of the three-day National Hunt Festival separately. The leading Festival trainer is Martin Pipe with 32 winners since 1981 (up to 2004). His successes include two Champion Hurdles and both the Mildmay of Flete Challenge Cup and Cathcart Challenge Cup Chase four times each. Next comes Nicky Henderson with 25 victories, including three Champion Hurdles in a row achieved 1985–87 by that well-remembered hero of the crowds, *See You Then*. He has also taken the Arkle Challenge Trophy three times. Top rider is Tony McCoy with 15 winners (up to 2004); then comes Mick Fitzgerald with 11 successes. In addition, McCoy (1998), Jamie Osborne (1992) and B.J. Geraghty (2003) share with Fred Winter (1959) the post-war record of five for the most Festival winners in one year. Nevertheless, none of them yet come near Pat Taaffe's record total of 25 Festival triumphs.

In 1996, the Irish, with seven winners, had their most successful Festival since 1977 (same total) and only one short of their best-ever: eight triumphs in 1958. In only two seasons post-war have they failed to send over at least one winner: in 1947 (when because of the severe winter the Festival races had to be reopened and compressed into one day in April) and in 1989.

2 miles   Champion Hurdle, Cheltenham, March

Like the Cheltenham Gold Cup, also run at the Festival Meeting, this is the National Hunt equivalent of a Classic race, and decides the Hurdles Championship of the year. The distance has varied over the years (up to 200 yards beyond 2 miles) but is now 2 miles and about 110 yards. Horses carry the following weights: 4-y-o, 11 st 6 lb; older horses (except mares), 12 st (the majority of runners); mares, 11 st 9 lb. The race was first run in 1927 as the Champion Hurdle Challenge Cup and is now called the Smurfit Champion Hurdle Challenge Trophy. Prize to the winner in 2004 was £174,000.

	Winner	Age	Trainer	Jockey	Ran	SP
1965	Kirriemuir	5	F.Walwyn	G.W.Robinson	19	50/1
1966	Salmon Spray	8	R.Turnell	J.Haine	17	4/1
1967	Saucy Kit	6	M.H.Easterby	R.Edwards	23	100/6
1968	Persian War	5	C.Davies	J.Uttley	16	4/1
1969	Persian War	6	C.Davies	J.Uttley	17	6/4 F
1970	Persian War	7	C.Davies	J.Uttley	14	5/4 F
1971	Bula	6	F.Winter	P.Kelleway	9	15/8 F
1972	Bula	7	F.Winter	P.Kelleway	12	8/11 F
1973	Comedy of Errors	6	F.Rimell	W.Smith	8	8/1
1974	Lanzarote	6	F.Winter	R.Pitman	7	7/4
1975	Comedy of Errors	8	F.Rimell	K.White	13	11/8 F
1976	Night Nurse	5	M.H.Easterby	P.Broderick	8	2/1 F
1977	Night Nurse	6	M.H.Easterby	P.Broderick	10	15/2
1978	Monksfield	6	D.McDonogh	T.Kinane	13	11/2
1979	Monksfield	7	D.McDonogh	D.Hughes	10	9/4 F

1980	Sea Pigeon	10	M.H.Easterby	J.J.O'Neill	9	13/2
1981	Sea Pigeon	11	M.H.Easterby	J.Francome	14	7/4 F
1982	For Auction	6	M.Cunningham	Mr C.Magnier	14	40/1
1983	Gaye Brief	6	Mrs M.Rimell	R.Linley	17	7/1
1984	Dawn Run (m)	6	P.Mullins	J.J.O'Neill	14	4/5 F
1985	See You Then	5	N.Henderson	S.Smith Eccles	14	16/1
1986	See You Then	6	N.Henderson	S.Smith Eccles	23	5/6 F
1987	See You Then	7	N.Henderson	S.Smith Eccles	18	11/10 F
1988	Celtic Shot	6	F.Winter	P.Scudamore	21	7/1
1989	Beech Road	7	G.Balding	R.Guest	15	50/1
1990	Kribensis	6	M.Stoute	R.Dunwoody	19	95/40
1991	Morley Street	7	G.Balding	J.Frost	24	4/1
1992	Royal Gait	9	J.Fanshawe	G.McCourt	16	6/1
1993	Granville Again	7	M.Pipe	P.Scudamore	18	13/2
1994	Flakey Dove (m)	8	R.J.Price	M.Dwyer	15	9/1
1995	Alderbrook	6	K.C.Bailey	N. Williamson	14	11/2
1996	Collier Bay	6	J.B.Old	G.Bradley	16	9/1
1997	Make A Stand	6	M.C.Pipe	A.P.McCoy	17	7/1
1998	Istabraq	6	A.P.O'Brien	C.Swan	18	3/1 F
1999	Istabraq	7	A.P.O'Brien	C.Swan	14	4/9 F
2000	Istabraq	8	A.P.O'Brien	C.Swan	12	8/15 F
2001	No race					
2002	Hors La Loi III	7	J.R.Fanshawe	D.Gallagher	15	10/1
2003	Rooster Booster	9	P.J.Hobbs	R.Johnson	17	9/2 2F
2004	Hardy Eustace	7	D.T.Hughes	C.O'Dwyer	14	33/1

m = mare

About 3 1/4 miles 22 fences   The Cheltenham Gold Cup,   March

The Cheltenham Gold Cup, centrepiece of the final day of the Festival Meeting, is to National Hunt racing what the Derby is to the Flat. Since *Red Splash* was the first winner, in 1924, the race has provided the entry to steeplechasing's hall of fame, and some illustrious names embellish its records, after many a thrill on the way to so doing: *Easter Hero* and *L'Escargot* (twice each), *Cottage Rake* and *Arkle* (three times each), and *Golden Miller* (five times), although the number of victories gives no indication of the immeasurable superiority of *Arkle* as the greatest of all chasers, and, before him, that of *Golden Miller*. Among other famous names, *Mandarin* won in 1962 not long before his sensational victory with a broken bridle in the Grand Steeplechase de Paris; the game little ex-hunter-chaser *Halloween* (partnered, like *Mandarin*, by the incomparable Fred Winter) was placed four times without winning; while *The Dikler* set the seal on his career and Fulke Walwyn's high opinion of him at the fourth attempt. More recently, *Dawn Run*, amid enthusiasm and sentiment not witnessed since *Arkle*'s day, became only the fourth mare to win, and the first horse to have succeeded in both Gold Cup and Champion Hurdle; in 1989, *Desert Orchid* set the seal on his fame with a courageous victory; while in 1982, Michael Dickinson had saddled the winner, *Silver Buck*, and runner-up, *Bregawn*, and the following year improved on that by being trainer of all five horses to finish, this time *Bregawn* being the winner, and *Silver*

Buck finishing fourth. In 1924, the value to the winning owner was £685; sponsored by the Tote, the equivalent figure in 2004 was £203,000.

	Winner	Age	Trainer	Jockey	Ran	SP
1960	Pas Seul	7	R.Turnell	W.Rees	12	6/1
1961	Saffron Tartan	10	D.Butchers	F.Winter	11	2/1 F
1962	Mandarin	11	F.Walwyn	F.Winter	9	7/2
1963	Mill House	6	F.Walwyn	G.W.Robinson	12	7/2 F
1964	Arkle	7	T.Dreaper	P.Taaffe	4	7/4 2F
1965	Arkle	8	T.Dreaper	P.Taaffe	4	30/100 F
1966	Arkle	9	T.Dreaper	P.Taaffe	5	1/10 F
1967	Woodland Venture	7	F.Rimell	T.Biddlecombe	8	100/8
1968	Fort Leney	10	T.Dreaper	P.Taaffe	5	11/2
1969	What A Myth	12	Ryan Price	P.Kelleway	11	8/1
1970	L'Escargot	7	Dan Moore	T.Carberry	12	33/1
1971	L'Escargot	8	Dan Moore	T.Carberry	8	7/2 JF
1972	Glencaraig Lady (m)	8	F.Flood	F.Berry	12	6/1
1973	The Dikler	10	F.Walwyn	R.Barry	8	9/1
1974	Captain Christy	7	P.Taaffe	H.Beasley	7	7/1
1975	Ten Up	8	J.Dreaper	T.Carberry	8	2/1 2F
1976	Royal Frolic	7	F.Rimell	J.Burke	11	14/1
1977	Davy Lad	7	M.O'Toole	D.Hughes	13	14/1
1978	Midnight Court	7	F.Winter	J.Francome	10	5/2 2F
1979	Alverton	9	M.H.Easterby	J.J.O'Neill	14	5/1 JF
1980	Master Smudge	8	A.Barrow	R.Hoare	15	14/1
	(Tied Cottage finished first, disqualified)					
1981	Little Owl	7	M.H.Easterby	Mr A.J.Wilson	15	6/1 2F
1982	Silver Buck	10	M.Dickinson	R.Earnshaw	22	8/1
1983	Bregawn	9	M.Dickinson	G.Bradley	11	100/30 F
1984	Burrough Hill Lad	8	Mrs J.Pitman	P.Tuck	12	7/2 2F
1985	Forgive 'n Forget	8	J.Fitzgerald	M.Dwyer	15	7/1
1986	Dawn Run (m)	8	P.Mullins	J.J.O'Neill	11	15/8 F
1987	The Thinker	9	W.A.Stephenson	R.Lamb	12	13/2 2F
1988	Charter Party	10	D.Nicholson	R.Dunwoody	15	10/1
1989	Desert Orchid	10	D.Elsworth	S.Sherwood	13	5/2 F
1990	Norton's Coin	9	S.Griffiths	G.McCourt	12	100/1
1991	Garrison Savannah	8	Mrs J.Pitman	M.Pitman	14	16/1
1992	Cool Ground	10	G.Balding	A.Maguire	8	25/1
1993	Jodami	8	P.Beaumont	M.Dwyer	16	8/1 J2F
1994	The Fellow	9	F.Doumen(Fr)	A.Kondrat	15	7/1
1995	Master Oats	9	K.C.Bailey	N.Williamson	15	100/30 F
1996	Imperial Call	7	F.Sutherland	C.O'Dwyer	10	9/2 2F
1997	Mr Mulligan	9	Noel Chance	A.P.McCoy	14	20/1
1998	Cool Dawn	10	R.H.Alner	A.Thornton	17	25/1
1999	See More Business	9	P.F.Nicholls	M.A.Fitzgerald	12	16/1
2000	Looks Like Trouble	8	Noel Chance	R.Johnson	12	9/2 2F

2001	No race					
2002	Best Mate	7	Miss H.Knight	J.Culloty	18	7/1
2003	Best Mate	8	Miss H.Knight	J.Culloty	15	13/8 F
2004	Best Mate	9	Miss H.Knight	J.Culloty	10	8/11 F

m = mare

Favourites Not, overall, a race for favourites, nor altogether a reliable race for backers, the reason partly being that progressive, youngish chasers (see table) frequently upstage better-backed horses with established reputations. As can be seen, since 1960, 11 7-y-o have prevailed. Only 22.5% of favourites/joint-favourites succeeded between 1960 and 2000, and 47% of favourites or second-favourites. A total of 72% of winners, nevertheless, were in the first 4 in the betting.

CHEPSTOW   Left-hand   Flat and National Hunt

Draw: A slight advantage to high numbers on the straight course

Chepstow racecourse is only 78 years old and has come up in the world since its early days when, nevertheless, Gordon Richards put it, in 1933, into the record books by riding 11 consecutive winners there. For its rise to prosperity, the enterprise and imagination of its late and sadly missed Clerk of the Course for 20 years, John Hughes, must primarily be thanked, particularly in the area of attracting sponsors, but his good foundations have been enthusiastically built on by the present incumbent, Rodger Farrant. Also the opening of the Severn Road Bridge has brought easy access via the M4, not least for competing horses, in particular those from the Lambourn training area. Picturesque parkland surroundings and good racing make for an enjoyable time at Chepstow races. There is a mile course, quite straight, with undulations, and the round course is an oval joined to the straight course about 2 miles in circumference. And improvements are on the way with a £10 million redevelopment scheme now in progress. Its provisions include a new weighing room and Members' and brand new other stands.

National Hunt racing takes place on the oval course and as a result of its switchback nature the going can vary from fast down the back straight to wet in the dips; the fences are very fair, but the course itself demands abundant stamina, particularly when the ground becomes testing. The undulating nature of the course in the home straight also presents problems and demands on riding skill at the fences, the last of which is right in front of the stands. And for the horse on the Flat there is a stiffish 2 furlong rise where the two courses join. Big races include – Nov: Tote Silver Trophy Handicap Hurdle (2 m 4 f+, £22,073 to the winner); Dec: Western Daily Press Finale Juvenile Hurdle (2 m+, £21,420 to the winner); Dec: John Hughes Rehearsal Chase (3 m, £23,800 to the winner); and the Welsh National Handicap Chase, first run over 2 m 4 f at Cardiff in 1895, moved to Chepstow in 1949 and now, over 3 m 5 f, sponsored by Coral with a first prize of £43,500. Distinguished past winners include Aintree heroes *Rag Trade*, *Corbiere* and, most recently, *Earth Summit* as well as *Crudwell*, *Burrough Hill Lad*, *Bonanza Boy* (twice) and *Peaty Sandy*, who in 1981 walked to the course through the snow.

Martin Pipe has a remarkable record in the race, with five winners since 1988 and a runner-up. The average prize-money for National Hunt racing is far greater than for Flat racing at Chepstow and the quality of the jumping races is impressive. Horses that like to make the running do well over the jumps here.

Leading trainers: *Flat*   B.J. Meehan and B. Palling (10 winners each up to 2003); E.A. Dunlop (9); John Dunlop and P.D. Evans (8 each); Richard Hannon (7); H. Candy (6); J.M. Bradley and Mick Channon (5 each).

National Hunt   Paul Nicholls (35 winners up to 2003); Martin Pipe (15); P.J. Hobbs (13); J.J. O'Neill (7); Miss Venetia Williams and R.H. Alner (6 each).

Leading jockeys: *Flat*   Dane O'Neill (13 winners up to 2003); D. Kinsella and Seb Sanders (9 each); S. Drowne, K. Fallon and F. Norton (7 each); W. Supple (6); T. Quinn (5).

National Hunt   T.J. Murphy (19 winners up to 2003); Richard Johnson and A.P. McCoy (14 each); R. Walsh (10); P. Flynn, A. Thornton and T. Scudamore (6 each).

CHESTER   Left-hand   Flat only

Draw: The draw is of crucial importance on this course. Because of the conformation of the track, low numbers are very much favoured in races from 5 furlongs to 7 furlongs 122 yards. Conversely, if there is a biggish field for a sprint, a high number draw is often the kiss of death.

Racing began in Chester on the Roodeye within the city walls in the reign of Henry VIII, the prize being a silver bell. The Mayor of Chester at the time was one Henry Gee, who died in 1645, and until recently his name was commemorated still by a race. Chester thus boasts the oldest racecourse in the land, as well as the smallest, the most unusual, and, these days, one of the most popular. Only Ascot and York among racecourses staging Flat racing have a higher daily average attendance. Matching the bustling prosperity of the city, with its thriving tourist trade and crowded shops, racing on the Roodeye has seen bigger and yet bigger crowds over the past few years. In 1995 the first Sunday meeting was held and it drew an astonishing, record-breaking crowd of 38,000.

At one time there was only one three-day meeting at Chester, centred round the 2 1/4 mile-plus Chester Cup, first run in 1824 and including among its winners famous stayers such as *Brown Jack, Trelawny, Sea Pigeon, Major Rose* and Sir Peter O'Sullevan's *Attivo*, as a result of whose victory in 1974, his owner generously provides the press room with Cheshire cheese and wine annually on Chester Cup day. This meeting in May is still the big event of the year, and although not all the shops now put up their shutters on Chester Cup day as once used to happen, many still do. In addition to the main meeting, however, there are additional fixtures, including evening racing, in June and July. The course is usually described as circular (which makes it unique in this country), 1 mile 73 yards round (which makes it the smallest circuit), with a straight side from the 7 furlong start and a short very slightly curving run-in of only 2 furlongs from the final proper bend. This, quite apart from making the draw important, also means that a horse who likes to make all the running is well suited at Chester. The conformation of the course also dictates an advantage to the horse who gets a fast start in sprints, which start on the bend.

The Chester Cup (sponsored by the Tote) was worth £69,600 to the winner in 2004. It is invariably run at a cracking pace from start to finish and therefore, despite the sharpness of the track, is an exceptional test of stamina in which the runners pass the stands three times. Valuable Group Three events in May are the Chester Vase and the Ormonde Stakes. The Chester Vase, in particular, has long been used as a try-out race for Classic candidates, and, despite the emergence of other trials, is still so used today. Chester Vase winners who have gone on to win the Derby include Lord Derby's great racehorse *Hyperion* (1933), *Windsor Lad* (1934) and, more recently, *Henbit* (1980) and poor, ill-fated *Shergar* (1981); in 1989 *Old Vic* went on to capture both the Prix du Jockey-Club (French equivalent of the Derby) and the Irish Derby and in 1995 *Luso* went on to take the Derby Italiano at the start of a fabulous overseas career engineered by his Newmarket trainer, Clive Brittain, in which he eventually earned nearly £2 million in Italy, Germany and Hong Kong. Meanwhile, in the year 2000, the Chester Vase winner, *Millenary*, later captured the St. Leger. In the listed Dee Stakes, an historic race for 3-y-o over an extended 1 m 2 f, dating back to 1814, Barry Hills has a remarkable training record, having saddled no fewer than 11 winners since 1970, among them *Sir Harry Lewis*, Irish Derby winner in 1987, and *Blue Stag*, Derby runner-up in 1990. In addition, Barry Hills is the top trainer at the main three-day meeting at Chester in May. His record is remarkable not only in the Dee Stakes but also in the Cheshire Oaks, in which he has six times saddled the winner. In addition, he has had four successes in the Chester Vase and three in the Chester Cup. When *High and Low* won the Cheshire Oaks in 1998, Hills passed the previous best post-war record for the main three-day meeting, held by the late Sir Jack Jarvis. Hills's total for this main meeting is now no fewer than 51 (up to and including 2004).

Geoff Wragg is another who, like Hills, has a great affection for Chester and he, too, has a good record in the Dee Stakes, having sent out three winners. He has also been successful four times in the Cheshire Oaks, most recently in 2004. Another trainer to look out for on this unique track is, in the Lily Agnes Stakes, the traditional 2-y-o opener for the main meeting, Richard Hannon (five winners since 1993).

Leading trainers: (2001–04) B.W. Hills (21 winners); P.F. Cole (9); G.A. Butler and Sir Michael Stoute (8 each); E.J. Alston and Richard Hannon (7 each); W.M. Brisbourne (6).

Leading jockeys: (2001–04) Kieren Fallon (22 winners); D. Holland (16); K. Darley (13); W. Supple (10); R. Hills (9); M. Hills and F. Norton (8 each); E. Ahern (7).

DONCASTER   Left-hand   Flat and National Hunt

Draw: Difficult to assess accurately. For years on the straight mile (where the Lincoln Handicap is run) high numbers had a distinct pull except on soft going. But in recent years this has not been the case, and it is difficult to suggest reliable guidelines.

Records of racing at Doncaster go back as far as 1595. The oldest Classic, the St. Leger (as a humble, unnamed 25-guinea sweepstakes) was first run here, on Cantley Common, near the present site at Town Moor, in 1776, and was won by the Marquis of Rockingham's filly, later named *Allabaculia*. Despite the superb racing, the facilities at Town Moor were rather spartan until improvements began in the late 'sixties, when new stands and facilities hauled the track into the 20th century. The course is a very fair one, a pear-shaped oval about 1 mile 7 furlongs in circumference, flat throughout, except for a slight hill on the far side about 1 1/4 miles from the winning-post. There are two 1 mile courses, a straight mile on which the Lincoln Handicap is run, and one which starts on an arm at a tangent to the round course. Town Moor very much favours long-striding stayers with its great width and its long run-in of nearly 5 furlongs. The final and longest Classic of the season, the St. Leger, is only one of several top-class races at the September meeting, which also features the Group Two Doncaster Cup over 2 m 2 f, which with the Ascot Gold Cup and Goodwood Cup forms a corner of the Triple Crown for stayers and, first run in 1801, is actually the oldest of the three races. Horses since the war to have won all three in the same season are *Double Trigger* (1995), *Le Moss*, who, incredibly, performed the feat two years running (1979 and 1980), *Longboat* (1986), *Souepi*, who dead-heated for his Doncaster Cup in 1953, and *Alycidon* (1949). Other top stayers to have won the Doncaster Cup during the period include *Raise You Ten* (1963), *Proverb* (1974), *Ardross* (1982), *Further Flight* (1992) and *Persian Punch* (2003). *Double Trigger*, besides his 1995 Triple Crown success in the Doncaster Cup also triumphed in 1996 and again, with a thrilling and heart-warming performance, as a 7-y-o in 1998, thus becoming the only horse to record more than two victories in the race since the legendary *Beeswing* won four times between 1837 and 1842.

Other highlights of a well-balanced and immensely entertaining programme over the four days of the St. Leger meeting: the Group Three Park Hill Stakes is for fillies only 3-y-o and upwards at weight-for-age over the St. Leger distance. Distinguished 20th-century winners include *Pretty Polly* (1904); *Selene* (1922), later a most celebrated broodmare with a profound influence on the stud-book (dam of *Hyperion*, and therefore grand-dam of, to name a few, *Aureole*, *Sun Chariot* and *Owen Tudor*; also from whom, through another line, *Sea Bird II* was descended); and, from the late Mr R. Hollingsworth's famous *Felucca* family, *Ark Royal* (1955), *Kyak* (1956) and *Cutter* (1958). The Portland Handicap over 5 furlongs, sponsored by the Tote, is a highly competitive sprint.

In addition, there is a rich variety of 2-y-o events. Oldest established (in 1823) is the Group Two Champagne Stakes, now run over 7 furlongs and since 1988 confined to 2-y-o colts and geldings. Its later history fizzes with the names of subsequent Classic winners from *La Flèche* (1891) and *Ladas* (1893) right up to

Don't Forget Me (1986) and *Rodrigo de Triano* (1991). Some of the fastest horses in Turf history are on its roll of honour, including *The Tetrarch* (1913), his offpsring *Tetratema* (1919) and *Mumtaz Mahal* (1923) and his later descendant, *Abernant* (1948). The Group Two Flying Childers Stakes over 5 furlongs commemorates the colt of that name foaled in 1715, sired by the Darley Arabian – the first truly great racehorse, possessed of phenomenal speed. It was first run in 1967, and notable winners include *Mummy's Pet* (1970), *Green Desert* (1985) and *Paris House* (1991). The Group Two May Hill Stakes is for 2-y-o fillies over a mile. Henry Cecil has a quite remarkable record in this race, with 12 winners and three runners-up from 17 runners since 1978. His *Reams of Verse* (1996) went on to success in the Oaks, while another winner, *Midway Lady* (1985), trained by Ben Hanbury, won both the 1000 Guineas and Oaks the following season. A recent addition to the 2-y-o programme has been the £200,000 St. Leger Yearling Stakes over 6 f with a prize to the winner of no less than £142,000.

The March meeting features two races taken over from Lincoln when racing on the Carholme ceased in 1964. First, the Lincoln Handicap, over the straight mile. Originally, as the Lincolnshire Handicap, it had a splendidly raffish history of spectacular ante-post plunges and successful coups plotted over the winter months. The most celebrated gamble of the re-born race occurred when Barry Hills, then the late John Oxley's travelling head lad, in 1968 won enough on the stable's runner, *Frankincense*, to set up as a trainer in his own right. However, the Lincoln these days – known recently as the Freephone Stanley Lincoln Showcase Handicap and worth £65,000 to the winning owner – does not have the appeal it once had. The effect of the draw, as ever, is a great imponderable, but now is more unpredictable than ever it was. The other race transferred from Lincoln has certainly suffered a sad and disastrous decline in prestige. This is the Brocklesby Stakes for 2-y-o over 5 furlongs, a £7,969 race in 2004. A century ago, the Brocklesby (named after the Lincolnshire hunt of that name) was one of the top dozen 2-y-o races in the Calendar and offered a prize of £995, equivalent to approximately £50,000 in today's money.

At the other end of the season, the Racing Post Trophy, in late October, is the most important contest. It is a Group One event for 2-y-o over a mile (round course) worth £151,500 prize-money to the winner in 2003. Henry Cecil possesses yet another remarkable record, with ten winners in this race, the idea for which was originally conceived in 1961 by the late Phil Bull of *Timeform* as the Timeform Gold Cup. There were subsequently other sponsors, culminating in the present incumbents, but the object has always remained the same: to provide a valuable race that would indicate possible Classic winners for the following season, particularly potential stayers. In its early years it was highly successful in this aim. *Noblesse* (1962), *Ribocco* (1966), *High Top* (1971) and *Green Dancer* (1974) became Classic successes in England, Ireland and France, while *Vaguely Noble* (1967), not entered in the Classics, triumphed in the Prix de l'Arc de Triomphe. Later, *Reference Point* (1986) went on to win the Derby and St. Leger and other top races, while most recently, *High Chaparral* (2001) went on to win the Derby, Irish Derby and the Breeders Cup Turf the following season and *Brian Boru* (2002) followed up by triumphing in the St. Leger.

The steeplechase course is also one of the fairest in the country. One of its most attractive feature races is the Great Yorkshire Handicap Chase over 3 miles, worth £29,000 to the winner in 2004; it was won by *Freebooter* in 1950 before his Grand National victory, and *Knock Hard* in 1953 before winning the Cheltenham Gold Cup. Other valuable jumping events include the Grimthorpe Chase (3 m) sponsored in 2003 by Sainsbury's and worth £22,750 to the winner.

Leading trainers: *Flat*   Mark Johnston (23 winners); B.W. Hills (17); Mick Channon (11); M.A. Jarvis (10); T.D. Easterby (9); Sir Michael Stoute (7).

National Hunt   J.J. O'Neill (11 winners); Martin Pipe (9); Mrs. Reveley (8); Nicky Henderson (6); T.D. Easterby (5).

Leading jockeys: *Flat*   Darryll Holland (15 winners); Kevin Darley (14); Kieren Fallon (13); P. Robinson (11); L. Dettori and J. Fanning (10 each).

National Hunt   L. Cooper (8 winners); A.P. McCoy, R. Guest and R. Thornton (6 each); J.A. McCarthy and J.P. McNamara (5 each).

1 ³/₄ miles   St. Leger, Doncaster, September

Sponsored 2004 by Seabiscuit; worth £240,000 to the winner.

	Winner	Sire	Trainer	Jockey	SP
1970	Nijinsky	Northern Dancer	M.V.O'Brien(Ire)	L.Piggott	2/7 F
1971	Athens Wood	Celtic Ash	H.Thomson Jones	L.Piggott	5/2 2F
1972	Boucher	Ribot	M.V.O'Brien(Ire)	L.Piggott	3/1 2F
1973	Peleid	Derring-Do	W.Elsey	F.Durr	28/1
1974	Bustino	Busted	W.R.Hern	J.Mercer	11/10 F
1975	Bruni	Sea Hawk	H.R.Price	A.Murray	9/1
1976	Crow	Exbury	A.Penna(Fr)	Y.Saint-Martin	6/1 JF
1977	Dunfermline (f)	Royal Palace	W.R.Hern	W.Carson	10/1
1978	Julio Mariner	Blakeney	C.Brittain	E.Hide	28/1
1979	Son of Love	Jefferson	R.Collet(Fr)	A.Lequeux	20/1
1980	Light Cavalry	Brigadier Gerard	H.Cecil	J.Mercer	3/1 2F
1981	Cut Above	High Top	W.R.Hern	J.Mercer	28/1
1982	Touching Wood	Roberto	H.Thomson Jones	P.Cook	7/1
1983	Sun Princess (f)	English Prince	W.R.Hern	W.Carson	11/8 F
1984	Commanche Run	Run The Gantlet	L.Cumani	L.Piggott	7/4 F
1985	Oh So Sharp (f)	Kris	H.Cecil	S.Cauthen	8/11 F
1986	Moon Madness	Kalamoun	J.Dunlop	P.Eddery	9/2 3F
1987	Reference Point	Mill Reef	H.Cecil	S.Cauthen	4/11 F
1988	Minster Son	Niniski	N.A.Graham	W.Carson	15/2
1989*	Michelozzo	Northern Baby	H.Cecil	S.Cauthen	6/4 F
1990	Snurge	Ela-Mana-Mou	P.F.Cole	T.Quinn	7/2 3F
1991	Toulon	Top Ville	A.Fabre(Fr)	P.Eddery	5/2 F

1992	User Friendly (f)	Slip Anchor	C.Brittain	G.Duffield	7/4 F
1993	Bob's Return	Bob Back	M.H.Tompkins	P.Robinson	3/1 F
1994	Moonax	Caerleon	B.W.Hills	P.Eddery	40/1
1995	Classic Cliché	Salse	Saeed bin Suroor	L.Dettori	100/30 F
1996	Shantou	Alleged	J.Gosden	L.Dettori	8/1
1997	Silver Patriarch	Saddler's Hall	J.Dunlop	Pat Eddery	5/4 F
1998	Nedawi	Rainbow Quest	Saeed bin Suroor	J.Reid	5/2 F
1999	Mutafaweq	Silver Hawk	Saeed bin Suroor	R.Hills	11/2 2F
2000	Millenary	Rainbow Quest	J.L. Dunlop	T.Quinn	11/4 F
2001	Milan	Sadler's Wells	A.P. O'Brien(Ire)	M.J.Kinane	13/8 F
2002	Bollin Eric	Shaamit	T.D. Easterby	K.Darley	7/1
2003	Brian Boru	Sadler's Wells	A.P. O'Brien(Ire)	J.P.Spencer	5/4 F
2004	Rule of Law	Kingmambo	Saeed bin Suroor	K.McEvoy	3/1 JF

*Run at Ayr.   f = filly

EPSOM   Left-hand   Flat only

Draw: Low numbers up to 1¹/₄ m; middle numbers for the Derby course.

Epsom is synonymous with Derby Day, and Frith's great painting of that title, in the Tate Gallery, still has power to conjure up that particular atmosphere of peculiarly English carnival existing on that and no other day in the year. The costume has changed since Victorian times, but the faces haven't, nor the gipsies with lucky white heather, the bookmakers in the centre of the course, and the sense that one horse will go into the history books within an hour or so. Added today are the jellied eel stalls, the helter-skelters, the blare of fairground music, but still, also, the dips, the wide boys, the tipsters.

Epsom, still an important training centre, although at present under threat as such, is as integral to the British racing scene as Newmarket, but so very different. The Derby winner occupies a place in Turf history as no other horse ever does. To see it all in perspective, it is quite an experience to walk up the course to near Tattenham Corner station and watch the start of a 2-y-o race, such as the Woodcote Stakes, or a 5 furlongs sprint: the stalls rattle asunder, the horses plunge down the dip, and disappear in a blur of silks towards the winning-post in the far distance. From here you get a hint of the challenge of the Derby.

The intricacies of the course round a kind of devil's cauldron cleft in the Epsom Downs are well advertised: the long uphill rise after the start, the sweep of descent into Tattenham Corner, the dip a hundred yards from the winning-post and the uphill finish. These are ingredients which, in one form or another, have for more than two centuries dictated the searching severity of the race as a test for three-year-olds.

There is, however, an additional factor: the camber of the track running the length of the straight from the stands side. It is at its most severe in the dip, opposite Tattersalls' enclosure. At this point, the head of a racegoer standing next to the far rails would be below the ground-level of the bookmakers' pitches opposite. According to a survey conducted by the racecourse in 1978, the precise fall here is 7.49 feet. At the winning-post the course still slopes across significantly, by 5.86 feet. This is an unknown quantity for the majority watching the great annual spectacle, for the camber is invisible from a certain height in the stands; but it is also an 'X' factor to which the riders are well alerted. Walter Swinburn, successful in the Derby on *Shergar, Shahrastani* and *Lammtarra*, says: 'It's very much a problem if a horse is getting tired and tends to hang in but also if you go to make a challenge from that side, the camber can make you come across sharper than intended.'

Geoff Lewis, rider of one of the 20th century's great winners, *Mill Reef*, explains that the secret of dealing with the sideways slope is knowing how and when to pull the whip through, and equally, in certain circumstances, 'when to put your stick down'. Nonetheless, Epsom, where he trained until recently, remains emphatically his favourite course: 'It brings out the best in horses and the best in jockeys. It's like a moderate horse. It needs all the concentration and attention you can muster as well as a little bit of luck. But in the end it's all feel, it all comes down to that. Epsom needs more feel than any other track. And the camber takes no prisoners.'

The Derby apart, the same meeting features the Coronation Cup for older horses and the Oaks for 3-y-o fillies only, both races over the Derby course and distance. The Spring Meeting, after a lapse, has been restored as a one-day fixture and features the two old and famous handicaps, The City and Suburban (1 m 2 f) and the Great Metropolitan. This race, now reduced in distance to 1 m 4 f, no longer plots a fascinating and tortuous course over the Downs, but these two contests, in fact, can claim to be the earliest-ever commercially sponsored handicaps.

In the mid-19th century, a Cheapside publican, Samuel Beeton, knowing that Epsom was short of funds for a new race, opened a subscription list in his ale-shop and raised £300 for what became known as 'the Great Met'. The following year £500 was raised, and such was the success that in 1851, suburban publicans joined in and the 'City and Sub' came into being. Such was the versatility of horses in those days that, in 1854, the celebrated filly *Virago*, owned by the odious moneylender Henry Padwick (see under **Names** in Chapter One), won both the City and Suburban and the Great Metropolitan (then over a distance of 2 m 2 f) on the same afternoon.

Another of Epsom's meetings takes place on August Bank Holiday and this features the Moet and Chandon Silver Magnum Gentlemen's Handicap over the Derby course. The first running of this event had a fitting result: an easy win by a favourite of the crowds, *Thames Trader*, ridden by the Hon. John Lawrence (later Lord Oaksey) and owned by Stanley Wootton. Six years later, Wootton, who owned the greater part of Epsom's Walton Downs, assigned to the Levy Board the Walton Downs gallop, thus helping to assure Epsom of its continuity as a training centre. Lawrence, meanwhile, rode four winners of this race, a record later matched by Philip Mitchell, who now trains at Epsom.

Leading trainers: D. Nicholls (10 winners); John Dunlop, Richard Hannon and Mark Johnston (8 each); Mick Channon (7); S.C. Williams and I.A. Wood (6 each).

Leading jockeys: Kieren Fallon (14 winners); L. Dettori (13); C. Catlin (12); Martin Dwyer (11); T. Quinn and Darryll Holland (9 each); Seb Sanders (7).

An indispensable guide to the drama of the Derby over more than two centuries is the late Roger Mortimer's *History of the Derby Stakes*. Just as indispensable in attempting to put the finger on the winner is the form book. With its help, and taking some other factors into consideration, this is not the impossible task that is sometimes imagined. A great deal of ballyhoo surrounds the Derby, and rightly so because of its prestige, value as a unique test of the thoroughbred and its high prize-money, which has more than doubled in the past decade and is now over £1 million. In 2004, sponsored by Vodafone, it was worth £804,118 to the winning owner. Yet if the following points, based on an analysis of the past decade, are carefully evaluated in relation to the race, a fair proportion of winners can be guaranteed in the future.

Form
Only one maiden has ever won the Derby, so it is hardly surprising that every one of the ten most recent winners had previous winning form. However, *Dr. Devious, Generous, Lammtarra* and *Shaamit* went against the usual pattern in that none had winning form as a 3-y-o. Only seven other colts since the war belong to this category. *Commander-in-Chief* was, moreover, a comparatively rare instance of a colt not having had a run as a 2-y-o; only *Morston* (1973) and *Phil Drake* (1955) since 1946 won the Derby after a first racecourse appearance at 3-y-o. Against this, it is significant that *Dr. Devious, Generous* and *Benny The Dip* had busy and successful 2-y-o careers, starting as early as May, thus recalling, however temporarily, a reversal of modern practice and a time when the Coventry Stakes at Royal Ascot in June was frequently a starting point for a Derby triumph the following season. Both *Dr. Devious* and *Generous* were runners-up in that prestige contest. Before them, *Mill Reef* (1971) was the most recent Coventry Stakes success to take the Derby subsequently. By contrast, in the early years of the Coventry Stakes no fewer than five colts, from *Ladas* in 1893 to *Cicero* in 1904 (both, coincidentally, owned by Lord Rosebery), captured both Coventry Stakes and the Derby.

Previous races
The Dewhurst Stakes (2-y-o, 7 f Newmarket, October) has pointed to eight Derby winners in the past 50 years and a runner-up. *Pinza* (1952), *Crepello* (1956), *Nijinsky, Mill Reef, Grundy, The Minstrel, Generous* and *Dr. Devious* won the Dewhurst and the Derby the following year. *El Gran Senor* (1983) scored at Newmarket and was Derby runner-up.

The 2000 Guineas (3-y-o, 1 mile Newmarket, April/May) enjoys a poor reputation as a Derby guide, partly owing to a succession of winners, such as *Tudor Minstrel*, who were made favourite for the Derby just after the war but failed to stay. In fact, since 1946, and up to 2003, 33 Guineas winners have run in the Derby, 16 of them starting favourite. There have been six winners (*Nashwan* the latest, 5/4 favourite in 1989) and nine colts placed in the first four home; 18 were unplaced.

Staying potential is the obvious crucial factor in determining a Guineas winner's likelihood of going on to success at Epsom – vide *Nashwan, Nijinsky, Royal Palace* (1967) and *Crepello* (1957) for example; ignoring this factor has in consequence led to some expensive failures.

In the run-up to the Derby, the Lingfield Derby Trial (approximately $1^1/2$ miles over a course with some similarities to Epsom) has a good record. Since the war, six of its winners have gone on to capture the Derby: *High-Rise, Kahyasi, Slip Anchor, Teenoso, Parthia* (1959) and *Tulyar* (1952); two were runners-up – *Silver Patriarch* (1997) and *Aureole* (1953) – and five others reached the first three at Epsom. The Dante Stakes at York, over slightly longer than 1 m 2 f, and first run in 1958, has now done even better, with seven winners: *St Paddy* (1960), *Shirley Heights, Shahrastani, Reference Point, Erhaab, Benny The Dip* (1997) and, most recently, *North Light* (2004).

The Chester Vase in recent years has not been such a successful pointer as it used to be. The last two Chester Vase winners who went on to achieve Derby success were *Shergar* and *Henbit*, while *Law Society* (1985) was its most recent Derby runner-up. Similarly, *Shahrastani* in 1986 is the last winner of the Classic Trial run at Sandown in April under a succession of sponsorships to take the Derby, following *Shergar, Henbit* and *Troy* in successive seasons. Nevertheless, *Benny The Dip* was a recent runner-up who went on to win at Epsom. He was trained by John Gosden, who is worth following in this particular trial (four winners in the past decade). *Sakhee*, the winner in 2000, was also a Derby runner-up.

Ireland
Ireland has sent over 12 winners since *Hard Ridden* in 1958, the most recent being *High Chaparral* (2002).

France
France has had eight successes in the same period, but none since *Empery* (1976) and before that, *Sea Bird II* (1965).

Stamina and breeding
No less an authority than Vincent O'Brien, who remains the outstanding modern Derby trainer, considers that the ideal horse for Epsom is a top-class 1 m 2 f colt. He certainly proved it (with the help of Lester Piggott) with *Sir Ivor*. Much of the pre-race discussion in the press as to whether or not a colt will stay the Derby distance (if he has not already proved it on the racecourse) will be settled only on the day, partly by breeding but also by the pace and the way in which the Derby is run.

The pre-eminence of the great American stallion *Northern Dancer* with his son *Nijinsky* is a factor to note within the general ascendancy of American sires; as well as the fact that since 1970 eight successful colts were either by previous Derby winners or by sires who had already got at least one Derby winner.

Trainers
Henry Cecil and Sir Michael Stoute: four winners each; Luca Cumani, John Dunlop and A.P. O'Brien: two each.

Fillies
Only six fillies have ever won, the last being *Fifinella* in 1916 (see Chapter One under **Classics**).

Betting
Despite the vivid memories of occasional very long-priced winners such as *Psidium* at 66/1 and *Snow Knight* at 50/1, the Derby in recent years has been an excellent race for punters concentrating on the best-backed horses – provided they have not jumped in too early on the ante-post market. When the various trials are sorting themselves out is the time to have a bet. The market is a good guide to the Derby. As the table shows, in 35 runnings since 1970, there have been 11 winning favourites and 11 winning second-favourites, some at rewarding prices. Altogether, in that same period, 29 winners (85%) have come from the first five in the betting.

1 1/2 miles   The Derby, Epsom, early June

	Winner	Sire	Owner	Trainer	Jockey	SP
1970	Nijinsky	Northern Dancer	C.W.Engelhard	M.V.O'Brien(Ire)	L.Piggott	11/8 F
1971	Mill Reef	Never Bend	Paul Mellon	I.Balding	G.Lewis	100/30 F
1972	Roberto	Hail to Reason	J.W.Galbreath	M.V.O'Brien(Ire)	L.Piggott	3/1 F
1973	Morston	Ragusa	A.Budgett	A.Budgett	E.Hide	25/1
1974	Snow Knight	Firestreak	Mrs N.Phillips	P.Nelson	B.Taylor	50/1
1975	Grundy	Great Nephew	Dr C.Vittadini	P.Walwyn	P.Eddery	5/1 2F
1976	Empery	Vaguely Noble	N.Bunker Hunt	M.Zilber(Fr)	L.Piggott	10/1 2F
1977	The Minstrel	Northern Dancer	R.Sangster	M.V.O'Brien(Ire)	L.Piggott	5/1 2F
1978	Shirley Heights	Mill Reef	Lord Halifax	J.Dunlop	G.Starkey	8/1 J2F
1979	Troy	Petingo	Sir M.Sobell	Major W.R.Hern	W.Carson	6/1 2F
1980	Henbit	Hawaii	Mrs A.Plesch	Major W.R.Hern	W.Carson	7/1 2F
1981	Shergar	Great Nephew	HH Aga Khan	M.Stoute	W.Swinburn	10/11 F
1982	Golden Fleece	Nijinsky	R.Sangster	M.V.O'Brien(Ire)	P.Eddery	3/1 F
1983	Teenoso	Youth	E.Moller	G.Wragg	L.Piggott	9/2 F
1984	Secreto	Northern Dancer	L.Miglitti	D.O'Brien(Ire)	C.Roche	14/1
1985	Slip Anchor	Shirley Heights	Lord H. de Walden	H.Cecil	S.Cauthen	2/1 F
1986	Shahrastani	Nijinsky	HH Aga Khan	M.Stoute	W.Swinburn	11/2 2F
1987	Reference Point	Mill Reef	L.Freedman	H.Cecil	S.Cauthen	6/4 F
1988	Kahyasi	Ile de Bourbon	HH Aga Khan	L.Cumani	R.Cochrane	11/1
1989	Nashwan	Blushing Groom	Sheikh Hamdan al-Maktoum	Major W.R.Hern	W.Carson	5/4 F
1990	Quest for Fame	Rainbow Quest	Khaled Abdulla	R.Charlton	P.Eddery	7/1

1991	Generous	Caerleon	Fahd Salman	P.F.Cole	A.Munro	9/1
1992	Dr. Devious	Ahonoora	Sidney H.Craig	P.Chapple-Hyam	J.Reid	8/1 2F
1993	Commander-in-Chief	Dancing Brave	Khaled Abdulla	H.Cecil	M.J.Kinane	15/2 2F
1994	Erhaab	Chief's Crown	Sheikh Hamdan al-Maktoum	J.Dunlop	W.Carson	7/2 F
1995	Lammtarra	Nijinsky	Saeed Maktoum al-Maktoum	Saeed bin Suroor	W. Swinburn	14/1
1996	Shaamit	Mtoto	Khalifa Dasmal	W.J.Haggas	M.Hills	12/1
1997	Benny The Dip	Silver Hawk	Landon Knight	J.Gosden	W.Ryan	11/1
1998	High-Rise	High Estate	S.Mohammed Obaid al-Maktoum	L.Cumani	O.Peslier	20/1
1999	Oath	Fairy King	Thoroughbred Corporation	H.Cecil	K.Fallon	13/2 J2F
2000	Sinndar	Grand Lodge	HH Aga Khan	J.Oxx(Ire)	J.P. Murtagh	7/1
2001	Galileo	Sadler's Wells	Mrs J.Magnier/ M.Tabor	A.P.O'Brien(Ire)	M.J.Kinane	11/4 JF
2002	High Chaparral	Sadler's Wells	Mrs J.Magnier/ M.Tabor	A.P.O'Brien(Ire)	J.P.Murtagh	7/2 2F
2003	Kris Kin	Kris S	Saeed Suhail	Sir M.Stoute	K.Fallon	6/1
2004	North Light	Danehill	Ballymacoll Stud	Sir M.Stoute	K.Fallon	7/2 JF

1¹/₂ miles   The Oaks, Epsom, early June

First run as the Oakes Stakes in 1779, for 3-y-o fillies only. The weight carried is 9 st, and has been since 1892, but previously there were several fluctuations, from 8 st 4 lb originally, down to 8 st, then progressively upwards. During both World Wars the race was transferred to the Newmarket July Course and run as the New Oaks Stakes. As the Vodafone Oaks, the prize to the winner in 2004 was £203,000.

	Winner	Sire	Owner	Trainer	Jockey	SP
1981	Blue Wind	Lord Gayle	Mrs B.Firestone	D.Weld(Ire)	L.Piggott	3/1 JF
1982	Time Charter	Saritamer	R.Barnett	H.Candy	W.Newnes	12/1
1983	Sun Princess	English Prince	Sir M.Sobell	Major W.R.Hern	W.Carson	6/1
1984	Circus Plume	High Top	Sir R.McAlpine	J.Dunlop	L.Piggott	4/1 2F
1985	Oh So Sharp	Kris	Sheikh Mohammed	H.Cecil	S.Cauthen	6/4 F
1986	Midway Lady	Alleged	HH Rainier	B.Hanbury	R.Cochrane	15/8 F
1987	Unite	Kris	Sheikh Mohammed	M.Stoute	W.R. Swinburn	11/1
1988	Diminuendo	Diesis	Sheikh Mohammed	H.Cecil	S.Cauthen	7/4 F
1989	Snow Bride*	Blushing Groom	Saeed al-Maktoum	H.Cecil	S.Cauthen	13/2
1990	Salsabil	Sadler's Wells	Sheikh Hamdan al-Maktoum	J.Dunlop	W.Carson	2/1 F

1991	Jet Ski Lady	Vaguely Noble	Maktoum al-Maktoum	J.Bolger(Ire)	C.Roche	50/1
1992	User Friendly	Slip Anchor	W.J.Gredley	C.Brittain	G.Duffield	5/1 3F
1993	Intrepidity	Sadler's Wells	Sheikh Mohammed	A.Fabre(Fr)	M.Roberts	5/1 2F
1994	Balanchine	Storm Bird	Maktoum al-Maktoum	H.Ibrahim	L.Dettori	6/1 3F
1995	Moonshell	Sadler's Wells	Godolphin	Saeed bin Suroor	L. Dettori	3/1 2F
1996	Lady Carla	Caerleon	Wafic Said	H.Cecil	P.Eddery	100/30 2F
1997	Reams of Verse	Nureyev	K.Abdulla	H.Cecil	K.Fallon	5/6 F
1998	Shahtoush	Alzao	Mrs D.Nagle/ Mrs J.Magnier	A.P.O'Brien(Ire)	M.J.Kinane	12/1
1999	Ramruma	Diesis	Prince Fahd Salman	H.Cecil	K.Fallon	3/1 2F
2000	Love Divine	Diesis	Lordship Stud	H.Cecil	T.Quinn	9/4 F
2001	Imagine	Sadler's Wells	Mrs D.Nagle/ Mrs J.Magnier	A.P.O'Brien(Ire)	M.J.Kinane	3/1 F
2002	Kazzia	Zinaad	Godolphin	Saeed bin Suroor	L.Dettori	100/30 F
2003	Casual Look	Red Ransom	W.Farish III	A.M.Balding	M.Dwyer	10/1
2004	Ouija Board	Cape Cross	Lord Derby	E.A.L.Dunlop	K.Fallon	7/2

Aliysa, the 11/10 favourite, owned by the Aga Khan, trained by Michael Stoute and ridden by Walter Swinburn, was first past the post, but was controversially disqualified following a dope-test and Jockey Club deliberations lasting many months. This caused the Aga Khan to withdraw his horses from his English trainers and cease racing in this country until 1995, when his popular colours made a welcome return. *Snow Bride*, originally second, was made the winner instead of *Aliysa*.

Favourites 8 favourites have been first past the post since *Oh So Sharp* in 1985; 7 winners in the same period from the second and third market choices similarly tells its own story.

Trainers Henry Cecil, even though one of his successes was the promoted *Snow Bride*, has by far the best record, with 7 winners; Saeed bin Suroor, John Dunlop, A.P. O'Brien and Sir Michael Stoute have each saddled 2 winners.

GOODWOOD   Right-hand, but long-distance races starting in the straight swing left-handed first   Flat only

Draw: High numbers in sprint races, except in soft going.

Goodwood earned its title of 'Glorious' because of the exceptional racing during its big meeting, its unmatched pastoral setting on a fold of the Sussex Downs with distant views of hay-making, the fizz of champagne and creaking open of luncheon baskets, and (except when storm clouds gathered over Trundle Hill) a sense of unending summer – the Panama Hat to the Grey Toppers of Ascot and Derby Day. Today, the racing is better than ever, spread over five days for the main meeting and with other fixtures throughout the season, and no fewer than

12 Pattern races to attract enthusiasts. The course, laid out on the Duke of Richmond's estate five miles from Chichester, and with which Lord George Bentinck had much to do in the beginning, is a complicated one, full of bends and turns on the downland loop, favouring handy horses, and with a fast switchback and downhill stretch for the 6 furlong straight. Jockeyship is of enormous importance on the part of the track away from the sprint course, and top jockeys win most of the races. The main races include: the Group One Sussex Stakes (see table); Goodwood Cup (one of the three 'legs' of the stayers' crown: in 1998, *Double Trigger* became the first horse ever to win it three times); King George Stakes (a top race for sprinters); Nassau Stakes (1 m 2 f, fillies, now promoted to Group One); Gordon Stakes (1 m 4 f, 3-y-o); Stewards' Cup (see table) and Richmond Stakes (2-y-o); also, away from the main meeting, the Celebration Mile and Classic trials such as the Lupe Stakes and Predominate Stakes. The last-named commemorates a Goodwood favourite, *Predominate*, who, owned by 'Jim' Joel and trained by Ted Leader, won the 2 m 3 f Goodwood Stakes three seasons running 1958–60 (twice under 9 st 5 lb) and at the advanced age of nine, in 1961, captured the Goodwood Cup.

Leading trainers: (2001–03) Richard Hannon (20 winners); Mick Channon (18); John Gosden (17); Mark Johnston (16); D. Elsworth, Mrs A.J. Perrett and M.P. Tregoning (14 each); B.W. Hills and Sir Michael Stoute (12 each); John Dunlop (11).

Leading jockeys: (2001–03) Kieren Fallon and R. Hughes (22 winners each); D. Holland (20); J.P. Spencer (17); L. Dettori (16); T. Quinn and R. Hills (15 each); J. Fortune (14); Seb Sanders (13); Kevin Darley, Martin Dwyer and Dane O'Neill (12 each).

6 furlongs Hcp   The Stewards' Cup, Goodwood, late July

First run in 1840. Sponsored by Vodafone; worth £58,000 to the winner in 2003.

	Winner	Age	Wt	Trainer	Jockey	Ran	SP
1977	Calibina	5	8.5	P.Cole	G.Baxter	24	8/1 F
1978	Ahonoora	3	8.0	B.Swift	P.Waldron	23	50/1
1979	Standaan	3	7.10	C.Brittain	P.Bradwell*7	16	5/1 F
1980	Repetitious	3	7.2	G.Harwood	A.Clark*7	28	15/1
1981	Crews Hill	5	9.9	F.Durr	G.Starkey	30	11/1 2F
1982	Soba	3	8.4	D.Chapman	D.Nicholls	30	18/1
1983	Autumn Sunset	3	8.2	M.Stoute	W.Carson	23	6/1 F
1984	Petong	4	9.10	M.Jarvis	B.Raymond	26	8/1 JF
1985	Al Trui	5	8.1	S.Mellor	M.Wigham	28	9/1 F
1986	Green Ruby	5	8.12	G.B.Balding	J.Williams	24	20/1
1987	Madraco	4	7.2	P.Calver	P.Hill*5	30	50/1
1988	Rotherfield Greys	6	8.6	C.F.Wall	N.Day	28	14/1

1989	Very Adjacent	4	7.4	G.Lewis	Dale Gibson*5	22	12/1
1990	Knight of Mercy	4	9.0	R.Hannon	B.Raymond	30	14/1
1991	Notley	4	8.7	R.Hannon	R.Perham*5	29	14/1
1992	Lochsong	4	8.0	I.A.Balding	W.Carson	30	10/1 3F
1993	King's Signet	4	9.10	J.Gosden	W.Carson	29	16/1
1994	For The Present	4	8.3	T.D.Barron	J.Fortune	26	16/1
1995	Shikari's Son	8	8.13	J.White	R.Hughes	27	40/1
1996	Coastal Bluff	4	8.5	T.D.Barron	J.Fortune	30	10/1 JF
1997	Danetime	3	8.10	N.A.Callaghan	Pat Eddery	30	5/1 F
1998	Superior Premium	4	8.12	R.A.Fahey	R.Winston*5	29	14/1
1999	Harmonic Way	4	8.6	R.Charlton	R.Hughes	30	12/1 3F
2000	Tayseer	6	8.11	D.Nicholls	R.Hughes	30	13/2 2F
2001	Guinea Hunter	5	9.0	T.D.Easterby	J.P.Spencer	30	33/1
2002	Bond Boy	5	8.2	B.Smart	C.Catlin	28	14/1 J3F
2003	Patavellian	5	8.11	R.Charlton	S.Drowne	29	4/1 2F
2004	Pivotal Point	4	8.11	P.J.Makin	S.Sanders	30	7/1 JF

* Apprentice allowance claimed in lb

Favourites The Stewards' Cup is a popular big handicap sprint at the main Goodwood summer meeting, attracting big fields which start out of sight in a dip in the course and are first seen like Indians in pursuit of Custer as they breast the rise. Wokingham failures pay to follow in the Stewards' Cup, and several have done well recently: *Patavellian* (2003) and *Guinea Hunter* (2001) were both unplaced (5th and 9th respectively) in the Wokingham; *Superior Premium* (1998) was 3rd in the Wokingham, *Danetime* (1997) 2nd, *Lochsong* (1992) and *Notley* (1991) both 4th, and *Very Adjacent* (1989) 5th. All went on to take the Stewards' Cup. Recent Wokingham winners which have gone on to complete the double in the Stewards' Cup are *Calibina* (1977), *Petong* (1984) and *Knight of Mercy* (1990). Only 5 favourites and 2 joint-favourites winning in the past 25 seasons and a fair share of outsiders makes the Stewards' Cup the sort of race that led to the advice 'Never bet in a handicap', though in the period under review 64% of winners started at 14/1 or less.

Trainers T.D. Barron, Richard Hannon and Sir Michael Stoute have saddled 2 winners each.

Jockeys R. Hughes: 3 winners; J. Fortune: 2. Claiming apprentices do well.

Weights and Draw The winning weights cover the entire handicap range with no preponderant group. The draw similarly defies analysis.

1 mile Conditions Race 3-y-o+ The Sussex Stakes, Goodwood, late July

The Sussex Stakes was first run in 1841, although then, and up to 1959, it was for 3-y-o only, and subsequently until 1974 for 3-y-o and 4-y-o only. Now, with Group One status, it is one of the most important all-aged mile events in Europe and certainly the highlight of the principal Goodwood meeting in terms of quality. It was worth £174,000 to the winning owner in 2004. The post-war roll-call of success is impressive and includes *My Babu, Palestine, Petite Etoile, Brigadier Gerard* (and his sire, *Queen's Hussar*), *Romulus, Reform, Sallust* and *Humble Duty*, apart from those below.

	Winner	Age/Sex	Owner	Trainer	Jockey	SP
1976	Wollow	3c	C.d'Alessio	H.Cecil	G.Dettori	10/11 F
1977	Artaius	3c	Mrs G.Getty II	M.V.O'Brien(Ire)	L.Piggott	6/4 F
1978	Jaazeiro	3c	R.Sangster	M.V.O'Brien(Ire)	L.Piggott	8/13 F
1979	Kris	3c	Lord H.de Walden	H.Cecil	J.Mercer	4/5 F
1980	Posse	3c	Ogden Phipps	J.Dunlop	P.Eddery	8/13 F
1981	King's Lake	3c	J.P.Binet	M.V.O'Brien(Ire)	P.Eddery	5/2 2F
1982	On the House	3f	Sir P.Oppenheimer	H.Wragg	J.Reid	14/1
1983	Noalcoholic	6h	W.du Pont III	G.Pritchard-Gordon	G.Duffield	18/1
1984	Chief Singer	3c	J.Smith	R.Sheather	R.Cochrane	4/7 F
1985	Rousillon	4c	Khaled Abdulla	G.Harwood	G.Starkey	2/1 F
1986	Sonic Lady	3f	Sheikh Mohammed	M.Stoute	W.R.Swinburn	5/6 F
1987	Soviet Star	3c	Sheikh Mohammed	A.Fabre(Fr)	G.Starkey	3/1 2F
1988	Warning	3c	Khaled Abdulla	G.Harwood	P.Eddery	11/10 F
1989	Zilzal	3c	Mana al-Maktoum	M.Stoute	W.R.Swinburn	5/2 2F
1990	Distant Relative	4c	Wafic Said	B.W.Hills	W.Carson	4/1 3F
1991	Second Set	3c	R.L.Duchossois	L.Cumani	L.Dettori	5/1 3F
1992	Marling	3f	E.J.Loder	G.Wragg	P.Eddery	11/10 F
1993	Bigstone	3c	D.Wildenstein	E.Lellouche(Fr)	D.Boeuf	14/1
1994	Distant View	3c	Khaled Abdulla	H.Cecil	P.Eddery	4/1 2F
1995	Sayeddati	5m	Sheikh Hamdan al-Maktoum	C.Brittain	B.Doyle	11/2
1996	First Island	4c	Moller Racing	G.Wragg	M.Hills	5/1 2F
1997	Ali-Royal	4c	Greenbay Stables	H.Cecil	K.Fallon	13/2 3F
1998	Among Men	4c	M.Tabor/Mrs Magnier	M.Stoute	M.J.Kinane	4/1 2F
1999	Aljabr	3c	Godolphin	Saeed bin Suroor	L.Dettori	11/10 F
2000	Giant's Causeway	3c	M.Tabor/Mrs Magnier	A.P.O'Brien(Ire)	M.J.Kinane	3/1 F
2001	Noverre	3c	Godolphin	Saeed bin Suroor	L.Dettori	9/2 3F
2002	Rock of Gibraltar	3c	Mrs J.Magnier/Sir Alex Ferguson	A.P.O'Brien(Ire)	M.J.Kinane	8/13 F
2003	Reel Buddy	5h	Speedlith Group	R.Hannon	Pat Eddery	20/1
2004	Soviet Song	4f	Elite Racing Club	J.R.Fanshawe	J.P.Murtagh	3/1 2F

c = colt, f = filly, h = horse, m = mare

The table speaks for itself concerning the likely prices of winners of the Sussex Stakes.

Trainers Henry Cecil has sent out 5 winners from *Bolkonski* (1975) onwards; Sir Michael Stoute: 3; A.P. O'Brien, Saeed bin Suroor and Geoffrey Wragg: 2 each.

Jockeys L. Dettori and M.J. Kinane: 3 winners each.

HAYDOCK PARK   Left-hand   Flat and National Hunt

Draw: Races over 6 furlongs and further, low numbers. When the ground is soft, high numbers have an advantage over 5 and 6 furlongs.

An attractive course in the industrial hinterland of Lancashire with a particularly pleasant paddock and good amenities, making it a favourite day out from Manchester or Liverpool or farther afield, with easy access from the M6 motorway. Racing is always entertaining, and National Hunt especially is excellent, making Haydock one of the leading jump courses in the country. The circuit is undulating and one which suits a galloper. There is a gradual rise over the 4 furlong run-in, and the fences, which have a slight drop on the landing side, make Haydock a good course for an Aintree preliminary, because they are also fairly stiff. Some main races: Flat – Sept: Sprint Cup (Group One, 6 f, £130,500 in 2003 sponsored by Stanley Leisure); July: Lancashire Oaks (Group Three, 1 m 4 f, 3-y-o fillies); Aug: Rose of Lancaster Stakes (Group Three, 1 m 2 f+, 3-y-o); July: Old Newton Cup (£36,700 Hcp); and May: Tote Credit Silver Bowl (£46,400 Hcp). National Hunt – Nov: Tim Molony Memorial Hcp Chase (3 m 4 f+); Nov: Edward Hanmer Memorial Chase (3 m, £30,000); Dec: Tommy Whittle Chase (3 m, £31,000); Jan: Peter Marsh Hcp Chase (3 m, £34,800); Jan: Tote Premier Long Distance Hurdle (2 m 7 f+); Mar: Red Square Vodka Gold Cup Chase (3 m 4 f+, £63,800 in 2003; latest successor to the old traditional Grand National Trial); May: Swinton Handicap Hurdle (2 m, £40,600).

Leading trainers: *Flat* (2002–03) Mark Johnston (13 winners); Mick Channon (12); T.D. Easterby, John Gosden and Sir Michael Stoute (9 each); Luca Cumani, B.W. Hills and M.A. Jarvis (7 each); John Dunlop (6).

National Hunt (2000–01 – 2002–03) Jonjo O'Neill (16 winners); Mrs Reveley (11); Mrs Sue Smith and Miss Venetia Williams (10 each); Martin Pipe (9); Ferdy Murphy (7).

Leading jockeys: *Flat* A. Culhane and K. Darley (12 winners each); J. Fanning (11); W. Supple (10); F. Norton (9); K. Fallon, T. Quinn and J.P. Spencer (8 each).

National Hunt L. Cooper, B.J. Crowley and A. Thornton (9 winners each); Tony Dobbin and Richard Johnson (7 each); R. Garrity and Warren Marston (6 each).

LIVERPOOL   Left-hand   National Hunt only

The Aintree racecourse, home since 1839 of the most spectacular steeplechase in the world, the Grand National, has had its fair share of misfortune in recent years, among them the doubts over the future of the race and the death in 1988 of its immensely popular and go-ahead Clerk of the Course and my old friend, John Hughes, or 'Hughsie' as he was known.   He was the true architect of the resurgence of the National and the rescue of the course from what someone once described as 'a derelict prairie'.   Hughsie's death was a bitter and untimely blow which was followed by another, that in early 1993 of his successor, John Parrett, who had carried on with enthusiasm and overseen the building of new stands, the reshaping of the separate Mildmay Course, the work to make Becher's Brook safer, and an eventually successful campaign to stage an autumn meeting once again.   This was closely followed by the fiasco of the void National in the confusion of false starts, the second of which was not recalled.   However, with new starting equipment and extra contingency precautions, the National under the sponsorship of Martell (see end of Grand National details) bounced back triumphantly, despite a bomb-scare in 1997 causing the race to be abandoned and run the following Monday.   Not only that, the Aintree Festival once more consolidated its position as a superb three days of National Hunt racing with a consistently high level of prize-money to match.   By 2003, the attendance figures for the meeting were 140,000 – a huge increase in only 20 years.   Its attractions, Grand National apart, include the Aintree Hurdle, a contest of Champion Hurdle standard won four times in a row 1990–93 by the Champion Hurdler of 1991, *Morley Street*; the Topham Chase over a circuit of the National course and, similarly over those fences, the Foxhunters Chase for amateur riders.   The November meeting features the Becher Chase over 3 m 3 f of the National course. Sponsored by the Tote, it was worth £37,700 to the winner in 2003.

The actual races apart, Aintree is shortly to undergo a major £30 million facelift and re-vamp of its facilities.   It will be goodbye to its tents, temporary structures and the famous low-roofed winner's enclosure familiar to millions of television viewers (although, pleasingly, its famous structure is to be kept and converted into a champagne bar).   This welcome preservation aside, there are planned to be two new grandstands built next to the Queen Mother Stand, a re-located parade ring, and winner's and unsaddling enclosures, and a new weighing room and stable complex.   A new permanent Aintree Pavilion with facilities for up to 10,000 racegoers will replace the existing temporary structures for Tattersalls' customers, and the plan is to have all this complete in time for the 2007 Grand National fixture.

Leading trainers: Jonjo O'Neill (12 winners); Martin Pipe (8); Miss Venetia Williams (6); Tim Easterby, Philip Hobbs and Paul Nicholls (5 each); Nicky Henderson and Ferdy Murphy (4 each); F. Doumen (3).

Leading jockeys: A.P. McCoy (11 winners); Tony Dobbin (10); Ruby Walsh (7); B.J. Crowley, Mick Fitzgerald and Richard Johnson (5 each).

4 ¹/2 miles   The Grand National, Aintree, April

From 1992, the Grand National enjoyed an enlightened period of sponsorship under Martell. Sadly, this came to an end in 2004. In their final year of sponsorship, the National prize-money reached a staggering £600,000, including £348,000 to the winner and no less than £132,000 to the runner-up. What it is likely to be under a new sponsor is impossible to guess. It has been reported that there were no fewer than six applicants.

	Winner	Age	Wt	Trainer	Jockey	Ran	SP
1973	Red Rum	8	10.5	D.McCain	B.Fletcher	38	9/1 JF
1974	Red Rum	9	12.0	D.McCain	B.Fletcher	42	11/1
1975	L'Escargot	12	11.3	D.Moore(Ire)	T.Carberry	31	13/2
1976	Rag Trade	10	10.12	T.F.Rimell	J.Burke	32	14/1
1977	Red Rum	12	11.8	D.McCain	T.Stack	42	9/1
1978	Lucius	9	10.9	G.Richards	B.R.Davies	37	14/1
1979	Rubstic	10	10.0	S.J.Leadbetter	M.Barnes	34	25/1
1980	Ben Nevis	12	10.12	T.Forster	Mr C.Fenwick	30	40/1
1981	Aldaniti	11	10.13	J.Gifford	R.Champion	39	10/1
1982	Grittar	9	11.5	F.Gilman	Mr C.Saunders	39	7/1 F
1983	Corbiere	8	11.4	Mrs J.Pitman	B.de Haan	41	13/1
1984	Hallo Dandy	10	10.2	G.Richards	N.Doughty	40	13/1
1985	Last Suspect	11	10.5	T.Forster	H.Davies	40	50/1
1986	West Tip	9	10.11	M.Oliver	R.Dunwoody	40	15/2
1987	Maori Venture	11	10.13	A.Turnell	S.Knight	40	28/1
1988	Rhyme 'n Reason	9	11.0	D.Elsworth	B.Powell	40	10/1
1989	Little Polveir	12	10.3*	G.Balding	J.Frost	40	28/1
1990	Mr Frisk	11	10.6	K.Bailey	Mr M.Armytage	38	16/1
1991	Seagram	11	10.6	D.Barons	N.Hawke	40	12/1
1992	Party Politics	8	10.7	N.Gaselee	C.Llewellyn	40	14/1
1993	Race void after false starts						
1994	Miinnehoma	11	10.8	M.C.Pipe	R.Dunwoody	36	16/1
1995	Royal Athlete	12	10.6	Mrs J. Pitman	J.F.Titley	35	40/1
1996	Rough Quest	10	10.7	T.Casey	M.A.Fitzgerald	27	7/1 F
1997	Lord Gyllene	9	10.0	S.Brookshaw	A.Dobbin	36	14/1
1998	Earth Summit	10	10.5	N.Twiston-Davies	C.Llewellyn	37	7/1 F
1999	Bobbyjo	9	10.0	T.Carberry(Ire)	P.Carberry	32	10/1
2000	Papillon	9	10.12	T.M.Walsh(Ire)	R.Walsh	40	10/1 2F
2001	Red Marauder	11	10.11	N.B.Mason	R.Guest	40	33/1
2002	Bindaree	8	10.4	N.Twiston-Davies	J.Culloty	40	20/1
2003	Monty's Pass	10	10.7	J.J.Mangan(Ire)	B.J.Geraghty	40	16/1
2004	Amberleigh House	12	10.10	D.McCain	G.Lee	39	16/1

* including 3 lb overweight

Cheltenham Gold Cup winners   Only 7 horses since the war have attempted the Gold Cup/Grand National double in the same year. None have succeeded. Nearest was *Garrison Savannah*, runner-up to *Seagram* in 1991. Others were *Prince Regent* (1946 fav, 3rd); *Davy Lad* (1977, fell); *Alverton* (1979 fav, fell); *Cool Ground* (1992, 10th), *The Fellow* (1994, fell) and *Master*

Oats (1995, 7th). Dorothy Paget's *Golden Miller* in 1934 is the only horse ever to have achieved this double in the same season, although Raymond Guest's *L'Escargot* in 1975 won the National, having captured the Gold Cup in 1970 and 1971.

Greys Only 2 greys have ever won the National: *The Lamb* (1868 and 1871) and *Nicolaus Silver* (1961).

Previous winners *Red Rum*, whose imposing and lifelike statue rightly commands the Aintree paddock area, is the only horse ever to have won the National 3 times (as well as being twice runner-up, in 1975 and 1976). Since the illustrious reign of this popular hero, who died, aged 30, in 1995 and was buried by the Aintree winning-post, many other winners have tried again but none have succeeded: *Rag Trade, Rubstic* (2 attempts), *Aldaniti, Corbière* (4 attempts), *West Tip* (4 attempts), *Mr Frisk, Seagram, Miinnehoma, Party Politics* (2nd in 1995 and unplaced in 1996), *Rough Quest, Earth Summit, Bobbyjo, Papillon, Bindaree* and *Monty's Pass*.

Previous fallers A fall in the National in a previous season is no bar to success as *West Tip* and, most recently, *Red Marauder* have proved.

Handicap Only 4 horses set to carry the minimum 10 stone have won in recent years: *Rubstic* (1979), *Little Polveir* (1989), who also carried overweight, *Lord Gyllene* (1997) and *Bobbyjo* (1999). The other 24 all had proper marks in the handicap, which in most years narrows the field of winning possibilities to about the top dozen or so horses. This is by far the most important point to consider when trying to sort out the National.

Betting The most likely price of the winner is between 13/2 and 16/1 (23 winners in the period). There were only 7 outsiders, 3 of them, significantly, when the going was heavy: *Ben Nevis* (1980, 40/1), *Little Polveir* (28/1) and *Red Marauder* (33/1). Yet favourites do not do well (see overleaf, and table above).

Age Nine-year-olds, despite a gap between 1988 and 1997, still have the best record since the war, partly because they numerically have the majority of entries, but from the table it will be seen that the 11-y-o age group have been catching up from 1981, the year of the fairy-tale success of *Aldaniti* and Bob Champion: 6 successes since then, including *Red Marauder* in 2001. Also there have been no fewer than 6 12-y-o from *L'Escargot* in 1975 to, most recently, *Amberleigh House* in 2004. Modern records are against the 7-y-o. There have been 24 unsuccessful runners of this age since 1971, although *Black Secret* was an unlucky runner-up by a neck to *Specify* in 1971. Before the war, however, this age group had an impressive record with, for example, *Forbra, Kellesboro Jack* and *Golden Miller* in successive years 1932–34 and, in the 'twenties, *Troytown* and *Gregalach*. But *Bogskar* in 1940 was the last 7-y-o to win. In 2001, in addition, there were two unsuccessful 6-y-o and in 2004, a further 6-y-o, the French-trained *Kelami*, was unluckily brought down at the first fence. In the 19th century there were quite a number of winners from this age group, but today it is considered generally that 6 is too young for the National. Nevertheless, the 20th century produced two winning 6-y-o, the latest being *Ally Sloper* in 1915 and, before that, *Ambush II* in 1900, owned by Edward, then Prince of Wales, and the only horse ever to carry the royal colours to victory under National Hunt rules. The oldest winner in the records, at 15, was *Peter Simple* in 1853, while *Manifesto*, the hero of both 1897 and 1899 (when he carried 12 st 7 lb to a 5-length victory), was also placed 3rd under even more punishing weights at the ages of 12 and 14, and was 3rd yet again aged 15. In 1904, ridden by Lester Piggott's grandfather, Ernie Piggott, this great steeplechaser made the last of his 8 Aintree appearances. He was then 16 and a large crowd gathered at the racecourse that da⋅ to see him do his early work. Among them was the famous Flat-race jockey Mornington Canno⋅ (also Lester Piggott's great-uncle), who begged to be allowed to sit for a few minutes on thi equally famous old horse's back.

Mares The National has been won on 12 occasions by a mare, but only 3 times in the 20tl century, the last time being by *Nickel Coin* (1951) and before that by *Sheila's Cottage* (1948) an⋅ *Shannon Lass* (1902). The late Jack O'Donoghue had some fascinating recollections of *Nickel Coi⋅* the 40/1 chance he sent out from his Reigate yard. It was the year of the notorious pile-up at th⋅ first fence where, after a Light Brigade charge, 12 out of 36 came down. By the end of the firs⋅ circuit a bare half dozen were still standing and, by the last fence, only 2: *Nickel Coin* and *Roy⋅ Tan* (whose turn was to come in 1954), ridden by Vincent O'Brien's brother, 'Phonsie'. *Royal Ta⋅* hit the top of the fence, sprawled badly and left *Nickel Coin*, ridden by Johnny Bullock, to com⋅ home as she pleased. *Derrinstown*, remounted, was a bad third and the only other finisher. Tha⋅ much is on record, but Jack O'Donoghue was able to embellish the tale. 'She was beautifull⋅ bred,' he once said, 'by *Pay Up* [2000 Guineas winner in 1936], but when she was foaled, *Nicke⋅ Coin* was so weak she couldn't stand up and the vet said "Have her put down, you'll never d⋅ anything with her." Now, there was an old housemaid who used to work for Mrs Barlow, wh⋅ bred her, and she said, "If you put that foal down, I'm going to leave...you give her to me, I'⋅ look after her." And she got some bandages and two bits of boards and made crutches, so sh⋅ walked on the boards keeping her feet three inches off the ground. And, you know, she was fe⋅ on a bottle. She had no mother. This old housemaid kept her in the kitchen by the fire and th⋅ foal used to sleep there on a mattress.' So, at the start of her life, unexpected luck for *Nickel Coi⋅* which was redoubled in the National 9 years later. Nor was keeping out of trouble her only goo⋅ fortune: Jack O'Donoghue also used to relate somewhat thoughtfully, 'I came over from Irelan⋅ in 1929. I was born on the 29th August. The number of my cottage is 29 and *Nickel Coin'⋅* number on the racecard was...29.'

Jockeys Carl Llewellyn has ridden 2 winners (1992 *Party Politics* and 1998 *Earth Summit*) and ha⋅ once been 3rd. Other riders of winners are Paul Carberry, J. Culloty, Tony Dobbin, Mic⋅ Fitzgerald, B.J. Geraghty, G. Lee, Jason Titley and Ruby Walsh.

Trainers D. McCain has a record 4 successes; N. Twiston-Davies: 2.

Fate of the favourites since 1994

1994	5/1 F	Moorcroft Boy 9-10.0	(Promising staying chaser but true handicap weight 9 st 8 lb)	3rd
1995	5/1 F	Master Oats 9-11.10	(Gold Cup and Welsh Grand National winner; unbeaten during season up to this point)	7th
1996	7/1 F	Rough Quest 10-10.7	(Runner-up in Gold Cup; winner Racing Post Trophy)	WON
1997	7/1 F	Go Ballistic 9-10.3	(4th in Gold Cup; Ascot NH specialist)	Pulled up before 2 out
1998	7/1 F	Earth Summit 10-10.5	(Winner Welsh and Scottish Nationals)	WON

1999	6/1 F	Fiddling The Facts 8-10.3	(Game staying mare; runner-up Welsh National)	Fell Becher's 2nd circuit
2000	9/1 F	Dark Stranger 9-10.1	(Useful chaser: success at Cheltenham in Mildmay of Flete Challenge Cup)	Unseated rider 3rd fence
2001	10/1 JF	Edmond	(Winner Welsh National)	Fell 15th
	10/1 JF	Moral Support	(Runner-up Welsh National)	Refused 8th
	10/1 JF	Inis Cara	(Ex-Irish, last-minute gamble)	Fell 4th
2002	8/1 F	Blowing Wind 9-10.6	(Third in 2001 after being remounted)	3rd
2003	7/1 F	Shotgun Willy 9-11.9	(Runner-up Scottish National)	Pulled up after 21st
2004	10/1 JF	Clan Royal 9-10.5	(Aintree specialist; wins include Becher Chase)	2nd
	10/1 JF	Jurancon 7-10.7	(Proven at extreme distances)	Fell 4th
	10/1 JF	Joss Naylor 9-10.11	(Runner-up Hennessy Chase)	Pulled up before 19th
	10/1 JF	Bindaree 10-11.4	(Winner Grand National 2002 and Welsh National 2003)	Pecked badly Becher's and unseated rider

Shortest price favourite: 2/1 F *Golden Miller* in 1935. This great steeplechaser, winner of the National the previous year and already winner of the Cheltenham Gold Cup 4 times in a row (to be followed by a further victory in 1936), was top of the handicap with 12 st 7 lb. First time round, however, he jumped badly at the fence after Valentine's and unseated his rider, Gerry Wilson. The race provided the first of *Reynoldstown*'s 2 successive victories. 27 ran.

Shortest price winning favourite: Poethlyn 1919 at 11/4. 22 ran.

Longest price favourites: 100/7 Joint-Favourites in 1964. *Time* (fell 4 fences from home), *Pappageno's Cottage* (finished 10th), *Flying Wild* (fell at the 1st fence) and HM The Queen Mother's *Laffy* (fell at the 4th fence). The race went to *Team Spirit*, then 12 years old, who was on his 5th attempt at Aintree. 33 ran.

As far as the general public are concerned, the Grand National provides the biggest annual flutter of all, more popular even than the Derby. Bookmakers' and Tote turnover on that day in early April easily tops 7 figures, with punters undaunted by the cold statistics furnished by the race. In the interests of safety the field is now restricted to a maximum of 40 runners (regulations also, mercifully, have been tightened concerning inexperienced riders). Fewer horses fall in the National these days than used to be the case and the average number to finish has been steadily climbing over the past decade (although both these observations took a knock in the heavy going of 1994, 1998 and 2001). Also, more horses than used to be the case are now pulled up when their chance is hopeless. Nevertheless, of 40 starters very roughly 16 will complete the course, 10 will fall, 1 will be brought down, 3 will unseat their riders, 2 will refuse to jump a fence at some stage of the race, and 7 will be pulled up before the finish. At least, these are the average figures, rounded up or down, over the past few years.

The Grand National, the future of which was in the 1970s for so long in the balance, is assured now to give its annual spectacle of courage, skill, narrow escapes and hard luck, triumph and tragedy. No amount of plain statistics nor proliferating valuable jumping races can rob the race of its place still close to the heart of the National Hunt sport. It still remains, too, a summit of owners', trainers', and riders' ambitions, and a huge attraction, in which television has played an important part, to a public far greater than that which normally goes racing on a cold winter's afternoon. In the past, when the Grand National dominated the chasing scene, a horse (for example *Golden Miller* or *Freebooter*) would be said to be 'an Aintree type'. These days, the ability to jump well still remains paramount (even though Becher's Brook has been filled in), but greater need seems to be required for a turn of foot on the long run-in than just stamina to last it out. Such is the variety of good opportunities for staying chasers these days that there are no longer outstanding 'key' races leading to the National, although those horses who do well at Haydock Park are still worth following at Aintree, and if they have class, so much the better.

Seagram and the enthusiasm of their then Chairman, Ivan Straker, deserve immense credit for financially underpinning not only the National, but enthusiastically supporting with their sponsorship from 1984 the concept (see above) of an Aintree Festival; from 1992, until 2004, their subsidiary, Martell, took over and also enhanced the sponsorship with equal keenness.

***The definitive work on this great sporting event is: *The History of the Grand National: A Race Apart* by Reg Green (Hodder and Stoughton). It is a detailed account of every National from *Lottery*'s victory in 1839 to modern times.

NEWBURY   Left-hand   Flat and National Hunt

Draw: Doubtful advantage

With its own railway station alongside the course, and easy access to the M4 motorway, the big and attractive Berkshire course is deservedly popular with London racegoers, and equally so with the great number of trainers whose stables are also in very easy reach from the Lambourn area. Another reason for its popularity and the size of its fields is that the oval track and the 1 mile straight which joins it are wide and only gently undulating, providing an extremely fair test of a horse, but one which, with a long run-in, favours the horse that likes to stride out. The steeplechase and hurdle courses are similarly fair, and spectators can see all the running from the recently rebuilt stands. Newbury racecourse was the idea of the great trainer John Porter of nearby Kingsclere, where Andrew Balding now trains. His original plan was turned down by the Jockey Club, but, supported by King Edward VII, was later adopted and racing began in September 1905. During both World Wars the course was turned over to the military. After the 1939–45 War, when a huge American Supply Depot had submerged the entire area in concrete, barrack blocks, hard standing, and 35 miles of railway line, prodigious feats of demolition, restoration and re-turfing had to be achieved before racing could start again. This did not take place until 1949, and National Hunt not until 1951. Some main races: Flat – Greenham Stakes, Fred Darling Stakes – these are both races over 7 furlongs for 3-y-o only (the latter confined to fillies), run in the spring and regularly providing trials for the 2000 Guineas and 1000 Guineas (but see under **Newmarket**). The main races for 2-y-o include – July: Weatherbys Super Sprint Stakes (5 f, £78,300); Sept: Haynes, Hanson and Clark Conditions Stakes (1 m straight). Not a valuable event, but result worth noting because in the past its placings have produced smart subsequent performers, e.g. 1993 winner *King's Theatre* (King George VI & Queen Elizabeth Diamond Stakes); 1992 third *White Muzzle* (Derby Italiano); 1985 runner-up *Shahrastani* (Derby); 1983 winner *Rainbow Quest* (Prix de l'Arc de Triomphe). Sept: Mill Reef Stakes (Group Two, 6 f, £33,350); Oct: Horris Hill Stakes (Group Three, 7 f). Events for older horses include: April: John Porter Stakes (Group Three, 1 m 4 f, 4-y-o+); May: Juddmonte Lockinge Stakes (Group One, 1 m straight, 4-y-o+, £116,000); Aug: Hungerford Stakes (Group Three, 7 f, 3-y-o+); Aug: Geoffrey Freer Stakes (Group Two, 1 m 5 f, 3-y-o+, £59,500); Sept: Courage Handicap (1 m 2 f, £58,000); Oct: St. Simon Stakes (Group Three, 1 m 4 f, 3-y-o+). In addition, and most important, Newbury stages a great number of maiden races for 2-y-o and 3-y-o throughout the season. These normally attract outsize fields with horses especially from stables close by. A notebook can quickly be filled with likely future winners. National Hunt – Hennessy Cognac Gold Cup Chase, one of the first sponsored races in the Calendar (winner £63,800 in 2003); Feb: Game Spirit Chase (2 m 1 f, £31,000); Feb: Aon Chase (3 m, £41,650); Feb: Tote Gold Trophy, formerly the Schweppes Gold Trophy (2 m+ Hurdle, £69,000 in 2003), which had a drama-ridden history. In addition there are numerous novice hurdles and novice chases which, like the equivalent maiden races on the Flat, also pay dividends if an intelligent eye is kept on them.

Leading trainers: *Flat*   Richard Hannon (23 winners); John Gosden and M.P. Tregoning (13 each); Mick Channon (12); R. Charlton and B.W. Hills (11 each); Sir Michael Stoute (9).

National Hunt   Nicky Henderson (24 winners; 5 on one card in December 2002); Martin Pipe (15); P.F. Nicholls (7); J.J. O'Neill and P.J. Hobbs (6 each).

Leading jockeys: *Flat*   R. Hughes (20 winners); Richard Hills (14); S. Drowne (13); Kieren Fallon and Dane O'Neill (12 each); Martin Dwyer and M. Hills (11 each).

National Hunt   A.P. McCoy (18 winners); M.A. Fitzgerald (16); T.J. Murphy (6); N. Fehily and Carl Llewellyn (5 each).

3 miles 2 furlongs   Hennessy Cognac Gold Cup (Handicap Chase), Newbury, November

	Winner	Age	Wt	Trainer	Jockey	Ran	SP
1983	Brown Chamberlin	8	11.8	F.Winter	J.Francome	12	7/2 F
1984	Burrough Hill Lad	8	12.0	Mrs J.Pitman	J.Francome	13	100/30 F
1985	Galway Blaze	9	10.0	J.G.Fitzgerald	M.Dwyer	15	11/2
1986	Broadheath	9	10.5	D.Barons	P.Nicholls	15	6/1
1987	Playschool	9	10.8	D.Barons	P.Nicholls	12	6/1

1988	Strands Of Gold	9	10.0	Martin Pipe	P.Scudamore	12	10/1
1989	Ghofar	6	10.2	D.Elsworth	H.Davies	8	5/1
1990	Arctic Call	7	11.0	O.Sherwood	J.Osborne	13	5/1
1991	Chatam	7	10.6	Martin Pipe	P.Scudamore	15	10/1
1992	Sibton Abbey	7	10.0	F.Murphy	A.Maguire	13	40/1
1993	Cogent	9	10.1	A.Turnell	D.Fortt	9	10/1
1994	One Man	6	10.0	G.W.Richards	A.Dobbin	16	4/1
1995	Couldn't Be Better	8	10.8	C.Brooks	D.Gallagher	11	15/2
1996	Coome Hill	7	10.0	W.W.Dennis	J.Osborne	11	11/2
1997	Suny Bay	8	11.8	C.Brooks	G.Bradley	14	9/4 F
1998	Teeton Mill	9	10.5	Miss V.Williams	N.Williamson	17	5/1
1999	Ever Blessed	7	10.0	M.Pitman	T.J.Murphy	13	9/2 F
2000	King's Road	7	10.7	N.Twiston-Davies	J.Goldstein	17	7/1
2001	Whats Up Boys	7	10.12	P.J.Hobbs	P.Flynn	14	14/1
2002	Be My Royal	8	10.0	W.P.Mullins(Ire)	D.J.Casey	25	33/1
2003	Strong Flow	6	11.0	P.Nicholls	R.Walsh	21	5/1 JF

The Hennessy Gold Cup, as it then was, was first run at Cheltenham in November 1957. Its £5,272 was historic as the biggest National Hunt prize ever, after that of the Grand National (compare 1956 King George VI Chase £2,915; 1957 Gold Cup £3,996, Grand National £8,868 and Whitbread £4,842). This helped to cause a subsequent prize-money shake-up and the Hennessy, together with the Whitbread, first run 8 months previously, were jointly responsible for setting the ball of commerical sponsorship rolling and a consequent racing revolution. Up to then, commercial sponsorship had been unknown. In 1960 the race moved to Newbury and many famous names embellish its records.

First, *Mandarin*, the gallant little horse owned, fittingly, by Mme Hennessy. Among his 17 victories over fences, including the Gold Cup and King George VI twice, he won the very first Hennessy in 1957, then won again in 1961 and in between was unplaced when favourite in 1958. *Arkle* was beaten into 3rd place by his original great rival *Mill House* in 1963, but won the Hennessy in the following 2 years. Then came 1966. Here is what I wrote in the *Evening Standard* (Heading: 'Arkle Humbled in Cup'): 'The impossible happened here this afternoon. The mighty Arkle was toppled... by the 25/1 outsider Stalbridge Colonist...to whom he was giving two and a half stone'.

Other famous winners: *Kerstin* (1959), *Spanish Steps* (1969), *Diamond Edge* (1981), *Bregawn* (1982), *Burrough Hill Lad* (1984), *One Man* (1994), *Suny Bay* (1997), while *Red Rum* was beaten on the post in a 1973 thriller by *Red Candle* to whom he was giving a stone. Meanwhile, *Whats Up Boys* was runner-up in the 2002 National. He was beaten only in the last 75 yards and thus narrowly missed being only the 3rd grey to win the National (see under **Liverpool**).

Trainers Best trainer by far is Martin Pipe – from 20 Hennessy runners: 2 winners (*Strands Of Gold* 1988 and *Chatam* 1991), 2 runners-up, 3 thirds, 1 fourth.

NEWCASTLE   Left-hand   Flat and National Hunt

Draw: No advantage, if the going is good. Low numbers are best on the straight course if the ground becomes soft, and progressively more so if the going becomes heavy.

There is a long history of racing at Newcastle dating back at least to the 17th century and well maintained at Gosforth Park today. *Beeswing* is the most celebrated horse at this course, up to recently fittingly commemorated by a Group Three event for 3-y-o over 7 f, but now, under new-broom management, this has been shamefully downgraded to a handicap, although retaining *Beeswing*'s name in the title. Ballads have also been written about the exploits of this remarkable 19th century race mare (see earlier references) and not a few pub signs also bear her name. As her owner-breeder, William Orde, of the ancient Durham-Northumbrian family, said: 'She belongs to the people of Northumberland.' The most famous event here is the Northumberland Plate, a handicap for stayers in late June, first run in 1833, and known as 'The Pitmen's Derby', when the course is packed. In 2004, sponsored by John Smith's, it was worth £104,400 to the winner. The track itself is pear-shaped, with a 7 furlong straight joining it 4 furlongs from the finish. A steady rise from the final turn to the winning-post, bends which are banked and can be taken at top speed thus giving no opportunity for a breather, and, in general, an uncompromising test make Newcastle no course for a horse lacking either stamina or will to win on the Flat or over jumps. Some main races, other than those already mentioned: Flat – June: Gosforth Park Cup (5 f Hcp, £20,300); Aug: Blaydon Race Nursery Hcp (1 m straight, 2-y-o, £13,364). National Hunt – Nov: 'Fighting Fifth' Hurdle (2 m, £45,000); Jan: Dipper Novices Chase (2 m 4 f, £40,000); Feb: Tote Eider National Handicap worth £62,000 to the winner over 4 m 1 f: a recognised Grand National trial.

Leading trainers: *Flat*   Mick Channon (14 winners); Tim Easterby (12); R.A. Fahey, W.J. Haggas, Sir Mark Prescott and Mrs Reveley (6 each).

National Hunt   The National Hunt scene at Newcastle is utterly dominated by Mrs Mary Reveley (16 winners); N.B. Mason (9); M.W. Easterby and Len Lungo (8 each); Tim Easterby (7).

Leading jockeys: *Flat*   Kevin Darley (16 winners); R. Winston (11); P. Hanagan (10); A. Culhane, D. Holland and J.P. Spencer (9 each); G. Duffield (8).

National Hunt   A. Dobbin (12 winners); A. Dempsey and Richard Guest (9 each); G. Lee (8); P. Aspell, K. Johnson and K. Fenwick (5 each).

NEWMARKET   Right-hand   Flat only

Draw: For most races, no appreciable effect (but see below for effect of the Draw in the Cambridgeshire).

Enough has already been written to obviate the necessity for rehearsing the history of Newmarket again, as well as to leave no doubt of its importance as Turf 'Headquarters'. Anyone who loves horses and racing derives a quite specific enjoyment from the meetings on its two courses, both from the sense of the continuity of Turf history, and from the no-nonsense professional aspect of the racing, particularly on the Rowley Mile course. This is the course (where, in fact, there are races of much longer than a mile) which stages the spring and autumn meetings. In addition to a wholesale shake-up in 2001 on the management side, there have also been recent impressive structural alterations, notably to the paddock area and weighing room, and a wholesale demolition and rebuilding of the grandstand on the Rowley Mile – the result, not to everyone's liking, arousing considerable controversy. But no amount of reconstruction will solve Newmarket's main problem – that is that the courses were laid out at a time when it was not thought necessary for grandstand spectators to follow every yard of the running (because, in any case, this object could be achieved by following the races on horseback). It may be that the round Sefton Course in front of the stands will be put back into service in the future, but at present several races in their early stages are out of range of even the most powerful U-boat binoculars, an extreme instance being the Cesarewitch, which, starting down by the Devil's Dyke, runs much of its course unseen to all but television and closed-circuit watchers. Fortunately, to the enthusiast, this is a shortcoming easily forgiven by the quality of racing, and, additionally, the fact that most of the real action is well within range and intensified as the horses reach 'the Bushes' and go into 'the Dip' (traditional marker points in the final stages of the Rowley Mile). Of the meetings on this course, the Craven Meeting, first of the season, can be recommended for those who want a look at early 2-y-o, and to see how 3-y-o have developed physically during the winter. As to atmosphere, Sir Alfred Munnings best captured forever on canvas what a Rowley Mile meeting is like, in the clear East Anglian light and between the infinite horizons of the Heath.

The July Course, which stages the important meeting in July (hence the name) as well as the regular weekend meetings during the summer, has a more relaxed atmosphere, an effect heightened by its thatched buildings. The early stages of longer races on both courses are run over the same ground, before joining the Rowley Mile proper or branching on to the final mile of the July Course. Both courses provide a comprehensive test of the thoroughbred, and horses require undoubted stamina to make the grade at the various distances. Some main races: *Rowley Mile* – Craven Stakes (1 m, 3-y-o), Free Handicap (7 f, 3-y-o), Nell Gwynn Stakes (fillies), 2000 Guineas, 1000 Guineas (both Group One, 3-y-o); Middle Park Stakes (6 f), Cheveley Park Stakes (6 f, fillies), Dewhurst Stakes (7 f) (all Group One, 2-y-o); Jockey Club Stakes (Group Two, 1 m 4 f, 4-y-o+), Palace House Stakes (Group Three sprint), Sun Chariot Stakes (Group Two, 1 m, fillies and mares), Jockey Club Cup (Group Three, 2 m), Champion Stakes (Group One, 1 m 2 f; sponsored by Emirates Airline, this in 2003 carried the richest prize on offer at Newmarket – £232,000 to the winner, no less than £88,000 to the runner-up and a total of £80,000 other prizes down to sixth place), Challenge Stakes (Group Two, 7 f), Cambridgeshire Handicap, Cesarewitch. *July Course* – July Cup (Group One, 6 f; another race considerably enhanced in value – in 2003 worth £145,000 to the winner and £55,000 to the runner-up), July Stakes (Group Two, 6 f, colts and geldings; oldest 2-y-o race in the Calendar, first run in 1786); Princess of Wales's Stakes (Group Two, 1 m 4 f, 3-y-o+), Bunbury Cup (7 f Handicap, 3-y-o+), Cherry Hinton Stakes (Group Two, 6 f, 2-y-o fillies).

Leading trainers: Richard Hannon (22 winners); John Dunlop (14); D.R. Loder, Mrs A.J. Perrett and Sir Michael Stoute (10 each); B.W. Hills (9); Mick Channon and J. Fanshawe (8 each).

Leading jockeys: Kieren Fallon (22 winners); L. Dettori (21); R. Hughes (19); J.P. Spencer (12); Richard Hills (11); P. Robinson (9); T. Quinn (8); D. Holland and W. Supple (7 each).

Rowley Mile   2000 Guineas, Newmarket, late April/early May

First run over 1 mile 1 yard in 1809, the race was varied twice in distance in the 19th century until standardised at a mile in 1902. The 2000 Guineas was originally open to colts, geldings and fillies. From 1904 geldings were excluded, and then as now the race was open only to 3-y-o colts and fillies. Colts carry 9 st, fillies 8 st 9 lb. In practice, these days, fillies normally go for the 1000 Guineas and leave the 2000 Guineas to the colts. A notable exception last century was *Sceptre* in 1902 (see under **Classics** in Chapter One). *Garden Path* won in 1944 when (from 1940–45) the war-time Guineas were run on the July Course (the Rowley Mile course being occupied by the military). These were the only fillies to win this race in the 20th century. In 2004, the prize to the winning owner was £174,000.

	Winner	*Sire*	*Trainer*	*Jockey*	*Ran*	*SP*
1970	Nijinsky	Northern Dancer	M.V.O'Brien(Ire)	L.Piggott	14	4/7 F
1971	Brigadier Gerard	Queen's Hussar	W.R.Hern	J.Mercer	6	11/2 3F
1972	High Top	Derring-Do	B.Van Cutsem	W.Carson	12	85/40 F
1973	Mon Fils	Sheshoon	R.Hannon	F.Durr	18	50/1
1974	Nonoalco	Nearctic	F.Boutin(Fr)	Y.Saint-Martin	12	19/2
1975	Bolkonski	Balidar	H.Cecil	G.Dettori	24	33/1
1976	Wollow	Wolver Hollow	H.Cecil	G.Dettori	17	Evens F
1977	Nebbiolo	Yellow God	K.Prendergast(Ire)	G.Curran	18	20/1
1978	Roland Gardens	Derring-Do	D.Sasse	F.Durr	19	28/1
1979	Tap On Wood	Sallust	B.Hills	S.Cauthen	20	20/1
1980	*Known Fact	In Reality	J.Tree	W.Carson	14	14/1
1981	To-Agori-Mou	Tudor Music	G.Harwood	G.Starkey	19	5/2 F
1982	Zino	Welsh Pageant	F.Boutin(Fr)	F.Head	26	8/1 J3F

1983	Lomond	Northern Dancer	M.V.O'Brien(Ire)	P.Eddery	16	9/1
1984	El Gran Senor	Northern Dancer	M.V.O'Brien(Ire)	P.Eddery	9	15/8 F
1985	Shadeed	Nijinsky	M.Stoute	L.Piggott	14	4/5 F
1986	Dancing Brave	Lyphard	G.Harwood	G.Starkey	15	15/8 F
1987	Don't Forget Me	Ahonoora	R.Hannon	W.Carson	13	9/1
1988	Doyoun	Mill Reef	M.Stoute	W.R.Swinburn	9	5/4 F
1989	Nashwan	Blushing Groom	Major W.R.Hern	W.Carson	14	3/1 F
1990	Tirol	Thatching	R.Hannon	M.J.Kinane	14	9/1
1991	Mystiko	Secreto	C.Brittain	M.Roberts	14	13/2 2F
1992	Rodrigo de Triano	El Gran Senor	P.Chapple-Hyam	L.Piggott	16	6/1 3F
1993	Zafonic	Gone West	A.Fabre(Fr)	P.Eddery	14	5/6 F
1994	Mister Baileys	Robellino	M.Johnston	J.Weaver	23	16/1
1995	Pennekamp	Bering	A.Fabre(Fr)	T Jarnet	11	9/2
1996	Mark of Esteem	Darshaan	Saeed bin Suroor	L.Dettori	13	8/1
1997	Entrepreneur	Sadler's Wells	M.Stoute	M.J.Kinane	16	11/2 2F
1998	King of Kings	Sadler's Wells	A.P.O'Brien(Ire)	M.J.Kinane	18	7/2 2F
1999	Island Sands	Turtle Island	Saeed bin Suroor	L.Dettori	16	10/1
2000	King's Best	Kingmambo	Sir M.Stoute	K.Fallon	27	13/2 3F
2001	Golan	Spectrum	Sir M.Stoute	K.Fallon	18	11/1
2002	Rock of Gibraltar	Danehill	A.P.O'Brien(Ire)	J.P.Murtagh	22	9/1
2003	Refuse To Bend	Sadler's Wells	D.K.Weld(Ire)	P.J.Smullen	20	9/2 2F
2004	Haafhd	Alhaarth	B.W.Hills	R.Hills	14	11/2

*Nureyev (USA) by Nijinsky finished 1st in 1980 but was disqualified.

Well-backed horses have a good record, as the table shows, over recent years, but the 1970s threw up some shock winners in this first Classic.

Past records   The Craven Stakes (3-y-o colts and geldings, Newmarket 1 mile, April). In the past 20 years this race has a fair record as a guide to the 2000 Guineas. *Shadeed* (1985), *Dancing Brave* (1986), *Doyoun* (1988), *Tirol* (1990) and *Haafhd* (2004) all won before going on to Guineas success. *Don't Forget Me* (1987) was runner-up to *Ajdal* in the Craven Stakes before winning the Guineas, and *King's Best* was runner-up before Guineas success in the year 2000.

The Greenham Stakes (3-y-o colts, Newbury 7 f, April) has never realised its intended value as a trial. Of the past 15 winners of the Greenham, 6 were sunk without trace in the Guineas, 4 did not run, and the nearest to success were *Celtic Swing* (1995) and *Bairn* (1985), both 2nd in the Guineas, *Barathea Guest* (2000) and *Redback* (2002), both 3rd, and *Rock City* (1990), 4th. *Wollow* (1976) was the most recent Greenham winner to take the Guineas as well, and before that *Tower Walk* (1969). Beyond that, *Kris, Mill Reef* and *Silly Season* won the Greenham and were 2nd in the Guineas, and *Rodrigo de Triano* (1992) and *Known Fact* (1980) were 4th in the Greenham and went on to capture the first Classic.

The Middle Park Stakes (2-y-o, Newmarket 6 f, October) has only *Rodrigo de Triano* (1992) to show in recent years. He also won the Champagne Stakes (2-y-o, Doncaster 7 f, September) as did *Don't Forget Me*. In the past 40-odd years, the Middle Park has declined from a glorious past when it was known as the 'Two-year-old Derby' and has produced but 5 winners who have gone on to take the 2000 Guineas. *Rodrigo de Triano* apart, the others are *Nearula* (1952), *Right Tack* (1968), *Brigadier Gerard* (1970) and *Known Fact* (1979).

Trainers Sir Michael Stoute: 5 winners; Richard Hannon 3; André Fabre (France), Saeed bin Suroor, A.P. O'Brien and Henry Cecil: 2 each.

Jockeys M.J. Kinane: 3 winners; L. Dettori, Kieren Fallon: 2 each.

Owners Khaled Abdulla: 3 winners; Godolphin, John Horgan, Mrs J. Magnier: 2 each.

Rowley Mile   1000 Guineas, Newmarket, late April/early May

First run at 7 furlongs 178 yards in 1814; became 1 mile from 1902. Run on the July Course, Newmarket, during the war years 1940–45. Winner's prize in 2004, £187,195. For 3-y-o fillies only, all carrying 9 st.

	Winner	Sire	Trainer	Jockey	Ran	SP
1974	Highclere	Queen's Hussar	W.R.Hern	J.Mercer	15	12/1
1975	Nocturnal Spree	Supreme Sovereign	H.V.S.Murless(Ire)	J.Roe	16	14/1
1976	Flying Water	Habitat	A.Penna(Fr)	Y.Saint-Martin	25	2/1 F
1977	Mrs McArdy	Tribal Chief	M.W.Easterby	E.Hide	18	16/1
1978	Enstone Spark	Sparkler	B.Hills	E.Johnson	16	35/1
1979	One In A Million	Rarity	H.Cecil	J.Mercer	17	Evens F
1980	Quick As Lightning	Buckpasser	J.Dunlop	B.Rouse	23	12/1
1981	Fairy Footsteps	Mill Reef	H.Cecil	L.Piggott	14	6/4 F
1982	On The House	Be My Guest	H.Wragg	J.Reid	15	33/1
1983	Ma Biche	Key To The Kingdom	Mme C.Head(Fr)	F.Head	18	5/2 F
1984	Pebbles	Sharpen Up	C.Brittain	P.Robinson	15	8/1 J2F
1985	Oh So Sharp	Kris	H.Cecil	S.Cauthen	17	2/1F
1986	Midway Lady	Alleged	B.Hanbury	R.Cochrane	15	10/1
1987	Miesque	Nureyev	F.Boutin(Fr)	F.Head	14	15/8 F
1988	Ravinella	Mr Prospector	Mme C.Head(Fr)	G.W.Moore	12	4/5 F
1989	Musical Bliss	The Minstrel	M.Stoute	W.R.Swinburn	7	7/2 J2F
1990	Salsabil	Sadler's Wells	J.Dunlop	W.Carson	10	6/4 F
1991	Shadayid	Shadeed	J.Dunlop	W.Carson	14	4/6 F
1992	Hatoof	Irish River	Mme C.Head(Fr)	W.R.Swinburn	14	5/1 J2F
1993	Sayyedati	Shadeed	C.Brittain	W.R.Swinburn	12	4/1 2F
1994	Las Meninas	Glenstal	T.Stack(Ire)	J.Reid	15	12/1
1995	Harayir	Gulch	W.R.Hern	R. Hills	14	5/1 J2F
1996	Bosra Sham	Woodman	H.Cecil	Pat Eddery	13	10/11 F
1997	Sleepytime	Royal Academy	H.Cecil	K.Fallon	15	5/1
1998	Cape Verdi	Caerleon	Saeed bin Suroor	L.Dettori	16	100/30 JF
1999	Wince	Selkirk	H.Cecil	K.Fallon	22	4/1 F
2000	Lahan	Unfuwain	J.Gosden	R.Hills	18	14/1
2001	Ameerat	Mark of Esteem	M.Jarvis	P.Robinson	15	11/1

2002	Kazzia	Zinaad	Saeed bin Suroor	L.Dettori	17	14/1
2003	Russian Rhythm	Kingmambo	Sir Michael Stoute	K.Fallon	19	12/1
2004	Attraction	Efisio	M.Johnston	K.Darley	16	11/2 2F

All but 6 of the most recent 15 winners of the 1000 Guineas have been in the first 2 in the betting.

Past records   The Nell Gwynn Stakes (7 f, Newmarket Craven Meeting) has become an increasingly suspect pointer since the heady days between 1976 and 1985 when no fewer than 5 winners of the event went on to take the Guineas. These (see table above for dates) were *Flying Water, One In A Million, Fairy Footsteps, Pebbles* and *Oh So Sharp*. Since then, amongst its winners, *Sonic Lady* (1986), *Heart of Joy* (1990) and *Crystal Gazing* (1992) have managed only a place and *Mehtaaf* was 4th, although *Sayyedati* was 3rd in the 1993 Nell Gwynn and went on for a thrilling victory in the Guineas.

In most recent years, the Fred Darling Stakes at Newbury has given more reliable indications, with *Wince* (1999), *Bosra Sham* (1996), *Shadayid* (1991) and *Salsabil* (1990) winning before Guineas success, and *Sleepytime* (1997) and *Lahan* being 4th. Before then, the results of the Fred Darling, like those of its colts' equivalent, the Greenham, were quite outstanding for speaking with forked tongue. Of the customary French trial for the '1000', the Prix Imprudence, the winner and 2nd in 1993, *Wixon* and *Elizabeth Bay*, both failed at Newmarket; *Hatoof* in 1992 reversed the Imprudence form with *Kenbu* in the '1000', while both *Ravinella* (1988) and *Miesque* (1987) completed the double.

Beyond these 3-y-o trials, encouragement is to be had from the results of certain key 2-y-o contests. Of these, it is remarkable that in the most recent 15 years it is a French race which has given a good indication to the 1000 Guineas. The race is the Prix Marcel Boussac (formerly the Criterium des Pouliches), Group One at Longchamp over a mile for 2-y-o fillies only, run now on the first Sunday in October, on the same day as the Prix de l'Arc de Triomphe. Since 1985 (trainers' names in brackets) 4 Boussac winners have scored the following year in the 1000 Guineas: *Midway Lady* (1985, Ben Hanbury), *Miesque* (1986, Francois Boutin), *Salsabil* (1989, John Dunlop), *Shadayid* (1990, John Dunlop). In 1991 *Culture Vulture* (Paul Cole) won the Boussac, narrowly beating *Hatoof* (Mme Head), who had been very unlucky in running and was in front of *Culture Vulture* 2 yards past the post. At Newmarket the following spring *Culture Vulture* was unplaced in the Guineas and *Hatoof* (who came back again in 1993 to triumph in the Champion Stakes) justly earned her revenge.

It is nevertheless sad that the Boussac competes with the 2-y-o Fillies Mile (also Group One, run at Ascot a week earlier, sponsored by the Meon Valley Stud and worth in 2003 £116,000 to the winner). This race not only has a more valuable prize than the Boussac, but also produces its share of winners with good credentials for the 1000 Guineas. Most recently, *Soviet Song* (2002) was 4th in the 1000 Guineas the following season; *Gossamer* (2001) won the Irish 1000 Guineas in 2002, and *Crystal Music* (2000) followed up with a 4th in the next year's '1000'. In the earlier years after its first running in 1973, the Fillies Mile, under various sponsorships and not yet Group One, produced *Quick As Lightning* (1979) and *Oh So Sharp* (1984), who later won the 1000 Guineas, while *Diminuendo* (1987) was placed. After that, the Fillies Mile sent out no positive signals for some time, but in 1995 *Bosra Sham* won and went on to Guineas success, while in 1996 *Sleepytime* was 3rd in the Fillies Mile and won the Guineas the following season. Nevertheless (and despite *Culture Vulture* capturing both races), the running of two Group One races over a mile for 2-y-o fillies within a week of one another is a matter to which the European Pattern Committee ought to pay urgent attention.

The traditional 2-y-o indicator to the 1000 Guineas is the Cheveley Park Stakes, run over 6 furlongs at Newmarket in October. Unlike its immediate equivalent for colts and geldings, the Middle Park Stakes, this contest has maintained a fair reputation as a Classic guide. It was first run in 1899 and its more recent winners who have gone on to score in the 1000 Guineas include *Night Off* (1964), *Fleet* (1966), *Humble Duty* (1969), *Waterloo* (1971), *Ma Biche* (1982), *Ravinella* (1987) and *Sayyedati* (1992), while *Marling* was runner-up in the Guineas in 1992 and went on to take the Irish 1000 Guineas, as did *Forest Flower*, first past the post in the 1986 Cheveley Park but disqualified. In addition both *Pebbles* (1983) and *On The House* (1981) were Cheveley Park runners-up who went on to greater glory in the 1000 Guineas the following year.

Other 2-y-o fillies' races worth looking at are the Lowther Stakes (6 f York, August) won by later Guineas winners *Pourparler* (1963), *Humble Duty* (1969), *Enstone Spark* (1977), *Harayir* (1995), *Cape Verdi* (1997) and *Russian Rhythm* (2002); May Hill Stakes (1 mile Doncaster, September) and the Moyglare Stud Stakes (6 f The Curragh, September).

Trainers Henry Cecil has saddled 6 winners; John Dunlop and Mme Criquette Head (France) have each sent out 3; Clive Brittain, Saeed bin Suroor and Sir Michael Stoute: 2 each.

Jockeys Kieren Fallon: 3 winners; L. Dettori and Richard Hills: 2 each.

Owners Sheikh Hamdan al-Maktoum: 4 winners; Maktoum al-Maktoum and Godolphin: 2 each.

1 mile 1 furlong Hcp   The Cambridgeshire, Newmarket, October

First run 1839. Worth £75,400 to the winner in 2004, sponsored by the Tote.

	Winner(Draw)	Age	Wt	Trainer	Jockey	Ran	SP
1973	Siliciana(32) f	4	8.5	I.Balding	G.Lewis	37	14/1
1974	Flying Nelly(29) f	4	7.7	W.Wightman	D.Maitland	39	22/1
1975	Lottogift(22)	4	8.2	D.Hanley	R.Wernham*5	36	33/1
1976	Intermission(18) f	3	8.6	M.Stoute	G.Starkey	29	14/1
1977	Sin Timon(11)	3	8.3	J.Hindley	A.Kimberley	27	18/1
1978	Baronet(15)	6	9.0	C.J.Benstead	B.Rouse	18	12/1
1979	Smartset(20)	4	8.8	R.Johnson Houghton	J.Reid	24	33/1
1980	Baronet(11)	8	9.3	C.J.Benstead	B.Rouse	19	22/1
1981	Braughing(5)	4	8.4	C.Brittain	S.Cauthen	28	50/1
1982	Century City(12)	3	9.6	L.Cumani	J.Mercer	29	20/1
1983	Sagamore(18)	4	7.8	F.Durr	M.L.Thomas	30	35/1
1984	Leysh(7)	3	8.7	S.G.Norton	J.Lowe	34	33/1
1985	Tremblant(21)	4	9.8	R.V.Smyth	P.Eddery	31	16/1
1986	Dallas(16)	3	9.6	L.Cumani	R.Cochrane	31	10/1
1987	Balthus(7)	4	8.1	J.A.Glover	D.McKeown	31	50/1
1988	Quinlan Terry(7)	3	8.5	Sir Mark Prescott	G.Duffield	29	11/1
1989	Rambo's Hall(19)	4	8.6	J.A.Glover	D.McKeown	34	15/1
1990	Risen Moon(2)	3	8.9	B.W.Hills	S.Cauthen	40	7/1 F
1991	Mellottie(27)	6	9.1	Mrs M.Reveley	J.Lowe	29	10/1 J2F
1992	Rambo's Hall(7)	7	9.3	J.A.Glover	D.McKeown	30	9/2 F
1993	Penny Drops(18) f	4	7.13	Lord Huntingdon	D.Harrison	33	7/1 F
1994	Halling(24)	3	8.8	J.Gosden	L.Dettori	30	8/1 F

1995	Cap Juluca(26)	3	9.10	R.Charlton	R.Hughes	39	11/1 2F
1996	Clifton Fox(17)	4	8.2	J.A.Glover	N.Day	38	14/1
1997	Pasternak(17)	4	9.1	Sir Mark Prescott	G.Duffield	36	4/1 F
1998	Lear Spear(33)	3	7.13	D.Elsworth	N.Pollard*5	35	20/1
1999	She's Our Mare (14) m	6	7.12	A.J.Martin(Ire)	F.Norton	33	11/1 3F
2000	Katy Nowaitee(34) f	4	8.8	P.W.Harris	J.Reid	35	6/1 2F
2001	I Cried For You(11)	6	8.6	J.G.Given	M.Fenton	35	33/1
2002	Beauchamp Pilot(26)	4	9.5	G.A.Butler	E.Ahern	30	9/1
2003	Chivalry(17)	4	8.1	Sir Mark Prescott	G.Duffield	33	14/1
2004	Spanish Don(3)	6	8.10	D.Elsworth	L.Keniry	32	100/1

* Apprentice allowance claimed in lb. f = filly, m = mare

Favourites   For the average backer, finding the winner of the Cambridgeshire is by far the harder problem of the 2 'legs' of the Autumn Double. The race is invariably a death or glory charge of outsize proportions spread across the galloping expanses of the Rowley Mile in sunshine whose paleness is matched only by punters' faces at the finish. Until very recent years, unlike the Cesarewitch, it has not in general been a race for the leading market fancies. Yet 5 favourites have won since 1970, all of them between 1990 and 1997, which shows at least a temporary swing in the punters' favour, although perhaps the leopard does not permanently change his spots overnight. There is an abundance of winners priced from 20/1 to 50/1: no less than 36.7% of the winners in the period – a percentage remarkably unchanged since the very earliest years of the last century when the pattern was different, and there were several well-gambled-on short-price winners such as *Ballantrae, Hackler's Pride, Velocity,* and *Polymelus* (at 11/10 the shortest-priced favourite of them all).

Trainers   J.A.Glover (Worksop) has no fewer than 4 victories to his credit, 2 of them with the evergreen *Rambo's Hall,* who in 1993 was 3rd in his attempt aged 8 under a big weight to make it a hat-trick. Sir Mark Prescott has saddled 3 winners and Luca Cumani 2.

Jockeys   George Duffield and Dean McKeown have each scored 3 times.

Age   3-y-o used to be twice as successful as 4-y-o. Cambridgeshire victories are now more or less evenly divided between these 2 age groups with a slight edge in favour of 4-y-o and with some older horses winning (including *Baronet* who won as a 6-y-o *and* 8-y-o, thus becoming the oldest to win during the 20th century).

Weight   Winners are spread throughout the entire handicap range, but unlike most big betting handicaps, very low weights these days do not generally win. The feather-weight of 6 st 3 lb carried by *Esquire* in 1945 is now no longer possible, but an all-round upward shift of the handicap scale only partly explains why the Cambridgeshire, formerly dominated by horses weighted under 8 st, now has an unusual (compared with similar handicaps) number of winners weighted 9 st and over. This is a handicap bracket not to be ignored when attempting to solve the Cambridgeshire puzzle. Eleven winners have come from this topmost section of the handicap since 1971.

Draw   The draw on the Rowley Mile is generally held to be of no great significance. The field for the Cambridgeshire often splits into 2 main groups (towards the stands side rails and far running rails) with sometimes a proportion running up the middle. These circumstances, added to marginal differences in going from one side of the course to the other, make it impossible to lay down any firm rule. Nevertheless those drawn with very low numbers on the stands rails have a relatively poor winning record. The best winning chances, in fact, appear to be held by horses from just under the middle of the draw to medium-high numbers, although high numbers also have a good record.

2 mile 2 furlong Hcp   The Cesarewitch, Newmarket, October

First run 1839 and sponsored since 1978 by the Tote, it was worth £75,400 to the winner in 2004. The name is a corruption of 'Tsarevich', a title given in honour of Alexander II of Russia who, before he was Tsar, donated £300 to the Jockey Club. In its earlier days, Classic winners were often among the runners. *Faugh-a-Ballagh* (1844), *The Baron* (1845), *Robert The Devil* (1880), and *St Gatien* (1884) are winning examples, but it is now a long time since a Classic horse took part.

	Winner	Age	Wt	Trainer	Jockey	Ran	SP
1976	John Cherry (6 lb+)	5	9.13	J.Tree	L.Piggott	14	13/2 2F
1977	Assured (6 lb+)	4	8.4	H.Candy	P.Waldron	11	10/1
1978	Centurion	3	9.8	Ian Balding	J.Matthias	17	9/2 F
1979	Sir Michael	3	7.8	G.Huffer	M.Rimmer*5	11	10/1
1980	Popsi's Joy	5	8.6	M.Haynes	L.Piggott	27	10/1 2F
1981	Halsbury	3	8.4	P.Walwyn	J.Mercer	30	14/1
1982	Mountain Lodge f (4 lb+)	3	7.10	J.Dunlop	W.Carson	28	9/1 2F
1983	Bajan Sunshine	4	8.8	R.Simpson	B.Rouse	27	7/1 JF
1984	Tom Sharp	4	7.5	W.Wharton	S.Dawson*5	26	40/1
1985	Kayudee	5	8.1	J.Fitzgerald	A.Murray	21	7/1 2F
1986	Orange Hill f	4	7.9	J.Tree	R.Fox	25	20/1
1987	Private Audition	5	7.9	M.H.Tompkins	G.Carter	28	50/1
1988	Nomadic Way (4 lb+)	3	7.9	B.W.Hills	W.Carson	24	6/1 JF
1989	Double Dutch m (4 lb+)	5	9.10	Miss B.Sanders	W.Newnes	22	15/2 3F
1990	Trainglot	3	7.12	J.Fitzgerald	W.Carson	25	13/2 2F
1991	Go South	7	7.11	J.R.Jenkins	N.Carlisle	22	33/1
1992	Vintage Crop	5	9.6	D.Weld(Ire)	W.R.Swinburn	24	5/1 F
1993	Aahsaylad	7	8.12	J.White	J.Williams	31	12/1
1994	Captain's Guest	4	9.9	G.Harwood	A.Clark	32	25/1
1995	Old Red	5	7.11	Mrs M.Reveley	L. Charnock	20	11/1
1996	Inchcailloch	7	7.10	J.S.King	R.Ffrench	26	20/1
1997	Turnpole	6	7.10	Mrs M.Reveley	L. Charnock	29	16/1
1998	Spirit of Love	3	8.8	M.Johnston	O.Peslier	29	11/1
1999	Top Cees	9	8.10	Ian Balding	K.Fallon	32	7/1 2F
2000	Heros Fatal	6	8.1	M.C.Pipe	G.Carter	33	11/1
2001	Distant Prospect	4	8.8	Ian Balding	Martin Dwyer	31	14/1
2002	Miss Fara m	7	8.0	M.C.Pipe	R.L.Moore	36	12/1
2003	Landing Light	8	9.4	N.J.Henderson	Pat Eddery	35	12/1
2004	Contact Dancer	5	8.2	M.Johnston	R.Ffrench	34	16/1

+ Penalty carried. * Apprentice allowance claimed in lb. f = filly, m = mare

Favourites The Cesarewitch is not a race usually won by an outsider although, against the normal trend, there have been 4 in the most recent 15 runnings.

Changes in the minimum handicap rating make it difficult to draw any useful conclusion about likely winning weights, but the handicap range between 7 st 8 lb and 8 st 4 lb provided 53.8% of winners from 1960 onwards. Relatively fresh horses are worth looking at for the Cesarewitch, a principle held by Ryan Price. *Major Rose*, runner-up in 1967 and winner in 1968, had only 3 and 2 previous outings, respectively, during those seasons.

Others: 2000 *Heros Fatal* 2 runs; none since 1 July (unplaced in Northumberland Plate); June (3rd in Ascot Stakes).

1999 *Top Cees* 2 runs; September (winner at Ayr); August (unplaced at Chester).

1992 *Vintage Crop* 1 run; 19 September (5th in Irish St. Leger)

1985 *Kayudee* 2 runs; early October (5th) and early September (unplaced)

1984 *Tom Sharp* 2 runs; early October (unplaced) and mid-August (unplaced)

Trainers There have been no outstanding trainers since the late Ryan Price sent out 3 winners in the 1960s although Mrs Reveley and Martin Pipe have each had 2 successes. There are 2 salient points to observe, however: first, that this race is one which big stables do not monopolise; and second, Newmarket yards do not have the success that might be expected in a 'local' race – they have had only 5 victories since 1960. In the same period, the number of winners from Epsom (7) with fewer runners should be noted and although there was a decline in the fortunes once enjoyed by Yorkshire yards in the Cesarewitch – between 1945 and 1969 they sent no fewer than 9 winners down south – the balance has swung again in their favour with *Spirit of Love* (1998), *Turnpole* (1997), *Old Red* (1995) and *Trainglot* (1990).

Jockeys Lindsay Charnock and Gary Carter have each ridden 2 winners but no one at present looks to be a candidate for matching the extraordinary success of the Smith brothers. In 32 seasons up to 1966, Eph Smith (4) and Doug Smith (6) rode just under a third of all the Cesarewitch winners. A final point worth noting is that senior jockeys put up overweight on 7 occasions during the period, and their horses still won.

Age No firm pattern emerges from a study of ages. More 4-y-o are successful than any other age group, but this is simply because of the number of 4-y-o entered relative to other ages. On comparing entries and number of winners from a particular age group, 3-y-o have a slight edge (26% of total winners against 23% proportion of entries). A good improving 3-y-o too, e.g. *Spirit of Love* in 1998, is a likely Cesarewitch candidate because he keeps ahead of the handicapper, but veterans should not be ignored. They make up a small proportion of the total entry, but the victories of the 8-y-o *Persian Lancer* (1966), *Ocean King* (1974) and, most recently, *Landing Light* (2003) are in the records; also the 7-y-o *Go South*, *Aahysaylad*, *Inchcailloch* and *Miss Fara*, while gallant *Top Cees*, twice a hero of the Chester Cup when trained by Mrs Ramsden, at the age of 9, saddled by Ian and Andrew Balding, stole with a game performance the title of oldest Cesarewitch winner on record.

SANDOWN PARK   Right-hand   Flat and National Hunt

Draw: Round course, no advantage. Straight course, if soft, high numbers are best.

Sandown, near Esher in Surrey, was the first racecourse in the country to be entirely enclosed. It opened in 1875, and was immediately popular, with a frequent train service bringing racegoers from London in 20 minutes. The original stands lasted for almost a century on the top of a hill and gave a marvellous vantage point for seeing every detail of the running. The new stands, opened in 1973 by HM The Queen Mother, whose chasers won many races at the course, incorporate an entirely enclosed betting hall with Tote and SP facilities. The view from them is as good as ever though lacking entirely the faded Edwardian charm of the old buildings, and with the paddock area now transformed in concrete it somewhat resembles an annexe to London Airport. The oval circuit, which is crossed by a 5 furlong straight across the middle, has fairly easy gradients but a very stiff uphill finish (for both tracks), which makes Sandown a tough course, demanding on stamina, and favouring the horse which likes to stride out. Equally, the fences are stiff for the jumpers, and, coming in fairly rapid succession in the back straight beside the railway, allow no room for indifferent performers or inexpert riding. Front runners do well at Sandown. Some main races: Flat – Sandown has a fair share of Pattern and Listed races throughout the season, with its most important event the Eclipse Stakes, sponsored by Coral. This is a 1 m 2 f 'semi-Classic' first run in 1886, and the list of its past winners is a Turf roll-call of honour. Outstanding horses to have won it recently include *Pebbles, Dancing Brave, Nashwan, Daylami* and *Giant's Causeway;* its illustrious past includes the names *Isinglass, Diamond Jubilee, Persimmon, Ard Patrick* and *Bayardo* up to *Blue Peter, Tulyar, Royal Palace, Mill Reef* and *Brigadier Gerard.* Other races include in April: Classic Trial run under various sponsorships (Group Three, 1 m 2 f, 3-y-o); Esher Cup (1 m Handicap, 3-y-o); Gordon Richards Stakes (Group Three, 1 m 2 f, 4-y-o+); May: Temple Stakes (Group Two, 5 f, 3-y-o+, winner £58,000); Henry II Stakes (Group Two, 2 m, 4-y-o+, winner £58,000); Brigadier Gerard Stakes (Group Three, 1 m 2 f, 4-y-o+); August: Solario Stakes (Group Three, 7 f, 2-y-o, winner £23,000). The Solario Stakes is a race which used to produce its share of subsequent Classic winners, including *Oh So Sharp* and *To-Agori-Mou,* and earlier, *Scratch II, Charlottown* and *Athens Wood.*

The National Hunt programme includes the Imperial Cup, run in March. Now sponsored by Sunderlands and worth £29,000 to the winner, it is one of the oldest established (first run in 1907) hurdle events in the Calendar. Sandown is also the home of the Grand Military Meeting and Royal Artillery Meeting, while other feature races include: Dec: Mitsubishi Shogun Tingle Creek Trophy Chase (2 m, £59,500), named after the unforgettable, record-breaking Sandown specialist trained by 'Tom' Jones who continued until he died not long ago to make his annual journey from Newmarket to Sandown to appear, ebullient as ever, before his own race; Dec: William Hill Handicap Hurdle (2 m, £40,600). Martin Pipe has saddled no fewer than six winners of this event since 1988. Feb: Tote Scoop6 Sandown Handicap Hurdle (2 m 6 f, £34,800); Feb: Scilly Isles

Novices Chase (2 m 4 f+, £34,100); Feb: Agfa Diamond Limited Handicap Chase (3 m+, £29,000). The eventual replacement for the much-lamented Whitbread Gold Cup as Sandown's richest National Hunt event remains to be seen. In 2003, worth £87,000 to the winner, it was run as a 'Gold Cup Chase' sponsored by the now defunct Attheraces.

Leading trainers: *Flat*	Richard Hannon and Sir Michael Stoute (13 winners each); Mark Johnston (10); A.C. Stewart (9); John Gosden and M.P. Tregoning (8 each); B.W. Hills and T.G. Mills (7 each).
National Hunt	Nicky Henderson (20 winners); Martin Pipe (17); Paul Nicholls (15); Jonjo O'Neill (7); Miss Henrietta Knight (5); Philip Hobbs and Miss Venetia Williams (4 each).
Leading jockeys: *Flat*	Kieren Fallon (22 winners); L. Dettori (18); Darryll Holland (16); T. Quinn (15); Richard Hills, R. Hughes and Dane O'Neill (13 each); Martin Dwyer (11).
National Hunt	A.P. McCoy (20 winners); Mick Fitzgerald (18); Richard Johnson (7); R. Walsh (6); J. Culloty, B. Fenton and R. Thornton (5 each).

1 mile 2 furlongs Weight-for-Age 3-y-o+   Eclipse Stakes, Sandown Park, July

First run in 1886, the Eclipse was the first £10,000 race in this country (worth in today's terms approximately half a million pounds – compared with the £409,000 total prize-money of the Coral-sponsored Group One equivalent in 2004). The race was partly inspired by one of the founders of Sandown Park, Chairman and Clerk of the Course for 50 years Hwfa Williams. The money was put up by Leopold de Rothschild, later the owner of such famous Classic winners as *St Frusquin* and *St Amant*, and the name of the race neatly commemorates not only the great horse *Eclipse*, but also an intention to 'eclipse' the Derby prize-money, which it did with no difficulty whatsoever. The Derby in 1886, won by *Ormonde*, was worth £4,700, all in entries and forfeits (it was not until *Captain Cuttle*'s year, 1921, that the Derby first achieved a five-figure prize). The Eclipse therefore became the most valuable race in the Calendar. That position has long since been forfeited; yet, in 2004, worth £237,220 to the winner and no less than £89,980 to the runner-up, the Eclipse still remains an eminently worthwhile prize. Also, the name of Hwfa Williams until a few years ago was annually commemorated with a memorial race at Sandown. Sadly, that has fallen victim to the expediency of satisfying sponsors, and Sandown ought to consider restoring this event under its proper title and thereby once again give just tribute to the man on whom its prosperity was originally founded.

	Winner	Derby place*	Age	Owner	Trainer	Jockey	SP
1976	Wollow**	5	3	C.d'Alessio	H.Cecil	G.Dettori	9/4 F
1977	Artaius	2FrD	3	Mrs G.Getty II	M.V.O'Brien(Ire)	L.Piggott	9/2 3F
1978	Gunner B		5	Mrs P.Barratt	H.Cecil	J.Mercer	7/4 F
1979	Dickens Hill	2,2IrD	3	Mme J.Binet	M.O'Toole(Ire)	A.Murray	7/4 2F
1980	Ela-Mana-Mou		4	S.Weinstock	Major W.R.Hern	W.Carson	85/40 F

1981	Master Willie		4	R.Barnett	H.Candy	P.Waldron	6/4 F
1982	Kalaglow		4	A.Ward	G.Harwood	G.Starkey	11/10 F
1983	Solford		3	R.Sangster	M.V.O'Brien(Ire)	P.Eddery	3/1 2F
1984	Sadler's Wells	2FrD	3	R.Sangster	M.V.O'Brien(Ire)	P.Eddery	11/4 2F
1985	Pebbles (f)		4	Sheikh Mohammed	C.Brittain	S.Cauthen	7/2 2F
1986	Dancing Brave	2	3	Khaled Abdulla	G.Harwood	G.Starkey	4/9 F
1987	Mtoto		4	Sheikh Ahmed al-Maktoum	A.C.Stewart	M.Roberts	6/1 J3F
1988	Mtoto		5	Sheikh Ahmed al-Maktoum	A.C.Stewart	M.Roberts	6/4 F
1989	Nashwan	Won	3	Sheikh Hamdan al-Maktoum	Major W.R.Hern	W.Carson	2/5 F
1990	Elmaamul	3	3	Sheikh Hamdan al-Maktoum	Major W.R.Hern	W.Carson	13/2 3F
1991	Environment Friend	11	3	W.J.Gredley	J.R.Fanshawe	G.Duffield	28/1
1992	Kooyonga (f)		4	Mitsuo Haga	M.Kauntze(Ire)	W.O'Connor	7/2 F
1993	Opera House		5	Sheikh Mohammed	M.Stoute	M.Kinane	9/2 3F
1994	Ezzoud		5	Maktoum al-Maktoum	M.Stoute	W.Swinburn	5/1 2F
1995	Halling		4	Godolphin	Saeed bin Suroor	W.Swinburn	7/1
1996	Halling		5	Godolphin	Saeed bin Suroor	J.Reid	100/30 2F
1997	Pilsudski		5	Lord Weinstock	M.Stoute	M.J.Kinane	11/2 2F
1998	Daylami		4	Godolphin	Saeed bin Suroor	L.Dettori	6/4 F
1999	Compton Admiral	8	3	E.Penser	G.A.Butler	D.Holland	20/1
2000	Giant's Causeway		3	Mrs J.Magnier/ M.Tabor	A.P.O'Brien(Ire)	G.Duffield	8/1
2001	Medicean		4	Cheveley Park Stud	Sir M.Stoute	K.Fallon	7/2 3F
2002	Hawk Wing	2	3	Mrs J.Magnier	A.P.O'Brien(Ire)	M.J.Kinane	8/15 F
2003	Falbrav		5	Scuderia Rencati	L.Cumani	D.Holland	8/1
2004	Refuse To Bend		4	Godolphin	Saeed bin Suroor	L.Dettori	15/2

* Unsuffixed figures indicate English Derby positions; FrD = French Derby; IrD = Irish Derby.
** *Trepan* was first past the post, but disqualified. f = filly

Derby runners-up Nine have succeeded in the same season in the Eclipse: *St Frusquin* (1896), *Hapsburg* (1914), *Buchan* (1919), *Craig an Eran* (1921), *Gulf Stream* (1946), *Migoli* (1947), *Dickens Hill* (1979), *Dancing Brave* (1986), and *Hawk Wing* (2002). (A further 5 Derby runners-up were Eclipse winners as 4-y-o, including *Buchan* who won again in 1920.) In recent years only 4 Derby winners have competed in the Eclipse. *Nashwan* had an easy victory in 1989, but two seasons before that, *Reference Point* was beaten over this shorter distance by *Mtoto*. In 1994 *Erhaab* was 3rd and in 1997 *Benny The Dip* was runner-up.

Fillies The only fillies in the history of the race to have won are *Pebbles* (1985) and *Kooyonga* (1992), but a lot of good fillies have been beaten, including, in 1903, *Sceptre* as a 4-y-o, when *Ard Patrick* got up to beat her in the last few strides by a neck; more recently *Park Top* (1969), *Dahlia* (1974), *Time Charter* (1983), and *Triptych* (1986–88) were all beaten.

Prices The longest-priced winner of the last century was *Coup de Feu*, 33/1 in 1974. There has been 1 28/1 winner, *Environment Friend* in 1991, and 1 25/1 winner, *Caerleon* (1931), owned by Lord Derby, trained by the Hon. George Lambton, and after whose victory there were unpleasant scenes, with the crowd unjustly giving connections the bird (to put it mildly). There have also been 5 20/1 winners: *Saltash* (1923), *Boswell* (1937), HM The Queen's *Canisbay* (1965), the German-trained *Star Appeal* (1975), and *Compton Admiral* (1999). Against this, since 1975, 11 favourites, 7 second-favourites and 5 third- or joint third-favourites have been successful.

Age Only 12 horses older than 3 or 4 have ever won the race in 106 runnings (there were no races in 1887, 1890, 1915–18, 1940–45). *Bendigo*, owned by Major H.T. Barclay and trained by Charles Jousiffe at Seven Barrows, is the sole 6-y-o: he won the very first Eclipse in 1886.

Eleven 5-y-o have won: *Wolver Hollow* (1969), *Connaught* (1970), *Coupe de Feu* (1974), *Star Appeal* (1975) – apart from those in the table. Of the rest, 4-y-o have a slight advantage over 3-y-o.

Trainers Alec Taylor sent out a record 6 winners from Manton between 1909 (*Bayardo*) and 1923 (*Saltash*). Most successful present-day trainers are Sir Michael Stoute and Saeed bin Suroor with 4 winners each, Henry Cecil with 3 and A.P. O'Brien and A.C. Stewart with 2 each.

Owners Eleven of the most recent Eclipse winners have been owned by the Maktoum family (see table). But they individually have yet to equal the record of Lord Astor whose horses captured this race 5 times between 1919 (*Buchan*) and 1936 (*Rhodes Scholar*).

YORK   Left-hand   Flat only

Draw: When the going is soft or heavy, low numbers are best on the straight course.

York has widely been referred to as 'the Ascot of the North', which is an insult as far as Yorkshire people are concerned, since they regard Ascot as 'the York of the South'. Records of racing at York go back as far as 1530, and Charles I is known to have watched a horse race on Acomb Moor in 1633, but according to an article in *The British Racehorse* by Patricia Smyly, racing was transferred from Clifton Ings to the present site on the Knavesmire after the floods of 1731. The first grandstand went up a quarter of a century later, and today the facilities at York are among the best in the country, with a quality of racing to match. The 2 mile course is wide, completely flat, with easy sweeping turns. The 7 furlong straight joins the round course just under 5 furlongs from home, and the entire course provides an extremely fair test for the thoroughbred. The main meetings take place in May and August, the latter commonly known as the 'Ebor' Meeting when the big handicap of that name takes place as well as the Gimcrack Stakes for 2-y-o, commemorating the game little grey horse *Gimcrack* of the 18th century whose popularity led to the foundation of the Gimcrack Club at York. This is said to be the second oldest race club in the land after the Jockey Club, and the Gimcrack Stakes over 6 f is now a Group Two event, worth £72,500 to the winner in 2003. Other top-class races at this meeting include three Group One events – the Juddmonte International Stakes (1 m 2 f, 3-y-o+, winner's prize in 2004 £266,800); the Nunthorpe Stakes (5 f, 2-y-o+, worth £116,000 to the winner); and the Yorkshire Oaks (1 m 3 f, 3-y-o fillies and mares, £145,000 first prize in 2004). Another important race at the meeting, widely recognised as a trial for the

St. Leger, is the Group Two Great Voltigeur Stakes for 3-y-o colts and geldings over 1 m 3 f with a first prize of £87,000. July sees the John Smith's handicap for 3-y-o and upwards over 1 m 2 f+ with a £91,000 prize to the winner. It was formerly known as the Magnet Cup and 2004 saw the 45th running of this highly popular crowd-puller and betting opportunity. York's well-patronised Spring Meeting in May, meanwhile, features the Derby and Oaks trials, the Group Two Dante Stakes and the Group Three Musidora Stakes, both over 1 m 2 f, as well as the Group Two Yorkshire Cup for 4-y-o and upwards, over 1 m 5 f and worth £81,200 to the winner in 2003. Big crowds come to the Knavesmire to enjoy the high-grade racing, superb facilities and the strong betting markets.

Leading trainers: Mark Johnston and Sir Michael Stoute (18 winners each); Tim Easterby (15); Barry Hills (12); Mick Channon (10); Paul Cole, D.R. Loder, D. Nicholls and Saeed bin Suroor (9 each).

Leading jockeys: Kieren Fallon (33 winners); Kevin Darley (27); L. Dettori (15); T. Quinn (14); J.P. Spencer (12); M. Hills (11); George Duffield and R. Hughes (9 each).

1 mile 6 furlongs Ebor Handicap, York, August

First run in 1843. Sponsored since 1976 by the Tote. The prize to the winner in 2004 was £130,000. Famous past winners include *Lily Agnes* and *Isonomy* (1874), who was the diminutive and versatile hero of two Ascot Gold Cup wins and many other cup races, and eventually sire of two Triple Crown winners, *Isinglass* and *Common*.

	Winner	Age	Wt	Trainer	Jockey	Ran	SP
1976	Sir Montagu	3	8.0	H.R.Price	W.Carson	15	11/4 F
1977	Move Off	4	8.1	J.Calvert	J.Bleasdale*5	14	9/1 4F
1978	Totowah	4	8.1	M.Jarvis	P.Cook	22	20/1
1979	Sea Pigeon	9	10.0	M.H.Easterby	J.J.O'Neill	17	18/1
1980	Shaftesbury	4	8.5	M.Stoute	G.Starkey	16	12/1
1981	Protection Racket	3	8.1	J.Hindley	M.Birch	22	15/2 2F
1982	Another Sam	5	9.2	R.Hannon	B.Rouse	15	16/1
1983	Jupiter Island	4	9.0	C.Brittain	L.Piggott	16	9/1 J4F
1984	Crazy	3	8.13	G.Harwood	W.Swinburn	14	10/1 J4F
1985	Western Dancer	4	8.6	C.Horgan	P.Cook	19	20/1
1986	Primary	3	8.7	G.Harwood	G.Starkey	22	6/1 2F
1987	Daarkom	4	9.3	A.C.Stewart	M.Roberts	15	13/2 3F
1988	Kneller	3	8.1	H.Cecil	Paul Eddery	21	9/1 J2F
1989	Sapience	3	8.4	J.Fitzgerald	Pat Eddery	18	15/2 3F
1990	Further Flight	4	8.8	B.W.Hills	M.Hills	22	7/1 JF
1991	Deposki	3	7.3	M.Stoute	F.Norton*5	22	12/1
1992	Quick Ransom	4	8.3	M.Johnston	D.McKeown	22	16/1
1993	Sarawat	5	8.2	R.Akehurst	T.Quinn	21	14/1
1994	Hasten to Add	4	9.3	Sir Mark Prescott	G.Duffield	21	13/2 F
1995	Sanmartino	3	7.11	B.W.Hills	W. Carson	21	8/1
1996	Clerkenwell	3	7.11	M.Stoute	F.Lynch	21	17/2

1997	Far Ahead	5	8.0	J.L.Eyre	T.Williams	21	33/1
1998	Tuning (f)	3	8.7	H.Cecil	K.Fallon	21	9/2 F
1999	Vicious Circle	5	8.4	L.Cumani	K.Darley	21	11/1
2000	Give The Slip	3	8.8	Mrs A.J.Perrett	Pat Eddery	22	8/1 2F
2001	Mediterranean	3	8.4	A.P.O'Brien(Ire)	M.J.Kinane	22	16/1
2002	Hugs Dancer	5	8.5	J.G.Given	D.McKeown	22	25/1
2003	Saint Alebe	4	8.8	D.Elsworth	T.Quinn	22	20/1
2004	Mephisto	5	9.4	L.Cumani	D.Holland	19	6/1 2F

* Apprentice allowance claimed in lb.   f = filly

Favourites This popular stayers' handicap at the York August Meeting started as the Great Ebor and was the only race at the meeting then worth more than £100 added prize-money. The number of winning favourites (6 between 1960 and 1976) has declined in recent years. Only 3 clear favourites and 1 joint-favourite have prevailed since 1975. Yet 14 winners (48%) in the period have come from the first 4 market prices. However, too many longer-priced winners make the Ebor, these days, not an easy task for backers.

Trainers Sir Michael Stoute has saddled 3 winners; Henry Cecil, Michael Jarvis, Barry Hills and Luca Cumani each have 2.

CHAPTER NINE
Owners, Trainers and Jockeys

Racing cannot exist without horses, so equally it would not take place without owners. Racehorse owners today provide more of a mirror to the times and society in general than they used to. Even after the Industrial Revolution, the ownership of horses and the sport of racing was overwhelmingly the preserve of a landowning aristocracy who bred, for the most part, their own horses. The echoes of the Industrial Revolution did not make themselves heard in racing until long after it had happened. In the first 50 years of the Derby, 1780–1829, the race was won on only 13 occasions by a mere Esquire. By the later years of the 19th century, owners included rich industrialists and bankers, from the admirable Baron Meyer de Rothschild among the latter, to the egregious Scottish ironmaster James Merry among the first named. The Rothschild horses *Favonius* and *Hannah* won all but one of the Classics in 1871, while three years later Merry's horses won three out of five. Royal interest in racing was rekindled towards the end of the century by the Prince of Wales, later King Edward VII. He owned three Derby winners – *Minoru*, after he was crowned, and before that *Persimmon*, and *Diamond Jubilee* who won the Derby in 1900, the same year in which the Prince's horse *Ambush II* won the Grand National. The first half of the 20th century saw the zenith of great owner-breeders, such as the Joel brothers, the Aga Khan, Lord Derby, Lord Rosebery and Sir Victor Sassoon.

The scene today is barely recognisable when compared with those earlier days, so drastically has a hurricane of social change, and squalls of taxation, blown through the parks and paddocks, particularly in the past three decades. True, HM The Queen more than maintains royal interest. But the present era in racing is dominated, as far as horse owners are concerned, by the Arab influence. The extent of that domination may be appreciated by a glance at the tables of big-race results in Chapter Eight, particularly those for the Oaks and the Eclipse Stakes. It is an astonishing fact that of the 601 yearling entries for the £1 million Vodafone Derby of the year 2000, no fewer than 197 (almost one-third) were made on behalf of colts owned by the Maktoum family. From that family, Sheikh Mohammed was annually the leading owner in the United Kingdom on the Flat continuously from 1985 to 1993, with the exception of one season: that exception being when his brother, Sheikh Hamdan al-Maktoum, largely because of the prodigious exploits of *Nashwan*, was top of the list in 1989. Beyond that, the Maktoums have continued their domination, with Sheikh Hamdan at the top in 1994 and 1995; Sheikh Mohammed again in 1997; and the family 'business' of Godolphin in 1996, 1998 and 1999. The only break in this relentless sequence came when the Aga Khan at last ousted the Maktoums from the top of the owners' list in 2000. However, normal service was resumed subsequently with Arab owners once again at the top of the lists: 2001 Godolphin; 2002 Sheikh Hamdan; 2003 Khaled Abdulla.

The whole business, from this angle, looks, in fact, like an equine game of Monopoly, with the odds stacked heavily in favour of the Arabs. They don't, of course, own any railway stations. Instead, they have the equivalent in studs. Everything else, almost, on the board is theirs. Most recently, the Godolphin operation has gone even further in its rapacious pursuit of acquisitions. It has taken to buying up every leading two-year-old in sight. Alan Lee strongly deplored this 'regrettable trend' in *The Times*: 'There is apparently no truth in the old saying about money not buying happiness. Money, it seems, can buy anything in racing if you have the bottomless funds and ruthless ambition of the Godolphin operation. No trainer can now feel safe from the royal blue plundering and the worst of it is that most feel they must suffer in silence, accepting it as a hazard of the territory.' He concluded: 'The Maktoums have done much to nourish British racing in recent decades, but the tactics now being employed by their flagship operation mean, inevitably, that many in the sport will silently cheer when they are beaten.' Indeed it all causes some bitter comments, particularly from those not favoured with their patronage. Nevertheless, against the carping and griping and muttering that goes on, it has to be said that first and foremost, the average punter not only couldn't care less about the criticism they face but also is actually pleased that they have given him (and her) superb horses to watch and back: over the years *Oh So Sharp*, *Pebbles, Nashwan, Dayjur, Dancing Brave, Opera House, Swain* and *Daylami* to name a selection of Arab-owned horses who have been superlative. And there have been plenty of others in recent years in evidence of the fact that the Arab effect has been unequivocally to rescue British bloodstock breeding and racing, give or take some mistaken sales to Japan.

In addition it should be borne in mind that, undeniably, without the original Arab stallions, racing would not exist in its present form. Also, that it was the internal combustion engine which ousted the horse as a means of transport, so it is an interesting if ironic paradox that oil profits are now responsible for helping to keep at least one branch of horse activity in business.

The Arabs apart, the feature of recent years, and a true mirror of social change, has been the widening of the boundaries of ownership. Until the late 1960s, only private individuals could own racehorses. Since then the Jockey Club has progressively altered its rules, so that now a horse may be owned jointly (by up to 12 people), or by a club, or a commercial company. The Rules of Racing in the now defunct *Ruff's Guide* relating to ownership in 1964 took up no more than two lines in a simple definition. Thirty years later they more than covered three pages. In this exercise in democratisation, many members of the public who would not otherwise be able to afford it are now able to have an interest in the buying and running of a horse. Sometimes, individuals may get together and independently go into ownership; or they may answer one of the frequent advertisements in the sporting press offering a share in a horse; or they may join one of the many organisations such as the Elite Racing Club or Peter Harris Racing Stables.

The joy and excitement of this sort of ownership has seldom been better illustrated than at the 1994 Cheltenham Festival when the 2/1 favourite, *Mysilv*, put up a thrilling display of jumping and was never out of the first two in the Daily Express Triumph Hurdle. Her victory, quite apart from costing book-makers nationwide an estimated £2 million, made the day for her owners: no fewer than 160 of them, all members of the Million In Mind partnership run by the Newmarket bloodstock agent David Minton. At the same time, Cheltenham, including this triumph for democracy, once again demonstrated that in National Hunt racing you don't have to be among the big battalions in order to win the best races. In 1994, Richard Price had only ten horses in his yard at Leominster, Herefordshire. One of them, *Flakey Dove*, was the courageous 9/1 heroine of the Champion Hurdle and her win realised his wildest dreams. The Price family bred, owned and trained *Flakey Dove* on their dairy farm, and her breeding was as romantic as her Cheltenham victory, since on her dam's side she goes back to *Cottage Lass*, foaled in 1940, whom Richard Price's grandfather, Tom, bought for £25 and saved from the knacker's yard. *Flakey Dove* not long ago had a foal by *Alderbrook* who also won the Champion Hurdle (the year after she did): unique and historic breeding indeed.

Trainers

A good trainer may make a better horse out of a moderate one; a bad trainer, equally, is capable of turning a potentially good performer into a poor creature who is useless on the racecourse. Likewise, one of the marks of a good trainer is that he or she is able to get a horse to maintain winning form and run up a sequence of firsts, a feat usually beyond the abilities of an indifferent trainer, for whom a horse's one win, if any, signals the end of the line. To gain an idea as to which trainers are the most successful it is necessary to study the form books and the various statistical compilations concerning trainers' performance (see Chapter Four).

It is beyond the scope of this book or knowledge of the author to deal with the kaleidoscopic variations in methods of training racehorses, but some appreciation of the business is necessary for anyone who goes racing and/or has a bet, not least as a help to understanding what a trainer may say to the press after a race. Jack Leach (in *Sods I Have Cut On The Turf*) defines the one object of training as: '...to produce the animal fit, well, and feeling as if it could lick creation on the day of the race'. Exactly how this object was achieved in the past was the subject of much secrecy, leading to a common supposition that racehorse training was no more or less than a black art. Fortunately, today, there are books in existence which partially lift the veil, and three I would particularly recommend: *The Brigadier* by John Hislop, which gives much enlightenment on the details of how *Brigadier Gerard*, one of racing's heroes, was prepared for his astonishing career of 18 races in which he was beaten only once; *The Story of Mill Reef* (trained by Ian Balding) by John Oaksey; and *My Greatest Training Triumph*, edited by John Hughes and Peter Watson. This book provides a remarkable spy hole on the previously arcane world of training, with 24 leading trainers, both on the Flat and over jumps, writing about their hopes, despairs, problems, methods, and much else besides.

The following are some of the fascinating observations by Henry Cecil, addressed in 1988 to those attending the Hong Kong Racehorse Owners' dinner:

'Happy horses – I think you've got to have a very contented staff. Happy horses – contented staff, it's very important. It doesn't matter how much ability a horse has, if he's not happy and genuine he's no good to anybody. To get the best out of a horse you've got to give the best. Staff, feed, training and everything. Horses must be relaxed in their work. I think horses that are too free – you get a lot of morning glories – are not really any good. Distance-wise, I feel that a horse either stays or it doesn't stay. You can't make a horse stay. If he's bred to stay he'll stay. If he stays, then I think the secret may be to work him the shortest possible distance without souring him up. After all, it's the horse with a turn of foot that wins the race. I think that is very important. I don't believe in trial gallops. I like working my horses on the bit. I think you can tell quite a lot by just working a horse on the bit – you don't have to try a horse.

'I like an honest, broad head, and I like the eyes to be well apart, after all do we ever trust humans when their eyes are too close together? A wide muzzle – I've never found the horses I've been lucky enough to have, have ever been any good with small muzzles and narrow heads. I like a strong head. I think it's important, I really do. The next point is short necks. I don't like short necks and don't like swan necks. I feel that the windpipe is restricted. I think that a dipped back or swayed back leads to trouble with the muscles behind the saddle. Legs – over the knee sign of strength, back of the knee sign of weakness. Back of the knee leads to problems with the tendon. Tendons obviously are the trainer's nightmare. I know over jumps they seem to be able to patch up tendons and they can still run, but on the Flat, I've never, ever had a horse that's come right with a tendon. To me if I have a horse with a tendon, that is the end. The blood supply of the tendon is so minute, and the heart is so far away from the leg, the repair is very minimal. Short cannon bones – a horse with short pasterns, they don't seem to break down as much as horses with long pasterns although horses with long pasterns seem to have more spring and they're better movers, but on the other hand a really good mover doesn't have that extra gear. I like a deep girth in yearlings but unfortunately it's something that seems to develop between two and three, so when you're buying a yearling you're rather in trouble. When a horse walks away from you it wants to have that lovely swing, getting its hocks underneath it. I think if you're going to try to detect any error in a horse when you're buying – look through its back legs when it's walking away from you. You will see things that are wrong much easier than if it's walking towards you.

'The thing with a top-class horse, you've got to try and produce him six or seven times a year at his best, which is always very difficult because you know even with a human athlete it isn't easy. Some horses you can let them down in the middle of the season and give them a rest, but often they don't come back. They rarely come back to their best. So somehow you've got to keep them quietly ticking over. If you let a horse down too much, sometimes he just doesn't come back. *Reference Point* was very tough. He never did more than he had to do, he looked after himself. Probably when you asked him for 80 per cent, he always gave about 50 per cent at home. There's always a little bit in the tank. In every race really, once he got over his illness, he improved and improved and we thought he was probably as well, if not better, when he went for the Arc than he had been all year. But unfortunately he had an abscess brewing up in his foot.

I'm not sure whether it was from a flint or what caused it. It may be because of the time of the year, you get a tiny bit run down, humans get boils on their necks, but when he was in the race, he hit the ground and it triggered it off. Even looking at the film afterwards he was definitely in trouble and very uncomfortable. I went home after the Arc thinking, "Well, I've made a terrible mistake, he should never have run, he was over the top." But in my own heart of hearts I couldn't believe it. Once I got home, I got a message saying he was so lame he couldn't put his foot on the ground and they thought he'd broken a bone in his leg. And then of course the abscess came out. Once that abscess had burst, about four days later we managed to get him home. Even when he went to stud, another one formed in his hind leg and he was lame. So it may have been something to do with just the time of year and his condition. But I do think when he went for the Arc he was very well. I would never have dared run him, he'd done enough already, the Arc was going to be a bonus. He'd won the King George, the Leger and the Derby, and the two main trials, and as far as I was concerned that was enough. I had no intention of having him shot at if he wasn't right. So I think that was definitely the reason.

'There were two horses walking round the paddock which to me were definitely over the top. They were worried, they were gone. Not only were they sweating between their back legs, which I always hate, but they were very nervous and tense and as they were walking round they were boring, pulling on the rope. It's always a sure sign, you know, when the head is nodding, nodding, nodding, that he's gone. Those horses ran and I thought, considering that they'd gone, they ran very well. I think one was last, but one beat one. I don't think those horses could have benefited by that. And I'd expect that now they'd need to be left alone and rested, and have quite a lot of confidence put back into them. Working them with very, very bad horses to let them go past and win a gallop so they think they are the bee's knees, otherwise I can't see much future for them. I think a horse has also got to be reasonably fit. A lot of people think you can train a horse on the racecourse. "Run him, he needs the race, doesn't matter, he'll win next time." I don't think that works. The horse, if he's genuine, he's doing his best, he gets tired and he's got two furlongs still to go and his lungs are hurting him and he's beginning to hate it, although he wants to do it. I don't see how the next time he can be in the right frame of mind.

'I think it's very important that when a horse is right, that's when you run him, not when it's wrong, just because the race is available. I mean that to me doesn't really seem to make sense. It would be rather nice if the programme could allow for a little more leeway. They're not machines. It's like people. It's like Sebastian Coe, he probably only really comes right once in every two years. It would be awful if he's at his best and he can't run, wouldn't it?'

On the gallops

Some horses thrive on work, and others don't need much; some trainers believe in a lot of work – Sir Jack Jarvis was renowned in Newmarket for the prodigious amount of work he gave his horses; others favour a less strenuous approach. Josh Gifford (in *My Greatest Training Triumph*) says, 'We're lucky with the ground at Findon [Sussex]: if it pours with rain for twelve hours, the horses cut through the grass on to the flints; but we know that if we don't get any more rain for twenty-four hours, it dries up and we've got perfect ground the following day. You don't have to work just for the sake of it. The younger horses have to be taught to gallop – you've got to be working them; but the older horses know how to gallop and jump and you can do just as much work with them trotting up and down the hills.'

Martin Pipe is a fitness fanatic and his astonishing record-breaking exploits bear handsome witness to his policy: undisputed champion trainer numerically over the jumps 16 seasons in a row from 1988–89 onwards; nearly 4,000 winners since he started in 1975, including the record for the most wins in any season Flat or National Hunt – 243 (in 1999–2000). But the question of how much work, like much else in training, is a matter of opinion. In the 18th and early 19th centuries the business of training expanded and flourished, but trainers were then what would be called today 'private trainers', i.e. they were in charge of the horses of one particular individual. But most trainers are what are known as 'public trainers', i.e. they charge fees to train the horses of any number of individuals.

The 'public trainer' has been a feature of the racing scene for not much more than a century, and when they first appeared there were still some fairly rudimentary (as well as cruel and ineffective) techniques commonly employed. One of these was bleeding a horse, in the way that physicians cupped humans as a cure-all. Fortunately, this medieval practice has long since disappeared, together with 'sweating' – exercising horses by subjecting them to long and punishing gallops in heavy rugs. Since those unenlightened times, training has taken great strides forward, and modern techniques include, in some big stables, the practice of weighing horses (the theory being that, like human athletes, they have a physical weight at which they race best). There are covered rides for use in times of frost and snow, as well as all-weather gallops and equine swimming pools.

Some trainers employ mechanical horse-walkers for exercise, and some set great store by blood counts, swimming and feed additives. A frequent explanation for a poor performance these days is: 'His blood was wrong'. Such modern refinements were, of course, unknown to the great 'Atty' Persse when he was at the zenith of his training career, and had they been known would doubtless have been ignored. 'Atty' captured the Great Jubilee Handicap at Kempton six times between 1908 and 1953; was a master at producing two-year-olds to succeed first time out; trained *The Tetrarch*, who was possibly the fastest 2-y-o in history (see Chapter Ten), as well as his son *Tetratema*, winner of the 2000 Guineas in 1920 and a champion sprinter, and his grandson *Mr Jinks*, who also took the 2000 Guineas, in 1929. Although numbers of horses (and 'lots') have increased, his observations on training are of interest today, and complement those above of Henry Cecil who himself admits to being an 'old-fashioned' trainer (even if his views on Trials do not coincide with Persse's):

The day's work
'As to the daily routine of training, when the head lad has got the string ready they file out singly and walk round in a circle until the trainer takes over. As the trainer does so he receives from the head lad a list of the animals that have not fed and any other necessary information as to their well-being.

'Having carefully scrutinised the horses as they circle round, the trainer then trots them to see if all are sound. When he is satisfied, which is usually about three-quarters of an hour after they have left the stables, he gives them their first canter. This is generally very slow for a distance of about three-quarters of a mile, and if possible up an incline. I like always to use the same cantering ground, as then the horses know they are not going to be jumped off for fast work, and so they do not get excited. I think it is never advisable to start off with fast work.

'The canter over, then the real work of the day begins. The trainer picks out the first lot, which may vary from two to six horses, changes the riding boys, and then the animals. Then accompanied by the head lad, or someone reliable who knows just what to do, they go down to where they jump off. After the gallop they pull up and come straight back to the trainer, who runs his eye over them and notes their condition. Then the riding boys are put on another batch, and so the work continues until all is gone through.

'Some horses require little, if any, training beyond sharp canters, and some excitable ones are better if worked alone. There is no hard-and-fast rule and the man who tries to make one will never become a successful trainer. When the work is done and the horses are safe back in their boxes they are dressed over, made comfortable and fed. Then the second lot, or, as they are called, "the spares", are made ready, brought out, and the same routine gone through again. After "the spares" are made comfortable and fed the boys go to their dinner and then rest or do whatever they like until four o'clock.

'At this hour they go to their horses, tie them up, and report to the head man which of them has left droppings, and the ones that have eaten up generally get what is known as a small "standing" feed. Then the boys go to their tea and return to dress their horses over.

'By 6.30 everything should be ready for the trainer's nightly inspection. He visits each in turn, notes how he looks, runs his hand over him and feels his legs carefully. This over, the horses are fed and shut up for the night.

'Some trainers work differently from others – some work on Mondays, Wednesdays and Saturdays. As a rule my work-days are Tuesdays, Thursdays and Saturdays.

'On Tuesdays I jump my two-year-olds off and come at a good three-parts speed for three or four furlongs. On Thursdays I let them come a bit steadier; but on Saturdays they come four furlongs fast. Yet these are not hard-and-fast rules, for, as I have said, some horses are better without so much work.

'The great thing in training a two-year-old is to keep his speed, and if he loses it he must be rested at once. The trainer must always be watching to see that these youngsters do not get tired and that they keep their condition – always on their toes, full of fire, ready to jump off at any time and to come all the way required of them.

'Every trainer knows it to be a great advantage to have a jockey ride a horse for a few times before he rides him in the race he is expected to win; for then the jockey knows the animal and is ready for any manifestation of eccentricity.

'Given a jockey who knows the horse I have rarely had any difficulty in getting a two-year-old to run up to his true form the first time out.

'Customs vary. Some trainers give their charges an easy race or two before asking them to come out and win. But to my mind, if a two-year-old is properly educated, there is no necessity for these easy preparatory races, as many of my two-year-olds have proved the first time out.'

Trials*

'To the uninitiated, trials seem to be something easy of accomplishment; but to the experienced trainer they are difficult and often impracticable.

'So often does one hear of the wonderful trials and of amazing results which, however, are never repeated in public. But I am now writing of the genuine trial, not of the mythical variety, spoken of with bated breath in the corner of the club smoking-room, or "after dinner when we are all together", or "of course it won't go any further".

'A trial never produces a certainty, though an approximation to the truth may be reached with a certain amount of accuracy. I have found two-year-old trials to be the most satisfactory, and the results come out more accurately in public than those with older horses. Two-year-olds are fresh to the game and so do all they can, whilst older animals need all the excitement of the racecourse to induce them to exert their utmost.

'Furthermore, it is a far simpler job to try horses over five or six furlongs than over the longer distances. But in these short trials the great difficulty (unless one has experienced jockeys up) is to get stable lads to balance their horses before sitting down to send them along. If he is not properly balanced a horse can beat himself in a furlong. [Balance: when a horse carries its own weight and the weight of its rider in such a way that it can use and control itself to best advantage at all paces and in all circumstances. See Lester Piggott's illuminating remarks on the subject on p.234.]

'The two greatest exponents of balancing whom I have seen were Carslake and the late Danny Maher. I have seen them win races by heads when some distance from home it has looked long odds against them. What a delightful jockey to watch was Danny Maher, and what a judge of pace. He always seemed to be part and parcel of a horse. But this is a divergence.

'In trials I prefer all jockeys to be riding or else all stable lads. When I say stable lads I mean those who are constantly riding fast work and trials. But I am not keen to have a crack jockey riding against stable lads, for it means allowing for his greater experience.

'In order to get a true result in short trials there must be no waiting about after the start. Once a horse is balanced he must come right through all the way.

'In a short-distance trial if, as sometimes happens, they go no pace for the first 150 or 200 yards, then the course is appreciably shortened, and a non-stayer may get the journey, though he would have failed to do so had the race been run from end to end.

'Many think that if a trainer has, say, twenty two-year-olds and wins a race with one of them he must know exactly how all the others stand with him. Nothing can be more fallacious.

'Probably when your early two-year-old winner was fit to try there were only two or three others fit to be tried with him. When the others have been made ready then those which were fit earlier on are now *hors de combat*.

---

* Atty Persse's trial-book is said to have had a hasp and lock on it to defeat prying eyes.

'It is wonderful how rumours get about. One has only to win with two or three two-year-olds off the reel when the next one produced must necessarily be at least ten pounds ahead of the last winner. The amount of nonsense that is talked and the ridiculous balderdash that is vouchsafed by professional tipsters to the unsuspecting public passes one's comprehension.

'As I have said, a long-distance trial is a far harder proposition from which to get a result than a sprint. One must have at least four or five good horses all fit and well in the gallop, and they must come along fast from end to end. Then the various horses have to be ridden in the way that suits them best.

'Giving orders to a bunch of jockeys in a trial is different from giving them just to one jockey in a race; there are so many more points for a harassed trainer to remember. Some horses have to be waited with; some go best when allowed to run along and not interfered with; and so on.

'Again, many old horses will not do anything like their best at home – so, altogether, a home trial is not so easy as it looks in a newspaper. The best stayer I ever trained was Mr Raphael's *Sanctum*, who won the Cesarewitch in a canter. He was as great a horse at home as he was in public. I had in the stable another horse, called *Aboukir*, who was also very reliable at home. If I remember rightly, *Aboukir*, in the Cesarewitch, was set to give *Sanctum* 10 lb. I tried them together with some others and set *Sanctum* to give *Aboukir* 14 lb over $2^1/2$ miles.

'This he did in a hack canter. As *Aboukir*, at the weights, would have had a good outside chance, it is obvious that *Sanctum*, as the saying goes, was a pretty good thing to job with. Had he not met with an accident which finished his racing career he would have been a certain Ascot Gold Cup winner. In the spring following his Cesarewitch win a two-year-old got loose and came at full speed towards the string, hitting *Sanctum* amidships and knocking him down. His back was hurt, and although every kind of remedy was tried he was never right again.

'Some horses have to be dead fit or else they will not show anything like their real form at home. *Apelle* and *Twelve Pointer* were rather typical examples of this. Unless they were really fit they would soon begin to tire and refuse to do anything. When first I got *Apelle* to train I thought that, as the saying goes, I had caught a lobster. One day when I had him, as I thought, going fairly straight, I slipped him along a good mile, but without going top speed. Imagine my surprise when, a couple of furlongs from home, he began to drop out, with his head turned round and his ears back, as though to say: "Thanks very much, but I do not want any more of that!"

'He blew a lot and so, in a couple of days, I gave him another similar spin. He went much better, so I continued the treatment, and in a few weeks he was totally different. He finished his gallops with his ears pricked and no gamer horse ever looked through a bridle.

'Another difficulty in trying a horse is to make the lads tell afterwards any little thing that may have escaped the trainer's notice. No matter how carefully one may watch a trial something is sure to happen, at the beginning or somewhere in the gallop, that the trainer has not seen, which may have militated against the horse's chance.

'The riders do not like to admit that anything went wrong with their mount for fear they may be blamed, which is of course foolish, as no trainer would be so silly as to blame a boy for getting crossed at the start, for his horse stumbling, or getting shut in, which are some of the many episodes that occur in a trial.

'Then there is the going – one may try a horse in good going, yet he may have to race on ground which is very heavy or very hard, and these things make all the difference. If all trials could be relied upon to produce the same result in public then the bookmakers' profits would be considerably curtailed – although I am always being told that, as things now are, they very seldom make money. Nevertheless they seem to get on very well. Just as most other people do who say they never make anything.'

H S Persse (1940)

As remarked earlier, the number of horses in any given yard was significantly fewer in 'Atty' Persse's time than is the case today. Even 30 years ago, the late Walter Nightingall, who specialised in Saturday winners at Sandown, Kempton and Hurst Park, had just over 50 at South Hatch, his Epsom stable (about average for the better stables for those times) and he was able to joke about François Mathet's 100-plus in France: 'I don't suppose he's able to feel all their legs at evening stables.' In 1962, on the Flat, the biggest Newmarket string was that of Geoffrey Brooke at Clarehaven. He had 82 horses. In 2004, according to *Horses in Training*, Mick Channon at West Ilsley had the biggest number of horses in the entire country: 203. Next came Barry Hills (Lambourn) with 186; then Sir Michael Stoute (Newmarket) with 184; Richard Hannon (Marlborough) 169; John Dunlop (Arundel) 155; David Loder (Newmarket) 144; Andrew Balding (Kingsclere) 128; Paul Nicholls (Shepton Mallet, Somerset) 121; Mrs A.J. Perrett (Pulborough, Sussex) 120; and E.A.L. Dunlop (Newmarket) 115. In France, Mathet's 100-plus is dwarfed by present-day big trainers such as André Fabre with 151; Mme Criquette Head-Maarek 124; Alain de Royer-Dupré (whose principal patron is the Aga Khan) 124; and Pascal Bary 109. In an interview for *The Sporting Life* by Simon Holt, John Dunlop had these remarks to make about numerically large strings:

'There is an economic argument for having more horses and that concerns the maintenance and construction of gallops, particularly all-weather gallops, which are very expensive. If you have 200 horses which are paying a gallop fee towards it, then it is obviously more viable than if you have 40 horses. With a small stable, it is very difficult to recover the normal everyday overheads.'

John Dunlop's remarks about the economic viability of smaller yards will be echoed by the professional trainers who run such establishments, as well as by those whom financial pressure has helped to force out of the training ranks. Yet for every trainer who counts his horses at more than 100, there are scores of individuals who operate on a far more modest scale. With many small yards, despite the all round increase in prize-money, it is still of paramount importance to have a betting 'touch' from time to time. Such 'touches' can be regarded as usually beyond the clairvoyance of newspaper experts, although the market may sometimes give a clue to racegoers and betting shop habitués. With smaller yards, it is worth studying the previous form of any horse for whom a leading jockey has been engaged, although the fact of an unusual, high-powered riding arrangement is there for all to see, so the bookmakers will not be likely to be offering bargain prices, and more likely the reverse in the opening stages of the market.

In National Hunt racing, the yards tend to be rather smaller than on the Flat. Martin Pipe provides, in parallel with most of what he does, a contrast to that usual perspective. In the 2004 edition of *Horses in Training*, he has an unusually large number of horses for, predominantly, a National Hunt trainer: no fewer than 165. Nicky Henderson (Lambourn) also has a relatively large number: 113; as does Philip Hobbs (Minehead, Somerset) 112. Then come Mrs Mary Reveley with 99 at her mixed yard at Saltburn, Cleveland; Ferdy Murphy (Leyburn, North Yorkshire) 97; and Miss Venetia Williams (Hereford) 87. In addition to professional licensed trainers, a good number of whom run very small operations, there are Permit Holders, who annually apply for a permit from the Jockey Club in order to be able to train a family horse or horses for competition over hurdles and fences under rules. Alas, the number of Permit Holders is declining. In 1979–80, there were 602. By contrast, in 1998–99, there were only 240 applications for Permits: a sad decrease of 60 per cent in only 20 years. Nevertheless, the big professional yards, such as those mentioned above, may often dominate the prize-money, but stables with only a few horses are still numerically in a majority, and send out their share of winners.

How many trainers, then, are there? *Horses in Training* for 2001 lists about 640 licensed trainers on the Flat and over jumps, or both (including some in France and Ireland). That may seem a large number, but, in fact, the total number given has declined in the past 30 or so years – the 1965 edition listed 750. By contrast, as outlined above, today's trainers are in charge of a far larger number of horses. The racehorse population explosion is matched in human terms only by the Third World. Around the beginning of the 20th century there were an estimated 3,000 racehorses. In 1946 (after an inter-war increase and a drop during the Second World War) the number was still only 4,000+, a guide by which to compare the mid-sixties figure of 9,000. In 1994 it stood at 14,500 and in 2004 at 17,000.

At the same time, there are in the United Kingdom only about 11,000 races on the Flat, over jumps and on the All-Weather to be won, so quite apart from a horse's ability and a trainer's skill, or lack of it, statistics alone dictate that a considerable number of disappointments, both equine and human, are inevitable. Many of those disappointments, sad to say, happen to the very small establishments, and with no disrespect to National Hunt Permit Holders and their often splendid success with a single much-loved animal, and to the one-off yards, which, if well chosen, can provide good betting opportunities, the most consistent success comes to the bigger yards. That does not mean, however, that they necessarily provide betting value with the same consistency. The *Trainers Record* some years ago gave the basis for useful advice, dividing stables into four categories:

1. The On-Course Gambling Stable: Easy to identify in weak markets where the price shifts are out of all proportion to the actual money put on a horse. Who is putting the money on is more important as a factor, moreover, than the money itself, an instance of bookmakers 'betting to faces'. False prices and poor value are often involved here, and the stables themselves likewise have a bad ratio of winners to runners.

2. The Off-Course Gambling Stable: Inspired stable money is placed through commission agents and other 'putters-on' with a view to disguising the source of the bet. This type of stable is difficult to distinguish from the non-betting stable but a general lack of complete outsiders in their record may give a clue, and the money is worth following.

3. Non-Gambling Stables: Only the biggest stables can afford not to gamble. Even if the guv'nor is not a betting man the lads and other connections often produce the same effect. The non-gambling stable is typified by long odd winners, apparently unfancied animals beating well supported stable companions, and a good profitability figure.

4. Stables with a Big Public Following: These are the big stables which get widely reported in the media and often have the top jockeys riding for them. Their exposure in the press often means false favourites, so take a careful look at the number of horses made favourite from the big yards and especially those which show level stakes losses. They can be expensive to follow.

Successful stables

Top 10 Flat Trainers 2003

Position	Trainer	Total Winners	Total Prize-Money
1.	Mick Channon	144	£2,029,232
2.	Mark Johnston	139	£2,048,883
3.	Richard Hannon	122	£1,686,519
4.	Sir Michael Stoute	115	£3,754,863
5.	Barry Hills	107	£1,458,844
6.	John Dunlop	85	£1,074,955
7.	John Gosden	72	£1,356,386
8.	T.D. Barron	71	£529,405
9.	David Loder	70	£1,088,317
10.	D. Nicholls	64	£735,636

Top 10 National Hunt Trainers:
Record over 5 years 1999–2000 – 2003–04

Position	Trainer	Total Winners
1.	Martin Pipe	1,011
2.	Philip Hobbs	576
3.	Paul Nicholls	569
4.	Jonjo O'Neill	431
5.	Nicky Henderson	389
6.	Mrs Mary Reveley	357
7.	Miss Venetia Williams	339
8.	Nigel Twiston-Davies	279
9.	Len Lungo	266
10.	Mrs Sue Smith	242

Women trainers

How women finally forced the Jockey Club into granting them trainers' licences is a depressing saga of male hypocrisy and Stone Age attitudes to women. The story is well told by Caroline Ramsden in her book *Ladies in Racing*. Norah Wilmot had trained from 1930 onwards; Mrs Florence Nagle had saddled her first winner *Thoroughwort* at Lingfield in 1947; and Helen Johnson Houghton (twin sister of the late Fulke Walwyn, mother of the present trainer Fulke Johnson Houghton, and, eventually, made a member of the Jockey Club) on the tragic death of her husband in 1952 took over the string and trained not only Dorothy Paget's *Nucleus* to win several high-class races at Ascot and Newmarket and to be runner-up to *Meld* in the St Leger, but also *Gilles de Retz*, winner of the 1956 2000 Guineas. Some records have now been suitably amended, but as originally published, they name 'C. Jerdein' as the trainer, and in this lies the clue to the two-faced way in which women trainers were then treated. The Jockey Club was perfectly aware that women were *de facto* trainers but refused to recognise them as such – a man had to hold the licence. So, the head lads of Mrs Johnson Houghton, Mrs Nagle, Norah Wilmot, Auriol Sinclair and others became literally 'front men', while in the case of Mrs Rosemary Lomax (later, when licensed, she trained the Ascot Gold Cup winner *Precipice Wood*) her husband held the licence. It took a long, hard campaign, an exchange of some bitter but pertinent letters and, finally, a High Court judgement before the Jockey Club caved in, thus ending in 1966 a situation which was Gilbertian in every sense except humour.

Today, following on from the early trail-blazers – such as those mentioned above, to say nothing of the veteran Mrs Dingwall, as well as Mrs Dickinson and Mercy Rimell (now both retired) – women are rightly prominent in the training field. Mary Reveley regularly achieves prodigious totals: 106 successes over the jumps in 1999–2000. Jenny Pitman sent out winners of two Grand Nationals (*Corbière* and *Royal Athlete*) and two Cheltenham Gold Cups (*Burrough Hill Lad* and *Garrison Savannah*). She retired in 1999 after saddling close on 800 winners. Other successful women trainers to have retired in the past few years include Mrs Julie Cecil. Lady Herries, meanwhile, achieved a tremendous victory when, sent to Australia, *Taufan's Melody* won the Foster's Caulfield Cup worth £327,381. In the overall list of all NH trainers based on numbers of winners, in 2002–03, Miss Henrietta Knight was top of the women trainers for prize-money (43 winners, £891,837 prize-money) and was sixth in the overall list of trainers. Next in that overall list, in seventh place, came Miss Venetia Williams (78 winners), then, in eighth place, Mrs Sue Smith (74 winners) and, in ninth place, Mrs Reveley (58 winners). So it can be seen that women more than hold their own with men in the highly competitive National Hunt field. An interesting footnote to all this is provided by the Ascot NH card for Saturday 10 January 2004. Of seven winners, no fewer than four were trained by women: Miss E.C. Lavelle, Miss Henrietta Knight, Miss Suzy Smith and Miss Venetia Williams. In addition, Rebecca Morgan, at 25, is Britain's youngest Clerk of the Course: appointed to office not long ago at Wincanton.

National Hunt training

National Hunt training, of course, has its own special characteristics. Here ar
some wise words by David Elsworth taken from an article he wrote in *The Time*
in 1989, the year after *Rhyme 'n Reason* had won the National for him an
when his stable stars *Desert Orchid* and *Barnbrook Again* were at the height c
their popularity:

'I started training in 1978 and when the 1980s began I probably had 25 jumper
in the yard. I now have 60, the maximum I can take, and we have won som
pretty good prizes along the way. But if I have learned anything in this game, i
is the need for patience, and no matter what strides are taken in the years aheac
that will never change.

'There are trainers from whom you learn what to do and then there are other
who teach you the pitfalls. I could name some pretty distinguished trainers whc
in my view, have erred by buying horses at high prices and then been too har
on them in a misguided effort to recoup the outlay. I believe in the methods c
Bob Turnell, who was never in a hurry. He would make a horse rather than tr
to buy the finished product; then, due to careful handling, he would keep hin
contentedly and successfully for years.

'Sir Hugh Dundas, one of my owners, came to me one day and said h
wanted a three-mile chaser. My reply was that you cannot buy one – you try t
create one and then you wait and hope. Sir Hugh had the necessary patienc
and, three years later, he got his three-mile chaser in *Ghofar*, winner of th
Hennessy Gold Cup this season.

'Of course, some owners have neither the resources nor the temperament to wai
so long and there will always be a market for essentially Flat race horses bein
turned to hurdles. This is a trend which has grown in popularity throughout th
1980s and can only continue to do so in the coming decade. It is possible to get
quick result this way, but in most cases it is manufactured and it is short-term.

'Those whose passion is for chasing will always need infinite patience, not t
mention the resilience to survive the inevitable setbacks. If they finish up with
decent horse they usually think it has been worthwhile, but the rewards availabl
for this type of owner – the sort who keeps the sport flourishing – remain a lon
way short of realistic.'

Early birds

A few horses, year after year, shine in the spring in particular; some, however, d
not produce their best form until the autumn. Older fillies, however, can be ver
unpredictable at this time of year, and lose their form entirely. A look through th
index of past form books will show, each year, which horses fall into whic
categories, and they are often well worth following at the appropriate time.

Correspondingly, some trainers regularly have their horses, especiall
two-year-olds, more forward in condition than those of other trainers (it is rar
for trainers such as Henry Cecil and Michael Stoute, for example, to have a two
year-old runner before May).

Here is a list of trainers who saddled more than five 2-y-o winners in Marc
and April in the five years from 1999 to 2003.

	2003	2002	2001	2000	1999	Total
M.R.Channon	4	4	0	4	7	19
W.G.M.Turner	4	2	5	3	1	15
R.Hannon	5	4	0	3	1	13
A.Berry	2	1	5	3	–	11
B.A.McMahon	0	2	4	2	1	09
P.D.Evans	1	3	2	1	1	08

Finally, a word or two about how *not* to train a racehorse. *Sceptre*, one of the greatest fillies in racing history, was bred and owned by the 1st Duke of Westminster. She was by *Persimmon*, the Prince of Wales's 1896 Derby winner and subsequent stayer (see introduction to Chapter Ten), out of *Ornament*, a full sister to *Ormonde*, who, a decade previously, had carried off the Triple Crown for the Duke. But the Duke died in late 1899 and all his bloodstock was sold the following year at public auction. *Sceptre*, as a yearling, was bought by the unsavoury gambler Bob Sievier, who happened to be on a winning streak at the time, for the astonishing sum for the times of 10,000 guineas (equivalent today to well over half a million pounds), which beat the previous record price for a yearling by no less than 4,000 guineas. As a 2-y-o, *Sceptre* was fairly successfully trained by Charles Morton at Wantage. Morton then became a private trainer and Sievier decided to handle *Sceptre* himself. He forthwith hatched a stupid plan, impelled by greed and his gambling urge. Despite the filly's obvious Classic potential he ran her at the first meeting of the new season in the Lincolnshire Handicap. His scheme to lift £30,000 out of the ring might even have succeeded had he not had to be in Paris for a fortnight not long before the race and an incompetent American he had left in charge not given *Sceptre*, even though she was a stuffy horse and needed a lot of work, far too severe a preparation. She was caught on the post by the 4-y-o *St. Maclou*. The rest of her 3-y-o career is a marvellous Turf legend: she ran in five Classics, winning all but the Derby, when a bruised foot and poor jockeyship on the part of the ex-amateur Herbert Randall contributed to her downfall. Yet a full record of that 1902 season and the proximity of some of her races one to another shows Sievier, despite *Sceptre*'s success, in an extremely dim light as a trainer:

18 March	1 m	Lincolnshire H'cap	6 st 7	11/4 F	2nd beaten a head by *St. Maclou* (7 st 12)
30 April	1 m	2000 Guineas	8 st 9	4/1 JF	Won 2 l from *Pistol* and *Ard Patrick* (9 st)
2 May	1 m	1000 Guineas	9 st	1/2 F	Won easily a length from *St. Windeline* (9 st)
4 June	1½ m	Derby	8 st 9	Evens F	4th behind *Ard Patrick* (9 st)
6 June	1½ m	Oaks	9 st	5/2 F	Won in a canter, 3 l from *Glass Jug* (9 st)
15 June	1 m 7 f	Grand Prix de Paris	8 st 13	3/1	6th behind *Kizil Kourgan* (level weights)
18 June	1 m	Coronation Stakes	9 st 10	9/4	5th behind *Doctrine* (8 st 10 – all 1st 4)

19 June	1 m	St James's Palace St	8 st 11	5/2	Won a length from *St. Windeline* (9 st) from *Flying Lemur* (9 st)
30 July	1 m	Sussex Stakes	9 st 5	8/13 F	2nd beaten 2 l by *Royal Lancer* (8 st 13)
1 Aug	1½ m*	Nassau Stakes	9 st 8	2/1	Won 4 l from *Elba* (8st 5)
10 Sept	1 m 6 f	St. Leger	8 st 11	100/30 F	Won in a canter 3 l fm *Rising Glass* (9 st)
12 Sept	1 m 6 f	Park Hill Stakes	9st 8	1/4 F	2nd beaten a length by *Elba* (8 st 10)

* For 3-y-o fillies, but now run over 1 m 2 f

The following season after running (and backing) *Sceptre* in the Lincoln yet again (fifth under 9 st 1 lb), Sievier sold her and, mercifully, she went to Manton for the more professional guidance of Alec Taylor. It is a matter of speculation as to what he or another proper trainer might have achieved with her as a 3-y-o. At stud (to anticipate the next chapter) *Sceptre*, as sometimes happens with hard raced mares, did not appear to have conspicuous success. Nevertheless, her descendants have since left an indelible mark on Turf history.

On the female side there was her foal *Maid of the Mist*, who bred *Craig an Eran* (1921 2000 Guineas; Eclipse Stakes), who himself sired *April the Fifth* (1932 Derby). *Maid of the Mist* also bred *Sunny Jane* (1917 Oaks) and the influential broodmare *Hamoaze*. *Hamoaze* was the dam of *Buchan*, winner in 1919 and 1920 of the Eclipse Stakes, also in 1919 of the Champion Stakes and in 1920 of the Doncaster Cup. In turn, *Buchan* sired the filly *Book Law* (1927 Coronation Stakes; St. Leger) who was eventually mated with *Nearco*. The result was *Archive*, foaled in 1941. He never won, but became the sire of *Arkle*, the century's greatest steeplechaser.

Among other important horses tracing their ancestry to *Sceptre* was *Grey Of Falloden* whose greatest victory was in the 1964 Cesarewitch under a then-record weight of 9 st 6 lb (see under **Stayers** in Chapter One). Also, through the mare *Relance III* in France, there have been the following in direct female line from *Sceptre*: *Relko* (1963 Derby; Prix Royal-Oak; 1964 Coronation Cup), *Match III* (1962 King George VI and Queen Elizabeth Stakes; Washington International), and his full brother, *Reliance II* (1965 Prix du Jockey-Club).

Jockeys

One of the best things to have happened on the Turf since this book was first published was the return of Lester Piggott in 1990. Not only that, it was clear that he intended to resume where he left off, even though he was within a fortnight of his 55th birthday. On his first day back he was swiftly off the mark with a double at Chepstow. Eight days later, he rode four winners at the Curragh, all for Vincent O'Brien. And then the following Saturday, for the same trainer, with whom he had had such a fruitful association in days gone by, he demonstrated emphatically that all the old fireworks were still there when he got *Royal Academy* home in the Breeders Cup Mile at Belmont Park, New York.

Already at the top of the table of jockeys with English Classic successes, he added one more when *Rodrigo de Triano* won the 2000 Guineas in 1992 and took his total to 30, and the following season he added to his considerable list of

Classic victories abroad. His win in Bratislava was on *Zimbalim* for Barry Hills in the Slovenske Derby.

Then, sadly, in 1995 when he reached the age of 60, he again retired, but in an interview with Kenneth Harris of *The Observer*, Lester once gave his views on being a jockey and they make worthwhile and fascinating reading:

'There's an advantage in being tall, big: I think it's my main one. A horse responds to a good weight on its back – live weight – no dead weight – lead, under the saddle – to make up the right scale. When a biggish jockey gets up, the chances are that the horse feels – well, the authority. Not always. There is a great American jockey, Shoemaker, and he's only seven stone. And Gordon Richards again – eight stone. If you've got a good length of leg, you can communicate more with the horse, squeeze him with your knees, control him generally – show him you are there.

'There's the other side, the disadvantages; I've got to earn my living in a pretty strenuous game working at about one and a half stone below my natural weight. Some people exaggerate how I live; I don't starve, and I don't live on cigars and the *Financial Times*, and I don't drive to every race meeting in a rubber suit. But you can't eat and drink what might come naturally to you.

'If I'm riding at eight stone six, I have a boiled egg and a bit of toast for breakfast. If I have to do eight stone five that day, I'll give up the egg. I have a sandwich in the jockeys' room after I've finished riding, and I'll always have a meal at night. You lose the habit of eating, really – the less you have, up to a point, the less you want.

'You were asking me about influences. Susan's a great influence on me. She's almost like my manager. She's a trainer's daughter, and she rides well, and if I can't hear somebody on a long-distance telephone call, Susan talks. Sometimes she persuades me to do things I don't want to. Like this interview, because she says it'll do me good to do something I don't normally do. And the two girls influence me – you know, Maureen and Tracy. If I'm getting a bit serious about something they come in and one of them's bound to say something that makes me laugh.

'You ask about being influenced by other jockeys. Race-riding changes with the years. Not all that much: you've always got a leg each side of the horse, but things do change. For instance we go much faster in the first two furlongs than they did fifteen years ago. It doesn't do to model yourself on your predecessors.

'Another disadvantage about being big is style. Style is how you look. If you're small, it doesn't matter too much how you look, there isn't so much of you to be seen. And your legs don't take up so much room. If you're big, you can be seen better, and there's less horse showing.

'It's difficult for me to look stylish because I like to ride short. People ask me why I ride with my bottom in the air. Well, I've got to put it somewhere.'

KH: *One of the things often said of you is that you're a tremendously 'strong' jockey. What does 'strength' mean? Is it the kind of strength that bends iron bars?*
LP: 'Well, you need muscular strength to hold a horse that's pulling for his head, a big horse and a real puller, on his way down to the post. And if a horse is big and broad, and he's lazy, and he needs to be squeezed and kicked

along to keep him exerting himself, a small, light jockey can't do it so well. But when you talk about a jockey being "strong" or being able to ride a strong finish, it's a bit different.

'It's like this: a lot depends on the horse's balance. If he loses balance, he loses speed and direction, and that might cost him the race – he'll lose his position, or just get passed in the last fifty yards. Part of a jockey's job is to get his horse running balanced, and keep him balanced, and this means you've got to be balanced yourself all the time to fit in with the horse.

'The horse has his own centre of gravity just behind his shoulders. The jockey has a centre of gravity. But the jockey can shift his, and the horse can't. At every stride the horse's centre of gravity is shifting in relation to the jockey's. Getting a horse balanced means keeping your balance, every stride, every second, to suit his.

'Where strength comes in is that to keep doing this all the time without throwing yourself about in the saddle needs a lot of muscle control – you've got to be holding yourself as still as you can while you're making the right movement. The more control you have of your body, the fewer movements you have to make but the more muscular effort you need: you need more strength to stand still on one leg than to walk down the street.

'No, I don't say it's the strength that bends iron bars. It's the strength of an acrobat on a tightrope. Or of a juggler.

'In the finish of the race as well as keeping your horse balanced you've got to be doing things with him. You've got to be encouraging the horse – moving your hands forward when his head goes forward, squeezing him with your knees, urging him on with your heels, flourishing your whip, maybe giving him a crack, and all this without throwing him off balance, which means doing all these things and not letting yourself be thrown around in the saddle.

'In a tight finish a strong jockey may seem to be doing nothing in the saddle except throwing his hands forward – that's all you'll see, but the horse is going flat out, and still going straight. In the same finish a "weaker" jockey will be throwing himself about in the saddle, and his horse will be rolling about off balance. Keeping the horse balanced in that last hundred yards, and making him put it all in, can take a lot out of a jockey. It's got to be there to start with.

'Weight and length come into it again. If a jockey is strong, and he's good, I reckon live weight is better than dead weight. If all of the weight the horse is carrying is live, and the jockey can put it in the right place at every stride, the horse runs freer than he would if part of the weight is in a fixed place, in a bag on his back.'

KH: *What other attributes must a jockey have?*
LP: 'A jockey has got to make horses want to run for him. Sometimes a horse and jockey won't hit it off.

'Then, you've got to have judgement – can you get through that gap or not? Is the pace too slow? Is it so slow that if I poach a lead of four lengths here, three furlongs out, I can hang on and win by a neck? And you've got to do your homework – find out as much as you can about the other horses, so that when you see one in front of you, you can guess what he can do.

'Sometimes you can work out tactics in advance, but sometimes you've got to change them. You've got to keep thinking about racing all the time – it's no good starting to think about a race just before you get up on the horse's back. That's one thing about not wanting to talk very much – I get time to read about racing, and to listen, and to think.'

KH: *How far do you think the discipline of having to keep your weight down to this unnatural level changes, perhaps detrimentally, your natural personality?*
LP: 'I don't think it does very much. I don't think I'd be very different from what I am now if I didn't have to keep thin. But it's hard to say. As soon as I grew up I had to watch my weight hard and I've done it ever since. So I don't really know if I'd be different if I started living normally.

'Wasting depresses a lot of people – it's the way you're made. They say Fred Archer committed suicide because having to keep his weight down got his mind down as well – got him so depressed he couldn't go on living.

'I'm lucky because, well, you might say I'm pretty quiet and restrained by nature. I've never been one for living it up. Some people work to earn enough money to have fun. I enjoy the work best of all. If you like racing more than anything else, it's easier to give up things. It's easier to keep up your regime, without breaking out, and the steadier you keep it up the easier it is to live with it.

'I told you when you asked about motor-car racing that I liked to compete, that I liked to try and win – the winning isn't all that important, it's the *wanting* to win that matters. The competition. It's competing more than winning, if you see what I mean.

'In keeping your weight down you're competing. You're competing with yourself. After a time it becomes a habit and you're in one long competition with yourself. And you only keep winning if you're trying to win all the time.

'If I got on the scales one morning intending to be 8 st 4 lb and I was 8 st 6 lb, and I hadn't meant to be, even if I wasn't being asked to ride at 8 st 4 lb, I'd want to get those two pounds off. You've got to get what you started to do. Otherwise you start getting beat. The others start to beat you when you start being beat by yourself.'

Lester Piggot was 11 times champion jockey on the Flat between 1960 and 1982. But he was never able to reach the magic total of 200, his best season numerically being 191 in 1966. Only seven jockeys have passed the 200 mark on turf alone. Kieren Fallon is the latest to have achieved the feat (in 1999 and 2003). Frankie Dettori preceded him (1994 and 1995), while Michael Roberts (206 in 1992) has also reached this landmark total. Before that, Sir Gordon Richards rode more than 200 winners in no fewer than a dozen years between 1933 and 1952. His finest season was 1947 with a record 269. Tom Loates's tally was 222 in 1893, while the great Fred Archer in his comparatively short and tragically ended career exceeded the double century eight times between 1876 and 1885, when he achieved his best total of 246.

On the National Hunt scene, only nine riders have ever ridden 1,000 or more winners. Of these, the foremost and most phenomenal without doubt is Tony McCoy. In only ten seasons since 1995, he has won the NH Jockey's Title no fewer than nine times, with a record-breaking top score of 289 in 2001–02. In January 2004, at Wincanton, he rode a four-timer and took his total of successes to 2,002, so becoming the first jump jockey ever to ride 2,000 winners: an astonishing achievement. By the end of the 2003–04 season, his total stood at 2,069. Behind McCoy in the records come Richard Dunwoody (1983–99) with 1,699 winners; Peter Scudamore (1978–93) 1,678; Richard Johnson (1994 up to April 2004) 1,183; John Francome (1970–85) 1,138; Mick Fitzgerald (1988 up to April 2004) 1,036; Stan Mellor (1954–72) 1,035; Adrian Maguire (1991–2002) 1,024; Peter Niven (1984–2001) 1,002; Norman Williamson (1989–2003) 966.

Other jockey statistics: Gordon Richards is at the top of the all-time jockey table with 4,870 winners between 1921 and 1954. Pat Eddery comes next with a total of 4,598 winners up to his retirement in 2003, then Lester Piggott with 4,493. Eddery reached the milestone of 4,000 victories when he rode *Silver Patriarch* to success in the 1997 St. Leger.

Meanwhile, in June 1992, Pat Eddery had broken a record which had stood since 1864 by becoming the first jockey ever to win seven races on one day, thanks to three successes at Newmarket in the afternoon and four at Newcastle the same evening. Here is the list of those whose records he had beaten on the Flat:

SIX WINS ON ONE CARD
No. of rides

9	George Fordham	Newmarket	28 October 1864
7	George Fordham	Stockbridge	18 June 1867
6	Fred Archer	Newmarket	19 April 1877
7	Mr Charlie Cunningham	Rugby (NH)	29 March 1881
6	Fred Archer	Lewes	5 August 1882
6*	Gordon Richards	Chepstow	4 October 1933
6*	Alec Russell	Bogside	19 July 1957
7	Willie Carson	Newcastle	30 June 1990

* went through the card

But impressive as Eddery's achievement and these previous records were, they were all destined to be surpassed yet again. On Saturday 28 September 1996 Frankie Dettori became the first jockey ever to ride the winner of all seven races on the same card. This astonishing feat took place at Ascot and became known appropriately as Frankie's 'Magnificent Seven'.

CHAPTER TEN
Breeding Pointers to Performance

Our English racehorses differ slightly from the horses of every other breed; but they do not owe their difference and superiority to descent from any single pair, but to continued care in selecting and training many individuals during many generations.

Charles Darwin *On the Origin of Species* 1859

Darwin was writing within a century of Sir Charles Bunbury's notable reforms under the aegis of the Jockey Club to alter the demands of English racing upon the thoroughbred. A blend of speed and stamina was always necessary to win races; with shortened races, as well as younger contestants, speed became of more importance. Today, almost 150 years after Darwin propounded his controversial theories, speed has overtaken stamina in the majority of our racehorses, at the same time with a loss of versatility, and, with less strenuous racing careers, a lessening of toughness in many animals. Even in Victorian times there were horses such as *Plaisanterie, Foxhall* and *Rosebery* who were capable of winning both the Cesarewitch and Cambridgeshire in the same season, within a fortnight. No horse in training today could do that, and some of the longer-distance races are being shortened. The Great Metropolitan, which used to wind its way over the Downs at Epsom not so long ago and rejoin the racecourse proper, has now been shortened from 2 1/4 miles to 1 m 4 f. The Brown Jack Stakes, named after the famous and greatly loved Ascot stayer, used to share with the Queen Alexandra Stakes, a race *Brown Jack* won so many times, the title of the longest race in the Calendar; it has now been shortened to 2 miles. So has the Goodwood Cup and, as previously recorded, an attempt has been made to pare the Queen Alexandra itself down to 1 m 2 f. This event, although its distance was saved by the splendid public campaign already mentioned in a footnote in Chapter Seven, may yet be in danger of being shortened. As outlined at the beginning of Chapter Eight, there are plans to realign the straight at Ascot which would involve clipping the Queen Alexandra from its present 2 m 6 f 34 yds to about 2 m 5 1/2 furlongs; this would mean that this historic event would lose its title of longest race in the Calendar to Pontefract's Tote Marathon Handicap run in April over 2 m 5 f 122 yds. The French, too, have shortened some stayers' races, notably the Grand Prix de Paris, which used to be only just short of 2 miles. It is now 1 m 2 f. The Prix Gladiateur is still a testing contest at 1 m 7 f+ although it was at one time 3 m 7 f! The oldest and longest Classic, the St. Leger, over 1 m 6 f, is no longer supported in the way it used to be, partly because fewer horses these days stay that distance than even 50 years ago, and partly because of competition from rich races taking place in Europe and America, notably the Prix de l'Arc de Triomphe at 1 m 4 f. No longer is the Derby winner automatically trained for Doncaster.

Nor is the Ascot Gold Cup any longer the natural and likely objective for Classic winners if kept in training in subsequent seasons. The final decade of the 19th century provided no fewer than three such winning candidates: *Isinglass* and *La Flèche* at the age of five and, at four, the Prince of Wales's *Persimmon,* who having taken the Gold Cup by an easy eight lengths in 1897 went on to demonstrate his versatility at half the distance by winning the Eclipse Stakes the following month. By contrast, since the 1939–45 war, only one colt has successfully followed this pattern, and that as long ago as 1945 when Lord Rosebery's *Ocean Swell,* winner of a war-time substitute Derby at Newmarket, cantered home in the Gold Cup the next season.

Of course, the early retirement to stud, particularly of Derby winners after their three-year-old careers, is partly – but only partly – to blame (although it is by no means a modern phenomenon). Since the year of *Ocean Swell*'s impressive victory, 15 out of 55 Derby winners have remained in training at the age of four. Only one of them, *Blakeney,* in 1970, contested the Gold Cup. More to the point, of the rest, only *Parthia* (1960), who won the 1 m 6 f Paradise Stakes at Hurst Park, *St. Paddy* (1961), winner of the Jockey Club Stakes, in those days at 1 m 6 f, and *Teenoso,* successful in the 1 m 5 f+ Ormonde Stakes at Chester ever attempted at that age a distance beyond a mile and a half. This is not to belittle the achievements at that distance of Derby winners who stayed in training, such as the diminutive but great *Mill Reef,* who in the Prix de l'Arc de Triomphe in 1971 confirmed that he was the best in Europe and, the following season, won the Coronation Cup at 1 m 4 f; or *Royal Palace,* unbeaten as a 4-y-o with victories mostly in top-class company; or *Relko* and *Charlottown,* also unbeaten; or, more recently, *Teenoso.* The fact that 1 m 4 f was the optimum distance for all of them, nevertheless, tells its own story. We have to go back only to the immediately pre-war years to find a significantly different picture. The 1939 Derby winner, *Blue Peter* (who sired *Ocean Swell,* and was likewise owned by Lord Rosebery and trained by Jack Jarvis), was an intended Gold Cup runner for 1940 but was retired because of the war. The 4-y-o objective of *Bois Roussel,* the 1938 Derby victor, was also the Gold Cup, but he became impossible to train. Another diminutive but great Derby winner was *Hyperion* (1933). He was also lazy at home and Colledge Leader, who had taken over his training from the Hon. George Lambton, failed to realise this. Hence, in the 1934 Gold Cup, *Felicitation* made every yard of the running while *Hyperion,* short of work, finished an exhausted third.

The late Sir Noel Murless had some wise words on the topic in his introduction to *The Golden Post* (1985 – see Bibliography):

'The recurring theme throughout the book is the startling values placed on young racehorses – $10 million here, $20 million there, $30 million somewhere else. My goodness, the first two home in the Derby this year, *Secreto* and *El Gran Senor,* are valued at something like $60 million, and neither one of them was sound enough to run one step in competition after the June of their three-year-old season.

'Personally, my own policy, both as a trainer, a breeder and a manager of Sir Victor Sassoon's stud, was to ensure that *none* of our horses were given inflated values because I always tried to run them again at four. Never having had the slightest inclination to breed to unsound stallions myself, neither did I wish my clients to do so. To this day I seldom breed to a stallion who did not race beyond the age of three.

'I am afraid that the modern policy of breeding for money, rather than for the quality of future runners, would probably prove beyond my comprehension now. My conversations used to revolve round breeding a mare to a certain stallion, and the myriad of reasons why this mating might throw a Classic horse. Today they breed because the ensuing yearling might fetch a million at the sales.

'I suppose I may be considered by some people to be eccentric in my choice of *Ardross*, the long-distance Cup horse, for our Classic-winning miler (*Caergwrle*). But I am not trying to earn a fortune at the sales, I am trying to acquire the toughness, the gallantry, the soundness and the quality of *Ardross*, and put it to the speed of *Caergwrle*...*

'In some ways the modern passion for lightly raced speed is taking the breed down a dangerous path, and I do not envy would-be breeders the millions they are currently spending.'

So, with the stayer identified as an endangered species (and extreme staying races, perhaps, even more under threat), here are some observations on recent stayers and their antecedents. The two most impressive stayers in the latter half of the 1990s were *Double Trigger*, trained by Mark Johnston, and *Further Flight*, trained by Barry Hills. Both horses followed the historical precedent of such redoubtable stayers as *Brown Jack*, *Predominate* and *Trelawny* and became, over the years, tremendous favourites of the racing crowds, who thrilled to their victories and shouted themselves hoarse when they won, particularly in the later years: who says that public enthusiasm is confined to old favourites in the National Hunt field? *Double Trigger*, between 1995 and 1998, won the Ascot Gold Cup once, and both the Goodwood Cup and Doncaster Cup three times each; as a three-year-old in 1994, he had also won the Italian equivalent of the St. Leger. He was very stoutly bred by *Ela-Mana-Mou* (1979 King Edward VII Stakes; 1980 King George VI and Queen Elizabeth Diamond Stakes – both 1 m 4 f at Ascot), who was out of a mare by *High Hat*, bred and owned by Sir Winston Churchill, who was a winner, fittingly, of the 2 mile Winston Churchill Stakes at Hurst Park in 1961. The sire of the dam of *Double Trigger* was *Gay Lussac*, who had captured the Derby Italiano in 1972.

The grey *Further Flight*, deservedly the apple of his trainer's eye, had a quite astonishing and wonderful career before retiring at the age of 12 in 1998, having won yet again first time out that season. His score-sheet from 1989 onwards includes the record-breaking sequence of five victories in the Jockey Club Cup 1991–95, which made him the only horse since the beginning of the Pattern in 1971 to have won the same Group race so many times. In addition, with triumphs in the Goodwood Cup twice, the Doncaster Cup and the St. Simon Stakes, nine wins at Group level put him sixth in the list of European Pattern race leaders behind *Brigadier Gerard*, *Ardross*, *Acetenango* and *Persian Punch* (each with 13 Group victories) and *Triptych* (10) (see Chapter One under **Pattern races**). In addition, having won the Ebor Handicap at the age of four, he was fourth in 1997 at the age of 11! Altogether, *Further Flight*, whose owner, Simon Wingfield Digby, sadly died in 1998, ran 70 times (ridden 64 times by Michael Hills), winning no

* The result of the mating was *St. Ninian*, owned, like *Caergwrle*, by the late Lady Murless. Trained by Peter Easterby in Yorkshire, he was a high-class mile handicapper who won half a dozen times, including, in 1991, the Kempton Park Jubilee and Newbury Spring Cup.

fewer than 24 races and being second and third seven times each. *Further Flight* was sired by the son of *Lyphard*, *Pharly*, out of *Flying Nelly*, who was by the 1966 Prix du Jockey-Club winner, *Nelcius*. The pedigree, for an out and out and remarkable stayer, has some interesting characteristics. *Pharly* performed fairly well in France in 1977 at a mile and 1 m 2 f, winning the Prix Lupin and Prix du Moulin, both Group One. *Flying Nelly*, who won the 1974 Cambridgeshire, was also best in a similar distance bracket. But *Flying Nelly*'s dam (who bequeathed the grey colour) went back through a family of pure sprinters tracing to *Vilmorin* and the famous *Gold Bridge*. So where did the staying power come from? It was partly through *Pharly*'s dam, *Comely*, whose great-grandsire was *Mourne*, whose other progeny included *Rock Roi*, the outstanding Cup horse of 1971. *Mourne* went back through his dam's line to *Finglas*, twice a winner of the 2 m 6 f Queen Alexandra Stakes in the late 'twenties, just before *Brown Jack* made that event his own, as well as being beaten by only a length in the Ascot Gold Cup and being third to *Kantar* in the 1928 'Arc', for which he was joint-favourite. But one extremely interesting fact is that *Finglas* appears additionally in the further reaches of the pedigree of *Nelcius*. His stamina qualifications also include those of his grandsire, *Goyama*, Marcel Boussac's 1949 Coronation Cup winner, going back to *Tourbillon*, a cornerstone of Boussac's breeding foundations and arguably the best French staying stallion of the 20th century. He was sired by the dual 'Arc' and Prix Royal-Oak winner *Ksar*, who helped to keep the male line of *Herod* (see Chapter Two) alive in France and thus gives *Further Flight* a rare and distinguished ancestor.

Beyond the antecedents of *Double Trigger* and *Further Flight*, a look at the extensive *Northern Dancer* details later in the chapter give plenty of other clues to possible sires of stayers, in particular *Caerleon*, *Niniski* and *Sadler's Wells*. *Northern Dancer* and his progeny apart, *Alleged* and *Rainbow Quest* (details on p.252) stand out. *Lear Fan*, sire of the 1998 Prix Royal-Oak and Prix Gladiateur winner, *Tiraaz* (as well as *Sikeston*, a leading performer in 1 m 4 f Gr1 races in Italy in 1990/91), must also be noted for Cup races in the future, as should *Mtoto* (also see p.255). Another recent sire worth a mention is *Sharrood*, responsible for *Grey Shot* (1995 Prix de Lutece, 1 m 7 f; 1996 Gr2 Goodwood Cup, 2 m; 1997 Jockey Club Cup, 2 m; and successful over hurdles).

Sprint sires

At the other end of the racing spectrum from stayers are sprinters. My enthusiasm for stayers does not prevent huge pleasure from watching what the late Jeremy Tree always referred to as 'fast horses'. No one who saw *Lochsong* make all the running over the five furlongs in the Prix de l'Abbaye de Longchamp in 1993 can fail to have marvelled at her. After only two furlongs there were murmurs of 'They'll never catch her'. Nor did they, and the scenes round the unsaddling enclosure were truly amazing as the British greeted a national heroine who in the space of only two seasons had improved from handicap status to Group level. *Lochsong*, who repeated her 'Abbaye' triumph in 1994, is high on my list of favourite sprinters, but there are many others, not all of them Pattern-race winners, who had the power to excite, such as, in recent years, *Young Inca*, winning his sixth Ascot sprint at the age of 11; and a long time before that, another old favourite, *Denikin*, the Rowley Mile specialist who went on to a great age and recorded no fewer than nine Newmarket victories. In the top bracket, and also from decades ago, the grey *Abernant* remains a scintillating memory ('The fastest horse I've ever seen, let alone trained,' said Noel Murless.) and in more recent seasons, the flying machine *Dayjur*, while other purely personal choices over the years include *Be Friendly, Boldboy, Burglar, Cadeaux Genereux, Constans, Creole, D'Urberville, Elbio, Hever Golf Rose* (see under **Sprinters** in Chapter One), *Mr Brooks*, who met such a sad end in America in 1992, *Sing Sing*, and *Sharpo*. The race details of the Prix de l'Abbaye (see Chapter Twelve) provide some pointers to sprint sires. Yet the efficacy of a sire at this or that distance is often a matter of pure speculation: a point which is well illustrated in later pages with the progeny of *Northern Dancer*.

Opinions on the subject constitute an extensive quicksand, while breeding dogma is a Grimpen mire. This may be seen in the case, for example, of *Keen Hunter*, the thrilling winner of the Prix de l'Abbaye in 1991, trained by John Gosden (who, as Jeremy Tree used to be, is a master at producing sprinters). Concerning *Keen Hunter*, it is worth noting that, paradoxically, both the staying *Reliance II* and the 2000 Guineas and Derby winner *Crepello* are close up in the dam's side of his sire's pedigree, while his own dam, *Love's Reward* (foaled in 1981), significantly, traces through the remarkable broodmare *Pelting* and via *Vilmorin* to *Gold Bridge*, who in the 1930s founded a prolific and famous line of sprinters.

On the other hand, *Ahonoora* (see p.258) is a case of a sprinter who has sired noteworthy winners at longer distances, one being *Dr. Devious* (1992 Derby) and the other *Don't Forget Me* (1987 2000 Guineas). Of course, the dam's influence is of prime significance, but that does not always fully explain how sprinters/milers are able to get progeny capable of further. *Bluebird*, also, has sired not only another top sprinter in *Lake Coniston* but also the Park Hill Stakes (1 m 6 f) winner *Delilah*. *Danzig Connection* has sired, likewise, *Iktamal* (Haydock Sprint Cup) and *Riszard* (Queen Alexandra Stakes, 2 m 6 f). Meanwhile, a much-overlooked but influential sire, himself a Wokingham winner, was *March Past* (foaled in 1950). His record at stud (see also Chapter One under **Gelding**) was astonishing, including the sprinter *Constans* and another Wokingham success, *Marcher*; plenty of milers, such as the Royal Hunt Cup winners *Smartie* and *Camouflage*, and *Queen's Hussar*, sire of *Brigadier Gerard* and *Highclere*, dam of *Height of Fashion*; right through middle distances to the extremes of the Chester Cup and Cesarewitch (1968) with *Major Rose*. The interesting point about *Major Rose*, out of *Rosefield*, was that he not only had a full brother, *Captain Rose*, who also won at 2 miles plus, but also a full sister, *March Rose*: her limit, nevertheless, was a mile and a quarter.

The original edition of this book listed sires for the minimum distances. These are not now included. But a study of the *Northern Dancer* details in later pages gives worthwhile indications as to leading sprint sires. *Danzig* and his son *Green Desert* are to be particularly noted, while *Bluebird, Dancing Dissident* and *Royal Academy* have also shown capabilities for siring first-class sprinters. Outside the *Northern Dancer* line, *Efisio, Sharpo* and *Warning* have done particularly well.

After the sprinters and stayers, now for the extensive middle ground occupied by those who excel from 1 m to 1¹/₂ m. This is the chosen territory for excellence in the thoroughbred. Comprehensive and detailed lists of sires and famous families who have contributed are beyond the scope of this book, but some hints may be obtained in the results of important races in Chapter Eight, as well as in the notes which follow concerning *Northern Dancer*. A word of warning, nevertheless. Just as sprinting sires and mares find their way into staying and middle-distance pedigrees, so, on the other hand, what appears to be an ancestry guaranteed for success at middle distances does not always work. A case in point is little *Tenby*, favourite for the 1993 Derby. He was by the 1983 Prix du Jockey-Club winner, *Caerleon*, out of a mare whose dam, *Idle Waters*, won the 1976 Park Hill Stakes (1 m 6 f). Alas, *Tenby* did not appear to get the trip either in the Derby, where he may not have coped too well with Epsom, or in subsequent outings.

On the brighter side, however, here is an examination of the greatest and, indeed, most astonishing influence in middle-distance competition over the past decade or so: *Northern Dancer*, who was Canadian-bred and certainly the greatest sire of modern times. He founded a dynasty unparalleled in the annals of the Turf. *Northern Dancer* was by *Nearctic*, who was by the great sire *Nearco*, out of *Natalma* by *Native Dancer*, the 1953 Belmont Stakes and Preakness Stakes winner. There is very much a fairy-tale element about the whole *Northern Dancer* saga. He might never have been born but for the fact that *Natalma* broke a knee when in training for the 1960 Kentucky Oaks. Her owner, E.P. (Eddie) Taylor, decided against surgery and had her covered, but too late in the breeding season for a fashionable sire. Hence she went to *Nearctic*, a home-bred stallion in his first season at stud.
   As a yearling, the little bay *Northern Dancer* was too undersized to attract a bid at auction. So Eddie Taylor turned his unwanted colt out into a paddock, hoping the Canadian winter might toughen him up. In the spring, he was sent to Horatio Luro to be trained. He was given time, then in August his phenomenal racing career began with seven wins and two seconds out of nine run as a 2-y-o in 1963. Then, the following season, *Northern Dancer* won the Kentucky Derby in record time and also captured the Preakness Stakes. But, made odds-on to complete the Triple Crown in the Stakes, he did not quite see the trip out. Back home in Canada, he ran away with the Queen's Plate (see Chapter Twelve), winning by more than seven lengths.
   It had been a wonderful racecourse career from unlikely beginnings, and his jockey, Bill Hartack, paid tribute to his qualities: 'He was easy to handle and you never had to hit him. And once you asked him for his run, you could never get him to slow down again.' So *Northern Dancer* went to stud, and if his deeds on the racecourse were memorable, his progeny made him nothing less than a phenomenon, bringing about a breeding revolution in which, with their inspired support at auction, Robert Sangster as owner and Vincent O'Brien as trainer played leading roles. *Northern Dancer* died in 1990 at the age of 29, leaving the general stud-book immensely and permanently altered by his rich and fruitful life.

The dynasty of *Northern Dancer*

The list below gives, in bold type, the most important horses *Northern Dancer* sired and the races they have won, mostly at Group One and Group Two level only. In turn, the succeeding progeny of these horses and some of the races they have won are given. The idea of the list, which does not pretend to be complete or exhaustive, is to give an indication of the wide spectrum of distances that *Northern Dancer* and his descendants command, and the extent of his and, in turn, their importance. In general, the Group status of a given significant race and its distance are given usually on the first mention of that race. Where no Group status is given in the first mention of a particular race, it can be assumed that it is at least a Group Three event. Fillies – unless otherwise pointed out, or winners of 1000 Guineas, Oaks and overseas equivalents etc. – are mostly marked (f) and mares (m).

Be My Guest

Won Gr2 Waterford Crystal Mile. Has sired *On the House* (1982 1000 Guineas; Gr1 Sussex Stakes, 1 m); *Assert* (1982 Prix du Jockey-Club [French equivalent of the Derby]; Irish Derby; Gr1 Benson and Hedges Gold Cup, 1 m 2 f [later Juddmonte International]); *Free Guest* (f) (1985 Gr2 Nassau Stakes; 1984 and 1985 Gr2 Sun Chariot Stakes – both races at 1 m 2 f for fillies/mares only); *Most Welcome* (1989 Gr2 Lockinge Stakes, 1 m); *Pentire* (1995 Gr2 King Edward VII Stakes, 1 m 4 f; 1996 Gr1 King George VI and Queen Elizabeth Diamond Stakes); *Valentine Waltz* (1999 French 1000 Guineas).

IN TURN   *Assert* has sired *Patricia* (1991 Park Hill Stakes, 1 m 6 f fillies/mares only).
Most Welcome has sired *Arctic Owl* (1998 Gr2 Prix Kergolay, 1 m 7 f; Jockey Club Cup, 2 m; 2000 Irish St. Leger).

Dixieland Band

Sire of *Drum Taps*, winner of the 1992 Coppa d'Oro, 1 m 7 f, Milan, and victorious twice in the Ascot Gold Cup, 1992 and 1993. (*Drum Taps* was the first English-trained runner in the Melbourne Cup, unplaced but not disgraced in 1993); *Egyptband* (2000 Prix de Diane).

El Gran Senor

2000 Guineas winner in 1984, beaten by a short-head in the Derby by *Secreto*, then won the Irish Derby. Sired *Belmez* (1990 King George VI and Queen Elizabeth Diamond Stakes); *Rodrigo de Triano* (1992 2000 Guineas; Gr1 Champion Stakes, 1 m 2 f).

Fairy King

Top sire of two-year-olds in 1993. Winners that season included *Fairy Heights* (Fillies Mile) and *Turtle Island* (Gimcrack Stakes), who ran away with the Irish 2000 Guineas in 1994 and, in turn, became the sire of the 1999 2000 Guineas winner, *Island Sands*. *Fairy King* has also sired *Helissio* (1996 Prix de l'Arc de Triomphe; 1996 and 1997 Gr1 Grand Prix de Saint-Cloud, 1 m 4 f); *Ya Malak* (1997

Gr1 Nunthorpe Stakes, 5 f); *Victory Note* (1998 French 2000 Guineas); *Oath* (1999 Derby); *Falbrav* (2003 Eclipse Stakes).

Lomond
Won 2000 Guineas 1983. Sired *Dark Lomond* (1988 Irish St. Leger); *Kneller* (1998 Ebor Handicap; Doncaster Cup, 2 m 2 f; Jockey Club Cup, 2 m); and *Marling* (1992 Irish 1000 Guineas; Gr1 Coronation Stakes, 1 m fillies; Sussex Stakes, 1 m), who traces over nine generations on her dam's side to the incomparable *Pretty Polly*.

Lyphard
Lyphard won the 1972 Gr1 Prix Jacques le Marois, 1 m; Prix Daru, 1 m 2 f; and Gr1 Prix de la Foret, 7 f. *Dancing Brave*, one of the outstanding colts of the 20th century, is *Lyphard*'s most distinguished offspring. He won the 2000 Guineas in 1986, was narrowly defeated after misjudged jockeyship in the Derby, then was triumphant in the Eclipse, King George VI and Queen Elizabeth Diamond Stakes and finally, with a breathtaking performance, in the Prix de l'Arc de Triomphe. Others of *Lyphard*'s sons include *Pharly* (1976, at 2-y-o, Prix de la Foret; 1977 Gr1 Prix Lupin, 1 m 2 f; Gr1 Prix du Moulin, 1 m – also see above under *Further Flight* in the section dealing with stayers); *Lydian* (1981 Gr1 Gran Premio de Milano, 1 m 4 f; Gr1 Grosser Preis von Berlin, 1 m 4 f); *Manila* (1986 Gr1 Breeders Cup Turf, 1 m 4 f); and *Alzao*. Meanwhile among a host of oustanding daughters are *Reine de Saba* (1978 Prix de Diane [French equivalent of the Oaks]); *Dancing Maid* (1978 French 1000 Guineas; Gr1 Prix Vermeille, 1 m 4 f fillies); *Three Troikas* (1979 French 1000 Guineas; Prix Vermeille; Prix de l'Arc de Triomphe); *Ensconse* (1989 Irish 1000 Guineas); *Gracefully*, dam of *Lypharita* who won the 1985 Prix de Diane; *Pearl Bracelet* (1989 French 1000 Guineas); *Jolypha* (1992 Prix de Diane); and *Ski Paradise* (1994 Gr2 Keio Hai Spring Cup, 7 f, Tokyo; Prix du Moulin, 1 m).

IN TURN   *Dancing Brave*, prematurely and foolishly exported to Japan, where he died, aged 17, in 2000, nevertheless sired *Commander-in-Chief* (1993 Derby; Irish Derby); *White Muzzle* (1993 Derby Italiano winner and 'Arc' runner-up; 1994 Gr2 Grand Prix de Deauville, 1 m 4 f); *Wemyss Bight* (1993 Irish Oaks); *Cherokee Rose* (f) (1995 Gr1 Haydock Park Sprint Cup, 6 f; Gr1 Prix Maurice de Gheest, 6 f); *Infrasonic* (1993 Queen's Vase, 2 m); also *Ivanka* (1992, at 2-y-o, Fillies Mile).

Wemyss Bight, meanwhile, was dam of *Beat Hollow* (2000 Grand Prix de Paris), and another of *Dancing Brave*'s offspring, *Ballerina*, was the dam of *Millenary* (2000 St. Leger).

Pharly has sired *Further Flight* (see above for outstanding staying record); *Le Nain Jaune* (1982 Gr1 Grand Prix de Paris, 1 m 7 f [before it was shortened]); *Phardante* (1986 Gr1 Grand Prix de Bruxelles, 1 m 3 f; 1987 Gr2 Jockey Club Stakes, 1 m 4 f); *Busy Flight* (1998 Gr2 Yorkshire Cup, 1 m 6 f).

Alzao has sired *Second Set* (1991 Sussex Stakes); *Bobzao* (1994 Gr2 Hardwicke Stakes, 1 m 4 f); *Wind In Her Hair* (1995 Gr1 Aral Pokal, 1 m 4 f, Gelsenkirchen); *Matiya* (1996 Irish 1000 Guineas); *Shahtoush* (1998 Oaks); *Winona* (1998 Irish Oaks); *Alborada* (1998 Gr2 Nassau Stakes, 1 m 2 f fillies/mares; Gr2 Pretty Polly Stakes, 1 m 2 f fillies/mares, Curragh; Gr1 Champion Stakes, 1 m 2 f); *Epistolaire* (1998 Grand Prix de Deauville); *Waky Nao* (1998 Gr1 Premio Vittorio de Capua, 1 m, Milan).

Manila has sired *Time Star* (1994 Derby Italiano) and *Aquarelliste* (2001 Prix de Diane and Gr1 Prix Vermeille, 1 m 4 f 3-y-o fillies; 2002 Gr1 Prix Ganay, 1 m 2 f+ 4-y-o+).

Night Shift
Sired *In The Groove* (1990 Coronation Cup); *Nicolotte* (1995 Gr2 Queen Anne Stakes, 1 m; Gr1 Premio Vittorio di Capua, 1 m, Milan); *Struggler* (1995 Prix de Saint-Georges, 5 f); *Eveningperformance* (1996 Flying Five, 5 f, Leopardstown); *Lochangel* (1998 Nunthorpe Stakes, 5 f); *Daryaba* (1999 Prix de Diane).

Nijinsky
The original prime standard-bearer for *Northern Dancer*, Canadian-bred by E.P. Taylor and trained in Ireland by Vincent O'Brien. Winner in 1970 of the Triple Crown and most recent to perform that feat (see Chapter One); in addition, in the same season, he captured the Irish Derby and King George VI and Queen Elizabeth Diamond Stakes. *Nijinsky*'s stud career, if anything, was even more brilliant than his outstanding racecourse achievements. A luminous roll-call of his progeny includes *Green Dancer* (1975 French 2000 Guineas; Prix Lupin); *Caucasus* (Ulster Harp Derby; Irish St. Leger); *Quiet Fling* (1976 Gr1 Coronation Cup, 1 m 4 f); *African Dancer* (f) (1976 Park Hill Stakes, 1 m 6 f); *Ile de Bourbon* (1978 King Edward VII Stakes; King George VI and Queen Elizabeth Diamond Stakes; 1979 Coronation Cup); *Niniski* (1979 Gr1 Prix Royal-Oak, 1 m 7 f+; Irish St. Leger); *Leap Lively* (f) (1980 Hoover Mile [now Fillies Mile] for 2-y-o); *King's Lake* (1981 Irish 2000 Guineas; Sussex Stakes); *Golden Fleece* (1982 Derby); *Caerleon* (1983 Prix du Jockey-Club); *Solford* (1983 Eclipse Stakes); *Shadeed* (1986 2000 Guineas; Gr1 Queen Elizabeth II Stakes, 1 m); *Ferdinand* (1986 Kentucky Derby, 1 m 2 f; Gr1 Breeders Cup Classic, 1 m 2 f dirt); *Shahrastani* (1986 Derby; Irish Derby); *Royal Academy* (1990 Gr1 July Cup, 6 f; Breeders Cup Mile); *Niodini* (f) (1992 Park Hill Stakes); *Romany Rye* (1992 Queen Alexandra Stakes, 2 m 6 f); *Lammtarra* (1995 Derby; King George VI and Queen Elizabeth Diamond Stakes; Prix de l'Arc de Triomphe).

Nijinsky, aged 25, had to be put down in his old age in April 1992 and is buried at Claiborne Farm, Kentucky.

IN TURN   *Green Dancer* has sired *Aryenne* (1980 French 1000 Guineas); *Dancing Rocks* (f) (1982 Nassau Stakes, 1 m 2 f); *Suave Dancer* (1991 Prix du Jockey-Club; Prix de l'Arc de Triomphe);

Green Tune (1994 French 2000 Guineas; 1995 Gr1 Prix d'Ispahan, 1 m 1 f); *Canon Can* (1997 Queen Alexandra Stakes, 2 m 6 f; Doncaster Cup, 2 m 2 f).

Ile de Bourbon has sired *Rejuvenate* (f) (1986 Park Hill Stakes); *Kahyasi* (1988 Derby; Irish Derby). *Kahyasi* in his turn has sired *Vereva* (1997 Prix de Diane); *Zainta* (1998 Prix de Diane) and *Enzeli* (1999 Ascot Gold Cup).

Niniski has sired *Petoski* (1985 Gr2 Princess of Wales's Stakes, 1 m 4 f; King George VI and Queen Elizabeth Diamond Stakes); *Minster Son* (1988 St. Leger); *Hernando* (1993 Prix du Jockey-Club); *Sapience* (1989 Ebor Handicap; 1990 Princess of Wales's Stakes; 1992 Gr2 Jockey Club Stakes, 1 m 4 f); *Alflora* (1993 Queen Anne Stakes); *Assessor* (1993 Doncaster Cup; Gr1 Prix du Cadran, 2 m 4 f); *San Sebastian* (1998 Ascot Stakes, 2 m 4 f Hcp; 1999 Queen Alexandra Stakes; 2000 Gr1 Prix du Cadran 2 m 4 f).

Leap Lively was the dam of *Forest Flower* (1987 Irish 1000 Guineas).

Caerleon has sired *Casey* (f) (1988 Park Hill Stakes); *Generous* (1991 Derby; Irish Derby; King George VI and Queen Elizabeth Diamond Stakes); *Only Royale* (1993 Gr1 Yorkshire Oaks); *Cuff Link* (1994 and 1995 Queen Alexandra Stakes); *Moonax* (1994 St. Leger); *Lady Carla* (1996 Oaks); *Shake the Yoke* (f) (1996 Coronation Stakes); *Amfortas* (1996 King Edward VII Stakes); *Cape Verdi* (1998 1000 Guineas); *Kissogram* (1998 Gr2 Sun Chariot Stakes, 1 m 2 f fillies/mares); *Claxon* (2000 Gr2 Premio Lydia Tesio, 1 m 2 f fillies/mares); *Marienbard* (2002 Gr1 Grosser Preis von Baden; Prix de L'Arc de Triomphe); *Warrsan* (2003 Gr1 Coronation Cup).

Shadeed has sired *Shadayid* (1991 1000 Guineas); *Sayyedati* (1993 1000 Guineas; Gr1 Prix du Jacques le Marois, 1 m).

Royal Academy has sired *Oscar Schindler* (1996 Hardwicke Stakes; 1996 and 1997 Irish St. Leger); *Sleepytime* (1997 1000 Guineas); *Ali-Royal* (1997 Sussex Stakes, 1 m); *Carmine Lake* (f) (1997 Gr1 Prix de L'Abbaye, 5 f); *Zalaiyka* (1998 French 1000 Guineas); *Bolshoi* (1998 Gr2 Temple Stakes, 5 f; Gr2 King's Stand Stakes, 5 f).

Generous has sired *Windsor Castle* (1997 Queen's Vase; Northumberland Plate); *Bahr* (1998 Gr2 Ribblesdale Stakes, 1 m 4 f fillies); *Lisieux Rose* (f) (Gr2 Blandford Stakes, 1 m 3 f Curragh).

Hernando, in turn, has sired *Holding Court* (2000 Prix du Jockey-Club) and *Sulamani* (2002 Prix du Jockey-Club).

Northern Baby
Won 1979 Champion Stakes, 1 m 2 f, and has sired *Bairn* (1985 Gr1 St. James's Palace Stakes, 1 m) and *Michelozzo* (1989 St. Leger).

Northern Trick
Won 1984 Prix de Diane.

Northfields
Sire of *Northern Treasure* (1976 Irish 2000 Guineas); *North Stoke* (1977 winner of six races in succession at 1 m 2 f, including Grand Prix de Bruxelles and Gr1 Joe McGrath Memorial Stakes); *Nanticious* (f) (1977 Ribblesdale Stakes); *Northjet* (1981 Prix Jacques le Marois; Prix du Moulin); *Open Day* (1982 King Edward VII Stakes); *Infantry* (1985 Dee Stakes, 1 m 2 f). Also sire of *Anjuli*, dam of *Kooyonga* (1991 Irish 1000 Guineas; Coronation Stakes; 1992 Eclipse Stakes) and sire of *Northern Sunset*, dam of *St. Jovite* (1992 Irish Derby; King George VI and Queen Elizabeth Diamond Stakes).

Nureyev
Disqualified after finishing first past the post in the 1980 2000 Guineas, has proved quite brilliant at stud: *Sonic Lady* (1986 Irish 1000 Guineas; Coronation Stakes; Sussex Stakes; Prix du Moulin etc. – all at 1 m); *Soviet Star* (1987 Sussex Stakes); *Theatrical* (1987 Turf Classic, $1^1/_2$ m); *Miesque* (1987 1000 Guineas; French 1000 Guineas); *Zilzal* (1989 Sussex Stakes; Queen Elizabeth II Stakes – both at 1 m); *Dancing Dissident* (1989 Temple Stakes); *Polar Falcon* (1991 Lockinge Stakes, 1 m; Ladbroke Sprint Cup); *Wolfhound* (1992 Prix de la Foret, 7 f; 1993 Haydock Sprint Cup); *Mehtaaf* (1994 Irish 1000 Guineas); *Spinning World* (1996 Irish 2000 Guineas; 1997 Prix du Moulin; Breeders Cup Mile); *Reams of Verse* (1997 Oaks); *Peintre Celebre* (1997 Prix du Jockey-Club; Prix de l'Arc de Triomphe).

IN TURN   *Miesque* became dam of *Kingmambo* (1993 French 2000 Guineas; St. James's Palace Stakes; Prix du Moulin – all at 1 m); and dam of *East Of The Moon* (1994 French 1000 Guineas; French Oaks).

Soviet Star has sired *Ashkalani* (1996 Prix du Moulin); *Soviet Line* (1996 Lockinge Stakes); *Starborough* (1997 Gr1 Prix Jean Prat, 1 m 1 f; St. James's Palace Stakes).

See p.257 under *Mr Prospector*.

Theatrical has sired *Madeleine's Dream* (1993 French 1000 Guineas); *Zagreb* (1996 Irish Derby); *Gordi* (1996 Queen's Vase); *Royal Anthem* (1998 King Edward VII Stakes; Gr1 Canadian International, 1 m 4 f, Woodbine).

Zilzal has sired *Always Loyal* (1997 French 1000 Guineas); *Faithful Son* (1998 Prince of Wales's Stakes); *Among Men* (1998 Sussex Stakes).

Dancing Dissident has sired *Don't Worry Me* (1997 King's Stand Stakes; Gr2 Jacobs Goldene Peitsche, 6 f, Baden-Baden).

Polar Falcon has sired *Pivotal* (1996 King's Stand Stakes; Nunthorpe Stakes); and *Exclusive* (1998 Coronation Stakes).

Sadler's Wells
Winner 1984 Irish 2000 Guineas and Eclipse Stakes. Has sired so far: *Prince of Dance* and *Scenic* (dead-heated, at 2-y-o, 1988 Gr1 Dewhurst Stakes, 7 f); *Old Vic* (1989 Irish Derby; Prix du Jockey-Club); *Braashee* (1990 Gr2 Yorkshire Cup, 1 m 6 f; Prix Royal-Oak dead-heat with *Indian Queen*); *In the Wings* (1990 Coronation Cup; Breeders Cup Turf); *Salsabil* (1990 1000 Guineas; Oaks; Irish Derby); *Stagecraft* (1991 Gr2 Prince of Wales's Stakes, 1 m 2 f); *El Prado* (1991, at 2-y-o, Gr1 National Stakes, 7 f, Curragh); *Johan Quatz* (1992 Prix Lupin); *Saddler's Hall* (1991 King Edward VII Stakes; 1992 Coronation Cup; Princess of Wales's Stakes); *Masad* (1992 Gran Premio d'Italia); *Fatherland* (1992, at 2-y-o, Gr1 National Stakes); *Opera House* (1993, at 5-y-o, Coronation Cup; Eclipse Stakes; King George VI and Queen Elizabeth Diamond Stakes); *Intrepidity* (1993 Oaks); *Barathea* (1993 Irish 2000 Guineas; 1994 Queen Anne Stakes; Breeders Cup Mile); *Sonus* (1993 Goodwood Cup); *Fort Wood* (1993 Grand Prix de Paris, 1 m 2 f); *Imperial Ballet* (1993 Royal Hunt Cup); *Thawakib* (1993 Ribblesdale Stakes, 1 m 4 f); *Foyer* (1994 King Edward VII Stakes); *Carnegie* (1994 Prix de L'Arc de Triomphe; 1995 Grand Prix de Saint-Cloud); *King's Theatre* (1994 King George VI and Queen Elizabeth Diamond Stakes); *Moonshell* (1995 Oaks); *Northern Spur* (1995 Breeders Cup Turf); *Muncie* (1995 Gr1 Prix St. Alary, 1 m 2 f; Prix Penelope, 1 m 2 f); *Dance Design* (1996 Irish Oaks); *Admiral's Well* (1996 Queen Alexandra Stakes; Brown Jack Handicap, 2 m, under top-weight); *In Command* (1996 Dewhurst Stakes); *Cloudings* (1997 Prix Lupin); *Ebadiyla* (1997 Irish Oaks; Prix Royal-Oak); *Entrepreneur* (1997 2000 Guineas); *Chief Contender* (1997 Prix du Cadran); *Crimson Tide* (1997 Gr2 Grosser Preis von Dusseldorf, 1 m+); *King of Kings* (1998 2000 Guineas); *Dream Well* (1998 Prix du Jockey-Club; Irish Derby); *Kayf Tara* (1998 and 2000 Ascot Gold Cup; 1998 and 1999 Irish St. Leger; 1999 Goodwood Cup; 2000 Yorkshire Cup); *Leggera* (f) (1998 Gr1 Prix Vermeille, 1 m 4 f; 2nd in the 'Arc'); *Insight* (1998 Gr2 Prix de l'Opera, 1 m 1 f fillies/mares); *Commander Collins* (1998, at 2-y-o, Gr1 Racing Post Trophy, 1 m); *Istabraq* (1998 and 1999 Champion Hurdle); and stable-companion *Theatreworld* (1997–99 Champion Hurdle runner-up three seasons running); *Montjeu* (1999 Prix du Jockey-Club, Irish Derby, Prix de l'Arc de Triomphe; 2000 King George VI and Queen Elizabeth Diamond Stakes, Grand Prix de Saint-Cloud); *Beat Hollow* (2000 Gr1 Grand Prix de Paris 1 m 2 f); *Daliapour* (2000 Coronation Cup); *Imagine* (2001 Oaks); *Galileo* (2001 Derby; Irish Derby; King George VI and Queen Elizabeth Diamond Stakes); *Milan* (2001 St. Leger); *High Chaparral* (2002 Derby; Irish Derby); *Islington* (2002 Gr1 Nassau Stakes; 2002 and 2003 Yorkshire Oaks; 2003 Breeders Cup Filly and Mare Turf); *Refuse To Bend*

(2003 2000 Guineas; 2004 Eclipse Stakes); *Brian Boru* (2003 St. Leger); *Doyen* (2004 King George VI and Queen Elizabeth Diamond Stakes).

IN TURN   *Old Vic* has sired *Orchestra Stall* (1997 and 2000 Prix Gladiateur and other Gr3 staying races) and *Dominant Duchess* (2000 Queen Alexandra Stakes).

In The Wings has sired *Winged Love* (1995 Irish Derby); *Singspiel* (1996 Canadian International; 1997 Coronation Cup; Juddmonte International Stakes; Dubai World Cup); *Central Park* (1998 Derby Italiano) and *Act One* (2002 Gr1 Prix Lupin, 1 m 2 f+ 3-y-o colts and fillies).

Saddler's Hall has sired *Silver Patriarch* (1997 St. Leger; 1998 Coronation Cup).

Secreto
Derby winner in 1984 and sire of *Mystiko* (1991 2000 Guineas).

Shareef Dancer
Won 1983 King Edward VII Stakes, 1 m 4 f, and Irish Derby. Sired *Possessive Dancer* (1991 Oaks d'Italia; Irish Oaks); *Rock Hopper* (1991 and 1992 Hardwicke Stakes; 1992 Yorkshire Cup); *Spartan Shareef* (1993 Gr3 Gran Premio Napoli, 1 m 2 f).

IN TURN   *Rock Hopper* has sired *Russian Hope* (1998 Prix de la Lutece, 1 m 7 f).

Storm Bird
1980 Dewhurst winner. Sire of *Indian Skimmer* (unbeaten as 3-y-o, including 1987 Prix de Diane; 1988 Champion Stakes; Phoenix Champion Stakes; 1989 Prix d'Ispahan, 1 m 1 f); *Bluebird* (1987 King's Stand Stakes); *Balanchine* (1994 Oaks; Irish Derby).

IN TURN   *Bluebird* has sired *Dolphin Street* (1993 Prix de la Foret, 7 f; 1994 Prix Maurice de Gheest, 6 f); *Lake Coniston* (1994 Gr2 Diadem Stakes, 6 f; 1995 July Cup, 6 f); *Fly To The Stars* (1998 Gr2 Prix du Rond-Point, 1 m); *Delilah* (1998 Park Hill Stakes, 1 m 6 f).

Topsider
Sired *Assatis* (1989 Gr2 Hardwicke Stakes; Gr1 Gran Premio del Jockey-Club Coppa d'Oro, 1 m 4 f, Milan); *Salse* (won five Group races at 7 f in 1988, including Gr2 Challenge Stakes and Gr1 Prix de la Foret).

IN TURN   *Salse* has sired *Lemon Souffle* (1993, at 2-y-o, Gr3 Moyglare Stud Stakes); *Luso* (prolific Group winner overseas, including 1995 Derby Italiano; 1996 Gr1 Aral Pokal, Gelsenkirchen, and 1998 equivalent; 1996 and 1997 Gr2 Hong Kong International Vase, 1 m 4 f); *Classic Cliche* (1995 St. Leger; 1996 Ascot Gold Cup); *Yeast* (1996 Royal Hunt Cup); *Air Express* (1997 Italian 2000 Guineas; Queen Elizabeth II Stakes).

Try My Best
Full brother to *El Gran Senor* (out of *Sex Appeal*). Won 1977 Dewhurst Stakes as 2-y-o. Has sired *Last Tycoon* (1986 King's Stand Stakes; William Hill Sprint Championship; Breeders Cup Mile); *My Best Valentine* (1998 Prix de l'Abbaye).

IN TURN   *Last Tycoon* has sired *Marju* (1991 St. James's Palace Stakes); *Monde Bleu* (1992 Palace House Stakes, 5 f; Prix du Gros-Chene, 5 f); *Bigstone* (1993 Sussex Stakes; Queen Elizabeth II Stakes); *Ezzoud* (1993 and 1994 Juddmonte International Stakes; 1994 Eclipse Stakes); *Taipan* (1997 Grand Prix de Deauville; 1997 and 1998 Gr1 Europa Preis, 1 m 4 f, Cologne).

Marju has sired *Sil Sila* (1996 Prix de Diane).

The Minstrel
1977 Derby and Irish Derby winner. Sired *L'Emigrant* (1983 French 2000 Guineas; Prix Lupin); *Musical Bliss* (1989 1000 Guineas); *Silver Fling* (1989 Palace House Stakes; Prix de l'Abbaye – both at 5 f).

Unfuwain
Half-brother to *Nashwan* (see below under *Blushing Groom*) out of *Height of Fashion* (see below under *Busted*). Won 1998 Princess of Wales's Stakes, 1 m 4 f, and 1989 Jockey Club Stakes, 1 m 4 f. Has sired *Bolas* (1994 Irish Oaks; Ribblesdale Stakes); *Dovedon Star* (1998 Queen Alexandra Stakes); *Petrushka* (2000 Yorkshire Oaks, Irish Oaks, Gr1 Prix de l'Opéra); *Lahan* (2000 1000 Guineas).

In addition to the mostly mile to middle-distance stallions above, two of *Northern Dancer*'s sons' connections are predominantly with shorter distances:

Ajdal
Winner of the Dewhurst as a 2-y-o and favourite for the 2000 Guineas in 1987. But he did not stay and, eventually, turned to sprinting, becoming outstanding, with victories in the July Cup and Vernons Sprint at 6 f and the Nunthorpe (then the William Hill Sprint Championship) at 5 f. His stud career was, sadly, only brief, as a result of a fatal accident, but one of his succcesses was *Cezanne* (1994 Magnet Cup, 1 m 2 f Hcp; Gr1 Guinness Irish Champion Stakes, 1 m 2 f; and a Group Three in Germany).

Danzig
A very successful sire, mostly of sprinters and milers, including *Dayjur* the champion sprinter of 1990; also *Green Desert* (1986 July Cup; Vernons Sprint Cup, 6 f); *Polonia* (1987 Prix de l'Abbaye); *Danehill* (1989 Cork and Orrery Stakes; Ladbrokes Sprint Cup, 6 f); *Shaadi* (1989 St. James's Palace Stakes; Irish 2000 Guineas); *Polish Precedent* (1989 Prix du Jacques le Marois; Prix du Moulin); *Polish Patriot* (1991 July Cup); *Hamas* (1993 July Cup); *Emperor Jones* (1994 Lockinge Stakes); *Maroof* (1994 Queen Elizabeth II Stakes); *Anabaa* (1996 July Cup; Prix Maurice de Gheest); *Blue Duster* (f) (1996 unbeaten at 2-y-o, including Cheveley

Park Stakes – sprinter); *Pas de Reponse* (f) (1997 Gr3 winner at 6 f in France); *Yashmak* (f) (1997 Ribblesdale Stakes; Gr1 Flower Bowl International Invitational, 1 m 2 f, Belmont Park); *Bianconi* (1998 Diadem Stakes, 6 f); *Elnadim* (1998 July Cup); *Agnes World* (1999 Prix de l'Abbaye; 2000 Gr1 July Cup, 6 f); *Golden Snake* (2000 Gr1 Preis von Europa, 1 m 4 f; Gr1 Gran Premio del Jockey Club, 1 m 4 f; Gr1 Prix Ganay). Also *Chief's Crown* (1982) and *Danzig Connection* (1983).

IN TURN   *Polish Precedent* has sired *Pure Grain* (1995 Irish Oaks); *Pilsudski* (1996 Gr1 Grosser Preis von Baden, 1 m 4 f; Breeders Cup Turf; 1997 Eclipse Stakes; Champion Stakes; Irish Champion Stakes); *Predappio* (1997 Hardwicke Stakes).

Green Desert has sired *Sheikh Albadou* (1991 Nunthorpe Stakes; Breeders Cup Sprint; 1992 King's Stand Stakes; Haydock Spring Cup); *Owington* (1994 July Cup); *Cape Cross* (1998 Lockinge Stakes); *Tamarisk* (Haydock Sprint Cup); *Desert Prince* (1998 Irish 2000 Guineas; Prix du Moulin; Queen Elizabeth II Stakes); *Oriental Express* (1998 Gr1 Queen Elizabeth II Cup, 1 m 2 f, Hong Kong); *Rose Gypsy* (2001 Poule d'Essai des Pouliches).

Danehill has sired *Kissing Cousin* (1994 Coronation Stakes) and (out of a mare by *Nureyev*) *Desert King* (1997 Irish 2000 Guineas; Irish Derby); *Tiger Hill* (1998 German 2000 Guineas; Gr1 Grosser Preis von Baden, 1 m 4 f; 3rd in the 'Arc'); *Banks Hill* (2001 Gr1 Coronation Stakes, 1 m 3-y-o fillies; Breeders Cup Filly and Mare Turf, 1 m 2 f); *Landseer* (2002 Poule d'Essai des Poulains); *Rock of Gibraltar* (2002 2000 Guineas; Irish 2000 Guineas; Gr1 St. James's Palace Stakes, 1 m; Gr1 Sussex Stakes, 1 m 3-y-o+; Gr1 Prix du Moulin, 1 m 3-y-o colts and fillies); *Clodovil* (2003 Poule d'Essai des Poulains); *Westerner* (2003 Gr1 Prix du Cadran, 2 m 4 f 4-y-o+; Gr1 Prix Royal-Oak, 1 m 7 f+ 3-y-o+); *North Light* (2004 Derby). Sadly, *Danehill* (named after a village in Sussex and owned during a distinguished racing career by Khaled Abdulla) died aged 17 in May 2003, after an accident at the Coolmore Stud, Ireland. He was on the brink of overtaking *Sadler's Wells* as the most prolific stallion and had been acclaimed as 'the best stallion in the world' by no less an authority than André Fabre. *Danehill* sired around the world no fewer than 51 Group One winners and a record 207 stakes winners overall.

Chief's Crown has sired *Grand Lodge* (1993 Dewhurst Stakes; 1994 St. James's Palace Stakes); *Erhaab* (1994 Derby).

Danzig Connection has sired *Riszard* (1993 Queen Alexandra Stakes, 2 m 6 f); *Polish Laughter* (1993, at 2-y-o, Gr2 Mill Reef Stakes, 6 f); *Iktamal* (1996 Haydock Sprint Cup, record time).

IN TURN
AGAIN

Grand Lodge has sired *Sinndar* (2000 Derby; Irish Derby; Prix de l'Arc de Triomphe); *Indian Lodge* (Gr1 Prix du Moulin, 1 m; Gr1 Prix de la Foret, 7 f) and *Grandera* (2002 Gr1 Prince of Wales's Stakes, 1 m 2 f 4-y-o+).

Now follow notes on some important horses and sires other than those of the *Northern Dancer* line:

Alleged
Trained by Vincent O'Brien, won the Prix de l'Arc de Triomphe two seasons running 1977–78. American-bred by *Hoist the Flag*, 1970 champion 2-y-o in the USA, and a grandson by *Tom Rolfe* of the incomparable *Ribot*, who also twice captured the 'Arc' and in an illustrious stud career sired no fewer than four winners of the St. Leger. *Alleged*, too, has become an outstanding sire of stayers: *Law Society* (1985 Irish Derby); *Leading Counsel* (1985 Irish St. Leger); *Midway Lady* (1986 1000 Guineas; Oaks); *Mazzacano* (1989 Goodwood Cup); *Miss Alleged* (1991 Breeders Cup Turf); *Beyton* (1992 King Edward VII Stakes); *Muhtarram* (1993 Gr1 Guinness Champion Stakes, 1 m 2 f; 1994 Gr1 Premio Presidente della Republica, 1 m 2 f, Rome; 1994 and 1995 Prince of Wales's Stakes); *Molesnes* (1994 Prix du Cadran); *Always Earnest* (1995 Prix du Cadran); *Strategic Choice* (1995 Irish St. Leger); *Tulipa* (f) (1996 Ribblesdale Stakes; Prix Penelope, 1 m 2 f); *Shantou* (1996 St. Leger; Gr1 Gran Premio del Jockey Club, 1 m 4 f, Milan; 1997 Princess of Wales's Stakes; Gr1 Gran Premio de Milano, 1 m 4 f).

Blushing Groom
Brilliant on the racecourse as a 2-y-o, owned by the Aga Khan and trained by Francois Mathet. He won the 1977 French 2000 Guineas, but in the Derby could not quite cope with the pace of *The Minstrel* and *Hot Grove*, finishing five lengths away third. Exported to the United States, his stud career took a little time to take off, but when it did, *Blushing Groom* proved quite spectacular at a variety of distances. In Europe, his stock includes *Rosananti* (1982 Italian 1000 Guineas); *Rainbow Quest* (1985 Coronation Cup; Prix de l'Arc de Triomphe); *Al Bahathri* (1985 Irish 1000 Guineas; Coronation Stakes); *Groom Dancer* (1987 Gr3 winner in France, 1 m 2 f); *Love The Groom* (1987 King Edward VII Stakes); *Nashwan* (1989 2000 Guineas; Derby; Eclipse Stakes; King George VI and Queen Elizabeth Diamond Stakes); *Kadissya* (dam of 1988 Derby winner, *Kahyasi*); *Arazi* (undefeated in 1991 as a 2-y-o, completing a clean sweep, just as his sire had done, of all the best French races for that age-group and culminating in an astonishing victory in the Breeders Cup Juvenile at Churchill Downs; 1992 Prix du Rond-Point, 1 m); *Gold Splash* (1993 Coronation Stakes); *Desert Team* (1993 Princess of Wales's Stakes).

IN TURN

Rainbow Quest has sired *Quest For Fame* (1990 Derby); *Saumarez* (1990 Price de l'Arc de Triomphe); *Knight's Baroness* (1990 Irish Oaks); *Sought Out* (1992 Prix du Cadran); *Bright Generation* (1993 Oaks d'Italia); *Raintrap* (1993 Prix Kergolay, 1 m 7 f; Prix Royal-

Oak, 1 m 7 f+; 1994 Gr1 Rothmans International, 1 m 4 f, Woodbine); *Wagon Master* (1994 Princess of Wales's Stakes); *Spectrum* (1995 Irish 2000 Guineas; Champion Stakes); *Sunshack* (1995 Coronation Cup; Prix Royal-Oak); *Croco Rouge* (1998 Prix Greffulhe, 1 m 2 f; Prix Lupin, 1 m 2 f); *Nedawi* (1998 St. Leger); *Edabiya* (1998 Gr1 Moyglare Stud Stakes, 7 f 2-y-o fillies); *Multicolored* (1998 Gr2 Geoffrey Freer Stakes, 1 m 5 f); *Special Quest* (1998 Gr2 Prix Noailles, 1 m 3 f); *Millennary* (2000 St. Leger).

Nashwan has sired *Swain* (1996 Coronation Cup; 1997 and 1998 King George VI and Queen Elizabeth Diamond Stakes); and *One So Wonderful* (1998 Juddmonte International Stakes).

Groom Dancer has sired *Pursuit of Love* (1992 Prix Maurice de Gheest, 6 f); *Another Dancer* (m) (1998 Gr2 Prix de Malleret, 1 m 4 f); *Lovers Knot* (f) (1998 Gr2 Falmouth Stakes, 1 m).

Mill Reef
Diminutive, tough little American-bred colt by *Never Bend* (see below). Owned by Paul Mellon and trained at Kingsclere by Ian Balding, *Mill Reef* captured public hearts with his victories in 1971, including the Derby, Eclipse Stakes, King George VI and Queen Elizabeth Diamond Stakes and Prix de l'Arc de Triomphe, as well as the 1972 Prix Ganay and Coronation Cup. His full racing details have been well and affectionately told by John Oaksey in *The Story of Mill Reef* (W.H. Allen, 1975). *Mill Reef* proved immensely successful at the National Stud and his death in 1986 was a sad blow to both connections and breeders in general. The first Derby (and Irish Derby) winner he sired was *Shirley Heights* (1978). Among *Mill Reef*'s other progeny are *Idle Waters* (1978 Park Hill Stakes); *Acamas* (1978 Prix du Jockey-Club); *Fairy Footsteps* (1981 1000 Guineas); *Glint of Gold* (1981 Derby Italiano; Grand Prix de Paris; Gr1 Preis von Europa, 1 m 4 f, Cologne; 1982 Grand Prix de Saint-Cloud; Grosser Preis von Baden); and his brother *Diamond Shoal* (1983 Grand Prix de Saint-Cloud; Grosser Preis von Baden); *Wassl* (1983 Irish 2000 Guineas); *Paris Royal* (1984 Oaks d'Italia); *Reference Point* (1987 Derby; King George VI and Queen Elizabeth Diamond Stakes; St. Leger); *Milligram* (1987 Queen Elizabeth II Stakes; Waterford Crystal Mile); *Ibn Bey* (1978 Gr1 Gran Premio d'Italia, 1 m 4 f; 1998 Gr2 Grand Prix de Deauville; 1989 Preis von Europa); *Doyoun* (1988 2000 Guineas). Among a host of successful mares sired by *Mill Reef* are *Bahamian*, dam of the 1993 Irish Oaks winner, *Wemyss Bight* (see also above under *Dancing Brave*), and *Mill Princess*, dam of *Last Tycoon*.

IN TURN   *Shirley Heights* has sired *High Hawk* (1983 Ribblesdale Stakes); *Darshaan* (1984 Prix du Jockey-Club); *Head for Heights* (1984 King Edward VII Stakes; Princess of Wales's Stakes); *Slip Anchor* (1995 Derby); *Perpendicular* (1992 Prince of Wales's Stakes); *Zinaad* (1993 Jockey Club Stakes); *Highflying* (1993 Northumberland Plate); *Arcadian Heights* (1994 Ascot Gold Cup;

Doncaster Cup); *Stelvio* (1995 Queen's Vase); *Top Cees* (1995 and 1997 Chester Cup; 1999 Cesarewitch).

Slip Anchor has sired *User Friendly*, the outstanding filly of 1992 (Oaks; Irish Oaks; St. Leger; and brave runner-up, beaten only by a neck by *Subotica*, in the 'Arc' that season; 1993 Grand Prix de Saint-Cloud); *Sarawat* (1993 Ebor Handicap); *Posidonas* (1995 Gr1 Gran Premio d'Italia, 1 m 4 f, Milan; 1996 Princess of Wales's Stakes; 1998 Hardwicke Stakes).

Doyoun has sired *Daylami* (1997 French 2000 Guineas; 1998 Eclipse Stakes; Gr1 Man O'War Stakes, 1 m 3 f, Belmont Park; 1999 Coronation Cup; King George VI and Queen Elizabeth Diamond Stakes; Gr1 Champion Stakes, 1 m 2 f; Breeders Cup Turf, 1 m 4 f). *Kalanisi* (2000 Champion Stakes; Breeders Cup Turf).

IN TURN
AGAIN   *Darshaan* has sired *Aliysa* (1989 Oaks winner but subsequently disqualified; see Chapter Eight); *Hellenic* (1990 Ribblesdale Stakes; Yorkshire Oaks); *Kotashan* (1993 Breeders Cup Turf); *Mark of Esteem* (1996 2000 Guineas; Queen Elizabeth II Stakes); *Key Change* (1996 Yorkshire Oaks); *Make No Mistake* (1998 Gr2 Royal Whip, 1 m 2 f, Curragh); *Sayarshan* (1998 Gr2 Prix Hocquart, 1 m 3 f); *Dalakhani* (2003 Gr1 Prix Lupin, 1 m 2 f+; Prix du Jockey-Club; Prix de l'Arc de Triomphe); *Mezzo Soprano* (2003 Gr1 Prix Vermeille, 1m 4 f).

Never Bend
Foaled in 1940, by *Nasrullah*, one of the greatest and most influential sires of the 20th century, and exported to the USA. *Mill Reef* apart (see above), *Never Bend* also sired *Riverman* (1972 French 2000 Guineas; Prix d'Ispahan, 1 m 1 f; Prix Jean Prat, 1 m 1 f).

IN TURN   *Riverman* has sired *Irish River* (1979 French 2000 Guineas; Prix Jacques le Marois; Prix du Moulin); *Policeman* (1980 Prix du Jockey-Club); *Detroit* (1980 Prix de l'Arc de Triomphe); *Gold River* (1980 Prix Royal-Oak; 1982 Prix du Cadran; Prix de l'Arc de Triomphe); *River Lady* (1982 French 1000 Guineas); *Rousillon* (1984 Waterford Crystal Mile; 1985 Queen Anne Stakes; Sussex Stakes; Prix du Moulin); *Triptych* (1985 Irish 2000 Guineas; 1986 and 1987 Champion Stakes; 1987 Gr1 Phoenix Champion Stakes; Matchmaker International; Gr1 Prix Ganay, 1 m 2 f; 1987 and 1988 Coronation Cup, 1 m 4 f) – one of the great fillies of recent times (see page 35); *Al Maheb* (1990 Prix Kergolay, 1 m 7 f; Northumberland Plate, 2 m; Doncaster Cup); *Lahib* (1992 Queen Anne Stakes; Queen Elizabeth II Stakes); *All At Sea* (1992 Prix du Moulin); *Bahri* (1995 St. James's Palace Stakes; Queen Elizabeth

II Stakes); *Kingfisher Mill* (1997 King Edward VII Stakes); *Loup Sauvage* (1998 Gr1 Prix d'Ispahan, 1 m 1 f).

Irish River has sired *Hatoof* (1992 1000 Guineas; Gr2 Prix de l'Opera, 1 m 1 f; E.P. Taylor Stakes, Woodbine, Toronto; 1993 Champion Stakes); and *Brief Truce* (1992 St. James's Palace Stakes).

Rousillon has sired *Vintage Crop* (see under *Busted*).

Busted
Owned by Stanhope Joel, *Busted* may never have achieved what he did nor produced his many winners at stud had his owner's original intentions come to fruition. Like *March Past*, he was yet another notable escapee from the vet's knife, to the immense benefit of thoroughbred breeding. (But see, in particular, *Height of Fashion* below. She was a beneficiary in this way on both sides of her pedigree, being by *Busted*'s son *Bustino*, out of HM the Queen's 1974 1000 Guineas and Prix de Diane winner, *Highclere*, who was a grand-daughter of *March Past*). Regarding *Busted*, Noel Murless was appalled at the idea of his being gelded (with a view to hurdling) and so he was trained as four-year-old and as such he was undefeated, winning four races, including the 1967 Eclipse Stakes and, later the same month, the King George VI and Queen Elizabeth Stakes. His progeny include *Weaver's Hall* (1973 Irish Derby); *Bustino* (1974 St. Leger; 1975 Coronation Cup; King George VI and Queen Elizabeth Diamond Stakes); *Crash Course* (1975 Doncaster Cup); *Tromos* (1978 Dewhurst Stakes); *Busaca* (1977 Yorkshire Oaks); *Mtoto* (1987 and 1988 Eclipse Stakes; 1988 King George VI and Queen Elizabeth Diamond Stakes).

IN TURN   *Weaver's Hall* has sired *El Badr* (1982 Prix du Cadran); and *Weaver's Pin* (1983 Northumberland Plate).

Bustino has sired *Alma Ata* (f) (1981 Park Hill Stakes); *Bustomi* (1981 King Edward VII Stakes); *Easter Sun* (1982 Coronation Cup); *Dish Dash* (f) (1982 Ribblesdale Stakes); *Height of Fashion* (f) (1982 Princess of Wales's Stakes); *Borushka* (1984 Park Hill Stakes); *Rakaposhi King* (1987 Ormonde Stakes, 1 m 5 f); *Terimon* (500/1 runner-up 1989 Derby); *Overplay* (dam of *Vintage Crop* who won the 1992 Cesarewitch; 1993 and 1994 Irish St. Leger; 1993 Melbourne Cup; 1995, at 8-y-o, Gr3 Curragh Cup); *Mysilv* (1994 Triumph Hurdle; 1995 Tote Gold Trophy).

Height of Fashion became the dam of *Unfuwain* (see under *Northern Dancer*) and *Nashwan* (see under *Blushing Groom*).

Mtoto has sired *Shaamit* (1996 Derby) and *Celeric* (1996 Northumberland Plate; Jockey Club Cup; 1997 Yorkshire Cup; Ascot Gold Cup); *Book at Bedtime* (f) (1997 Park Hill Stakes).

Sharpen Up

A grandson of *Native Dancer*. Unbeaten as 2-y-o in 1971, culminating in the Middle Park Stakes, he was not quite good enough in top sprinting company in 1972, but proved highly successful at stud with winning progeny at a surprising number of distances. Sprinters include *Sharpo* (1982 July Cup; 1980–82 Nunthorpe Stakes); milers include *Kris* (1979 champion, including Sussex Stakes, Queen Elizabeth II Stakes) and *Selkirk* (1991 Queen Elizabeth Stakes; 1992 Lockinge Stakes); and the list of impressive middle-distance performers includes the redoubtable heroine *Pebbles* (1985 Eclipse Stakes; Champion Stakes; Breeders Cup Turf); *Trempolino* (1987 Prix de l'Arc de Triomphe); and *Sanglamore* (1990 Prix du Jockey-Club). In addition *Sharpen Up* sired a full brother to *Kris*, also owned and bred by Lord Howard de Walden, out of *Doubly Sure* (by the French stayer of 1965 *Reliance II*). This was *Diesis,* whose career mirrored that of his sire in that he proved himself only as a 2-y-o, winning both the 1982 Gr1 Middle Park Stakes and Dewhurst Stakes, but then went on to distinguish himself at stud with winners over a variety of distances.

IN TURN   *Kris* has proved a prolific sire of Group winners over the entire stamina spectrum: *Oh So Sharp* (most brilliant filly of 1985 with 1000 Guineas, Oaks and St. Leger to her credit); *Sure Blade* (1986 St. James's Palace Stakes; Queen Elizabeth II Stakes); *Unite* (1987 Oaks); *Shavian* (1990 St. James's Palace Stakes); *Landowner* (1992 Queen's Vase); *Oh So Risky* (1993 Nassau Stakes, 1 m 2 f); *Single Empire* (1997 Derby Italiano); *Dr. Fong* (1998 St. James's Palace Stakes); *Balisada* (1999 Coronation Stakes).

Diesis has sired *Diminuendo* (1988 Oaks); *Keen Hunter* (1991 Prix de L'Abbaye); *Knifebox* (1992 and 1993 Select Stakes, 1 m 2 f 1993 Prix Dollar, 1 m 1 f+); *Enharmonic* (Gr3 at a mile in HM The Queen's colours in Germany and Spain 1992 and 1993); *Gneiss* (1994 Jersey Stakes, 7 f); *Halling* (1995 and 1996 Eclipse Stakes Juddmonte International Stakes); *Ramruma* (1999 Oaks); *Love Divine* (2000 Oaks).

Selkirk has sired *Wince* (1999 1000 Guineas).

Sharpo has sired *Risk Me* (1987 Gr1 Prix Jean Prat, 1 m 1 f; Grand Prix de Paris); *Sharp Prod* (1993 and 1994 various Listed and Pattern events at 6 f/7 f in Germany and Italy); *College Chapel* (1993 Prix Maurice de Gheest; Cork and Orrery Stakes, 6 f), *Penny Drops* (f) (1993 Cambridgeshire Handicap; 1994 Gardner Merchant Mile; 1995 various Listed and Pattern races in Italy and Germany); *Port Lucaya* (1993 Gr2 Grosser Preis von Dusseldorf, 1 m; 1994 Gr1 Premio Vittorio di Capua, 1 m); *Lavinia Fontana* (m) (1994 Haydock Park Sprint Cup); *Leap For Joy* (1995 and 1996 Gr3 Premio Omenoni).

Known Fact
Owned by Khaled Abdulla, became, in 1980, the first Arab-owned Classic winner in this country when awarded the 2000 Guineas on the disqualification of *Nureyev*. Later that season, he also won the Waterford Crystal Mile and Queen Elizabeth II Stakes. At stud he has sired *Warning* (1988 Sussex Stakes; Queen Elizabeth II Stakes; 1989 Queen Anne Stakes); *Markofdistinction* (1990 Queen Anne Stakes; Queen Elizabeth II Stakes); and *So Factual* (1995 Nunthorpe Stakes).

IN TURN   *Warning* has sired *Prophecy* (f) (1993, at 2-y-o, Cheveley Park Stakes); *Piccolo* (1994 Nunthorpe Stakes, 5 f; 1995 King's Stand Stakes, 5f); *Charnwood Forest* (1996 Queen Anne Stakes, 1 m; Gr2 Challenge Stakes, 7 f); *Averti* (1997 King George V Stakes, 5 f); *Decorated Hero* (1997 Gr2 Prix du Rond-Point, 1 m; 1998 Challenge Stakes); *Little Rock* (2000 Gr2 Princess of Wales's Stakes, 1 m 4 f) and *Give Notice* (2002 Gr1 Prix du Cadran).

Mr Prospector
Comes from the male line of *Native Dancer* (sire of *Northern Dancer*'s dam, *Natalma*), who is, via *Raise a Native*, the grandsire of *Mr Prospector*. *Mr Prospector* has sired *Miswaki* (1980, at 2-y-o, Gr1 Prix de la Salamandre, 7 f); *Gone West* (1984); *Woodman* (1985, at 2-y-o, Gr3 Ferrans Futurity, Curragh); *Machiavellian* (1989, at 2-y-o, Gr1 Prix Morny, 6 f; Gr1 Prix de la Salamandre, 7 f; runner-up 1990 2000 Guineas); *Placerville* (1993 Prince of Wales's Stakes); *Kingmambo* (1993 French 2000 Guineas; St. James's Palace Stakes; Prix du Moulin); *Macoumba* (f) (1994, at 2-y-o, Gr1 Prix Marcel Boussac, 1 m); *Distant View* (1994 Sussex Stakes); *Ta Rib* (1996 French 1000 Guineas). Also sired *Lion Cavern* and *Storm Cat*.

IN TURN   *Storm Cat* has sired *Black Minnaloushe* (2001 Irish 2000 Guineas; Gr1 St. James's Palace Stakes, 1 m); *Sophisticat* (Gr1 Coronation Stakes, 1 m 3-y-o fillies); *Nebraska Tornado* (2003 Prix de Diane; Gr1 Prix du Moulin, 1 m 3-y-o colts and fillies).

             Miswaki has sired *Midyan* (1987 Jersey Stakes, 7 f); *Urban Sea* (1993 Prix de l'Arc de Triomphe); *Misil* (1991 Italian 2000 Guineas; 1992 Gr1 Premio Roma, 1 m 2 f; 1993 Gran Premio del Jockey Club, 1 m 4 f, Milan); *Allied Forces* (1997 Queen Anne Stakes).

             Gone West has sired *Zafonic* (1993 2000 Guineas), who, in turn, has sired *Alrassaam* (2000 Gr2 Budweiser International Stakes, 1 m 1 f); also in 2000 several 2-y-o Pattern winners including *Count Dubois* (Gr1 Gran Criterium, Italy); *Endless Summer* (Gr2 Richmond Stakes) and *Clearing* (Gr3 Horris Hill Stakes), as well as *Zee Zee Top* (2003 Gr1 Prix de l'Opera, 1 m 2 f 3-y-o+ fillies and mares) and *Zafeem* (2003 Gr1 St. James's Palace Stakes, 1 m).

             Woodman has sired *Hector Protector* (1991 French 2000 Guineas; Prix Jacques le Marois), *Bosra Sham* (1996 1000 Guineas;

Champion Stakes; 1997 Prince of Wales's Stakes); *Hula Angel* (1999 Irish 1000 Guineas) and *Hawk Wing* (2002 Gr1 Eclipse Stakes, 1 m 2 f 3-y-o+; 2003 Gr1 Lockinge Stakes, 1 m 4-y-o+).

Machiavellian has sired *Invermark* (1998 Gr1 Prix du Cadran, 2 m 4 f); *Medicean* (2001 Gr1 Eclipse Stakes, 1 m 2 f) and *Patavellian* (2003 Goodwood Stewards' Cup; Gr1 Prix de l'Abbaye, 5 f).

Midyan has sired *Beauchamp Hero* (1995 Hardwicke Stakes; Princess of Wales's Stakes); *Alhijaz* (1993 Gr1 Premio Vittorio di Capua, 1 m, Milan); *Tioman Island* (1994 Coppa d'Oro di Milano, 1 m 7 f; Goodwood Cup, 2 m).

Lion Cavern has sired *Crimplene* (2000 Irish 1000 Guineas; German 1000 Guineas; Coronation Stakes).

Kingmambo sired *King's Best* (2000 2000 Guineas) and *Bluemamba* (2000 French 1000 Guineas); *Russian Rhythm* (2003 1000 Guineas; Gr1 Coronation Stakes, 1 m 3-y-o fillies; Gr1 Nassau Stakes, 1 m 1 f+ 3-y-o fillies and mares).

Ahonoora
Leading sprinter of 1979, winning both the sponsored equivalent of the Nunthorpe Stakes and the King George V Stakes. Has sired *Don't Forget Me* (1987 2000 Guineas; Irish 2000 Guineas); *Statoblest* (1989 King George V Stakes; 1990 Palace House Stakes, 5 f); *Indian Ridge* (1988 Jersey Stakes; 1989 King's Stand Stakes); *Dr. Devious* (1992 Derby; Irish Champion Stakes). *Ruby Tiger* was another great success sired by *Ahonoora*. Her victories at 1 m 2 f included the 1990 E.P. Taylor Stakes at Woodbine and the Gr2 Premio Lydia Tesio in Rome, as well as the Gr2 Nassau Stakes in 1991 and 1992.

IN TURN   *Indian Ridge* has sired *Ridgewood Pearl* (1995 Irish 1000 Guineas; Coronation Stakes; Prix du Moulin; Breeders Cup Mile); *Namid* (2000 Gr1 Prix de l'Abbaye, 5 f)

Efisio
Won the 1985 Challenge Stakes, 7 f; 1986 Gr1 Premio Emilio Turati, 1 m, Milan; 1987 Gr2 Premio Chiosura, 7 f, Milan. He has become an excellent sire of sprinters including the top-class *Hever Golf Rose* (1995 Gr1 Prix de l'Abbaye; Gr2 Goldene Peitsche, 6 f, Baden-Baden; plus 1994–98 wins in six other Group and five Listed sprints, and placed at Group level 11 times – total earnings £659,789. See also under **Sprinters** in Chapter One); *Pip's Pride* (1993 Grosser Preis von Berlin, 6 f); *Hello Mister* (1994 and 1995 Tote Portland Handicap, trained by then octogenarian, the late Jack O'Donoghue); *Young Ern* (1994 Prix du Palais-Royal; Hungerford Stakes – both at 7 f); *Tomba* (1997 Grosser Preis von Berlin; 1998 Gr2 Cork and Orrery Stakes, 6 f; Gr1 Prix de la Foret, 7 f); *Pearly Shells* (2002 Gr1 Prix Vermeille, 1 m 4 f 3-y-o fillies); *Attraction* (2004 1000 Guineas; Irish 1000 Guineas; Coronation Stakes).

Before leaving the Flat-race breeding scene, here are two comments, the first by the late John Hislop from his excellent book on *Brigadier Gerard*: 'Some breeders are prejudiced against old stallions, often wrongly.   Provided his health is unimpaired and his fertility is still good, a stallion is just as likely to get a good horse at twenty as at six. In fact, some have sired their best offspring in their last season at stud, for instance, *Donatello II*, whose best son, *Crepello*, was among his sire's last crop.'

Lastly, from the *Biographical Encyclopaedia of British Flat Racing* (see Bibliography) regarding that phenomenally fast horse, *The Tetrarch*, foaled 1911 (see under Atty Persse in Chapter Nine): 'His owner described *The Tetrarch's* attitude at the stud as "monastic in the extreme." In consequence *The Tetrarch* was a bad foal-getter and got steadily worse in that respect. He had been sterile for ten years before his death in 1935. He only got 130 foals altogether, of which 80 were winners. In his closing years this once phenomenal racehorse was completely white in colour, very dipped in the back, and used to be ridden with the letters down to the local post-office.'

That seems such a sad comment on a once-great racehorse, but the next paragraph corrects the impression: 'Considering how few foals he got, *The Tetrarch's* stud record was remarkably good. He was champion sire in 1919, twice third and once fourth. He got three St. Leger winners, *Caligula, Polemarch* and *Salmon Trout*. If those three inherited stamina, *The Tetrarch* imparted immense speed in *Tetratema*, later champion sire; and also to the brilliant *Mumtaz Mahal*, ancestress of *Mahmoud* and *Nasrullah*. *The Tetrarch*, in fact, made an immense contribution to bloodstock breeding...' Which goes to show that quality rather than quantity, happily, prevailed.

Top Six Sires of 2003 on the Flat

Stallion	Foaled	Sire	Wins	Earnings (£)
1. Sadler's Wells	1981	Northern Dancer	76	3,458,787
2. Danehill	1986	Danzig	56	1,459,082
3. Key Of Luck	1991	Chief's Crown	12	1,411,191
4. Kris S	1977	Roberto	9	1,303,850
5. Indian Ridge	1985	Ahonoora	49	880,308
6. Cadeaux Genereux	1985	Young Generation	41	817,698

The National Hunt scene

It is a widely held notion that the breeding of a jumper does not matter a great deal. The contrary is proved by sires such as *Vulgan*, who dominated the scene for many years and not only because of the great number of mares he covered. Similar proof was once given by the prolific National Hunt sire *Deep Run*.

Leading Jumping Sires 1999–2000

Stallion	Rnrs	Wnrs	W/R %	Wins	Earnings (£)	Top Earner
1. Be My Native	453	137	30.2	256	1,899,691	Native Upmanship
2. Strong Gale	291	103	35.4	204	1,542,550	Marlborough
3. Phardante	327	84	25.7	135	999,844	Niki Dee

4. Roselier	249	62	24.9	128	928,314	Bindaree
5. Supreme Leader	296	82	27.7	131	915,564	What's Up Boys
6. King's Ride	173	48	27.7	87	775,040	Mister Morose
7. Zaffaran	53	22	41.5	50	725,217	Looks Like Trouble
8. Orchestra	125	39	31.2	67	675,737	Dorans Pride
9. Montelimar	169	50	29.6	99	667,095	Youlneverwalkalon
10. Lafontaine	52	21	40.4	46	591,100	Papillon

Before leaving the National Hunt scene, a brief note on the proliferation o French-bred recruits to British jumping. This is something to watch out for, witl Martin Pipe having led the way buying over the Channel for some time, an Henrietta Knight (with for example, *Edredon Bleu*, Grand Annual Chase winne of 1998 and winner of 2000 Queen Mother Champion Chase) being anothe enthusiast for these well-schooled horses – and not forgetting Francois Doumei (winning trainer in the King George VI Chase five times) with his frequent an successful raids over here, which were a notable feature (with a double, fo example, at Aintree) of the 2000–01 NH season. In an article in *Horse and Houna* Sue Montgomery amplified the details of a growing trend:

'One of the features of the National Hunt scene in recent years has been th mark made by high-class French-bred horses. Steady progress by imports fron across the Channel during the 1990s climaxed in the 1999/2000 season with a bes ever 25 victories in pattern contests, the grade one, two and three races that forn the elite levels of the sport.

'During the current campaign, with most of the top races yet to come, they ha already notched 12 victories by the middle of last month and in *First Gold*, *Geos Edredon Bleu* and *Baracouda* have the first or second favourites for the four senio championships at the Cheltenham Festival.*

'It was the victory of unheralded *Nupsala* in the 1987 King George VI Chase when he had the temerity to interrupt *Desert Orchid*'s sequence of wins, that wa one of the catalysts for the invasion by the French foreign legions.

'With it came the dawning recognition that the best French jumpers Thoroughbreds and the indigenous half-bred Selle Français strain – were well u to taking on their counterparts in Britain and Ireland. British-based owners trainers and agents have taken the hint and a lively trade has developed.'

Postscript

In the foregoing chapter, the concentration has necessarily been on sires. Thi postscript is intended to redress the balance a little and acknowledge the par played by some wonderful broodmares and their families (and if anyone doubt their documented importance the various volumes of *Keylock's Dams of Winner* can be consulted). In Turf history there have been many famous broodmare including *Penelope* (1798), successful herself in 18 races and dam of the brother *Whalebone* and *Whisker*. Both were Derby winners, and had great influence i continuing the line of *Eclipse*. *Pocahontas*, meanwhile, was one of the longest-live as well as probably the greatest broodmare on record. She was 33 years old whei she died in 1870, having had a profound effect on thoroughbred breedin through her sons *Stockwell*, *Rataplan* and *King Tom*.

* Which, in the event, had to be cancelled because of foot-and-mouth disease.

But it is impossible here to pay tribute to all the important broodmare families, such as, for example, those descended from the royal mare *Feola* (1933), the Jim Joel mare *Picture Play* (1941), and the late Richard Hollingsworth's *Felucca* (1941). An entire book could be devoted to these and other famous families (e.g. at random, those including *Pretty Polly, Conjure, Lady Josephine, Selene, Weighbridge, Red Sunset, Double Life* etc., etc.).

So the following are a few of my own favourites, beginning with *Oh So Fair* (1967), whom I saw and who ransacked my wife's handbag for mints on a visit to Dalham Hall some years ago. She was a phenomenal broodmare, producing *Roussalka* (1975 Coronation Stakes) and *Etienne Gerard* (1977 Jersey Stakes) – therefore two Group winners at Royal Ascot; *Our Home*, runner-up in the 1000 Guineas of 1980; and the star of them all, *Oh So Sharp*, who in 1985 swept the Classic board with the 1000 Guineas, Oaks and St. Leger. Next comes the incredible *Mrs Moss* (1969), who was the apple of Lady Tavistock's eye at the Bloomsbury Stud, Woburn.   *Mrs Moss* produced *Jupiter Island* (1983 Ebor Handicap and several Group races, including the 1985 Hardwicke Stakes and 1986 Japan Cup), as well as other successes, including *Pushy* (1980 Queen Mary Stakes) and *Precocious* (1983 Gimcrack Stakes).   *Height of Fashion* (1979) has already been mentioned as dam of *Unfuwain* and *Nashwan*, while another of my favourites is *Slightly Dangerous* (1979), dam of the champion miler of 1988, *Warning*, and also (by *Dancing Brave*) of the 1993 Derby and Irish Derby winner, *Commander-in-Chief*.

Finally the story of Meon Valley Stud (who now sponsor the Group One Fillies Mile for 2-y-o at the Ascot Festival) makes heartwarming reading. Back in 1977, the textile businessman Egon Weinfeld invested in three yearling fillies to become eventually broodmares, for 'a bit of fun'. That expectation has been far exceeded, with spectacular success in produce for this small Hampshire stud and fame for the Helena Springfield colours, which the fillies advertised. The original fillies were *One In A Million, Reprocolor* and *Odeon. One In A Million* won the 1979 1000 Guineas. She produced *Milligram* (1987 Gr1 Queen Elizabeth II Stakes), and is grand-dam of *One So Wonderful* (1998 Gr1 Juddmonte International Stakes) and third dam of *Kissogram* (1998 Gr2 Sun Chariot Stakes). *Reprocolor* has produced *Colorspin* (1986 Irish Oaks) and *Cezanne* (Gr1 Irish Champion Stakes [see above under **Ajdal**]). *Colorspin* in turn has produced *Opera House* (1993 Coronation Cup; Eclipse Stakes; King George VI and Queen Elizabeth Diamond Stakes – all Gr1) and his full brother *Kayf Tara* (1998 and 2000 Ascot Gold Cup; 1998 and 1999 Irish St. Leger – both Gr1). Meanwhile *Odeon* is the grand-dam of *Lady Carla* (1996 Oaks).

Here is an up-date (2003) on the marvellous Meon Valley Stud: *Reprocolor* is still the main influence, but the emphasis has moved from her daughters to more distant descendants…moreover, *Colorspin* has conceived to *Galileo* and thus is carrying a very close relative of *Kayf Tara* and *Opera House*. What a wonderful advertisement for broodmares to conclude the chapter!

CHAPTER ELEVEN
Systems

Follow a winning two-year-old until it gets beaten, and then back the one that beats it.

There was a time when the affable face of Ralph Freeman used to look out from the advertisements in *Ruff's Guide*. He would be smoking a big cigar and proclaimed not only that he had laid and paid the owner of *Mill House* £50 each way at 200/1 for the Cheltenham Gold Cup (which the horse had won, SP 7/4 Fav) but that 'Large or Small. Ralph Freeman Ltd will operate Any Systems'. I know of no comparable advertisement today, which is a little odd, because as Jack Leach (author of the advice at the head of this chapter) wrote in *Sods I Have Cut On The Turf*: 'Systems? Bookmakers love them.'

Systems fall under three main headings:
1. Those which involve blind backing irrespective of a study of form or other considerations on the part of the backer. They are the horseracing equivalent of roulette systems and include all blind backing of favourites, second favourites etc., jockeys' mounts, trainers, newspaper naps, top-weights in Nursery Handicaps, low/high numbers in the draw, forecast betting involving the favourite to beat or be beaten by the field, second-favourite each way in fields of eight runners, 12-to-follow bets, and so on. The intrinsic flaw in such systems is that they do not offer the precise mathematical odds involved in winning or losing in a casino. The first factor contributing to this is the horse itself, which, unlike the roulette wheel, can have moods, pull a muscle, feel off colour, or, if a filly, come unexpectedly into season just before a race. The system also compels backing a horse regardless of whether it likes hard going or heavy ground; whether it is ridden by a Pat Eddery or an apprentice having his or her first ride in public; whether it is on a suitable galloping course or an unsuitable sharp track; whether it has no chance whatsoever on the form book. Systems involving favourites further suffer from and frequently founder on the surfeit of short prices inseparable from the operation.

In 1992 Craig Thake produced in the *Racing Post* an illuminating analysis of the dubious profitability of following favourites, beginning with these words: 'There can be no greater joy for a bookmaker than to see the word "favourite" on a betting slip, as such indiscriminate favourite-backing will always lose in the long run.' He went on to show that over the jumps, in only six out of 44 courses did the first market choice show an overall profit in the four-year period from August 1988 to August 1992. Similarly, on the Flat, on only six out of 35 courses did favourites return an overall profit in a similar four-season period. These were the 'winners':

Favourites (over jumps)

Aug 88–Jun 92	Per cent	£1 Stake
1. Fontwell	48%	+£34.29
2. Perth	51%	+£21.28
3. Haydock	51%	+£20.47
4. Taunton	41%	+£6.04
5. Cartmel	53%	+£4.58
6. Doncaster	48%	+£1.47

Favourites (Flat)

1988–91	Per cent	£1 Stake
1. Redcar	32%	+£41.26
2. Newcastle	44%	+£23.26
3. Southwell	40%	+£20.58
4. Ripon	38%	+£7.26
5. York	34%	+£2.06
6. Chepstow	36%	+£0.87

Favourites do best when the going is good or good to firm, and enough form is available of a consistent variety, but, in general, backing favourites doesn't pay in the long run, nor does blind backing of jockeys, trainers, or newspaper naps. Systems involving these inevitably strike long losing runs from time to time; some jockeys show sizeable profits at some courses, but far more show colossal losses to a level stake wagered on them every time they have a ride.

2. These 'systems' could perhaps best be called limited systems. They all involve a degree of selectivity and judgement on the part of the backer arising from a study of form and other factors. They are, essentially, an amendment of category 1. systems. For example, instead of backing every favourite irrespective of any factor other than it being the favourite, it is decided to limit the system to 'only on good or good to firm going, and only if ridden by one of the six most successful jockeys'.

3. The third category is not really a system as such, but is so-called as in the phrase, 'I've got a system', meaning, 'I've got a method of finding winners which seems to work'. Into this bracket comes following the market, following in-form trainers and jockeys, beaten favourites dropped in class, horses carrying penalties for easy wins on their previous outing, and so on.

Backing top-weights in Nursery Handicaps is thought to be a profitable system, and in some seasons this is the case. But in the majority of seasons it is not. There were 107 Nurseries run in 1993. Top-weights won 20 of them at prices ranging from 4/5 favourite to 14/1. Overall, a very small loss after tax (now abolished) would have been shown if every top-weight had been backed off-course. In 1998, there were 101 Nurseries. In 20 cases, the top-weight was made favourite, but of the 20 only seven succeeded. Altogether, there were only 14 winners out of the 101. Despite some rewarding prices – 11/1, 10/1, 8/1, for example – backing every top-weight for a £1 win stake would have produced an overall loss of £21.62.

Forecast betting
Any systems based on forecast betting are not to be recommended from the outset, whether Tote Dual Forecast or the Bookmakers Computer Straight Forecast. Systems involving fields of four, five and six runners have been tested. None of them pay off, and in fields beyond these small numbers of runners, when dividends may be higher, the outlay is too great to justify a system.

Second-favourite each way in fields of eight runners
This system cannot be operated 'blind' – i.e. with unnamed second-favourites – since bookmakers will not take bets on such selections except win only. The system depends therefore on observation of the market. Backing second-favourites each way in fields of eight runners gives three chances of some success to five chances of failure. This was highly profitable in the days when book-makers paid a quarter of the odds a place in fields of eight runners. Today it is less so, because bookmakers pay only one-fifth of the odds a place in such fields. So, an 11/2 place horse is required to break even, and far fewer second-favourites start at that price than at 4/1, which was the old break-even figure.

To illustrate how bookmakers have closed down on what used to be a 'knocking' bet, these are the results from one summer month in the days when good profits could be expected by backers using the 'system':

22 placed second-favourites (July 1962)
Prices 6/1, 11/2, 5/1 x 3, 9/2, 4/1 x 9, 7/2 x 3, 11/4, 15/8, 7/4, 6/4
Resulting in at a quarter of the odds a place: six marginal winners, nine break even, seven losers.
But today at one-fifth of the odds, these figures would become: one marginal winner, one break even, 20 losers.

Today this system can still be expected to be profitable, though not as handsomely as before. However, observation of the market in itself presents an occasional danger that the wrong 'second-favourite' will be chosen. Last-second shifts in the betting might make what appears to be a firm second-favourite into a favourite (particularly in a weak market). Alternatively it might be displaced out to third-favourite, but this does not happen often enough to invalidate the general strategy.

Finally, outside all the categories come some systems which, without putting a single coin on a horse, might avoid losses, and thus be judged to turn in a consistent profit. Negative systems such as these will make no appeal to the majority of punters, who, like Oscar Wilde, can be relied on to resist anything but temptation. Nonetheless the following methods have stood the test of time in helping to avoid an examination in bankruptcy:

Odds-on favourites
These do not generally appeal to small backers, but the prices of the next best in the market often do, irrespective of the merit of the horses concerned. The system here is not to oppose an odds-on favourite, because the next best is 5/1 against. Better no bet than a 5/1 loser, backed on the previous principle that the

favourite's odds are too short to warrant an interest. In any case, remembering, for example, *Brigadier Gerard*'s odds-on victories, it was pleasure enough just to see him win.

The eight-race card
Normally there are six races on a card, often there are seven when races have to be divided, and sometimes eight. Eight betting opportunities, it seems, but, in fact, there may be none at all. The system here is not to have a bet in every race simply for the sake of it and in recognition that the opportunity is there.

The getting-out stakes
Traditionally the last race on the card, when every fancied runner has gone down in the previous five races: the bookmakers are as near to dancing on their boxes as they ever will be; the floor of Tattersalls' Ring is knee deep in lost hopes in the shape of torn-up losing tickets; and punters turn to the last race as the final desperate resort. Like temptation itself, difficult to resist, but a winning system here is to remember the old song: 'There's Always Tomorrow'.

Beware get-rich-quick schemes
As an appropriate finale to this chapter, here is an article from the *Racing Post* (January 1999) by that doughty campaigner for the punter, David Ashforth. It appeared under the heading '"Winning system" is an old formula' and is reprinted by kind permission of the *Racing Post*'s editor:
'Over 30 years ago, me and my mate Len invented a system. At least, we thought we had invented it. It was based on Lester Piggott. The first thing you did was decide how much you wanted to win. We decided £2. Then you backed Lester's first mount, to win £2. If it won, you started again. If it lost, you put enough on Lester's next mount to win £2 plus what you had lost on the first bet.
'Lester was champion jockey, and rarely had a long run of losers. That was the theory. Piggott's next seven mounts lost. So we backed mount eight and, when it won, claimed our net £2 profit, and heaved a mighty sigh of relief, because our pockets were empty.
'We had spotted a flaw in the system. Later, I realised that our idea wasn't original. The system, capable of countless variations, was older than Lester himself, so it comes as a surprise to learn that an organisation called Tic-Tac is charging £1,995 a year for what seems to me to be a variation on the same theme.
'Tic-Tac advertises "A Dynamic Money Making Method That You Have Never Seen Or Heard About Before. Since January 1 1998 you could have won over £58,000. You could have a very good Christmas in 20 days. Yes, just think, £2,000–£10,000 right there now in only 20 days. You owe it to yourself and your family to take this opportunity right now."
'To reassure waverers, there is a money-back guarantee. If the "Tic-Tac Daily Profit Plan" shows a loss in more than one of its first seven days, then the subscription will be refunded. Those who lash out £1,995, or £1,495 for four months, receive a brief "Profit Plan". The apparent novelty in the system is that Tic-Tac suggests which meetings clients get involved with, "but it is your choice

in the end". There may well be other refinements. If not, it is a familiar version of the ancient formula, based on favourites at a particular meeting.

'The Plan explains that, if you decide you want to win £100 a day, and the first favourite is 5-2, you need to stake £40. If the favourite wins, that is it for the day. If the favourite loses, Tic-Tac seems to believe that, to reach your daily profit target of £100, with the second race favourite at evens, "that would mean we need to win £240 which is £120 stake, that is £40 lost on the first race, and we need to win our £100 for the day".

'Tic-Tac's English and Maths have floored me. I thought you needed to win £140, made up of your £100 profit target plus the £40 lost on the first race. Your stake would therefore be £140, ignoring tax [now abolished]. The flaws in Tic-Tac's "Daily Profit Plan" are the same as the flaws in all its predecessors – or are they? Mike Bramley, a partner in Tic-Tac, is adamant that the system is profitable and that it is more than just a variation on our old Piggott system. "I am saying it works," Bramley told me, "and I can prove it works. Our clients are happy. Whether it's an old system or not, it's a winning system. There has not been a losing day since October and, last year, there were only nine losing days."

'Has Tic-Tac discovered gold, or only fool's gold? Had Nomura better get a move on with its flotation of William Hill, before it's too late? Without knowing which meetings Tic-Tac's clients have been advised to get involved with, and one or two other aspects of the system, it is impossible to know how well the Plan has been working, but anyone blindly pursuing the old-fashioned "cover-to-win" system may have made a good start to 1999.

'Sixty-six meetings have been staged since January 1, and a clear favourite has won at least one race at 64 of those meetings. A joint-favourite was the only favourite to win at Uttoxeter on January 2, and every favourite at Plumpton failed on January 18. Money for the proverbial old rope? If, on January 18, you had decided to win £100 by backing favourites on a "cover-to-win" basis at all three meetings, you would have won your £100 at Doncaster and Southwell but lost £2,433 at Plumpton.

'That would have wiped out the profit from 24 winning meetings, but still left you well up – in theory, at least. At Doncaster that day, the first six favourites lost. If you were betting tax-free, you would have found yourself putting roughly £1,040 on *All Gong*, the 11-10 favourite in the seventh and final race, at which point you would have staked over £2,000 during the afternoon, to win £100. Let's hope you had £2,000, and your nerve held out.

'At Southwell, where the first five favourites failed, you would have gone through similar torture, staking £1,100 on *China Castle* at 10-11 in order to net your £100. Again, you would have needed a bank of £2,000 to keep going – much more if you were also betting at Doncaster and/or Plumpton.

'Tic-Tac may have steered its clients away from Plumpton, perhaps from Doncaster and Southwell, too, but January 18 illustrates the two major flaws in "cover-to-win" systems. First, sooner or later, there will be a nasty losing run, and a losing run can quickly wipe out your profits. Second, if your bank isn't big enough, you may still lose even on what, in theory, was a winning day.

'Those aren't the only problems. You need to be available throughout each race meeting, and to be certain that you can get your money on. If the medium you choose is favourites, then flip-flopping favourites, joint-favourites and long odds-on favourites complicate matters, as does betting tax.

'For days, weeks, even months, all may go well. But there only needs to be a handful of meetings without a winning favourite for it all to collapse. Maybe Tic-Tac has solved those problems, and a new version of an old system has turned iron pyrites into gold. Maybe.'

CHAPTER TWELVE
Racing Round The World

In Budapest they call it the Magyar St. Leger, and in Denmark, Norway and Sweden respectively, the Dansk, Norsk and Svenskt St. Legers. Germany holds its Deutsches St. Leger, while in Turin not long ago they celebrated the centenary of the St. Leger Italiano.

Australia, fittingly for a country which was quick out of the starting-gate behind England herself in the field of horseracing, stages no fewer than five different St. Legers, from the Group Two Australian Jockey Club event at Randwick in Sydney, to the most humble version at Mowbray in Launceston, Tasmania. Equally, and hardly surprising in view of the foundations of the British Raj, India also boasts five. New Zealand puts on its own St. Leger in windy Wellington, while nearly 7,000 miles east across the Pacific, Chile is a country which holds a race bearing no national attribution whatsoever, being entitled simply: 'St. Leger'.

Yet none of this astonishing international activity would be taking place today were it not for an event held in 1776 on Cantley Common, Doncaster, in Yorkshire: 'A Sweepstakes', distance two miles, open to three-year-old colts, fillies and geldings for a purse of £131. The race was won by the 2nd Marquis of Rockingham's brown filly later given the weird name of *Allabaculia*, starting at 2/1 on and beating four opponents.

At a time of intense British colonial expansion and with a far-flung British army greatly reliant on cavalry, it might be expected that not only trade, but horseracing would also follow the flag. This, indeed, was the case. Australia, for example, inaugurated a St. Leger in 1841. But the gathering fame and prestige of the five British Classic races spread far beyond the bounds of the Empire as it then was. The USA had not long since achieved independence, so it is perhaps surprising that British titles were adopted for its own races. Most of Europe, Scandinavia, China and South America did likewise.

At present, at least 176 races worldwide possess titles which incorporate in some form the names of these original historic contests, their exotic A–Z ranging from the Alberta Derby to the Zimbabwe Guineas. There are no fewer than 74 Derbys, including El Derby (Chile), the Derby Nacional (Peru), the Derby Club (Brazil), the Derby Mexicano and, in America, there are more Derbys than anywhere else in the world, a staggering total of at least 24. The most famous of them, of course, is the Kentucky Derby, dating from 1875.

This, then, is the debt owed and acknowledged by international racing to Britain. On the obverse of the coin, as far as this country looking outwards is concerned, there has never been a greater success in sending horses to compete abroad, chiefly in Europe (although new ground was broken in 1993 when *Drum Taps* was sent to run in the Melbourne Cup), nor a greater return to the benefit of the balance of payments. It was not so half a century ago and for the change in attitude and widening of horizons a major share of credit must go to that brilliant former jockey and equally brilliant trainer, the late Harry Wragg. At Abington Place, Newmarket, where his son, Geoffrey, now trains, the walls are lined with photographs of winners sent out by his father to win abroad, particularly in Germany in the 1960s, although Geoffrey now warns: 'Before you send a horse abroad these days, you've got to be pretty sure it's going to run into a place because the transport costs have really escalated.' This is a statement amplified by Paul Cole: 'It's no good going abroad without a decent horse these days as the standards in Italy and Germany have improved considerably in the last few years.'

Be that as it may, John Dunlop in particular has been a great raider for years, especially in Italy, although he is now extending his net as far as Turkey, where in 1997, when his *Sandstone* won the £47,000 Topkapi Trophy in Istanbul, the first three home were all British-trained. Richard Hannon, Paul Cole, Clive Brittain, Luca Cumani, Barry Hills, Saeed bin Suroor and Henry Cecil are also prominent trainers who reap great rewards abroad.   There were record earnings of £11,295,984 in 1996.   In 1998, the overseas prize-money brought back to this country amounted to £6,795,395, harvested from 14 different countries: well down on the £10 million level of the previous two seasons.

So where does this leave the punter? Answer: fairly well out in the cold, because bookmakers in this country tend to ignore most racing abroad, with the notable exceptions of a good deal of Irish racing, some French, particularly the 'Arc' weekend, and the Breeders Cup in the United States. But, to their credit, they have now also opened up on the Melbourne Cup, Japan Cup and Dubai World Cup.

Of all these, certainly the most popular with British racegoers is the first weekend in October, when the Prix de l'Arc de Triomphe is run, and thousands of British invade Longchamp, many of them with the organisation Horse Racing Abroad, and a fair number preferring Eurostar to the hassle of independent air travel. So here is a look at racing in France.

FRANCE
To most English enthusiasts, French racing is represented above all by that first weekend in October and its entire programme of predominantly important Group races, including the outstanding sprint, the Prix de l'Abbaye de Longchamp, in which our own trainers have an astonishing record of success (see below for 'Arc' and 'Abbaye' details and notes). *Les Anglais* invade Paris in their thousands. As can be seen from the 'Arc' records, the weather is variable, but, if lucky, they will be rewarded with a golden autumn day in the Bois de Boulogne, the grass strewn with fallen horse-chestnuts; with the sight of the unbelievably wide emerald sweep of the courses themselves (three plus a sprint track), overlooked by the ivy-covered old windmill and, more distantly, by the Eiffel Tower. The fronts of the stands are bright with tier upon tier of geraniums; there are parades up the course of military bands, sometimes that of the Cavalerie de la Garde Republicaine, sometimes, say, that of a Guards regiment or of the 17th/21st Lancers complete with drum horses, who are liable to render 'Colonel Bogey' for the benefit of the visitors. The visitors themselves, in turn, help to give atmosphere to Longchamp which, without bookmakers and left to its own

devices, can be dauntingly antiseptic in aspect, however theoretically marvellous the horses and racing. And here a word of warning, there are *two* winning-posts, the farthest of them, when used, indicated in the racecard as '2e Poteau'.

Other disadvantages, which once pointed out need not spoil a marvellous experience: the course commentary, delivered, these days, at a break-neck babble, is unintelligible to all but super-tuned French ears and provides a sad contrast to the lugubrious, leisurely and enjoyable performance of a former commentator who while understandably fracturing names such as *Vaguely Noble* ('Vaggerly Nobluh') also relied heavily not so much on horses' names as the easily recognisable orange-with-grey cap of the then leading owner: '...et en entrant la ligne droite c'est *Fantomas*...suivi par...par..BOUSSAC...' (for graphically reinforcing this recollection, I am obliged particularly to Sir Peter O'Sullevan, who has done more than any man alive to make the English aware of French racing).

In addition, the queues for the Pari-Mutuel (PMU) before the 'Arc' are long and taxing to the patience; the wait between race-finish and pay-out is even longer, and quite unbelievable to the English, who are now used to almost instant declaration of dividends from the Tote at home. The suggestion that the Pari-Mutuel still use ready-reckoners may be unkind; the fact is that their computerised operation, not quite geared across the board to the volume of betting that takes place on 'Arc' day, simply gets swamped, as it has been for at least the past 30 years. Although for most races the PMU booths work well enough, the best advice for the 'Arc' is to take a price ante-post with a book-maker before leaving home.

From 1988 to 1993, the entire weekend's racing was sponsored, indeed, pulled together as a fabulous package of high-class events by the International Hotel Group Ciga under the chairmanship of the Aga Khan (before their sponsorship, nothing much happened on the Saturday; under their aegis, Group events were drafted in from other points of the French Calendar). After Ciga pulled out, Forte's resumed sponsorship, but their contract lasted only until 1996. All the races on 'Arc' day are now sponsored by Lucien Barrière, the leading French casino and hotel group, and once again there has been a reshuffle to make a card, as from the year 2000, with no fewer than five Group One contests including, of course, the 'Arc' itself. Among the changes are the inclusion (from the former Saturday programme) of the long-distance Prix du Cadran and recently up-graded Prix de l'Opéra. In addition there has been a prize-money boost to make it the richest single day's racing in Europe: worth just over £1.5 million, with the 'Arc' alone carrying added money of £1.1 million, including £593,662 to the winner in 2003.

Transport to the races: there are free buses (Navettes Gratuites) running between the Métro station Porte d'Auteuil and the racecourse every 15 minutes from 12.45 pm and every five minutes from 1.30 pm. They return similarly from 4.30 pm onwards up to half an hour after the last race. There are also plentiful buses for return to the Porte d'Auteuil, Porte Maillot and Etoile, but beware rip-off operators.

Racecard: there are two kinds, both free at the gate. First, the old-fashioned two-sided single card the size roughly of a charter of independence and, secondly, on 'Arc' weekend, a lavish production with some useful English translation, particularly concerning Pari-Mutuel betting (see below).

Announcements on 'Arc' weekend are helpfully in English as well as French and also, in a very thoughtful gesture, racing including the Cambridgeshire is relayed promptly from Newmarket.

Newspapers: the well-established *Paris-Turf* is required reading, and also the imaginative colour tabloid *Weekend*. For those with little or no French, the *Racing Post* is plentifully present by the gates.

Longchamp is run by the Société d'Encouragement pour l'Amélioration des Races de Chevaux en France, known more usually as the Société d'Encouragement. It is by far the most important course in France, dating from 1857 and, quite apart from the 'Arc', puts on a superb spring, early summer and autumn programme, including the French equivalents of the Guineas and St. Leger, the Grand Prix de Paris, now sadly axed in distance, notable Derby trials, such as the Prix Lupin, and, later, 'Arc' trials, including the Prix Vermeille for fillies and Prix Niel. The Société's other responsibilities include Auteuil, nearby in the Bois, jumping only, over a figure-of-eight course, where *Mandarin* performed wonders with a broken bridle and Fred Winter to win the Grand Steeplechase de Paris in 1962; this is also where a gallant horse called *Al Capone* became a legend and subject of great and much-deserved adulation. In no fewer than seven seasons in succession he won the same race, the Prix La Haye Jousselin, over the big Auteuil jumps. He took part yet again, at the age of 12, in November 2000, in a brave attempt to create a world record for consecutive victories in the same event. Sadly, it was not to be, but that did nothing to diminish *Al Capone*'s reputation, nor the tremendous applause that greeted him even in defeat. He is now retired but, fittingly, there is to be a statue of him on the course he made his own.

The Société's other courses include: Chantilly, a quite beautiful course with resident chateau for horses, Les Grands Ecuries, at the main French training centre north of Paris; it is the home of the Prix du Jockey-Club of which HH the Aga Khan has owned no fewer than five winners, from *Top Ville* in 1979 to *Dalakhani* in 2003. Chantilly also stages the equivalent for fillies of our Oaks, the Prix de Diane, and was fortunately reprieved not long ago from closure; Saint-Cloud in the suburbs of Paris; and Deauville where magnificent racing takes place throughout August by the seaside in Normandy. Deauville has just heralded the dawn of a new era with the opening in June 2003 of its new all-weather track: an innovation indeed. About 20 per cent of the races at Deauville are now scheduled to take place on the All-Weather. Elsewhere, France abounds in provincial racecourses, both Flat and jumping, which far outnumber the total in Britain.

Betting in France: at the betting windows it will be indicated what stake is taken at that window, but any amount can be staked by simply multiplying up. As with our own Tote, the changing approximate odds are shown on video screens.

Win only, place only, each-way bets, forecasts and tricasts can be made. A silver-coated ticket of the kind shown below will be issued. Make sure the details are correct, then keep it safe and uncrumpled, because if it is a winner this slip has to go back through the machine in order for the cash to be paid out.

For win bets only, some horses will be coupled if in the same ownership. If, for example, there were three horses running in Daniel Wildenstein's colours, a win only bet on any one would succeed should any of the three come home first, but the dividend would be less than if individual odds had been obtainable.

Win only
At the window, say first 'Gagnant' followed by the racecard number in French of the horse. Example: you want to back No. 4 to win. Simply say: 'Gagnant le quatre'. Backing No. 1 is a little different, though. Say 'Gagnant l'as' – 'l'as' is French for 'the ace'. On the ticket the letters GAG will indicate a win only bet.

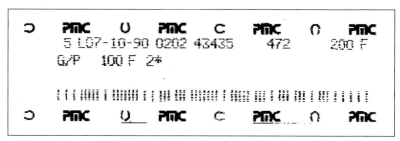

Place only
Similarly, 'Place' followed by racecard number. On the ticket the letter P will indicate a place only wager.

Each-way
'Gagnant et place' followed by racecard number. G/P on the ticket stands for each-way.

Forecasts
First comes Le Pari Jumelé Gagnant. In races of fewer than four runners, no forecast pool operates. In races of four to seven runners the forecast has to be in correct order (the equivalent of a 'straight forecast'). Say 'Jumelé en ordre exact' followed by the racecard numbers of the horses in the order expected, e.g. 'Jumelé en ordre exact le cinq et le sept'. In races of eight or more runners, the Pari Jumelé works exactly like a dual forecast on the Tote. Simply say 'Jumelé' followed by the chosen two racecard numbers, and similarly for combination forecasts involving three or more horses, where the stake will be accordingly increased. JU will be printed on the ticket.

Next comes Le Pari Jumelé Placé. This is a place dual forecast which operates on all races with eight or more runners. It involves the choice of two or three horses. If at least two are in the first three in any order, the bet is a winner. Say 'Jumelé Placé' followed by the racecard numbers of the horses involved.

Tricast

This is Le Pari Trio. Races for which this type of pool operates are indicated 'Pari Trio' on the racecard. The bet involves choosing three horses to finish in the first three irrespective of order. Give the racecard numbers of the three horses and then say 'Trio'.

Should you have a winning bet and forget to collect, all is not lost. The racecard gives a Pari-Mutuel address in Paris to which, within a time-limit of about two weeks, you can post your winning ticket and get paid out.

In addition, members of the Tote Credit Club can place bets on their account at Pari-Mutuel prices in the Tote office on the racecourse and Horse Racing Abroad badge holders can do so within the HRA pavilion.

Weights and distances in France are metric. Here is how they translate from lb and furlongs:

WEIGHTS

GB	FRANCE	GB	FRANCE
St-lb	Kgrams	St-lb	Kgrams
10st	63.5	9-0	57.2
9-13	63.0	8-13	56.7
9-12	62.6	8-12	56.2
9-11	62.1	8-11	55.8
9-10	61.7	8-10	55.3
9-9	61.2	8-9	54.9
9-8	60.8	8-8	54.4
9-7	60.3	8-7	54.0
9-6	59.9	8-6	53.5
9-5	59.4	8-5	53.1
9-4	59.0	8-4	52.6
9-3	58.5	8-3	52.2
9-2	58.1	8-2	51.7
9-1	57.6	8-1	51.3

8-0.....................50.8	7-10................................49.0		
7-13..................50.3	7-9..................................48.5		
7-12..................49.9	7-8..................................48.1		
7-11...................49.4	7-7..................................47.6		

DISTANCES

Furlongs   Metres

5 1,000	10 2,000	15 3,000	20 4,000
6 1,200	11..................2,200	16 3,200	21 4,200
7 1,400	12 2,400	17 3,400	22 4,400
8 1,600	13 2,600	18 3,600	
9 1,800	14 2,800	19 3,800	

Finally a few French words which may be useful on the racecourse: *les courses*, the races; *le pari*, the bet; *le départ*, the start; *l'arrivée*, the finish, the result; *le poteau*, the winning-post; *les tribunes*, the stands; *le rond de présentation*, the parade ring; *les palmarès*, past records; *carrière*, career; *les casaques*, jockeys' silks; *places louées*, reserved seats; *location jumelles*, binocular hire; *les oeillères*, blinkers; *poids*, weight; *cheval*, horse; *chevaux*, horses; *poulain*, colt; *pouliche*, filly; *jument*, mare; *hongre*, gelding; *un défilé sur la piste*, parade in front of the stands; *élevé par*, bred by; *vainquer lauréat*, winner; *gagner, remporter* (fig), to win; *vaincu*, beaten; *léger*, firm going; *assez souple*, good going; *souple*, soft going; *collant*, holding going; *lourd*, heavy going.

1 1/2 m Conditions Race 3-y-o+ Prix de l'Arc de Triomphe, Longchamp

The Prix de l'Arc de Triomphe was conceived as an international race in the gloomy days following the First World War but, at first, received little support from outside France, those being days when English trainers, in particular, were predominantly disposed to stay at home. Nevertheless, an exception was Peter Gilpin, who, from Newmarket, sent *Comrade* (owned, it is true, by a Frenchman, Evrémond de St. Alary) to win the first contest in 1920. Another English-trained horse, *Parth*, won in 1923 and there were two subsequent Italian-trained victors before the Second World War caused a temporary interruption, but only for a couple of seasons. The occupying Germans were in favour of racing and allowed it, eventually, to continue; indeed, they encouraged bloodstock activities, no doubt with an eye to their own main chance, and therein lies part of an explanation of why French-trained horses in the immediate post-war years reaped a harvest in England, where racing and breeding had been severely restricted during hostilities. But it was only after the war that the 'Arc' took off and fulfilled its original object. The table below gives some idea of how it has become a European autumn championship, but, before then, some of the greatest horses of the 20th century were successful, including *Tantième* (1950–51), *Ribot* (1955–56) and *Sea Bird II* (1965), whose victory had to be seen to be believed.

Winner	Age/Sex	Sire	Trainer	Country	Jockey	Going	Approx. SP
1968 Vaguely Noble	3c	Vienna	E.Pollet	(Fr)	W.Williamson	Dead	5/2 F
1969 Levmoss	4c	Le Levanstell	S.McGrath	(Ire)	W.Williamson	Good-Firm	52/1
1970 Sassafras	3c	Sheshoon	F.Mathet	(Fr)	Y.Saint-Martin	Good	19/1
1971 Mill Reef	3c	Never Bend	I.A.Balding	(GB)	G.Lewis	Good	4/6 F
1972 San San	3f	Bald Eagle	A.Penna	(Fr)	F.Head	Good	18/1
1973 Rheingold	4c	Faberge	B.W.Hills	(GB)	L.Piggott	Yielding	8/2 F
1974 Allez France	4f	Sea Bird II	A.Penna	(Fr)	Y.Saint-Martin	Soft	1/2 F
1975 Star Appeal	5h	Appiani	T.Grieper	(Ger)	G.Starkey	Soft	119/1
1976 Ivanjica	4f	Sir Ivor	A.Head	(Fr)	F.Head	Holding	7/1
1977 Alleged	3c	Hoist The Flag	M.V.O'Brien	(Ire)	L.Piggott	Good	6/4 F
1978 Alleged	4c	Hoist The Flag	M.V.O'Brien	(Ire)	L.Piggott	Yielding	6/4 F
1979 Three Troikas	3f	Lyphard	Mme C.Head	(Fr)	F.Head	Good	9/1
1980 Detroit	3f	Riverman	O.Douieb	(Fr)	P.Eddery	Fast	7/1
1981 Gold River	4f	Riverman	A.Head	(Fr)	G.W.Moore	Good-Soft	5/1
1982 Akiyda	3f	Labus	F.Mathet	(Fr)	Y.Saint-Martin	Heavy	11/1
1983 All Along	4f	Targowice	P-L.Biancone	(Fr)	W.R.Swinburn	Good-Firm	17/1
1984 Sagace	4c	Luthier	P-L.Biancone	(Fr)	Y.Saint-Martin	Holding	3/1
1985 Rainbow Quest*	4c	Blushing Groom	J.Tree	(GB)	P.Eddery	Firm	7/1
1986 Dancing Brave	3c	Lyphard	G.Harwood	(GB)	P.Eddery	Firm	2/1 F
1987 Trempolino	3c	Sharpen Up	A.Fabre	(Fr)	P.Eddery	Good-Firm	20/1
1988 Tony Bin	5h	Kampala	L.Camici	(It)	J.Reid	Good-Firm	14/1
1989 Carroll House	4c	Lord Gayle	M.Jarvis	(Ire)	M.Kinane	Good-Soft	19/1
1990 Saumarez	3c	Rainbow Quest	N.Clement	(Fr)	G.Mossé	Good	15/1
1991 Suave Dancer	3c	Green Dancer	J.Hammond	(Fr)	C.Asmussen	Good-Soft	7/2 2F
1992 Subotica	4c	Pampabird	A.Fabre	(Fr)	T.Jarnet	Soft	9/1
1993 Urban Sea	4f	Miswaki	J.Lesbordes	(Fr)	E.Saint-Martin	Holding	37/1
1994 Carnegie	3c	Sadler's Wells	A.Fabre	(Fr)	T.Jarnet	Soft	3/1 F
1995 Lammtarra	3c	Nijinsky	Saeed bin Suroor	(GB)	L.Dettori	Soft	3/1 F
1996 Helissio	3c	Fairy King	A.Fabre	(Fr)	O.Peslier	Good-Soft	2/1 F
1997 Peintre Célèbre	3c	Nureyev	A.Fabre	(Fr)	O.Peslier	Good-Firm	2/1 F
1998 Sagamix	3c	Linamix	A.Fabre	(Fr)	O.Peslier	Soft	5/2 F
1999 Montjeu	3c	Sadler's Wells	J.E.Hammond	(Fr)	M.J.Kinane	Heavy	6/4 F
2000 Sinndar	3c	Grand Lodge	J.Oxx	(Ire)	J.P.Murtagh	Good	6/4 2F

2001 Sakhee	4c	Bahri	S.binSuroor	(GB)	L.Dettori	Holding 22/10
2002 Marienbard	5h	Caerleon	S.binSuroor	(GB)	L.Dettori	Good 158/10
2003 Dalakhani	3c	Darshaan	A.deRoyer-Dupre	(Fr)	C.Soumillion	Holding 9/4 2F
2004 Bago	3c	Nashwan	J.Pease	(Fr)	T.Gillet	Good 10/1

* *Sagace* was first past the post but demoted to second place after a successful objection by Pa
Eddery for bumping in the final furlong.   c = colt, f = filly, h = horse

Four horses only have won both the Derby and the 'Arc': *Sea Bird II* (1965), *Mill Reef* (1971),
Lammtarra (1995) and *Sinndar* (2000). But a total of 18 Derby winners (16 at 3-y-o, 4 at 4-y-o) have
failed in 20 attempts (*Blakeney* was 9th in 1969, 5th in 1970 and *High Chaparral* was 3rd in
2002 and 2003). The most expensive failure in this category recently was *Generous*, in 1991. He
was sent off a fractionally odds-on favourite in a field shining with stars: apart from him, there
were winners of 6 other Classics. However, he could finish only 8th behind the Prix du Jockey
Club winner, *Suave Dancer*, whom he had beaten convincingly in the Irish Derby. Several
theories were brought out in explanation, the most likely being that either he was over the top
or, not having run since July (see below for 'Arc' preparation) was lacking the edge (which *Suave
Dancer* had) that a more recent sharpening-up race might have given him.

His jockey, Alan Munro, was also criticised for being too near the front too soon and for too
long. But the truth is that no hard and fast rules can be set concerning tactics in the 'Arc', which
is often a rough race and in which luck in running significantly plays its fickle hand. The
fashion in most recent years has been to play a waiting game. *Montjeu, Peintre Célèbre, Urban Sea,
Subotica* and *Suave Dancer* all had a lot of ground to make up at the final bend and delivered their
efforts in the closing stages. *Saumarez*, on the other hand, from a prominent position all the way
took the lead entering the straight, while both *Ribot* and *Allez France* had gone ahead before the
straight, and *Helissio*, in 1996, led from start to finish.

Finding the winner of the 'Arc' is no light task, as the approximate prices in the table amply
demonstrate, and what a jockey's tactics might be add a further complication. However, what
undoubtedly should be considered is the kind of preparation a horse has for the race, and, in this
respect, it is noteworthy that French trainers who have the 'Arc' as their ultimate target do not
these days run their horses in our own mid-season championship race, the King George VI and
Queen Elizabeth Diamond Stakes in late July. The late François Boutin stated the case after
Hernando won the Prix du Jockey-Club in June 1993: 'Top races in July are fatal for the three-year-
olds, so after the Grand Prix de Paris [also in June], it would be my idea to rest him until
September, when he could be prepared for the Arc de Triomphe in the Prix Niel.' This is what
happened, but, in the event, *Hernando* could not cope with the heavy ground on 'Arc' day.
Moreover, bearing in mind what *Mill Reef, Dancing Brave* and *Lammtarra* achieved as three-year-
olds – victory both in the King George and the 'Arc' – Boutin's statement should be amended,
perhaps, to exclude exceptional 3-y-o performers who have by-passed the St. Leger.
Nevertheless, his ideas accord with what the majority of French-based trainers think both about
3-y-o and 4-y-o. That they target the 'Arc' and nothing else (to the detriment of the King George)
from June/early July is proved by most modern records. For example, *Montjeu, Peintre Célèbre,
Helissio, Subotica* and *Suave Dancer* all followed the general scheme of no racing between late
June/early July and a 'prep' race in September for the 'Arc'. *Sinndar*, too, although trained in
Ireland, also conformed to this pattern: in his case, no race between winning the Irish Derby
in early July 2000, and his pre-'Arc' race in September. Meanwhile, *Urban Sea*, 4-y-o in 1993,

provided the only striking variant to this kind of run-up in recent years. Jean Lesbordes, after sending her to Royal Ascot in June, where she was beaten by only a neck by *Placerville* in the Prince of Wales's Stakes (1 m 2 f), chose to run her the following month at a French provincial track, Le Lion-d'Angers on 11 July, when she won the 1 m 2 f Prix du Fonds. And on 21 August she went to Deauville, winning the 1 m 2 f Group Three Prix Gontaut-Biron. This was her final appearance before her 'Arc' victory six weeks later. Other points to note on 'Arc' form: no horse has won the St. Leger in September and then the 'Arc' in the same season, although *Ballymoss* (St. Leger 1957) triumphed in the 'Arc' the following year. It is arguable that several horses have left behind their 'Arc' chances with their victories at Doncaster, among them *Premonition* (1953), *Ribero* (1968), *Nijinsky* (1970), *Dunfermline* (1977), *Reference Point* (1987) and, game runner-up though she proved, *User Friendly* (1992). In addition, no St. Leger winner has run in the 'Arc' since 1993 (*Bob's Return*, unplaced). The Prix du Jockey-Club (French Derby), on the other hand, offers more reliable pointers. Since 1950, this race has contributed 9 'Arc' winners and a dozen other places from its first 3. In the same period, 3 'Arc' runners-up (*Nuccio*, *Allez France* and *Tony Bin*) have succeeded the following year, while *Pilsudski* was second 2 years in succession, but 9 other runners-up were unplaced at their next attempt. Meanwhile, since *Alleged* triumphed 2 seasons running in 1977–78, 6 others have tried the double but failed. Nearest was *Sagace* (see table). *All Along* was 3rd in 1984 and the rest unplaced. More to the point, all but *Sagace* (co-favourite) were second-favourites second time round: not good value when considering a bet. As can be seen from the table, fillies have an excellent record.

Betting The market has proved a good guide in recent years.

Trainers André Fabre, with 6 winners, holds the record; Saeed bin Suroor, with 3 successes, comes next.

Jockeys Frankie Dettori and Olivier Peslier have 3 successes each; M.J. Kinane: 2.

Finally, *The Grand History of the Prix de l'Arc de Triomphe* by Arthur Fitzgerald (Genesis Publications) is a wonderful, exhaustive guide to the race from its beginnings up to 1997.

5 f All-aged Conditions Race   Prix de l'Abbaye de Longchamp

A sprint of the first importance which (see table below) the British have made their own. Since *Be Friendly*, ridden by Geoff Lewis, consolidated his championship in this race for Sir Peter O'Sullevan in 1968, a further 25 winners (including a dead-heat) trained in this country have captured the prize worth, in 1998, just over £50,000 to connections of *My Best Valentine*. He, with his game, exhilarating victory and pointed reminder never to overlook the old and bold, made history by becoming the first 8-y-o ever to win a Group One race since the Pattern began in 1971. It may seem strange that the French do not win more often on their home ground, but there are fewer first-class opportunities, hence far fewer top sprinters in France. As can be seen, fillies, as in the 'Arc', as well as mares, have a good record in the 'Abbaye', winner's prize-money for which, in 2004, was £80,479.

	Winner	Age/ Sire Sex		Trainer	Jockey	Owner
1978	Sigy	2f	Habitat	Mme C.Head(Fr)	F.Head	Mme A.Head
1979	Double Form	4c	Habitat	R.F.Houghton	J.Reid	Baronne H. Thyssen-Bornemisza

1980	Moorestyle	3c	Manacle	R.Armstrong	L.Piggott	Moores Furnishings
1981	Marwell	3f	Habitat	M.Stoute	W.R.Swinburn	E.Loder
1982	Sharpo	5h	Sharpen Up	J.Tree	P.Eddery	Miss M.Sheriffe
1983	Habibti	3f	Habitat	J.Dunlop	W.Carson	M.A.Mutawa
1984	Committed	4f	Hagley	D.Weld(Ire)	S.Cauthen	R.Sangster
1985	Committed	5m	Hagley	D.Weld(Ire)	M.Kinane	A.Paulson
1986	Double Schwartz	5h	Double Form	C.Nelson	P.Eddery	R.Sangster
1987	Polonia	3f	Danzig	J.Bolger(Ire)	C.Roche	H.de Kwiatowski
1988	Handsome Sailor	5h	Some Hand	B.W.Hills	M.Hills	R.Sangster
1989	Silver Fling	4f	The Minstrel	I.A.Balding	J.Matthias	G.Strawbridge
1990	Dayjur	3c	Danzig	Major W.R.Hern	W.Carson	Sheikh Hamdan al-Maktoum
1991	Keen Hunter	4c	Diesis	J.Gosden	S.Cauthen	Sheikh Mohammed
1992	Mr Brooks	5h	Blazing Saddles	R.Hannon	L.Piggott	Paul Green
1993	Lochsong	5m	Song	I.A.Balding	L.Dettori	J.C.Smith
1994	Lochsong	6m	Song	I.A.Balding	L.Dettori	J.C.Smith
1995	Hever Golf Rose	4f	Efisio	T.J.Naughton	J.Weaver	M.P.Hanson
1996	Kistena	3f	Miswaki	Mme C.Head(Fr)	O.Doleuze	Wertheimer Brothers
1997	Carmine Lake	3f	Royal Academy	P.Chapple-Hyam	J.Reid	R.Sangster
1998	My Best Valentine	8h	Try My Best	V.Soane	R.Cochrane	The Valentines
1999	Agnes World	4c	Danzig	H.Mori(Japan)	Y.Take	T.Watanabe
2000	Namid	4c	Indian Ridge	J.Oxx(Ire)	J.P.Murtagh	Lady Clague
2001	Imperial Beauty	5m	Imperial Ballet	J.E.Hammond(Fr)	Y.Take	Mrs J.Magnier/ M.Tabor
2002	Continent	5g	Lake Coniston	D.Nicholls	D.Holland	Lucayan Stud
2003	Patavellian	5g	Machiavellian	R.Charlton	S.Drowne	D.J.Deer
2004	Var	5h	Forest Wildcat	C.Brittain	L.Dettori	Mohammed Rashid

c = colt, f = filly, h = horse, m = mare, g = gelding

Aside from the 'Arc' and 'Abbaye' it is worth noting that between 1999 and 2003, John Dunlop twice sent out the winners of the Gr1 2 m 4 f Prix du Cadran and Sir Michael Stoute saddled 2 winners of the Gr1 1 m 2 f fillies and mares race, the Prix de l'Opéra. Also, in 2003, John Gosden added to his Longchamp success (which includes the Prix Dollar 3 times since 1993) with a second victory in the Gr1 1 m race for 2-y-o, the Prix Marcel Boussac. Meanwhile, one to put in the notebook for the Prix du Jockey-Club (the French equivalent of the Derby) is the French trainer Pascal Bary, who has saddled the winner no fewer than 5 times in 10 years since 1994.

In conclusion, French racing now has its own attractive website at: http://www.frenchbloodstock.com

IRELAND

In a country where there is a deep passion for and knowledge of the horse, it is hardly surprising that the racing is plentiful, rich and varied both on the Flat and over the jumps. It goes further than that: whereas, for example, at Royal Ascot, the social aspect and corporate entertainment figure high on the scale, in Ireland the horses, the racing and, as they would say, 'the crack' are of far more importance. Plus, of course, beating the bookmakers, who tend to offer, very often, more tempting odds than can be had on this side of the water. The Irish Classics at the Curragh are run significantly later than in England, and all attract fields of international class, with the Budweiser Irish Derby in the lead, having been worth more than (Ir)£486,753 to the winner in 2003. But there is far more to racing in Ireland than the Classics, or the other important races at the Curragh. Only six miles from the heart of Dublin is the beautiful setting of Leopardstown (which also boasts an on-course pub, 'The Goat'). This first-class course is the home of the Irish Champion Hurdle, the Ladbroke (Hurdle) and Hennessy Cognac Gold Cup Chase as well as Group races on the Flat, including the Irish Champion Stakes now that Phoenix Park, sadly, has closed.

Festivals abound. Punchestown, where *Arkle*'s great rival, *Mill House*, was bred, lies picturesquely beneath the Wicklow mountains, and puts on its best, and quite superb, racing in late April, with the local towns, Naas and Newbridge, contributing plenty to the festivities. Ireland's equivalent of Cheltenham, the racing embraces everything from the Heineken Gold Cup – recently made the richest race of its kind in Ireland, worth (Ir)£120,000 (£73,000 to the winner) – and 4-y-o Champion Hurdle to the unique La Touche Cup, over natural countryside (as the Grand National originally was). Said to date from the 12th century, its course includes a double bank, a stone wall (also like the first Grand National), a drain, and a timber rail, as well as regulation fences over a distance of four miles and a furlong.

Galway on the west coast stages its famous six-day Summer Festival in July (like most of such events with roots in the old horse fairs), featuring the Galway Plate, while its Autumn Festival (September) appropriately coincides with the opening of the Galway oyster season. On the west coast, farther south, Tralee in August is also the scene of determined festivities, Kerry style, over six days of racing, coinciding with the Rose of Tralee beauty competition. These apart, there is even further variety of racing on Ireland's 27 courses, from the rural setting of Down Royal (which stages the Ulster Derby, the start of which in 1988 was delayed by a flock of sheep on the course) in the north to the outstandingly attractive Killarney in the south-west. Enormous crowds watch the Irish Grand National on Easter Monday, the first day of the three-day Festival at Fairyhouse, which in 1851 became the first officially enclosed steeplechase course in Ireland. Fairyhouse is 15 miles north-west of Dublin.

1 ¹/2 m   The Budweiser Irish Derby, The Curragh, late June/early July

	Winner	Sire	Trainer	Jockey	SP
1986	Shahrastani	Nijinsky	M.Stoute	W.R.Swinburn	Evens F
1987	Sir Harry Lewis	Alleged	B.W.Hills	J.Reid	6/1
1988	Kahyasi	Ile de Bourbon	L.Cumani	R.Cochrane	4/5 F
1989	Old Vic	Sadler's Wells	H.Cecil	S.Cauthen	4/11 F
1990	Salsabil (f)	Sadler's Wells	J.Dunlop	W.Carson	11/4
1991	Generous	Caerleon	P.Cole	A.Munro	Evens F
1992	St. Jovite	Pleasant Colony	J.Bolger(Ire)	C.Roche	7/2
1993	Commander-in-Chief	Dancing Brave	H.Cecil	Pat Eddery	4/7 F
1994	Balanchine (f)	Storm Bird	H.Ibrahim	L.Dettori	5/1
1995	Winged Love	In The Wings	A.Fabre(Fr)	O.Peslier	5/1
1996	Zagreb	Theatrical	D.K.Weld(Ire)	P.Shanahan	20/1
1997	Desert King	Danehill	A.P.O'Brien(Ire)	C.Roche	11/2
1998	Dream Well	Sadler's Wells	P.Bary(Fr)	C.Asmussen	2/1 F
1999	Montjeu	Sadler's Wells	J.E.Hammond(Fr)	C.Asmussen	13/8 F
2000	Sinndar	Grand Lodge	J.Oxx(Ire)	J.P.Murtagh	11/10 F
2001	Galileo	Sadler's Wells	A.P.O'Brien(Ire)	M.J.Kinane	4/11 F
2002	High Chaparral	Sadler's Wells	A.P.O'Brien(Ire)	M.J.Kinane	1/3 F
2003	Alamshar	Key Of Luck	J.Oxx(Ire)	J.P.Murtagh	4/1 2F
2004	Grey Swallow	Daylami	D.K.Weld(Ire)	P.J.Smullen	10/1

f = filly

The Irish Derby was first run in its present form in 1866 but was given a great boost in 1962 by Irish Hospitals Sweepstakes founding father Joe McGrath as the Irish Sweeps Derby, when its prize-money exceeded that at Epsom and it became, as it is today, a major international event. It has been sponsored by Budweiser since 1986. It used to be an automatic next race for Derby winners or those placed at Epsom. Since 1964, 14 colts have won both at Epsom and the Curragh, including *Santa Claus*, *Nijinsky*, *Grundy*, *The Minstrel*, *Shergar* and, most recently, *Sinndar*, *Galileo* and *High Chaparral*. A further 11 placed in the first 4 at Epsom have won, notably *Meadow Court*, second to *Sea Bird II* in 1965, and other Derby runners-up *El Gran Senor* (1984) and *St. Jovite* (1992). However, 8 Derby winners have been beaten at the Curragh from *Larkspur* (1962) to *Dr. Devious* (1992), including such apparent certainties in the Irish equivalent as *Sir Ivor* (1968). On a more positive note, the French have been taking a more lively interest in the Irish Derby than used to be the case. For many years it was ignored by connections of the winner of the Prix du Jockey-Club (although *Tambourine II* was 4th in that race in 1962 and won the first Sweeps Derby). The late Robert Sangster, however, set the ball rolling by taking both races with *Assert* in 1982. The following season his *Caerleon* won at Chantilly and was runner-up at the Curragh. Since then, *Old Vic*, *Dream Well* and *Montjeu* have won both races, while *Suave Dancer* (1991), *Hernando* (1993) and *Dalakhani* (2003) were Curragh runners-up after success in the Prix du Jockey-Club. This today is a race not to miss when assessing the form. In 2004, the prize to the winner was (Ir)£736,600, and £251,000 went to the runner-up.

Trainers Sir Michael Stoute (including *Shergar* 1981 and *Shareef Dancer* 1983) and A.P. O'Brien: 3 winners each; H. Cecil, J. Dunlop (including *Shirley Heights* 1978), R.F. Johnson Houghton, John Oxx, D.K. Weld and Peter Walwyn: 2 each.

AUSTRALIA

The first recorded meeting in Australia took place in Hyde Park, Sydney, in 1810, organised by officers of the 73rd Regiment; but before this, and not so long after *Allabaculia*'s victory, there are references to meetings at Parramatta and Hawkesbury, both in New South Wales, as early as 1800. The horses were of mixed breed, but mostly Arab stock imported from the Cape of Good Hope. Meanwhile, the first English stallion had arrived in 1799, and from 1825 onwards more and more English thoroughbreds were shipped in.

The oldest Australian Classic, as in England, is the St. Leger, first run at Homebush in 1841 and won by *Eleanour*. The St. Leger was eventually incorporated into the Australia Jockey Club's fixtures at Randwick.

But Classic-named races proliferated in states other than New South Wales. In Victoria, the first meeting at Flemington, in Melbourne, was in 1840, and the Victoria Derby was established in 1856, when it was won by H.N. Simson's *Flying Doe*. The VRC St. Leger also dates from the 1850s, and is older than the Melbourne Cup itself.

The great Australian national hero and one of the greatest horses of all time in any hemisphere, *Phar Lap*, as a 3-y-o in 1929–30, won both Derbys and both St. Legers in Sydney and Melbourne. At Flemington, his bronze statue now overlooks the present-day crowds, who still pay homage to this great horse. A similar feat to *Phar Lap*'s had been performed in 1906–07 by the outstanding stayer *Poseidon*, while a post-war Australian favourite, *Tulloch*, in 1957–58, achieved not only this record, but also won the Queensland Derby and Caulfield Guineas in his career of 36 victories.

Racing today, as ever, flourishes all over Australia, with bookmakers on-course and pari-mutuel betting only off-course: an arrangement that works exceedingly well. Melbourne Cup day is a public holiday in the state of Victoria, and in 1993, for the first time, horses were sent from England and Ireland; a welcome step forward and widening of international horizons which caused, also for the first time, British bookmakers to lay odds on the race. *Drum Taps*, twice the Ascot Gold Cup winner, ridden by Frankie Dettori, was out of the frame but not disgraced and the £590,000 first prize went to *Vintage Crop*, 1992 Cesarewitch and 1993 Irish St. Leger victor, trained to the minute in Ireland by the brilliance of Dermot Weld. *Vintage Crop* followed up by being fourth in 1994 and third in 1995. Then, in 1998, Lady Herries caused a sensation by sending *Taufan's Melody* to lift the £327,381 prize for the Foster's Caulfield Cup at 66/1, then saddled him just over two weeks later to be fourth in the Melbourne Cup, also sponsored by Foster's (for a further £41,667). He was one of three British-trained horses in the first five, all earning prizes; the other trainers were David Elsworth (third with *Persian Punch*: £79,365) and Paul Cole (fifth with *Yorkshire*: £29,762). The first two home were from New Zealand and the nearest home-trained runner was sixth, a result which, to put it mildly, did not go down well down under but delighted punters in the UK and gave much encouragement for the future, particularly since the Tote paid out 12/1 fourth place for *Taufan's Melody* even though the Australian equivalent did not pay out beyond third place; bookmakers in this country also, with varying conditions, paid out handsomely on the first four. The year 2002, meanwhile, proved to be an excellent one for overseas runners in the Melbourne Cup: they provided three of the first four home. The winner was *Media Puzzle*, trained by Dermot Weld in Ireland. He also saddled the fourth. Between them, these two took home more than £900,000 in winnings. Third place was taken by *Beekeeper*, trained by Saeed bin Suroor. In 2003, the first prize for the Melbourne Cup, sponsored by Toohey's, the Australian brewery firm, had risen to an astonishing £985,915 but this time it did not go abroad but stayed firmly at home, courtesy of the 6-y-o mare *Makybe Diva*. Even so, the third, *Jardines Lookout*, trained by A.P. Jarvis and ridden by Darryll Holland, improved our balance of payments by no less than £117,958.

JAPAN

Racing is booming in Japan, although it takes place only at the weekends and the governing body, the Japan Racing Association, was formed as recently as 1954. The Fuchu racecourse in Tokyo regularly attracts crowds of more than 100,000. On the breeding side the Japanese have made determined inroads into high-class European bloodstock. *Dancing Brave* (who died in 2000), his Derby-winning son, *Commander-in-Chief*, as well as *Dr. Devious* and *Rodrigo de Triano* were among the latest to stand there. Nevertheless, reciprocity does not extend very far in the field of European participation in their races. The list open to the West has recently been extended, but still comprises only a handful of events. The most important (total prize-money in 1998, £1,632,905) is the Japan Cup, on which British bookmakers usually advertise prices. Held in Tokyo since 1981 in late November, it is an invitation race over $1^{1}/_{2}$ miles for the horses deemed by the Japan Racing Association to be the best in Europe, Australasia and the United States against their chosen home team. So far, the sole British success in this tough contest, which, like the Breeders Cup series (see below), comes at the wrong time of year, has been Lord Tavistock's *Jupiter Island* (1986), ridden by Pat Eddery and trained by Clive Brittain. Other valuable races open to overseas runners include the Group One Yasuda Kinen over a mile in May/June (£581,000 to the winner in 2000); the Group Two Keio Hai Spring Cup over 7 f (£363,000); and, at Kyoto, the Group One Mile Championship (£446,889). At the same time, the Japanese have begun to have, in the past year or so, some notable victories in Europe, and they are now no longer to be ignored in big races. *Seeking The Pearl* made history in 1998 by becoming the first Japanese-trained horse to win a European Group One event, the Prix Maurice de Gheest at Deauville. Further Group One success quickly followed at Deauville, then, more recently, the Japan Cup victor, *El Condor Pasa*, impressively beat a field including Derby and 'Arc' winners in the 1999 Grand Prix de Saint-Cloud; *Agnes World* later that season won the Abbaye, and in the year 2000 added to his Group One laurels by capturing the July Cup.

DUBAI

This is where the horses owned by the Maktoum family, in particular those who carry the highly successful blue colours of Godolphin, are over-wintered prior to their assaults on major European events. There is also an ambition to make Dubai itself the centre of the horseracing world, centred on the luxuriously appointed racecourse at Nad Al Sheba with both turf and dirt tracks. Here, in March, there takes place the world's richest race day, the so-called 'Horse Racing Olympics', worth no less than (US)$15 million in 2001. At the top of the winning list, the USA alone took home more than £3.76 million in sterling terms in prize-money under the floodlights of Nad Al Sheba, including the world's richest prize, which went to *Captain Steve*, winner of the flagship race, the Gr1 Emirates Dubai World Cup. Inaugurated only in 1996, the event has quickly gained an enviable reputation, with the first winner being the great American horse *Cigar*, with *Singspiel* following up for Great Britain in 1997. In 1999, an increase of no less than $1 million to a total of $5 million restored the status of the race as the world's richest once again. Sorting out the possible winner (the popular *Swain* in the home-trained Godolphin colours was an unlucky second in 1998) is difficult because it involves trying to tie together American, UK, French, German and Japanese form-lines. But, with television coverage and a betting market, the Dubai World Cup generates plenty of public interest in the UK. In 2003, the Dubai World Cup was consolidated once again as the richest race in the world: Gr1 over 1 m 2 f and worth a total of £3,750,000 prize-money, including £2,250,000 to the winner. It was, however, kept firmly in the family as *Moon Ballad*, owned by Godolphin, trained by Saeed bin Suroor and ridden by Frankie Dettori, captured this astonishing rich bounty.

In addition, launched in March 1999, there is now an Emirates World Series, seen as a 'global world championship' and sponsored by Emirates Airline. Awards are made on a points basis to horses, jockeys and trainers. *High Chaparral* ridden by Mick Kinane took the World Series Championship in 2003. The races involved in 2004 are:

Queen Elizabeth II Cup	Sha Tin, Hong Kong	25 April
Singapore Airlines International Cup	Singapore Turf Club	16 May
King George VI and Queen Elizabeth Diamond Stakes	Ascot	24 July
Arlington Million	Arlington Park	14 August
Grosser Bugatti Preis	Baden-Baden	5 September
Irish Champion Stakes	Leopardstown	11 September
Canadian International	Woodbine	30 September
Prix de l'Arc de Triomphe Lucien-Barrière	Longchamp	3 October
Cox Plate	Moonee Valley	23 October
Breeders Cup Classic	Grand Prairie, Texas	30 October
Breeders Cup Turf	Grand Prairie, Texas	30 October
Japan Cup	Tokyo	28 November
Hong Kong Cup	Sha Tin	12 December

HONG KONG

For the historical information, I am indebted to Austin Coates's illuminating, erudite and entertaining book *China Races*, which was published by Oxford University Press in 1984 to commemorate the centenary of the Royal Hong Kong Jockey Club. It tells an amazing tale of how racing flourished in China before the Communist regime, on 25 racecourses and in particular in Shanghai (which had the largest grandstand in the world) on an unprecedented financial scale. More particularly, it tells how the site of the first racecourse in Hong Kong, Happy Valley, where racing started in 1846, was ironically named because of its terrible reputation for death and disease. But today, with the addition in 1978 of Sha Tin – the largest racecourse in China, on 250 acres of reclaimed land – racing flourishes under the floodlights with tremendous prize-money and an astronomical betting turnover from both courses which is a vital factor in the municipal economy of the island. Hundreds of millions of Hong Kong dollars are ploughed back from betting into hospitals, clinics, parks, schools, swimming pools and other worthy projects. The annual betting turnover recently was the equivalent of £7,319 million, which generated more than £966 million for government funding. Even so, there was plenty left over for the fanatical local punter and for prize-money which averaged just short of £30,000: an enviable situation brought about by the fact that racing is the only legal basis of betting in Hong Kong and there are no bookmakers creaming off huge profits. British-based jockeys regularly ride there, and not long ago Kieren Fallon completed three successful months, becoming a favourite with the local racegoers. Not only that, British-based horses also race there, and valuable races (over and above the predominant handicaps) which attract international fields at Sha Tin include the Group One Queen Elizabeth Cup over 1 mile 2 furlongs in April and other important international races. The Hong Kong Derby at Sha Tin takes place in March. Total prize-money in Hong Kong in 2000 reached the impressive figure of £6.36 million.

CHINA

An Irish trainer, Kevin Connolly, has big plans to revive thoroughbred racing on mainland China. With backing from a Hong Kong tycoon, he has built China's biggest racecourse, the Beijing Jockey Club, on a 395-acre greenfield site near the capital and is betting on a change in the law which forbids gambling.

The course has three international standard racetracks, two turf and one dirt track. As the law stands at the moment, the Chinese are not allowed to bet on horses but may 'guess' which horse will win and put money down on that basis. Only members of the Jockey Club can take part and there are no bookies.

The Beijing Jockey Club is at present the only licensed racetrack in China. Current attendances are about 1,500 per meeting which Mr Connolly hopes to see dramatically improved. There are eight races on the card on Saturdays and racing is about to take place on a twice-weekly basis with a total of £5 million prize-money available for 2004. There are also plans for other courses at Hangzhou, Wuhan and Nanjing.

Says Mr Connolly: 'Horse racing is really a whole new industry in China and it's been so far very exciting in every respect. Any disappointments have been far outweighed by the successes.'

CANADA

Racing in Canada has a history appropriately dating back to the pioneering days of the late 18th and early 19th centuries. In 1771, five years before the first St. Leger was run at Doncaster, horseracing was banned by authorities in Halifax on the grounds that it was turning citizens into 'idle, immoral gamblers'. But the proscription in Nova Scotia did not last long. Today, racing flourishes in Canada. In the west, from British Columbia to Manitoba, there are at least four different versions of the Derby. For European horses, however, most interest is focused farther east in Ontario, particularly on Woodbine racecourse in north-west Toronto. Among its prestige races is the oldest annual sporting event on the American continent, the Queen's Plate. It was inaugurated in 1860 with the approval of Queen Victoria, who had been petitioned, and was originally run at the now defunct Carleton course. It is now a Group One event run at Woodbine, and one of its most famous winners was, in 1964, the legendary *Northern Dancer* (see Chapter Ten) bred by E.P. Taylor. He was the phenomenal driving force who, from the late 1940s onwards, propelled Ontario racing to its present success. In 1994, at Woodbine, the extremely attractive new turf track, laid out on European lines and named in his honour, was opened. It regularly attracts runners from England, France and Ireland. The Canadian International is one of the Grade One events which brings in competition from across the Atlantic. In 2003, it was worth £358,366 to the winner when *Phoenix Reach*, trained by Andrew Balding, took the prize. Other European successes over the years have included *Ballingarry* (2002, trained in Ireland by A.P. O'Brien); *Mutamam* (2001); *Mutafaweq* (2000); *Singspiel* (1996) and the St. Leger winner *Snurge* (1992) from England, as well as that great filly *Dahlia* (1974) and the 'Arc' victor *All Along* (1983) from France. Another top-class race is the E.P. Taylor Stakes (Grade 1, 1 m 2 f 3-y-o+ fillies and mares) worth £179,283 to the winner in 2003. The previous season, this race was captured by *Fraulein*, trained by Ed Dunlop. In 1996, Woodbine was host to the Breeders Cup series when *Pilsudski*, trained by Sir Michael Stoute, beat his stable-companion *Singspiel* for the Breeders Cup Turf.

USA

The only American racing in which the undoubtedly insular British punter takes an interest and on which bookmakers here lay odds is the Breeders Cup series (worth a total of £4,455,063 in winners' prizes alone in 2003). These have taken place annually since 1984 in early November on various US courses and, in 1996, at Woodbine, Toronto. There have been but eight English-trained Breeders Cup winners beginning with that gallant heroine *Pebbles* in 1985. No fewer than five of those successes were achieved in the Breeders Cup Turf: *Pebbles* (trained by Clive Brittain); *Pilsudski* (1996, Sir Michael Stoute); *Daylami* (1999, Saeed bin Suroor); *Kalanisi* (2000, Sir Michael Stoute); and *Fantastic Light* (2001, Saeed bin Suroor). In addition, *Sheikh Albadou* (A.A. Scott) won the Breeders Cup Sprint in 1991; *Barathea* (Luca Cumani) captured the Breeders Cup Mile in 1994; and *Islington* (Sir Michael Stoute) the Breeders Cup Filly and Mare Turf in 2003. The successes of Sir Michael Stoute and Saeed bin Suroor speak for themselves. But they pale beside the exploits of A.P. O'Brien. In only four seasons 2000–03, O'Brien sent out from Ireland three winners in the Breeders Cup series, including *High Chaparral* who took the Breeders Cup Turf both in 2002 and 2003. In addition, in those four seasons, O'Brien had four runners-up, three thirds, three fifths and only seven of his runners were unplaced. His total winnings were £3,186,774. Despite this, it has to be said that the Breeders Cup comes at the end of our Flat season when some horses have had enough for the year (although this does not explain the fact that French-trained runners, with ten victories, have performed rather better than ours). There is, nevertheless, in addition, long-distance air travel and inability to acclimatise to heat on the West Coast (we perform better when the venue is in the east of the States). But above all, perhaps, there is the tightness of American tracks, which bear a distinct resemblance to Hackney dog-track and certainly are a sharp contrast to the galloping expanses of Newmarket.

At Santa Anita, for example, the turf circuit is a perfect oval under one mile round. It lies immediately inside the dirt track. Both would fit quite comfortably and with plenty to spare at, say, Newbury or York. For the mile race there, the tightness of the circuit means two turns. As John Gosden, who used to train successfully in the States, once explained: 'There is a huge difference in running a two-turn mile and running a mile at Ascot. It's two different ball games.' I suppose we shall continue yearly with this 'Mission Improbable', but there is little useful advice that can be given and all that is left for me to do is to remind the punter that bets can be settled at bookmakers' offered prices, but if no price is taken, they will be settled at the US returned pari-mutuel (PMU) odds. Punters must be sure to state which option they want to take. If no preference is stated, bets will generally be settled at PMU odds, which for European runners are often longer than the odds offered by British bookmakers. If choosing PMU odds, punters should note that some horses in common ownership are 'coupled'. At PMU odds, all dividends are declared to a $2 stake. A further complication involves the US system of declaring dividends, which features three possibilities, namely win, place (just referring to the one-two) and show (one-two-three). The Tote and Tote Direct bookmakers also offer a Placepot on races two to seven. There are special rules in the Placepot so read these carefully when doing this bet. Finally, should the urge still continue to plunge on the Breeders Cup events, a historic cautionary tale. It concerns *Papyrus* who won the Derby in 1923. In the St. Leger he was beaten two lengths by Lord Derby's filly *Tranquil*. After the Leger he was shipped out (in a special padded box) on board the Cunard liner *Aquitania* for a match with the American champion *Zev*, to be held on dirt over $1^1/_2$ miles at Belmont Park under the auspices of the Westchester Racing Association. The prize for the winner was £20,000; £5,000 for the runner-up.

August Belmont, head of the Westchester Association (and owner of the 1903 Triple Crown winner *Rock Sand*), thought up the idea, which was to promote interest in racing in New York, then nothing like as popular as it is today. This object was certainly realised with a good deal of pre-race publicity and ballyhoo. Damon Runyon wrote: 'Much excitement in horse circles because *Papyrus*, the English horse, shows a fast work-out. The handlers of *Papyrus* probably do not intend betting on their horse as it appears to have been an honest work-out. They might have taken a leaf from the book of certain crafty, conniving American horsemen, disguised the real speed of *Papyrus*, sent out lies as to the horse's condition, expressed doubt, uncertainty.'

Papyrus had sailed, with work companion *Bar of Gold*, on 22 September. The match was due to be held on Saturday 20 October.

On Friday evening, after a long dry spell, heavy rain unexpectedly fell, turning Belmont into a quagmire which a roller had smoothed to the consistency of French mustard. Basil Jarvis was advised to have *Papyrus* re-shod with special shoes which would grip the slop, otherwise 'He won't have a million to one chance. He won't see the way *Zev* goes.'

But Jarvis chose to ignore the advice, and the forecast came true. Earl Sande, the leading American jockey, set a strong gallop on *Zev*, and *Papyrus* was never in the hunt, with Donoghue easing him long before the post. Commonly described as 'a farce', the match did, nevertheless, achieve one good result: it very much strengthened transatlantic racing relationships. And, of course, it also set a strong precedent for our continual whitewashes in the Breeders Cup, the latest of which, at Churchill Downs in 1998, involving the utter defeat of 11 of our runners, was aptly described by Henry Cecil as 'a disaster'.

But to end on a happier note and illustrate that all excursions across the Atlantic need not end in tears: *Running Stag*, winner of the 'Winter Derby' on the All-Weather at Lingfield and the Group Three Prix Gontaut-Biron at Deauville, was trained at Epsom by Philip Mitchell and owned by Richard Cohen. In the autumn of 1998 he gave them both the thrill of a lifetime in New York and great acclaim from the locals when he was a marvellous third to America's most recent equine hero and wonder-horse, *Skip Away*. This was in the Grade 1 Woodward Stakes at Belmont Park, and on the same track two weeks later he again helped to exorcise the memory of *Papyrus* when he was fourth in the Jockey Club Gold Cup, once more just behind *Skip Away*, and took his worldwide earnings to just over £127,000.

This, however, was not the end of the story. In June 1999, *Running Stag* was sent to America yet again and pulled off a devastating seven-length victory in the Grade 2 Brooklyn Handicap at Belmont. The prize was £126,000, so *Running Stag* in one blow doubled his overseas earnings, and Philip Mitchell began to have even bigger ambitions for this undoubted star who flew the flag so triumphantly for England. These were more than justified. In September 1999, *Running Stag* captured the Saratoga Breeders' Cup worth £108,434. Then, the following season, he had an even more triumphant time in the United States with his biggest-ever victory, the Massachusetts Handicap in Boston, worth no less than £243,902, among another success at Belmont and places in the Arlington Million and at Saratoga. Altogether, this admirable and doughty campaigner was a credit to his trainer: and a profitable one for Great Britain, too. Before he retired, aged six, his American earnings amounted to no less than an astonishing £695,505. What a wonderful career!

APPENDIX A
Rules on Betting

1. Tattersalls' Committee have authority to settle all questions relating to bets, commissions for bets and any matters arising directly or indirectly out of wagers or gaming transactions on horseracing, to adjudicate on all cases of default, and *at their discretion*, to report defaulters to the Jockey Club. If a defaulter is a partnership or limited company all or any of the partners or their agents and all or any of the shareholders, directors, officers or agents of the defaulting company may be reported to the Jockey Club.

   Upon an application being made to the Committee in any case to admit or hear further evidence, the Committee may at its discretion decide to re-hear such case and upon such re-hearing may admit such further evidence and uphold, reverse or amend its original decision or adjudication as it may think fit.

2. In all bets there must be a possibility to win when the bet is made.

3. No betting first past the post will be recognized by the Committee.

4. All bets made, stand and are subject to official 'Weigh In' with the following exceptions:
   (a) Single ante-post bets, being bets made before 10 a.m. on the day of the overnight declarations will be void under the following circumstances:
      1) If the race is abandoned
      2) If the race is declared void
      3) If the 'Conditions' of the race entry are changed prior to the horses coming under Starter's orders
      4) If the venue is altered
      5) If a horse is eliminated under Jockey Club Rule 125
      However in any such circumstances accumulative ante-post bets (win or place) will stand and be settled at the ante-post price(s) laid on the remaining horse(s).
      Any race in which a horse is suppplemented does not affect Rule 4 (a).
   (b) Bets other than ante-post bets will be void if the race is abandoned or declared void. If postponed to another day and overnight declarations stand, then bets stand, and if the original overnight declarations do not stand, bets will be void. Bets on a horse which does not come under Starter's orders or on a horse declared by the Starter 'not to have started' will be void. Bets on the distance are void if the first or second horse is disqualified, or the placings are reversed.
   (c) In the case of bets made at a price on the day of the race before it has been officially notified that a horse has been withdrawn before coming under

289 RULES ON BETTING

Starter's orders or has been declared 'not to have started', the liability of a layer against any horse remaining in the race, win or place, will be reduced in accordance with the following scale depending on the odds current against the withdrawn horse at the time of such official notification:

(a) 3/10 or longer odds on by 75p in the £
(b) 2/5 to 1/3 by 70p in the £
(c) 8/15 to 4/9 by 65p in the £
(d) 8/13 to 4/7 by 60p in the £
(e) 4/5 to 4/6 by 55p in the £
(f) 20/21 to 5/6 by 50p in the £
(g) Evens to 6/5 by 45p in the £
(h) 5/4 to 6/4 by 40p in the £
(i) 13/8 to 7/4 by 35p in the £
(j) 15/8 to 9/4 by 30p in the £
(k) 5/2 to 3/1 by 25p in the £
(l) 10/3 to 4/1 by 20p in the £
(m) 9/2 to 11/2 by 15p in the £
(n) 6/1 to 9/1 by 10p in the £
(o) 10/1 to 14/1 by 5p in the £
(p) If over 14/1 the liability would be unchanged
(q) In the case of two or more horses being withdrawn before coming under Starter's orders, the total reduction shall not exceed 75p in the £

In the case of withdrawals in reformed markets, the total deduction over the two or more horses (i.e. one in the original and one in the reformed market) will be calculated on the prices applicable in the original market. For bets placed in subsequent markets deductions over withdrawn horses in these markets will be calculated on the prices applicable in these markets. Bets made at starting price are not affected, except in cases where insufficient time arises for a fresh market to be formed, when the same scale of reductions will apply. In the event of the withdrawal of one or more runners in circumstances which would lead to only one runner and therefore a 'walkover', all bets on the race will be void. The race will be considered a 'walkover' for the purpose of settling bets.

For the purpose of this rule, the non-appearance of the number of a declared runner in the number board shall be held to be an official notification of the withdrawal of such horse before coming under Starters's orders. In the case of a horse declared by the Starter 'not to have started' the racecourse announcement will be made to that effect. This official announcement will be made before the race result is displayed.

(d) In the event of an announcement being made that the provisions of Rule 4 (c) do not apply on the grounds that no market had been formed at the time of withdrawal of an overnight declared runner or in the event of the number of an overnight declared runner not appearing in the number board, all bets (other than ante-post bets) made at a price prior to either eventuality shall be settled at starting price with the exception of bets struck at nationally advertised or publicly transmittted prices when Rule 4 (c) will operate, based on the advertised price of the withdrawn horse(s).

(e) In the event of a horse or horses being withdrawn under Jockey Club Rule No. 125 (limitation of the number of runners in a race), all ante-post bets on such horse(s) shall be void and the liability of a layer against any horse(s) remaining in the race, win or place, will be reduced in accordance with a rate to be announced before the race by Tattersalls' Committee, dependent on the odds current against the withdrawn horse(s) at the time of such official withdrawal.

(f) In the event of a reserve horse replacing a declared runner all bets, other than ante-post bets, struck prior to such a replacement and a new market being formed will be settled at starting price.

5. When the 'Weighed In' announcement has been made as provided for in Rule 162 of the Rules of Racing, or such other rule being in identical terms which may be substituted for it, the bets go to the horses as officially announced. Objections or disqualifications after the 'Weighed In' announcement has been made, do not change the result of the race for betting purposes.

6. Bets made on one horse against another or that one horse beats another, are determined by the official result. Unless agreed it is not indispensable that both horses should start.

7. Dead Heats. Where a dead heat is declared, a bet on one of two horses that dead heat loses half the stake, with full odds being applied to the remaining half (if a triple dead heat or more, reduction in proportion).

(a) In the event of a double and the first selection dead heats, then the stake is halved and full odds applied. This then becomes the stake on the second selection. Should the second selection also dead heat then the stake is again halved.

(b) In the event of any withdrawals, Tattersalls' Rule 4 (c) reductions will apply to the winnings from the reduced stake.

(c) Un-named favourites finishing joint will be subject to the same rule as if they dead heated. Where an un-named favourite both dead heats and is returned joint in the market, then the stake is halved in the proportion of one fourth to the backer and three fourths to the layer.

8. If odds are laid without mentioning the horse, the bet must be determined by the state of the odds at the time it was made. Bets made after a race that a horse will be disqualified stand, even if no objection be made.

9. Any bet made from signal or indication when the race has been determined, will be considered fraudulent and void.

10. Subject to Rule 4 (a) accumulative bets are not determined until the last event has been run.

11. Bets made on horses, jockeys, trainers etc. winning any number of races within the year shall be understood to mean between 1 January and 31 December, both dates inclusive for flat racing. For jump racing the recognised National Hunt season will apply.

12. In the event of a race being ordered to be run again, or of a false start or break-away, starting price bets shall be regulated by the price current at the time of the original 'off', false start or breakaway. All bets in favour of any horse which started on the first but did not go to the post on the second occasion in the case of a race run over again, or in favour of any horse not returning to the post (by permission) in the case of a false start or breakaway are lost, except when such a horse has not come under Starter's orders.

13. No bet can be declared off except by mutual consent but on any allegation of fraud or corrupt practice, the Committee may investigate the case and may declare the bet void. Either of the bettors may demand stakes to be made on proving to the satisfaction of the Committee, or any two of them, that he has just cause for doing so, and, *if ordered*, the bets must be covered or sufficient security given within the time specified in such order, in default whereof the bets will be off.

14. In the case of a photo finish, all bets made will be settled in the same way as if they had been made on the result of the race.

15. If any extraordinary occasion should arise, in cases of notorious or palpable fraud, or it should come to the notice of the Committee that the wager or gaming transaction involved either or both of the parties in an illegal act under the current legislation in respect of betting and gaming, any of the before-mentioned rules may be suspended by the Committee, and any of the before-mentioned rules may be altered or added to by a simple majority of the Committee.

APPENDIX B
How to Read *RACEFORM*

Introduction

2001 was the 68th year that *Raceform* has been published, now with the new styl Form-Book and Note-Book combined.

Race details contain speed figures for every horse that clocks a worthwhile time weight-for-age allowances, stall positions for every race and the starting pric percentage, in addition to the traditional features. The extended Note-Bool comments are printed below each race and cover all horses which are considered worthy of inclusion by our expert race-readers. For race winners, the comment provide an in-depth analysis of the winning performance and, where applicable explain possible reasons for improvement. For the other runners, the race readers will combine information gained on the day of racing with historical rac performances and attempt to explain why any horse failed to run to its best. More importantly, our on-course team will also provide indications of how horses can be placed to future advantage. Any horse with a sufficient market move is also included under the Note-Book comments.

RACEFORM
The Official Form Book

RACEFORM, THE OFFICIAL FORM BOOK, records comprehensive race details o every domestic race, every major European Group race and every foreign even in which a British-trained runner participated. Extended notes are given to runners, during the turf season, worthy of a mention, including all placed horse and all favourites. Generally speaking, the higher the class of race, the greater the number of runners noted.

MEETING BACK REFERENCE NUMBER is the Raceform number of the last meeting run at the track and is shown to the left of the course name. Abandoned meeting are signified by a †.

THE OFFICIAL GOING, shown at the head of each meeting, is recorded as follows

Turf:	Hard; Firm; Good to firm; Good; Good to soft; Soft; Heavy.
All-Weather:	Fast; Standard; Slow.

THE **WEATHER** is shown below the date.

THE **WIND** is given as a strength and direction at the Winning Post, classified as follows:

Strength:	gale; v.str; str; fresh; mod; slt; almost nil; nil.
Direction:	(half) against; (half) bhd; (half) across from or towards stands.

VISIBILITY is good unless otherwise stated.

RACEFORM GOING, which may differ from the Official Going, now appears against each race to allow for changing conditions of the ground. It takes into account the race times compared with the Raceform Standard Times, the wind and other elements, and is recorded in the following stages:

Turf:	**HD** (Hard); **F** (Firm); **GF** (Good to firm); **G** (Good); **GS** (Good to soft); **S** (Soft); **HY** (Heavy).
All-Weather:	**FST** (Fast); **STD** (Standard); **SLW** (Slow).

THE **POSITION OF THE STARTING STALLS** is shown against each race, in the form of: High (H), Centre (C) or Low (L). The actual position of the stalls can make a vital difference to a runner's chances and reference should be made to the *Effect of the Draw* summary when assessing a horse's performance.

THE **RACE DISTANCE** is given for all races, and is accompanied by (straight) for all races run on straight courses and (round) for courses where there is a round track of comparable distance. Tracks which are identified by a specific name i.e. (Rowley) (July) and (Jubilee) are also indicated. On All-Weather courses (Fibresand) or (Equitrack) indicates the nature of the artificial surface on which the race is run.

PRIZE MONEY shows penalty values down to sixth place (where applicable).

COMPETITIVE RACING CLASSIFICATIONS are shown on a scale from Class A to Class G. All Pattern races are Class A.

WEIGHT-FOR-AGE allowances are given where applicable for mixed-age races.

RACE NUMBERS for Foreign races carry the suffix 'a'.

IN THE RACE RESULT, the figures to the left of each horse show the race number of its most recent listing in Raceform. A figure in *italics* indicates the previous performance was recorded on an All-Weather course. The superscript figures indicate its finishing position in that race and are coded as follows:

* – winner;
2.40 – finishing positions second to fortieth;
b – brought down; **c** – carried out; **f** – fell; **p** – pulled up;
r – refused (to race); **ro** – ran out; **s** – slipped up; **u** – unseated rider;
v – void race; **w** – withdrawn.

A figure to the left of the *Raceform Note-Book* comment is the last race in which the horse warranted an extended comment.

THE ADJUSTED OFFICIAL RATING is the figure in **bold type** directly after the horse's name in the race result. This figure indicates the Official BHB rating, at entry, after the following adjustments had been made:

(i)   Overweight carried by the rider.
(ii)   The number of pounds out of the handicap (if applicable).
(iii) Penalties incurred after the publication of the weights.

However, **no** adjustments have been made for:

(i)   Weight-for-age.
(ii)   Riders' claims.

THE TRAINER is shown in brackets for every runner.

THE HORSE'S AGE is shown immediately before the weight carried.

WEIGHTS shown are actual weights carried. A figure next to the weight with ᵒʷ is the amount of overweight put up by the jockey, e.g. ᵒʷ4.
Allowances are shown between the weight and the jockey name, e.g. **8-10** ⁽³⁾ S. Copp.

LONG HANDICAP WEIGHTS for runners allotted a lower-than-minimum weight at entry **(handicaps only)** are shown directly after the breeder of the winning horse in each race, and above the *Note-Book* comments.

APPRENTICE ALLOWANCES The holders of apprentice jockeys' licences under the provisions of Rule 60(iii) are permitted to claim the following allowances in Flat races: 7lb until they have won 20 Flat races run under the Rules of any recognised Turf Authority; thereafter 5lb until they have won 50 such Flat races; thereafter 3lb until they have won 95 such Flat races.
These allowances can be claimed in the Flat races set out below, with the exception of races confined to apprentice jockeys:

(a) All handicaps other than those Rated stakes which are classified as Listed races.
(b) All selling races.
(c) All weight-for-age races classified C, D, E, F and G.

HEADGEAR is shown after the actual weight carried and expressed as: **b** (blinkers); **v** (visor); **h** (hood); **e** (eyeshield); **c** (eyecover).

THE DRAW for places at the start is shown after each jockey's name in brackets.

THE OFFICIAL DISTANCES between the first six horses are shown on the right-hand side immediately preceding their position at the finish. Distances beyond sixth place may be shown after inspection of race-finish photographs.

STARTING PRICES (SP) appear to the right of the finishing position in the race result. The favourite indicator appears to the right of the Starting Price, [1] for the favourite, [2] for the second-favourite and [3] for third-favourite. Joint favourites share the same number.

RACEFORM RATINGS (RR), which record the level of performance attained in this race for each horse, are given to the right of the starting price. Reference to the *Raceform Ratings* page should be made for a full description of this feature.

SPEED FIGURES (SF) appear for every horse that clocks a sufficiently fast time, and appear in the column to the right of the *Raceform Ratings*. The figures are adjusted to 9st, and calculations made for going, wind, and distance behind the winner. To apply Speed Figures to future races, add 1 point for each 1lb below 9st, and deduct 1 point for each 1lb above 9st. The highest resultant figure is best.

WITHDRAWN horses which fail to come under orders after the jockey has weighed out are included in the index to past racing (with W after the race number); side reference, odds at the time of withdrawal and the reason for withdrawal (if known) are shown in the race comment for that horse.

STEWARDS' ENQUIRY, except in special circumstances, is included only if it concerns a prize winner. Objections by jockeys and Officials are included.

OFFICIAL EXPLANATIONS are included where the horse is deemed to have run well above or below expectation, unless the explanation is covered by the in-running or note book comment.

RACE TIMES in Great Britain, (except official times which are electronically recorded and shown to 100th of a second), are clocked by Raceform's own watch-holders. Figures in parentheses following the time show the number of seconds slower than the Raceform Standard Time for the course and distance.

RACEFORM STANDARD AND RECORD TIMES were originally compiled from times recorded on good to firm going after adjustments had been made for weights carried above or below a norm of 9st. Times equal to the standard are shown as (equals standard). Times under the standard are preceded by –, for instance, 1.8 seconds under the standard would be shown (–1.8). Record times are displayed either referring to the juvenile record (1.2 under 2y best) or to the overall record (1.2 under best).

STARTING PRICE PERCENTAGE is ranged right below the final finisher and gives the total SP percentage of all runners that competed.

TOTE prices include £1 stake. Dual Forecast dividends are shown in parentheses. The Computer Straight Forecast dividend is preceded by the letters CSF, Computer Tricast is preceded by CT and Tote Trio dividend is preceded by the word Trio. Jackpot, Placepot and Quadpot details appear at the end of the meeting to which they refer.

THE OWNER of the winner is shown immediately below the Tote returns together with the breeder, result of the auction for sellers, and details regarding any claimed horse. Friendly claims are not detailed.

Abbreviations and their meanings

Paddock Comments

gd sort	- well made, above average on looks
h.d.w	- has done well, improved in looks
wl grwn	- well grown, has filled to its frame
lengthy	- longer than average for its height
tall	- tall
rangy	- lengthy and tall but in proportion, covers a deal of ground
scope	- scope for physical development
str	- strong, powerful looking
w'like	- workmanlike, ordinary in looks
lt-f	- light framed, not much substance
neat	- smallish, well put together
leggy	- long legs compared to body
angular	- unfurnished behind the saddle, not filled to frame
unf	- unfurnished in the midriff, not filled to frame
narrow	- not as wide as side appearance would suggest
small	- lacks any physical scope
nt grwn	- not grown
lw	- looked fit and well
bkwd	- backward in condition
t	- tubed
swtg	- sweating
b. (off fore or nr fore)	- bandaged in front
b. hind (off or nr)	- bandaged behind

At the Start

stdd s	- jockey purposely reins back the horse
dwlt	- missed the break and left for a short time
s.s	- slow to start, left longer than a horse that dwelt
s.i.s	- started on terms but took time to get going
ref to r	- either does not jump off, or travels a few yards and then stops
rel to r	- tries to pull itself up in mid-race

Position in the Race

led	- in lead on its own
disp ld	- upsides the leader
w ldr	- almost upsides the leader
w ldrs	- in a line of three or more disputing the lead
prom	- on the heels of the leaders, in the front third of the field
trckd ldr(s)	- just in behind the leaders giving impression that it could lead if asked
chsd ldr	- horse in second place
chsd clr ldrs	- horse heads main body of field behind two clear leaders
chsd ldrs	- horse is in the first four or five but making more of an effort to stay close to the pace than if it were tracking the leaders
in tch	- close enough to have a chance
hdwy	- making ground on the leader
gd hdwy	- making ground quickly on the leader, could be a deliberate move
sme hdwy	- making some ground but no real impact on the race
stdy hdwy	- gradually making ground
ev ch	- upsides the leaders when the race starts in earnest
rr	- last of main group but not detached
bhd	- detached from the main body of runners
hld up	- restrained as a deliberate tactical move
nt rcvr	- lost all chance after interference, mistake etc.
wknd	- stride shortened as it began to tire
lost tch	- had been in the main body but a gap appeared as it tired
lost pl	- remains in main body of runners but lost several positions quickly

Riding

effrt	- short-lived effort
pushed along	- received urgings with hands only, jockey not using legs
rdn	- received urgings from the saddle, including use of the whip
hrd rdn	- received maximum assistance from the saddle, including use of whip
drvn	- received forceful urgings, jockey putting in a lot of effort and using whip
hrd drvn	- jockey very animated, plenty of kicking, pushing and reminders

Finishing Comments

jst failed	- closing rapidly on the winner and probably would have led a stride after the line
r.o	- jockey's efforts usually involved to produce an increase in pace without finding an appreciable turn of speed
r.o wl	- jockey's efforts usually involved to produce an obvious increase in pace without finding an appreciable turn of speed
unable qckn	- not visibly tiring but does not possess a sufficient change of pace
one pce	- not tiring but does not find a turn of speed, from a position further out than unable qckn
nt r.o	- did not consent to respond to pressure
styd on	- going on well towards the end, utilising stamina
nvr plcd to chal	- never apparently given the chance to make a challenge
nvr able to chal	- unable to produce a challenge without a specific reason
nvr nr to chal	- unable to produce a challenge, normally due to a slow start, stumbling etc.
nrst fin	- nearer to the winner in distance beaten than at any time since the race had begun in earnest
nvr nrr	- nearer to the winner position wise than at any time since the race had begun in earnest
rallied	- responded to pressure to come back with a chance having lost its place
no ex	- unable to sustain its run due to lack of strength or effort from the saddle, enthusiasm etc.
bttr for r	- likely to improve for the run and experience
rn green	- inclined to wander and falter through inexperience
too much to do	- left with too much leeway to make up

Winning Comments

v.easily	- a great deal in hand
easily	- plenty in hand
comf	- something hand, always holding the others
pushed out	- kept up to its work with hands and heels without jockey resorting to whip or kicking along and wins fairly comfortably
rdn out	- pushed and kicked out to the line, with the whip employed
drvn out	- pushed and kicked out to the line, with considerable effort and the whip employed
all out	- nothing to spare, could not have found any more
jst hld on	- holding on to a rapidly diminishing lead, could not have found any more if passed
unchal	- must either make all or a majority of the running and not be challenged from an early stage

Complete list of abbreviations

a	- always	ent	- entering	nk	- neck
a.p	- always prominent	ev ch	- every chance	no ex	- no extra
abt	- about	ex	- extra	nr	- near
appr	- approaching	f	- furlong	nrr	- nearer
awrdd	- awarded	fin	- finished	nrst fin	- nearest finish
b.b.v	- broke blood-vessel	fnd	- found	nt	- not
b.d	- brought down	fnl	- final	nvr	- never
bdly	- badly	fr	- from	one pce	- once pace
bef	- before	gd	- good	out	- from finish
bhd	- behind	gng	- going	outpcd	- outpaced
bk	- back	grad	- gradually	p.u	- pulled up
blkd	- baulked	grnd	- ground	pce	- pace
bmpd	- bumped	hd	- head	pl	- place
bnd	- bend	hdd	- headed	plcd	- placed
btn	- beaten	hdwy	- headway	plld	- pulled
bttr	- better	hld	- held	press	- pressure
c	- came	hmpd	- hampered	prog	- progress
ch	- chance	imp	- impression	prom	- prominent
chal	- challenged	ins	- inside	qckly	- quickly
chsd	- chased	j.b	- jumped badly	qckn	- quicken
circ	- circuit	j.w	- jumped well	r	- race
cl	- close	jnd	- joined	racd	- raced
clr	- clear	jst	- just	rch	- reach
comf	- comfortably	kpt	- kept	rcvr	- recover
cpld	- coupled	l	- length	rdn	- ridden
crse	- course	ld	- lead	rdr	- rider
ct	- caught	ldr	- leader	reard	- reared
dismntd	- dismounted	lft	- left	ref	- refused
disp	- disputed	m	- mile	rn	- ran
dist	- distance	m.n.s	- made no show	rnd	- round
div	- division	mde	- made	r.o	- ran on
drvn	- driven	mid div	- mid division	rr	- rear
dwlt	- dwelt	n.d	- never dangerous	rspnse	- response
edgd	- edged	n.g.t	- not go through	rt	- right
effrt	- effort	n.m.r	- not much room	s	- start

slt	- slight	swvd	- swerved	w	- with
sme	- some	t.k.h	- took keen	w.r.s	- whipped round
sn	- soon		hold		start
spd	- speed	t.o	- tailed off	wd	- wide
st	- straight	tch	- touch	whn	- when
stmbld	- stumbled	thrght	- throughout	wknd	- weakened
stdd	- steadied	trckd	- tracked	wl	- well
stdy	- steady	u.p	- under pressure	wnr	- winner
styd	- stayed	u.str.p	- under strong	wnt	- went
swtched	- switched		pressure	¹/₂-wy	- halfway

RACEFORM RATINGS

Raceform Ratings for each horse are listed after the Starting Price and indicate the actual level of performance attained in that race. The figure in the back index represents the **BEST** public form that our Handicappers still believe each horse is capable of reproducing.

To use the ratings constructively in determining those horses best-in in future events, the following procedure should be followed:

(i)   In races where all runners are the same age and are set to carry the same weight, no calculations are necessary. The horse with the highest rating is the horse best-in.

(ii)   In races where all runners are the same age but are set to carry different weights, add one point to the Raceform rating for every pound less than 10 stone to be carried, deduct one point for every pound more than 10 stone.

For example

Horse	Age & Weight	Adjustment from 10 stone	RR base Rating	Adjusted Rating
Convict	3-10-1	-1	78	77
Keyhole	3-9-13	+1	80	81
Blue Acara	3-9-7	+7	71	78
Firemouth	3-8-11	+17	60	77

Therefore Keyhole is top-rated (best-in)

(iii)   In races concerning horses of different ages the procedure in example (ii) should again be followed, but reference must also be made to the Official Scale of Weight-For-Age.

For example

12 furlongs July 20th

Horse	Age and wt fr 10 st	Adjust Rating	RPH Rating	Adjust deduct	W-F-A Rating	Final
Tapaculo	5-10-0	0	90	90	Nil	90
Oropendola	4-9-9	+5	83	88	Nil	88
Jacamar	3-9-4	+10	85	95	-12	83
Quetzal	4-8-7	+21	73	94	Nil	94

Therefore Quetzal is top-rated (best-in)

(A 3-y.o is deemed 12lb less mature than a 4-y.o or older horse on 20th July over 12f. Therefore, the deduction of 12 points is necessary).

The following symbols are used in conjunction with the ratings:

++	almost certain to prove better
+	likely to prove better
d	disappointing (has run well below best recently)
?	form hard to evaluate – rating may prove unreliable
t	tentative rating based on race-time

Weight adjusted ratings for every race are published daily in Raceform Private Handicap.

APPENDIX C
SELECT BIBLIOGRAPHY

Anthologies
Ed. by John Hislop and David Swannell. *The Faber Book of the Turf.* Faber, 1990.
Ed. by Sean Magee. *Runners and Riders.* Methuen, 1993.
Ed. by Lord Oaksey and Bob Rodney. *A Racing Companion.* Lennard Books for W.H. Smith, 1992.
Ed. by Alan Ross. *The Turf.* Oxford, 1982.

Betting
Alex Bird with Terry Manners. *The Life and Secrets of a Professional Punter.* Queen Anne Press, 1985.
Ed. by Richard Onslow. *Great Racing Gambles and Frauds.* Marlborough Press. Four volumes, 1991–94.
Charles Sidney. *The Art of Legging.* Maxline International, 1976.

Breeding
Michael Church. *The Classic Pedigree.* Racing Post, 1990.
Michael Church. *Dams of Classic Winners 1777–1993.* Racing Post, 1994.
Keylock's *Dams of Winners.* Various edns. Knapp, Drewett.
Sir Charles Leicester. *Bloodstock Breeding.* J.A. Allen, 1964.
Peter Willett. *An Introduction to the Thoroughbred.* Stanley Paul, 1966.
Peter Willett. *The Classic Racehorse.* Stanley Paul, 1981.

Historical
David Ashforth. *Ringers and Rascals – A Taste of Skulduggery.* Highdown, 2003.
Asa Briggs. *A Social History of England.* Weidenfeld, 1983.
Dennis Craig. *Horse-Racing.* J.A. Allen, 1963.
Arthur Fitzgerald. *The Arc* (Complete history of the Prix de l'Arc de Triomphe). Genesis Grand History Series, 1997.
Paul Mathieu. *The Druid's Lodge Confederacy.* J.A. Allen, 1990.
Roger Mortimer, Richard Onslow, Peter Willett. *The Biographical Encyclopaedia of British Flat Racing.* Macdonald and Jane's, 1978.
Roger Mortimer. *The Flat* (Flat Racing 1939–1978). Allen and Unwin, 1979.
Roger Mortimer. *The History of the Derby Stakes.* Michael Joseph, 1973.
Richard Onslow. *Headquarters: A History of Newmarket and Its Racing.* Great Ouse Press, 1983.
Richard Onslow. *Royal Ascot.* Crowood Press, 1990.
Vincent Orchard. *The Derby Stakes (1900–1953).* Hutchinson, 1954.
Chris Pitt. *A Long Time Gone* (A definitive history of racecourses that have closed). Portway Press, 1996.

George Plumptre. *Back Page Racing* (A Century of Newspaper Coverage). Queen
    Anne Press, 1989.
George Plumptre. *The Fast Set* (The World of Edwardian Racing). Deutsch, 1985.
Caroline Ramsden. *Ladies in Racing*. Stanley Paul, 1973.
Alexander Scott. *Turf Memories of Sixty Years*. Hutchinson, 1924.
Michael Seth-Smith. *A Classic Connection* (The friendship of the Earl of Derby and
    the Hon. George Lambton). Secker, 1983.
'Thormanby'. *Famous Racing Men*. James Hogg, 1882.
Howard Wright. *The Encyclopaedia of Flat Racing*. Hale, 1986.

Horses
Stephen Budiansky. *The Nature of Horses*. Weidenfeld and Nicolson, 1997.
Richard Burridge. *The Grey Horse. The True Story of Desert Orchid*. Pelham, 1992.
John Fairley. *Great Racehorses in Art*. Phaidon Press, 1984.
Clive Graham. *Great Horses of the Year 1954–55*. McGibbon & Kee, 1954.
John Hislop. *The Brigadier*. Secker and Warburg, 1973.
Henrietta Knight. *Best Mate: Chasing Gold*. Highdown, 2003.
David Livingstone-Learmonth and John Hislop. *Famous Winners of the British
    Turf 1949–55*. Hutchinson, 1956.
R.C. Lyle. *Brown Jack*. Putnam, 1934.
Ginger McCain. *Red Rum, A Racing Legend*. Weidenfeld and Nicolson, 1996.
Roger Mortimer. *Twenty Great Horses*. Cassell, 1967.
John Oaksey. *The Story of Mill Reef*. W.H. Allen, 1975.
Richard Stone Reeves and Patrick Robinson. *The Golden Past*. Fine Art
    Enterprises, 1985.
Julian Wilson. *100 Greatest Racehorses*. Queen Anne Press, 1987.

Jockeys
Edgar Britt. *Post Haste*. Muller, 1967.
Willie Carson and Brough Scott. *Carson Up Front*. Stanley Paul, 1993.
Pat Eddery with Alan Lee. *To Be A Champion*. Hodder and Stoughton, 1992.
Dick Francis. *Lester, the Official Biography*. Michael Joseph, 1986.
John Francome. *Born Lucky*. Pelham, 1985.
Jack Leach. *Sods I Have Cut On The Turf*. Gollancz, 1961.
Alan Lee. *Fred. The authorised biography of Fred Winter*. Pelham, 1991
Amanda Murray. *Race To The Finish – The Life and Times of Fred Archer*.
    Robson, 2003.
Lester Piggott and Sean Magee. *Lester's Derbys*. Methuen, 2004.
M. Seth-Smith. *Knight of the Turf* (Biography of Sir Gordon Richards). Hodder
    and Stoughton, 1980.
John Welcome. *Fred Archer, His Life and Times*. Faber, 1967.
Tommy Weston. *My Racing Life*. Hutchinson, 1952.

Journalism
Sidney Galtrey. *Memoirs of a Racing Journalist*. Hutchinson, 1934.
Quintin Gilbey. *Fun Was My Living*. Hutchinson, 1970.
John Oaksey. *Mince Pie For Starters – A Racing Life*. Headline, 2003.

Peter O'Sullevan. *Calling The Horses*. Stanley Paul, 1989.
Brough Scott. *On and Off The Rails*. Gollancz, 1984.

National Hunt
Michael Ayres and Gary Newbon. *Over The Sticks*. David & Charles, 1971.
Reg Green. *The History of the Grand National: A Race Apart*. Hodder, 1993.
John Hughes and Peter Watson. *Long Live The National*. Michael Joseph, 1984.
Alan Lee. *Cheltenham Racecourse*. Pelham Books, 1985.
Richard Pitman, John Oaksey, Gerry Cranham. *The Guinness Guide to Steeplechasing*. Guinness Superlatives, 1979.
Fred and Mercy Rimell. *Aintree Iron* (Autobiography). W.H. Allen, 1977.
Mercy Rimell. *Reflections on Racing*. Pelham/Stephen Greene Press, 1990.
Michael Seth-Smith, Peter Willett, Roger Mortimer, John Lawrence. *The History of Steeplechasing*. Michael Joseph, 1966.
Patricia Smyly. *The Encyclopaedia of Steeplechasing*. Hale, 1979.

Records and statistics
Edward Abelson and John Tyrrel. *The Breedon Book of Horse Racing Records*. Breedon Books, 1993.
John Randall and Tony Morris. *Horse Racing: The Records*. Guinness Books, 1985, 1988, 1990.

Training
William Day. *Reminiscences of the Turf*. Richard Bentley & Son, 1886.
Tim Fitzgeorge-Parker. *Ever Loyal* (The Biography of Neville Crump). Stanley Paul, 1987.
Bryony Fuller. *Fulke Walwyn: A Pictorial Tribute*. Lambourn Publications, 1990.
Ed. by John Hughes and Peter Watson. *My Greatest Training Triumph*. Michael Joseph, 1982.
Hon. George Lambton. *Men and Horses I Have Known*. J.A. Allen, 1963.
Jenny Pitman. *The Autobiography*. Partridge Press, 1998.
Peter Walwyn. *Handy All The Way – A Trainer's Life*. Metro, 2000.
Peter Willett. *Dick Hern – The Authorised Biography*. Hodder & Stoughton, 2000.

General
Julian Bedford. *The World Atlas of Horse-Racing*. Hamlyn, 1989.
Gerry Cranham and Christopher Poole. *The Guinness Book of Flat Racing*. Guinness, 1990.
George Ennor and Bill Mooney. *The World Encyclopaedia of Horse Racing*. Carlton Books, 2001.
Summerhays' *Encyclopaedia for Horsemen*. Warne, 1975.

PUNTER'S NOTES

PUNTER'S NOTES

PUNTER'S NOTES

PUNTER'S NOTES

PUNTER'S NOTES

PUNTER'S NOTES

PUNTER'S NOTES

PUNTER'S NOTES

PUNTER'S NOTES

PUNTER'S NOTES

PUNTER'S NOTES

PUNTER'S NOTES

PUNTER'S NOTES

PUNTER'S NOTES

PUNTER'S NOTES

PUNTER'S NOTES